Bernie Pearl was a pioneer of the Blues in Los Angeles. Before Bernie, Blues musicians earned $25 a night playing part-time at small clubs in South Central LA and Watts.

Then, Bernie started the radio show "Nothin' But the Blues", the Annual Blues Festivals, and broadcasting the radio show and the Blues Festivals on National Public Radio. As a result of this exposure, demand for the Blues grew at larger clubs on the west side of Los Angeles and for touring the US and Europe.

Blues musicians could earn a full-time living playing the Blues.

To the Blues ...

Sam King
The King Brothers Blues Band
drummer for Freddie King, Albert King, and Smokey Wilson

==

The name Bernie Pearl goes back to my earliest memories as a kid in Southern California. I remember getting a Walkman radio for Christmas around 1983 or so. I remember my folks talking about names like Howlin Wolf, Muddy Waters, Bobby Blue Bland and T Bone Walker. This was the music of their time and those names always fascinated me as a kid. So, one Saturday afternoon I'm scrolling through the radio dial, and I hear Howlin Wolf singing "Little Red Rooster" and Fred McDowell and so many others.

I was completely blown away! The man responsible for playing all this great music on the weekends was Mr Bernie Pearl. Bernie hosted a radio show called "Ain't nothing but the Blues" every weekend from Cal State Long Beach. That radio show changed my life. Bernie not only played the records, but also gave some insight on those great Bluesmen.

Bernie has always done so much for Blues music, like being involved with the Long Beach Blues Festival. If it weren't for these two things my career as a musician might've looked completely different.

I was doing a gig many years ago in a Gospel/Funk Band, Bernie and the late Harmonica Fats were on the bill, and it was one of the defining moments for me to focus on playing straight Blues. I respect so many things about Bernie Pearl and I will continue to try and inspire, just like Bernie did for me,

Thank you Bernie. All the best.

Kirk Fletcher
singer-songwriter-guitarist
former member, the Fabulous Thunderbirds, Joe Bonamassa

===

I was fourteen when I first saw Bernie Pearl accompanying Lightnin' Hopkins at The Ash Grove and I instantly wanted to grow up and be like him. From his early days playing with legends like Lightnin', Big Mama Thornton and Johnny Shines, to name a few, through his decades as a solo artist, Bernie's guitar mastery never fails to amaze, inform and inspire me. His smart, economical, soulful guitar work sets a standard that most of us six-string bashers still struggle to reach. His writing is the same, full of passion, respect and love for the blues. After all these decades, I still want to grow up and be Bernie Pearl.

Dave Alvin
Grammy Award winning singer-songwriter-guitarist

===

Bernie Pearl was clearly on his mission with a guitar and the Blues from the first time I encountered him at the Ash Grove ,8162 Melrose Avenue between La Jolla Street(Ave?) and Crescent Heights Boulevard! This was 1965. I'd just arrived in Cali from back east and I'm tellin' ya, he ain't slowed up yet!

His brother Ed owned and ran a fabulous one-of-a-kind club which had great supporters and staff and probably the best regularly appearing artists in the USA & California for that real down home earthy music of real people!

It was in this environment of constant incredible musical talent that Bernie honed his skills and harnessed his creativity!

Performer, band leader, teacher, team player, accompanist(duo or ensemble) knew how to "comp" and could go lick for lick or toe to toe with the best of 'em!

One of my favorite memories is of Bernie playing guitar and accompanying "Long Gone Miles" who sang and improvised not patterned Blues, but more often than not in odd time and rhythmic meter!

Bernie was the man who could play and arrange this man's music on the fly so the music made perfect sense and was an enjoyment for fan and listener alike! suspension!

It was a sight to behold and has been forever etched in my memory!

For sure, trust me, they don't make that no more, period!!

Aside from his very busy schedule, he has recently turned his attention to the lap steel guitar! Only time will tell what delightful music and sounds will be springing fourth from this lovely instrument in his capable hands!

Always a gentleman and "en forme!!"

You'll be enlightened by the stories and memoirs of this man and his life, mind! A hands-on history with this great music!!

Now!! Lemmee get out the way and let some other great folks shine their bright lights on Bernie!!

Peace

Taj Mahal
November, 2022

==

Years before I became Dr. Demento in 1970, I was Barret Hansen, a teenager from Minneapolis who had fallen in love with the blues. My dad had a few records by Lead Belly, and I read about Blind Lemon Jefferson in a magazine and bought a 10" LP by him, which I enjoyed, but when I was 14 I heard Joe Turner's "Shake, Rattle and Roll" and Little Walter's "Thunder Bird," I was hooked. In 1963 I arrived in Los Angeles for grad school at UCLA, which had a new M.A. program in "Folk Music Studies." I learned a lot there, but I learned a lot more at the Ash Grove, the legendary folk club where I heard, and met Brownie McGhee and Sonny Terry, Lightnin' Hopkins, Mississippi John Hurt, Mance Lipscomb, Bukka White and practically every Black blues artist who toured the USA in the 1960s.

At the Ash Grove I also met some of the many, mostly white people of my generation who were also becoming blues addicts. One of the first was Bernie Pearl, whose brother was the founder/owner of the Ash Grove. Bernie sang and played guitar, and had met and even jammed with many of the artists who performed at the club. He also liked to sing and play with people about his age, and soon became the co-founder of an electric blues band called King David and the Parables. Before long I also became a Parable, despite my numb fingers at the piano. We opened for a couple of acts at the Ash Grove, and played a couple of gigs at other places, before we all found more productive ways to express ourselves.

Bernie never stopped singing and playing the blues, and over the years he got better and better at it, becoming a stalwart of the L.A. live blues scene, which he remains today. In this book he shares his memories of the many blues greats he's known, and passes along some of their wisdom, their knowledge and their soulful spirit, as well as his own.

Barrett Hansen, Dr. Demento

...*sittin' on the Right Side of the Blues*

A Life in the Blues

BERNIE PEARL

with

BRUCE E. KRELL, PhD

Front Cover Images

Bernie Pearl Plays With Lightnin' Hopkins

    Courtesy: Phil Melnick

Performer

    Courtesy: Bernie Pearl

Host

    Courtesy: EK Waller, Bernie Pearl

Producer

    Courtesy: EK Waller, Bernie Pearl

Creator, Director

    Courtesy: James Tamburro

Back Cover Image

Blues Guitar Killers

    Courtesy: Edie Pearl

Author Contact Information

Bernie Pearl	Bruce E. Krell, PhD
BerniePearl@hotmail.com	bruce@la-blues.com

... sittin' on the Right Side of the Blues

A Life in the Blues

BERNIE PEARL

with

BRUCE E. KRELL, PhD

Copyright © 2025 Bernie Pearl and BM Krell Trust

All Rights Reserved. No part of this book may be reproduced in any form or by any electronic or mechanical means, including information storage and retrieval systems, without permission in writing from the author and copyright holder above, except by a reviewer who may quote brief passages in a review. Scanning, uploading, and electronic distribution of this book or any part of this book or the facilitation of such without the permission of the author and copyright holder is prohibited. Please purchase only authorized electronic versions, and do not participate in or encourage electronic piracy of copyrighted materials. Your support of the rights of the author and copyright holder is greatly appreciated.

Best efforts have been made to contact the photographers whose images are used throughout this book. For the most part, contacts were successful and permissions were given in writing. All contact efforts are well documented.

ISBN-13: 978-0-9966250-8-1

Library of Congress Control Number: 2025912201

Printed in the United States

Bernie Pearl and BM Krell Trust, Trustee Bruce Krell

Long Beach, CA

Dedications

Sam Lightnin' Hopkins
Lightnin taught me
to play the Blues.

Source: Wikipedia
Creative Commons License

Mance Lipscomb
Mance taught me to play and
to live the Blues.

Courtesy: Gerrie Blake
Newport Jazz Festival

Barbara Morrison
Barbara was my friend, my sister,
my boss, my mentor and mentee,
my teacher and my student.

Courtesy: Barbara Morrison Press Kit

Ed Pearl
Ed was my brother, my boss,
my biggest secret supporter.
He provided access to legends.
I was penniless but privileged,
in an elite setting he provided.

Courtesy: Bernie Pearl

A Special Dedication

Bernie Pearl   Barbara Morrison   Glenn McKinney

Remembering good times with Barbara Morrison and Glenn McKinney with fondness and gratitude.

Barbara for her perennial generosity and sharing of her immense talent.

Glenn for his enduring friendship and initiative in taking the crucial first steps in making this book a reality.

Good times remembered with a tear in my eye, wishing they were here for the party.

They loved a party. They deserved a party.

... sittin' on the Right Side Of The Blues

I have a little story I'd like to tell
About the music I love so well
I promise I won't take long
I'll get right down to the point of this song

I was young, eighteen or so
I met some Blues men you might know
Brownie, Sonny, Lightnin' Sam said
Learn this music and understand
It comes from true life into your heart
We're gonna help you make a start
On the right side, the right side of the blues
Just carry on when we are gone
Keep on sittin' on the right side of the blues

Daddy Mance come to town
He said c'mon sit down
Watch my fingers while I play
You hit the bass I will concentrate
He sang a song from long ago
About a rich man named Tom Moore
He closed his eyes, remembered the past
I got the message at long last
On the right side, the right side of the blues
I learned his style, it took a while
Sittin' on the right side of the blues

I saw him on a Lomax LP
Mississippi Fred spoke to me
He drank his water out a hollow log
He'd be her kid-man, wouldn't be no dog
When he got the blues late night 'fore dawn

Pick a tune, moan along
Sit and play into the night, when he arose he'd feel alright
On the right side, the right side of the blues
You must be true, don't care what you do
Keep on sittin' on the right side of the blues

Now, I don't know about Heaven or Down Below
Or if we come back once we go
But, if I had my 'druthers I would choose
Keep on sittin' on the right side of the blues
The Right side, I say the right side of the blues
Now my song is done, won't you come
Sit down on the right side of the blues, the right side of the blues
Down on the right side of the Blues.

Lyrics by Bernie Pearl

CD: *Sittin' On the Right Side of the Blues*

© 2011, All Rights Reserved

Table of Contents

The Blues Chooses Bernie 5

Who Is Bernie Pearl? 11

Who Is Bruce Krell? 17

The Origin Years (Prior To 1930) 23

The Pearl Family in the 1930s 39

Bernie Pearl Grows Up (1940s, Early 1950s) 43

The Kibbutz Years (1957-1958) 63

Early Years At The Ash Grove (1958 – 1961) 77

A Portrait in Black and White 87

Studying With The Masters (1958 – 1968) 99

Brownie McGhee and Sonny Terry 101

Performing At The Ash Grove (1964) 125

Encounters With Lightnin' Hopkins 135

Encounters With Mance Lipscomb 153

Encounters With MS Fred McDowell 161

Encounters with Doc Watson and Ravi Shankar 171

Encounters With Rev Gary Davis 177

Encounters With Some Other Notables 191

Encounters with Phillip Walker & Little Walter 197

Learning to Laugh to keep from Cryin' (1964) 201

On The Road With Long Gone (Summer, 1966) 207

Big Mama's in Town (Sept, 1966) 225

Visiting Mance and Lightnin' (Xmas, 1973) 251

Dylan in the Afternoon (Mid 1970s) 265

Terminal Island (Late 1970s) 267

The Smoke – Pioneer Club Blues (1978) 273

Playing The Blues (1979) 289

Impact of KLON & the Blues Festivals 309

Joining KLON (1980) 313

Bernie And The First Blues Festival (1980) 319

1980, 1st Annual KLON Blues & Gospel Festival 329

The Fruit Falls From the Tree 339

A Blues Society is Born (1980 – 1981) 343

The Play Is The Thing (1981) 347

More Blues Festivals Follow 375

Big Mama Drops In -- USC Extension II (1982) 377

1983 4th Annual Blues Festival Lineup 387

1983, 4th Annual Blues Festival Musicians 391

1983 4th Annual Blues Festival Details 397

Call Him "Mr. Harmonica Smith" **(1983)** 423

1984 5th Annual Long Beach Blues Festival 425

Big Mama Maybe Sings Her Last Song (1984) 441

1985 6th Annual Blues Festival Lineup 443

- Blues Guitar Killers (1985) 445
- Big Time Blues Productions (1986) 449
- George Smith Harmonica Blowdown (1987) 455
- Final Blues Festivals With Bernie Pearl 459
- Bernie and The Real Deal 461
- Harmonica Fats and Johnnie (1986 – 1999) 469
- Booksellers' Blues (The 1990s) 481
- We Go to Gemmrig – Where? (1993) 487
- 1993 Big Time Blues Festival: Artists 489
- 1996 Big Time Blues Festival: Artists 491
- 2001 Big Time Blues Festival: Artists 495
- Big Time Blues Gets The Blues (2002) 499
- Some Interesting Gigs 501
- And You Thought We Were Done! (2020-2021) 507
- Musicians I Have Known 529
- Epilogue 533
- Book References 535
- Barbara Morrison's Family and Early Life 539
- Endnotes 549

List Of Biographies

Who Was Jesse "Lone Cat" Fuller 6
Who Was Sonny Terry? 109
Who Was Brownie McGhee? 112
Who Were Sonny Terry and Brownie McGhee 115
Who Was Blind Boy Fuller? 120
Who Was Lightnin' Hopkins? 143
Who Was Howlin' Wolf 147
Who Was Hubert Sumlin? 151
Who Was Mance Lipscomb 157
Who Was MS Fred McDowell? 167
Who Was Rev Gary Davis? 181
Who Was Bukka White? 193
Who Was "Big Mama" Thornton? 229
Smokey Wilson and His Music 277
Who Was Smokey Wilson? 278
Who Was Freddie King? 293
Who Was Barbara Morrison? 353
Who Was Sippie Wallace? 382
The Blues Society Finally Takes Off (1983) 384
Who Was Albert King? 399
Who Was Bill Graham? 406
Who Was Willie Dixon? 410
Who Was Bobby "Blue" Bland? 416
Who Was BB King? 425

Acknowledgements

A number of people agreed to be interviewed during research for this book. Their contributions added depth, insight and personal experience to the events and to the people described in this pages.

Interviewees included Gordon Alexandre (The Ash Grove), Ray Bailey (the Blues in LA), Mike Barry (the Bernie Pearl Blues Band), Phil Boroff (Bernie as a musician), Barry "Dr Demento" Hansen (The Ash Grove and King David and the Parables), Joe Kincaid (the Pioneer Club and the Tiki Room), Jim Tamburro (the Southern CA Blues Society), Sam King (the King Brothers), Bobby Warren (Blues history of Los Angeles), and Cadillac Zack Slovinsky.

Many of the photographs that are used throughout this book were freely contributed by some of the observers of the events described. Special thanks to these contributors including David Horwitz, Erik Lindahl, Marc Canter, Phil Melnick, Sam King, Stan Weinstock, and Jim Tamburro.

Edie Pearl, wife of Bernie Pearl, deserves special credit. Edie encouraged this project from the beginning. She regularly urged Bernie to write his memories until he finally took action. Edie supported this project throughout the long period of development, never wavering in her support.

Michiko Krell, wife of Bruce Krell, smiled on this project from beginning to end, without reservation.

Last but not least, thanks to all of the Blues musicians, living and dead, that performed the music. Preparing this book required extensive time listening to a wide range of Blues across both rural and urban Blues subgenres. These musicians made a gift to humanity that can never be repaid. Many of them made the recordings in the face of real physical and emotional adversity.

We hope to honor and to pay homage to these musicians by incorporating their stories and their participation in these pages.

Preface By Bernie Pearl

I am sitting here into my 86th year on this earth (so incredible to me), intending to write my story mostly as it pertains to my relationship with the Blues. I find myself in physical good health, and as stable and focused mentally as I have ever been – which probably isn't saying that much.

I am married happily to Edie. We have two marvelous kids, now young adults, who are successfully making a place for themselves in the world. We own our own home after almost twenty years of paying as low a mortgage payment as possible. Our lot is large. We have had many summer music parties here and are not looking to stop partying any time soon. I play tennis with an informal bunch almost daily at our local park. Neither Edie nor I are on medication. We keep busy, each in our own spheres. We, well mostly she, constantly work at nest building and maintenance, while I do any demolition and ladder-climbing required. I also split wood for our fireplace and do dead rodent disposal, as needed. I always know what's up when she hollers, "Bernard Marven!"

I've frequently been asked by my kids, other relatives, and friends when I'm going to write a book on my experiences. My response is usually that I will when I'm better-known and there's a demand. But, the truth is, I've been writing in my head for a long time. I doubt that fame or even just general name recognition will happen anytime soon. But I am convinced that what I have lived is worth sharing. I believe ever more firmly in what I do. I have never lost interest in understanding and learning about the Blues. Quite unexpectedly, my ability to translate that understanding into musical expression continues to expand.

But, a catalyst (I'll ignore the impulse to make a religious pun) got me started. I recently received an e-mail from my long-time friend and colleague Mary Katherine Aldin regarding my 1966 trip to the Newport Folk Festival and to New York with Luke "Long Gone" Miles. I told Mary Kathryn the tale. She responded that the story was fascinating stuff. I should write my memoirs down before I forget too much. Thanks so much, pal, for the reminder that time is indeed marching onward! True, nonetheless. In fact when I re-

read what I wrote to Mary Kathryn, I found the writing fascinating too.

I regret that I did not keep after my father about his early history. Daddy was less forthcoming than Mama. But, Daddy's story was a dramatic, and in some ways, a heroic story as well. Blessed is their memory.

Here's my story.

Bernie Pearl

Preface By Bruce Krell

I have the great pleasure here to join with Bernie Pearl to write the story of his life in the Blues. I am uniquely qualified to participate. I was raised Jewish in the South by Beatrice Stallworth, a Black woman, who introduced me to Gospel. As a result of this foundation, I came to love the Blues and Gospel sung in Black churches. I spent many hours listening to the Blues in juke joints in rural MS. *For the period 1980 – 1987, I participated in many of the events that involved Bernie. I observed and participated in the growth of the Blues community in Los Angeles during those years.* Any observations that I make about that period are based on personal experience during that time period.

Bernie Pearl played a key role in the growth and evolution of the Blues in Los Angeles and southern CA. During the years 1980-1990, Bernie hosted the KLON radio show *Nothin' But The Blues*. He also served as Artistic Director and Master of Ceremonies for the KLON Long Beach Blues Festival during that same period. Through these activities, Blues activities grew extensively at clubs in the affluent areas of West LA and Hollywood. Before Bernie, Blues musicians played only in south central Los Angeles for $25 for a 4 hour show. Thanks to these activities, Blues musicians began to play shows on financial terms that more reflected the value of their music and its appeal at a personal level.

But, Bernie Pearl is so much more. He is a real Blues musician and producer of Blues by himself and other Blues musicians.

I always wondered how Bernie came to be in the position to help influence and to grow the Blues in Los Angeles, southern CA, and then throughout the US. When Bernie offered me the opportunity to collaborate on his autobiography, I jumped at the chance to learn about his life. Now, you can also experience the life of Bernie Pearl through this autobiography.

You won't be disappointed!

Bruce Krell, PhD

Our Objectives In These Pages

This book was written with a number of specific goals in mind.

- provide a biography of Bernie Pearl written by Bernie

- relate how and why the Blues chose Bernie

- offer short biographies and historical vignettes of the lives of national Blues musicians that interacted with Bernie

- illuminate aspects of and insights into the lives of Blues musicians that are not normally known

- through statements by the musicians and comments by others, give insight into the personal side of each Blues musician

- explain how to *play the shit* (meant in a complimentary way)

    o describe techniques Bernie learned from Lightnin' Hopkins, Mance Lipscomb, MS Fred McDowell and others

    o balance plain English and technical jargon

    o use simple terms that non-musicians can understand

Bernie Pearl, the meaning of "Playing The Shit"

Some years ago, a musician I knew, who had moved away from the area years prior, came into a place where I was playing. He said something like, *Wow, there's Bernie Pearl, still playing the shit!* It was meant as a sincere and high compliment. The meaning is musicians' code meaning something like, *There you are, still reveling in the real, low-down, and no bullshit guitar Blues.* A more polite description of that kind of music would be Deep Blues.

I've always tried to learn exactly what the masters I was listening to were doing to make their music resonate. It meant a lot of time training your fingers to move in new ways, often, in new and unfamiliar places on your axe, i.e. the instrument you use to chop your way through the forest of music.

The music was conceived and realized often decades before, in places you've never seen or even heard of. A complex music seemingly natural and effortless to the artists you admire and even idolize.

Someone who can listen to your interpretations and admire it as they would the playing of the masters from whom you learned, by recognizing it as *the real shit*, is your reward. Hearing that level of recognition and even adulation from a group of people gathered to listen is about as good as it gets, regardless of the level of monetary reward you receive.

But, there's nothing wrong with some bread in recognition of the kind of shit you're laying down.

Lightnin' Hopkins

Mance Lipscomb

MS Fred McDowell

Rev Gary Davis

...sittin' on the Right Side of the Blues
A Life in the Blues

Bernie Pearl

Long Gone Miles

Harmonica Fats

You don't choose the Blues. The Blues chooses you.

Sam King, the King Brothers (Aug 11, 2023)

I didn't want the Blues stuff. Wanted to be a soul singer. Kept running away from the Blues. But could only make money playing the Blues. The Blues chose me. I finally accepted that. I claimed what I was – a Bluesman.

Bobby Warren, The Real Deal Bluesman (Jan 24, 2024)

Smokey Wilson (guitar) and Sam King (drums)
1980 Blues and Gospel Festival
Source: Bernie Pearl

The Blues Chooses Bernie

K'far Blum, Israel, July, 1958

Sitting on my cot reading the latest letter from my mother. She had written that my brother Ed, with help from our two other brothers, Stan and Sherman, our brother-in-Law Bob, other family, and members of the folk music community had been working on opening a folk music coffee house. This letter told me that it was now open, The Ash Grove and Galleries. I had spent the previous 10 months on a kibbutz in the Upper Galilee largely doing agricultural work. I had put on several pounds of muscle, was tan and fit, and as much as I had thrived in this setting, I couldn't wait to pack my guitar and get back to see what was going on. I had no idea what awaited.

The Ash Grove Founded By Ed Pearl
Source: The Ash Grove Foundation

Los Angeles, September, 1958

Once back in L.A. I got in touch with two of my musical friends from our Habonim youth group, Lonnie and David, and we three went to my first show at the club. Featured artists were a popular folk duo, "Bud and Travis", and the place was packed with the folkies of 1958. No mention of the opening act until Jesse "Lone Cat" Fuller was introduced and took the stage with his amplified 12-string guitar, harmonica rack (which was reputed to have inspired Bob Dylan), which also held a kazoo.

Jesse removed his right shoe and sat down on a stool behind this contraption made of wood (it looked like a piece of furniture), and had a scraper on its' side, controlled by his left foot, while he played the pedals on the furniture piece with his stocking-clad right foot. His heel on a swivel, he produced a steady electric bass pattern while playing a song filled with harmonica riffs and guitar chords, and some solos on the kazoo. Singing songs like "John Henry", "Workin' on the Railroad", and his own immortal "San Francisco Bay Blues". He finished his set by standing up with his 12-string and harmonica rack, playing a lively tune and dancing the buck and wing (traditional dance) with taps on his shoes.

It was stunning, compelling, and rhythmic beyond anything I had ever experienced. The three of us were yelling, laughing, pounding the table unrestrainedly. I glanced around the room. Men in jackets, neatly attired women were sipping their cappuccinos and talking, oblivious to the magic happening before their eyes, had they cared to look. I was stunned. It was in that moment I decided, no, I was compelled, to embrace what Jesse Fuller was laying down, and to begin to move away from the "folk music" I had grown up with.

It was a moment that changed my life. Blues, how do you do?

Who Was Jesse "Lone Cat" Fuller

Jesse "Lone Cat" Fuller was born in Jonesboro, GA, on Mar 12, 1896. His father had disappeared. His indifferent mother gave Jesse away when he was seven years old. Jesse was mistreated by his adopted family. He found solace in creating his own mouth harp and guitar by the time he was 10. After graduating the third grade, Fuller ran away, drifting across Georgia and Alabama. During this period, Jesse worked mostly in manual labor jobs: laying down railroad tracks, sweating in a lumber factory, working as a canvas stretcher in a circus, and building chairs.[1]

Jesse Fuller left the South for Cincinnati where he spent time running a streetcar. When he turned 24, Jesse moved on to Los Angeles, California, hawking handmade wooden snakes in the streets. Later Jesse opened a shoeshine stand on a corner outside of the studios at United Artists. While shining shoes, Jesse befriended one of the silent screen's biggest stars, Douglas Fairbanks, Jr. Fairbanks gave Fuller work as an extra in such epics as *"The Thief of Bagdad"* and *"East of Suez."* Jesse opened a hot dog stand that was bankrolled by Fairbanks at his shoeshine corner. With the money earned by selling hot dogs, Jesse moved to Oakland. In Oakland, he toiled on the Southern Pacific Railroad.

By singing on street corners doing show tunes, gospel songs, ragtime, folk tunes and the blues, Jesse Fuller made extra money while working for the Railroad. Jesse did not have the confidence to succeed professionally as a musician until after World War II. With the end of the War, the railroad job ended. So, Jesse started another shoeshine business in Berkley. In the late 1940s and early 1950s, Fuller drew the attention of Bay area folk singers. These singers came to listen to Jesse as he shined shoes and sang songs that he had learned from his years on the road. Soon Jesse was performing at several Bay area bars and clubs. Finally, in 1958, at the tender age of 62, Jesse recorded his first album, entitled *Jazz, Folk Songs, Spirituals And Blues*, released on the Good Time Jazz Records label. During that same year, Bernie Pearl heard the performance of Jesse Fuller at the Ash Grove.

Note Written By Jesse Fuller

On Air Playlist

His best, most well-known song was the *San Francisco Bay Blues*, appearing on an album of the same name in 1963.

Jesse "Lone Cat" Fuller Mural
Source: Jonesboro Public Art Project

The Furniture Piece

Jesse Fuller was no ordinary country Blues musician. Most country Blues musicians played an acoustic guitar and beat the rhythm directly tapping a foot or banging a high-hat cymbal. Fuller was not satisfied with the depth of the sounds from those limited instruments. Jesse invented a headpiece rack that could hold a harmonica, kazoo, and microphone. Unhappy with the beat from tapping his foot or beating the cymbal, Jesse Fuller also invented the ***fotdella*** that produced a deep bass sound.[2] The fotdella was the furniture piece used by Jesse Fuller to produce that a **steady electric bass pattern** that Bernie Pearl heard that night.

Fuller developed the fotdella in the early 1950s. In the first version, a large upright box had a rounded top, shaped like the top of a double bass, with a short neck on top. Six bass strings were attached to the neck and stretched over the body. He later made five more models of assorted designs.

**Jesse Fuller
Playing A Fotdella
(Rectangular Box)**
Source: African American Museum at Oakland,
MS193_B01_025

To play the instrument, a homemade set of pedals was pressed. Each pedal brought a padded hammer to strike a string when the pedal was depressed, like the action of a piano. When the depressed pedal struck a spring, each spring produced a different bass note. With these six bass notes, Fuller could accompany himself on the 12-string guitar in several keys.

It took me a whole week one time when I wasn't doing anything, and I made the thing I call the Fotdella in my back room. I just got the idea lying' in my bed one night, just like I write songs. I lie down on the bed and write songs at night. I thought about doing' something like that (the Fotdella) so that I could have something to go along with me and help me out instead of another fellow.

I just took some Masonite, heated some wood in hot water and rounded it off around a wheel. I learned that in the barrel factory where I used to work – that is the way they do the staves. I tried to use bass fiddle strings, but they don't sound so good, they stretch out of tune, so I use piano strings. My wife named it the Fotdella because I play it with my foot, like, 'Foot diller'.[3]

While generally spelled fotdella, the instrument name is pronounced footdella. This name was coined by Jesse's wife, Gertrude; a foot-diller -- fot from foot and della from killer-diller, an old expression used by jazz musicians for something hip or cool. So, a foot diller is a hot foot, which Jesse had, while nimbly playing ragtime bass lines with his right foot.[4]

Using these inventions, Jesse Fuller was a one-man band. He simultaneously played a 12-string guitar, a harmonica, a kazoo, a high-hat cymbal played with the left foot and the fotdella played with the right foot. In addition, Jesse would generally include at least one tap dance, soft-shoe, or buck and wing in his sets, accompanying himself on a 12-string guitar as he danced. His style was open and engaging. In typical busker's fashion, he addressed his audiences as "ladies and gentlemen," told humorous anecdotes, and cracked jokes between songs. He told of his love of his wife and family, but some of his stories were anything but cheerful, often including recapitulations of his tragic childhood, his mother's illness and early death, his determination to escape the segregated racial system of the South, suicide, and death.[5]

The Blues Chooses Bernie Pearl

With this performance by Jesse Fuller, the Blues chose Bernie Pearl. Fuller's musical rhythm compelled listeners to react and to interact. Listeners responded by clapping, stomping and howling while Fuller performed. The feel of the music infected Bernie's body and soul. Lyrics sung by Fuller told stories about his life, his travels and his relationships. These lyrics related to the life experience of everyone. Bernie Pearl was hooked. He wanted to perform this same style of music – the Blues. Bernie wanted to have the same effect on a listening audience as did Jesse Fuller. Yep, the Blues chose Bernie.

Who Is Bernie Pearl?

Hearing Jess Fuller that fateful night in 1958 had a profound effect on the future of Bernie Pearl. When he heard this sound with the electric bass pattern, Bernie knew from that point in time that he wanted to play country Blues like Jesse Fuller and those who followed.

Start	End	Activity
1939	1953	Growing Up In Boyle Heights
1953	1957	Growing Up In West Adams
1957	1958	Serving On Kibbutz Kfar Blum, Israel
1958	1970	The Ash Grove
1958	1961	Los Angeles City College
1962	1965	UCLA, BA Degree
1966		NYC Trip, Long Gone Miles
1968	1970	KPPC, Nothin' But The Blues
1973		TX Trip, Lightnin' Hopkins, Mance Lipscomb
1980	1990	KLON, Nothin' But The Blues, Blues Festival
1981		Play: Yerma, Barbara Morrison
1981	1982	USC, Simply Blues
mid 1980s	1990	Ms Whis Gig
1986	1999	Harmonica Fats, Bernie Pearl Blues Band
1991	1995	Bee Bump Records
1991	1992	KCRW, The Blues Roll On
1993	2001	Big Time Blues Festival
2005		Play: Berlin Blues
2020	2021	Barbara Morrison Performing Arts Center

With the performance of Jesse Fuller at the Ash Grove, the Blues chose Bernie Pearl. Bernie decided to make playing the Blues the major emphasis of his life.

This life involved a number of accomplishments:

- Learning to play country Blues from some of the great country Blues musicians.
- Modernizing and orchestrating country Blues to emphasize the beat of the rhythm with a heavy bass.
- Hosting *Nothin' But the Blues*, the first all Blues FM radio show, in Los Angeles, on KPPC then later revived on KLON.
- Growing the awareness of the Blues to the large potential audience in the Los Angeles area
- Creating the outdoor Annual Long Beach Blues Festival with local, then national Blues musicians
- Helping establish a growing performance schedule at local clubs for local Blues musicians.
- Returning the country Blues tradition back to the Black community in Los Angeles.

Lightnin' Hopkins Mance Lipscomb MS Fred McDowell
Source: Wikipedia   Courtesy: Gerrie Blake Courtesy: Bernie Pearl
Commons License   Newport Jazz Festival

During his time at the Ash Grove, Bernie was mentored by Lightnin' Hopkins and Mance Lipscomb(East Texas Blues), MS Fred McDowell (MS Hill Country Blues), and Rev Gary Davis and Brownie McGhee (Piedmont Blues). As a result of this extensive mentoring, Bernie was able to make significant inroads into mastering these primary sources of The Blues.

As a result of this mentoring, Bernie orchestrated these older Blues songs for a modern Blues band. Extensive use was made of the bass guitar and the drum kit to emphasize the rhythm and beat of these older country Blues songs. This fresh playing of these updated versions brings a great appreciation to these old Blues songs.

At the Ash Grove, Bernie formed the band King David and the Parables. This band was the first white Blues band in Southern California.[6] Barrett Hanson was a member of this band. Barry went on to become the famed Dr. Demento.

**1st Annual Blues and Gospel Festival, 1980, Long Beach, CA
Courtesy: Bernie Pearl**

Bernie started the Annual Blues Festival in 1980. This 1st Festival utilized only local Blues artists. As the Festivals grew in attendance, Blues musicians from all over, including Chicago, appeared at the Festivals. In 1982, the Long Beach Blues Festival was broadcast on APR. These broadcasts created a nationwide interest in attending live Blues concerts. Blues musicians from Chicago were performing at the Annual Long Beach Blues Festivals. Not surprisingly, in 1984, Chicago inaugurated its own series of Annual Blues Festivals.

By 1984, the Festival had grown to a 3-day event with 13000 attendees. After this peak, attendance settled in at about 8500 per year for the remaining years the radio show and Annual Festival were hosted by Bernie Pearl.

At the time when Bernie moved the *Nothin' But the Blues* radio show to KLON and started the Blues Festivals, the only places to see the

Blues in Los Angeles were the clubs in South Central Los Angeles. As a result of the radio show and the Festivals, a large number of venues in West Los Angeles and Hollywood began to host Blues performances.

After leaving KLON and the Blues Festival, Bernie began the Big Time Blues Festival in 1992. This festival was held annually until 2001. These Festivals were smaller. However, interest in live Blues performances continued to grow based on these Festivals, continuation of KLON activities and growing Blues performances in southern CA clubs.

Before 1980, Blues performances generally were not given in the more affluent areas of Southern CA. From 1980 – 1990, Bernie Pearl hosted *Nothin' But The Blues* on KLON and conducted the Annual Blues Festivals.

In Jan 1995, 28 Blues radio programs were broadcast from radio stations throughout southern CA **every week**. These programs ran from 1 – 3 hours each. During That same month, 529 Blues performances were given in affluent areas across southern CA for that month of Jan, 1995. All 31 days of the month had live Blues performances at clubs in affluent areas. Even a weekday generally had 10 or more live performances at various club venues. The Bernie Pearl Blues Band was among those performers.[7]

**Bernie Pearl Blues Band
Courtesy: Bob Aisley**

**From Left To Right
Bernie Pearl
Hollis Gilmore
Harmonica Fats
Big Terry DeRouen
Mike Barry
Albert Trepagnier, Jr.**

Now affluent whites did not have to venture into south central Los Angeles, a predominately Black area, to hear the Blues. Such a significant growth in live Blues performances in affluent areas of

Southern CA was a direct result of the efforts by Bernie during the decade and the years of the Big Time Blues Festival.

Blues musicians benefited significantly from these extensive radio and live performances at annual festivals and club venues.

When a Blues musician performed in South Central Los Angeles, he/she was lucky to get $25 for a 6-hour session. Gigs in more affluent areas of southern CA, such as West LA, Santa Monica, and Hollywood were shorter and paid significantly more per hour. Better pay enabled Blues musicians to obtain better income for their performances. More opportunities for better pay were indicators of the growth of local Blues.

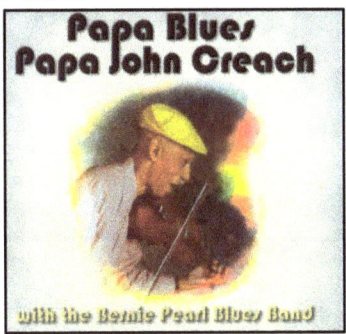

Front Cover, Papa Blues CD
Graphics, Photos Courtesy: EK Waller

This album received very positive feedback from reviewers.

By all rights this recording should have reset Papa's star in Jazz and Blues heaven. Unfortunately, his death in 1994 prevented his following up on this super disc.

But, thank the stars, we'll always have this one shining testament to his greatness.

Al Lubiejewski[8]

As a record producer, Bernie was able to preserve the Blues legacy of Papa John Creach and Harmonica Fats. Papa John was a member of a number of rock bands, such as Jefferson Airplane, Hot Tuna, Jefferson Starship, The Grateful Dead, and the Charlie Daniels

Band. His recordings with these groups did not really demonstrate the Blues capabilities of Papa John. In 1992, Bernie produced *Papa Blues*, featuring the Blues fiddle of Papa John front and center. These 13 recordings are the Blues legacy of Papa John Creach.

Who Is Bruce Krell?

Bruce is the everyman of Black Gospel music and its close cousin the Blues. When he listens to the Blues, he feels the music and the emotion behind the music. Bruce can sense when the music is "on" and is "off". This deep-seated intimacy with Black Gospel music and the Blues, its near cousin, was acquired from birth over his whole life.

Bruce can also be described as a Blues addict. He records video of live performances of Blues and Gospel performed in South Central Los Angeles. These videos are posted on YouTube for all to see.

Start	End	Activity
1949	1965	Raised In Klan Country By A Black Woman Singing Gospel
1955	1955	Attended Elvis Blues Concert, Forrest County Fairgrounds
1955	1958	Listened To "Race Records" -- Blues
1958	1964	Listened To Blues, Rockabilly, WXXX Radio
1965	1967	BB King, Bobby Bland At HiHat Club, Chitlin Circuit
1967	1973	New Orleans Blues In Unpromoted Neighborhood Clubs
1973	1977	Attended Last Freddie King Show At Liberty Hall, Houston
1981	1981	Discovered Nothin' But The Blues on KLON
1982	1982	Attended 3rd Annual Long Beach Blues Festival
1982	1988	Frequent Attendance At The Pioneer Club, Smokey Wilson
1983	1984	Volunteer Work At KLON FM - Flyers at Clubs
1983	1983	Volunteer 3rd Annual LB Blues Festival With Albert King
1983	1989	Tiki Room, Music Machine, China Club Blues Performances
1984	1984	Volunteer, KLON, Computer Work, 4th Annual Festival
1985	1989	Blues Clubs In Chicago On Business Trips

Bruce Krell was born Jewish in Hattiesburg, MS. Hattiesburg was in the heart of Klan country, only 20 miles from the national headquarters of the White Knights. Beatrice Stallworth, his Black mother, raised Bruce from birth to age 16. Beatrice used to stop Bruce from crying by rocking him and singing Gospel music. As she worked, Beatrice sang Gospel music. Thanks to Beatrice, Bruce listened to Gospel 8 hours a day, 6 days a week, for the first 6 years of his life. Gospel music was embedded in Bruce's DNA from an early age.

Beatrice Stallworth, Bruce and Ricky Krell, 1953
Courtesy: Bruce Krell

Elvis Presley introduced Bruce to the Blues. Bruce saw Elvis perform the Blues in 1955 at an unannounced concert at the Forrest County Fairgrounds. This location was in Petal, MS, just outside of Hattiesburg, where Bruce was born and grew up.

Elvis Presley In 1955

Courtesy: Graceland Museum

Notice the reddish blond hair!

Life was dangerous for Jews in south MS in the 1960s. Bruce formed an extended family with the children of Beatrice Stallworth and the Donald children, another Black family. Bruce regularly walked down the street in Klan country with his Black family and friends. This brazenness brought Bruce to the attention of several Klan groups. Bruce was chased and shot at by the Klan. He was personally threatened by two Imperial Wizards, Sam Bowers (White Knights) and Bobby Shelton (UKA).

Bruce has the experience of attending live concerts and interacting with the Kings of the Blues. As a teenager in Hattiesburg, MS, from 1965 – 1967, he watched and listened many times to BB King and others perform Blues at the Hi-Hat Club. This club in Palmers Crossing was one of the largest clubs on the famed Chitlin' Circuit.

**BB King At the HiHat Club
June 12, 1969**
Courtesy: Bruce Krell

I played the Hi-Hat Club so often that Hattiesburg was my home away from home.

BB King[9]

[Anniversary
Medger Evers Assassination
1963]

For 6 years, Bruce lived in New Orleans. During that period, he had the joy of seeing famous New Orleans Blues musicians perform in small neighborhood clubs. In these unpromoted performances, Bruce saw and heard Fats Domino, Allen Toussaint, Dr. John, Irma Thomas, James Booker, Earl King, and others. When living in Houston, TX, in 1976, Bruce attended the last concert by Freddie King at the famed Liberty Hall. Freddie died just 8 months after this concert.

Bruce served as a volunteer at the Long Beach Blues Festival in 1983. His job at the Festival was to be the "gofer" for Albert King. Bruce spent the day with Albert. He also saw Albert perform at several small clubs in MS after the Blues concert.

**Bruce Krell
Albert King
1983 Blues Festival
Long Beach, CA**

Courtesy: Bruce Krell

During the period 1985-1989, Bruce made numerous business trips to the East Coast. He often spent weekends in Chicago on his return trips. When in Chicago, Bruce attended concerts by Blues greats such as Son Seals and Buddy Guy in small clubs on the near north side, the west side, and the south side of Chicago.

Isaac/Yitzak Polinksy and Bracha/Bertha Medvinski
Grandparents of Bernie Pearl on Mother's Side
Ukrainian Ashkenazi Jews

The Origin Years (Prior To 1930)

Both the ancestors of Bernie Pearl and the Blues were born out of adversity. During the time period in which his ancestors faced violence and hatred, rural South and Southwest musicians were creating forms of music that reflected their own violent environments here in the US.

With this violent history absorbed into their DNA, most Jews, like Bernie Pearl, resonate with and feel the emotion upon hearing the threat of violence expressed in the lyrics, melody, harmony and rhythms of the Blues.

In 1904, the Polinsky family (Bernie's mother) emigrated from Ukraine in the Pale of the Settlement to Boyle Heights .The Pearl family (Bernie's father) emigrated to Boyle Heights in 1920.

The Old Country – The Pale of the Settlement

My parents were immigrants from the Ukrainian part of the Russian Empire.

Sara Polinsky Pearl

Courtesy: Bernie Pearl

My mother Sara, of blessed memory, came to America at around 4 years of age, from a little town in the area of Kiev, several years prior to WWI and the Bolshevik takeover. She entered via the port of Baltimore with her mother, father, older sister and brother, assisted by the money sent by Anna Pearl, who came earlier to work in America. They made their way to St. Louis.

They didn't just leave Russia, they fled it.

Although this was long before the calamity which came with WWII, there was poverty, oppression, and terror enough to motivate them, and millions of fellow Jews, get the hell out of there.

Jews had long been confined largely to small towns and villages in the "Pale of Settlement" generally to the west of Moscow, the Baltic countries, Ukraine, Belorussia, where they were subject to severe restrictions on land ownership, occupation, travel, forced conversion, and general abuse. And, just to make sure they remembered where they were, they endured periodic murderous rampages by their neighbors and armed gangs, called pogroms. Approved, fomented, or blind-eyed by the government and church.

Morris Pearl

Courtesy: Naturalization Application

The story of my father Maurice (Morris) was somewhat different. His family lived in Odessa, a cosmopolitan city on the north shore of the Black Sea. His father was a linguist and political activist. Odessa was a center of ideological ferment and was the center of the failed 1905 Socialist revolution. The triumph of the of the battleship Potemkin was short-lived, and my father, Maurice (Morris), of blessed memory, a boy of 10 or so, with his mother, father, and baby sister fled to Constantinople then to Egypt.

They lived in Cairo for a while, my grandmother running a small restaurant that catered to Jewish immigrants. My father, who was very close-mouthed about his early history, did tell us that he had been a payroll courier for Standard Oil. He recalled being beset once by a group of bandits who tried to pull him off his camel (I seem to recall that he said it was a donkey, but my brothers said, no, a camel) but he drove them off with his staff.

What a coincidence. I seem to recall that there was another Moses (Moshe is also my father's Hebrew name) some time ago who also used a staff to get out of hot water in Egypt.

His father is believed to have died in Cairo. Morris Pearl emigrated to the US, followed later by the rest of the family. My father was its adolescent head and provider. They entered at the port of NYC and headed for Philadelphia.

My parents met and married in Los Angeles. I am ever mindful that had they not immigrated and had I been born in Europe, I surely would be counted among the million and a half Jewish children who were hunted, trapped, and massacred by the Nazis and their many willing abettors in the Pale and across Europe.

A word on the phrase, *"of blessed memory"*. It is Jewish custom when writing the name of the departed to follow it with the abbreviation ז"ל. These are the first letters of the Hebrew words, zichrono (m), or zichrona (f) l'bracha: may his/her memory be for a blessing.

In recalling in these pages my many blues friends, teachers, and mentors who have passed, I would honor them with same respect. They were beloved contributors to my life, never to be forgotten.

Pearl/Polinsky Ancestral Rhythm

Bernie Pearl was born from the marriage between two Jewish families, the Pearls, and the Polinskys. Both of these families were members of a Jewish ethnicity commonly called Ashkenazi Jews.

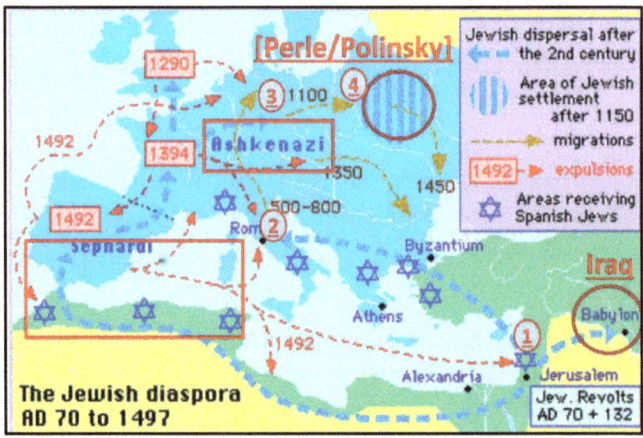

Jewish Migration Patterns

Prior to 132 CE (or AD), the Jews were concentrated in Canaan (now modern day Israel). Conquering forces resulted in Jews migrating from Canaan. This migration is called the Diaspora in Jewish history. In 63 BCE (or BC), Pompey conquered Jerusalem for the Romans. During the Roman occupation, many Jews were sent back to Rome as slaves (<u>1</u> above). From the beginning, the Jews did not go lightly. Various revolutions occurred. Around 133 CE (or AD), the Jew bar Kochba led the major revolution against the Romans. This revolution brought about the end of Roman occupation. Many Jews then began to voluntarily emigrate back to Rome. These Jews who emigrated from Rome during the period from 63 BCE until 150 CE are the source of the Ashkenazi Jews.

Once into Europe, the Jews were not well accepted. Jews were generally successful in business and were often blamed for the ills and failures of society. Between 500 CE and 800 CE, various government edicts drove the Jews from Italy up into Western Europe (<u>2</u> above), specifically Poland and Germany. Again, societal problems were blamed on the Jews. Another set of governmental edicts sent the Jews from Western Europe into Eastern Europe (<u>3</u> above). These Jews in Eastern Europe were pushed by the government in 2 directions around 1100 CE (<u>4</u> above).

One group of Jews was driven south into Southern Poland. This area was known as Galicia (<u>not shown</u>). The other area was eastward into

Russia (**4** above). But that was not the end of movement for the Jews in Russia.

Catherine II, Empress of Russia, created The Pale of the Settlement by decree on December 23, 1791. Additional decrees in 1793 and 1795 expanded the area incorporated into the Pale.[10]

The Pale of Settlement included all of Belarus and Moldova, much of Lithuania, Ukraine and east-central Poland, and relatively small parts of Latvia and what is now the western Russian Federation.[11]

The Pale of the Settlement

Error! Bookmark not defined. The Pale covered an area of about 386,100 sq. mi. from the Baltic Sea to the Black Sea. According to the census of 1897, 4,899,300 Jews lived in the Pale, forming 94% of the total Jewish population of Russia and 11.6% of the general population of this area.[12]

Ashkenaz is used in Hebrew and Yiddish sources from the Eleventh century onward to denote a region in what is now roughly Southern Germany.[13],[14] Ashkenazi Jews are the Jews who were pushed out of Poland and Germany and into the Pale of the Settlement and Galicia.

Facing A Hostile Environment

Simchah David Pearl and Isaac Polinsky were the grandfathers of Bernie Pearl. David Pearl, father of Morris Pearl, is believed to have been born in Odessa, Russia, around 1855. Issac Polinsky, father of Sara Polinsky, was believed to have been born in Stavidla, Russia, around 1860. Both of these cities are south of Kiev in the Pale of the Settlement, currently in Ukraine.

All Jews were limited to living and working within The Pale. Limiting Jews to specific geographical areas had two impacts on the Jews. Jews were subject to economic controls and limits. Jewish merchants were explicitly prohibited from trading within the inner provinces of Russia. Merchants within inner Russia did not have to face aggressive competition from Jewish merchants.[15]

As a result of these geographical limitations, Jews were restricted in their occupations. 72.8% of the total of persons engaged in commerce within the Pale of Settlement were Jews. Jewish artisans concentrated in certain branches of crafts (tailoring; shoemaking). Very few had the possibility of engaging in agriculture. The competition among the merchants, shopkeepers, and craftsmen was intense and gave rise to pauperization and the development of a Jewish proletariat which could not be integrated.[16]

However, the worst impact from concentration of the Jews was that Jews were easily targeted by violence. A Russian native could harass, murder, or beat a Jew walking down the street with impunity. Russian authorities ignored these activities and thus were complicit.

David Pearl was born in Odessa in The Pale around 1855. Manya Minnie Cosmandel Pearl was born in Stavidla in The Pale around 1860. **These grandparents of Bernie Pearl grew up, lived, and earned a living facing potential violence every day. Simply walking to work and shopping for groceries exposed the Pearls to a real threat of immediate violence.**

This violence was spurred by a growing belief that all of the ills of the Russian empire were attributed to the Jews. In reality, these ills were the result of the disruptive effects of industrialization and modernization. But, the Jews concentrated in The Pale and engaged as merchants were a convenient target for blame and violent actions.[17]

As anti-Jewish sentiment grew, so did the level of violence directed at the Jews confined to The Pale. Finally, the violence against the Jews erupted into pogroms. A pogrom is a riot in which a large number of angry people (a mob) directs violence at the Jews. This violence could take many forms: death, beatings, property damage, and property theft.

Easter was prime-time for pogroms. Priests riled the peasants with blame for the crucifiction of Jesus.

On March 13, 1881, Tsar Alexander II was assassinated. Some Russians blamed "agents of foreign influence," implying that Jews committed the murder.[18]

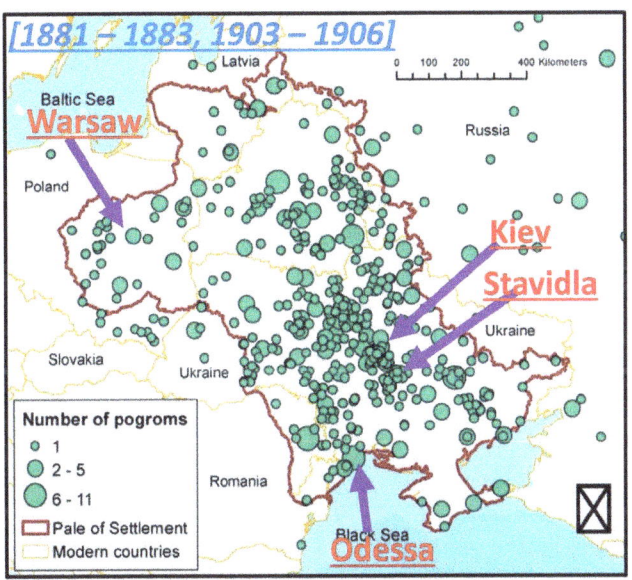

Pogroms Throughout The Pale
Source: Political and Economic Drivers of Pogroms[19]

A large-scale wave of anti-Jewish riots swept through The Pale from 1881 to 1883. More than 200 anti-Jewish events occurred in the Russian Empire. Pogroms which occurred in Kiev, Warsaw and Odessa were the most notable.[20] Altogether perhaps forty-five Jews lost their lives in these events, thirty-five in 1881–3 as well as the ten in Nizhny Novgorod in 1884. Many more were injured, and there was also considerable material damage.[21]

At the time of the 1881-1883 pogroms, David Pearl, the grandfather of Bernie Pearl, was growing up in Odessa. David was 13 years old. Grandmother Minnie Cosmandel Pearl, also growing up in Odessa at the time, was only 15 years old. Growing up in a violent environment seeps into your DNA. Hundreds of years of this violence directed at Jews are passed to subsequent generations through cultural and historical references and family tradition. Jews understand the feeling of the daily threat of violence. This feeling of the threat of violence was an important part of the original Blues. **With this violent history absorbed into their DNA, most Jews resonate and feel the emotion upon hearing the threat of violence expressed in the lyrics, melody, harmony and rhythms of the Blues.**

Escaping the Hostile Environment

Faced with increasing violence in The Pale, a large number of Jews chose to emigrate.

Sometime in 1903-1904, Grandfather David Pearl emigrated to Egypt with his wife Minnie Cosmandel Pearl. He was accompanied by his young son Morris, father of Bernie, born in 1892, and his daughter Mollie, born in 1902. Both Morris and Mollie had been born in Odessa.

The Pearl Family
Possibly David Pearl, Morris Pearl, Minnie Pearl
In Front: Mollie Pearl
Possibly Taken In Constantinople, Turkey
[Males Are Wearing Turkish Fez]
Source: Bernie Pearl

Grandfather David Pearl seems to have died in Cairo, Egypt in 1905. Grandmother Minnie and son Morris Pearl had to work in order to support the family. Morris was only 13 years old at the time.

In October, 1905, an extensive pogrom broke out in Odessa. *In the port city of Odessa alone*, the police reported that at least 400 Jews and 100 non-Jews were killed and approximately 300 people, mostly Jews, were injured, with slightly over 1,600 Jewish houses, apartments, and stores incurring damage.

These official figures underestimate the true extent of the damage, as other informed sources indicate substantially higher numbers of persons killed and injured. For example, Dmitri Neidhardt, City Governor of Odessa during the pogrom reported that over 800 were killed and another several thousand were wounded. Moreover, various hospitals and clinics reported treating at least 600 persons for injuries sustained during the pogrom. Jews of Odessa experienced the most violence and destruction of all the cities in the Russian Empire in 1905.[22]

Fortunately, the Pearls missed this extensive violence, having emigrated from Odessa via Constantinople to Egypt in 1903-1904. However, the Polinskys were not so fortunate.

Unfortunately, the violence was not restricted to Odessa. Surrounding small towns and cities were affected. Isaac Polinsky, grandfather of Bernie Pearl, wife Bertha Medvinski Polinsky, and daughter Sara Polinsky, mother of Bernie Pearl, lived in Stavidla, a small town in the Pale (now in southern Ukraine). In 1905, Sara, future mother of Bernie Pearl, was 3 or 4 years old. Fear of hiding from the ongoing pogroms was incorporated into her mental experience. **Feeling this fear is an example of the way in which these feelings get passed through the DNA from parent to child.**

Daughter Chana (Anna in English) Polinsky began the migration of the Polinsky family in 1906. Anna was only 15 years old at the time. Anna preceded the family to the US to establish an economic foothold. Jews often sent the oldest child to the US first, specifically for this purpose to ease the burden of emigration by the other family members.

Chana (Anna) Polinsky

Source: Bernie Pearl

Anna made her way to Rotterdam. She boarded the SS Potsdam to Ellis Island in NYC, arriving in July, 1906. From NYC, Anna made her way to St Louis.

Travel for Anna was in steerage class about the SS Potsdam. Steerage class was the cheapest form of travel on a ship.

... steerage passengers [are] crowded into the hold of ... [the ship. They] are positively packed like cattle, making a walk on deck when the weather is good, absolutely impossible, while to breathe clean air below in rough weather, when the hatches are down is an equal impossibility. The stenches become unbearable... [and the] division between the sexes is not carefully looked after, and the young women who are quartered among the married passengers have neither the privacy to which they are entitled nor are they much more protected than if they were living promiscuously. The food, which is miserable, is dealt out of huge kettles into the dinner pails provided by the steamship company.[23]

Imagine the bravery of a 15 year old girl travelling unaccompanied under these uncomfortable conditions!

In 1907, grandparents Issac and Bertha Polinsky, along with daughter Sara Polinsky and sons Phil and Louis, emigrated to the US from Stavidla, Ukraine.

Travel was in steerage class about the SS Frankfurt. This ship departed Bremen, Germany, and arrived in Baltimore, MD, in Nov, 1907. After leaving the ship in Baltimore, Issac, Bertha, Sara, Phil and Louis traveled to St Louis to join oldest daughter Anna Polinsky.

Morris Pearl, his mother Minnie and his sister Mollie, departed Egypt to emigrate to the US in 1913. This family traveled from Cairo, Egypt to Patras, Greece to NYC. In Oct, 1913, the family passed through Ellis Island and immediately moved to Philadelphia. Morris began work in Philadelphia as a machinist, in order to support his mother Minnie and his sister Mollie.

Boyle Heights In The 1920s

From 1900 to 1920, Los Angeles was the scene of frenzied activity in wildcat oil drilling, intense business speculation, religious excitement, extensive suburban development, the birth of the aircraft and film industries, and civic corruption. By 1920 southern California's population had surpassed that of northern California. In the next several years Los Angeles experienced the largest internal migration in the history of the American people. Hundreds of thousands of people arrived by automobile.[24]

New zoning and land use policies enacted by the Los Angeles City Council resulted in extensive building of production facilities. The number of rail yards, metal works, packing houses, and brick yards in the flats of Los Angeles grew. Boyle Heights' proximity to jobs in these facilities enticed an increasing number of working-class families to settle in the area.[25]

However, about 90% of housing stock in Los Angeles was governed by restrictive racial housing covenants. Boyle Heights was one of the few neighborhoods that did not have the covenants.

Boyle Heights In 1924
Source: Security National Pacific Collection, LA Library[26]

However, segregation did exist within Boyle Heights. Blacks had their own segregated section of Boyle Heights. Blacks called the segregated Jewish section of Boyle Heights *Jewtown*.

By 1920, the mostly white, affluent residents of Boyle Heights had subdivided their estates into smaller parcels and sold them off at more affordable prices.[27]

Immigrants moving to a new community tend to congregate together. A common foreign language and old country customs just made for a more comfortable life. Without the restrictive covenants, Jews migrated to and heavily settled into Boyle Heights. Jews in Boyle Heights were primarily working-class families of Eastern European descent, largely secular, and politically engaged.[28]

Boyle Heights became the largest Jewish community west of Chicago. Local businesses, such as restaurants and groceries, were needed to support residents and to the availability of homes.[29] Many Jews started these local businesses in the area. The Jewish population in Boyle Heights grew from less than 2,000 residents in 1920 to over 10,000 households in 1930.[30] Of the Jews residing in greater Los Angeles in the 1920s, at least one-third lived in Boyle Heights.[31] By the end of the 1930s, 50,000 Jews were concentrated in the Boyle Heights district.[32]

Pearl and Polinsky In Los Angeles

In 1920, the Breed Street Shul in Boyle Heights was the religious and cultural center for the Jews in Boyle Heights.

Breed Street Shul, 257 N Breed St, Boyle Heights

Orthodox Jews must walk to Sabbath morning services. Social activities often occur on the Sabbath as well as other days of the week. In the 1920s in Boyle Heights, the Breed Street Shul provided these activities for the Jews in Boyle Heights.

In late 1920/early 1921, both the Pearl and the Polinsky families independently relocated to Los Angeles. At this time, the families did not know each other. Both families moved into separate homes in Boyle Heights. These homes were fairly close together.

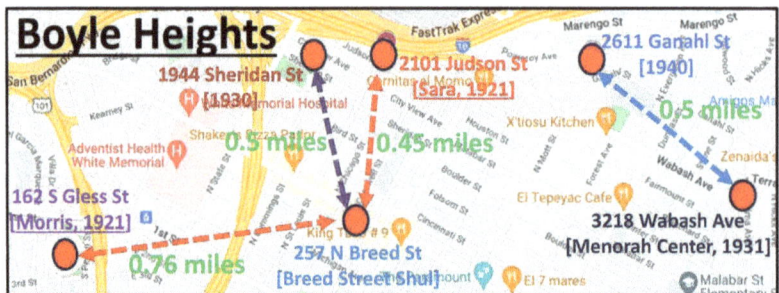

Pearl and Polinsky Homes During the Early Years In LA

In 1921, Isaac, Anna, Phil, Louie and Sara Polinsky were living together at the north end of Boyle Heights.

Polinsky Home, 2101 Judson St, Boyle Heights

Bertha Medvinksi Polinsky died on June 3, 1922. Isadore Polinsky, her husband, died a year later on June 8, 1923..

Not far away, Morris Pearl, Aunt Mollie and mother Minnie Cosmandel Pearl were living together on the west side of Boyle Heights, at the same time in 1921.

Pearl Home, 162 S Gless St, Boyle Heights

The Polinsky home was 0.45 miles from the Breed Street Shul. Morris and Minnie lived about 0.76 miles from the Shul. This home was still well within walking distance. By living within walking distance, both the Pearls and the Polinskys could participate in the Orthodox community life.

Given the importance of the Shul in their social lives, Morris Pearl met Sara Polinsky at event for a young peoples' group at the Shul. On August 16, 1925, Morris Pearl married Sara Polinsky.

Morris Pearl and Sara Polinsky

Marriage Picture, 8/16/1925

Courtesy: Bernie Pearl

After getting married, Morris and Sara Pearl chose to establish their own home within Boyle Heights.

1944 Sheridan Street, Boyle Heights

This house was about 0.5 miles form Breed Street Shul, again, well within walking distance. Bernice (1928), Stan (1930) were born in this house on Sheridan Street. Morris was working as a delivery man for the Sunny Coast Baking Company at 3600 Avalon Blvd.

The Pearl Family in the 1930s

In March 1931, Marco Newmark, president of the Federation of Jewish Welfare Organizations, presided over the official dedication of the new Menorah Center in Boyle Heights.[33]

The Menorah Center
3218 Wabash Ave, Boyle Heights

This new facility was to become the educational and cultural center for most working class Jews in Boyle Heights.

Classes aimed to soothe the "constant strife" between immigrant parents and their American-born children. As Jewish kids acquired "American ways of doing and thinking," the more traditional ways and customs of their often religiously-observant parents caused conflicts. These parent/child conflicts forced the kids on to the streets to be corrupted by all sorts of "anti-Jewish" influences[34]

Classrooms, offices, a large auditorium on the street-level and a large banquet hall on the ground floor below were all housed in the Menorah Center. A variety of social clubs for adults and children were conducted in the auditorium. Wrestling mats, boxing equipment, and a volleyball net enabled the auditorium to serve as a gymnasium.[35]

With the wide variety of classes and social functions at the Menorah Center, Morris and Sara wanted to move closer to the Center.

Pearl Family Home
2611 Ganahl St, Boyle Heights

Shortly after the opening of the Center, a new home was found for the Pearl family, closer to the Center. This home was only 0.5 miles from the Menorah Center. Morris, Sara and the kids could easily walk to this Center to participate in events. Morris and Sara had 3 more children in this home: Edwin (1932), Sherman (1934) and Bernard (1939). Brother Ed first abbreviated this name to Bernie when Ed introduced Bernie at Habonim Camp in 1952 or 1953.

Young Bernie Pearl and Siblings, circa 1946
Courtesy: Bernie Pearl

Bernie Pearl Grows Up (1940s, Early 1950s)

Boyle Heights and the Left

I was born in East Los Angeles, in 1939 in the Jewish enclave of Boyle Heights. During the 20's and 30's, this was where the Jewish community thrived and grew. The temples, the Yiddish and Hebrew schools, the gangsters, the rag and junk men and small businessmen (some of whom found great success) were all to be found there.

After WWII the community began to dissolve, moving to the Westside, Beverly-Fairfax, the San Fernando Valley (even). My community was blue-collar, often politically left and pro-union, We fit right in. My mother kept kosher and observant, my father was secular, skeptical of religion, if not an atheist. I recall the FBI vehicles parked in the neighborhood. One of our neighbors was a prominent Communist that the government wanted to arrest, which they eventually did, at the Wabash Theater watching the Saturday matinee with his kids. The Feds were the intruders, clamping down on political freedom, as far as I was concerned.

After WWII, the US became paranoid about the USSR, our WWII ally, and the witch-hunt for Commies was on. Notoriously manipulated by political charlatans like Sen. Joe McCarthy and the House Un-American Activities Committee (HUAC), the country lived under a sort of reign of terror, with many afraid to speak their mind. Many of those under federal scrutiny were Jews. Indeed, some of them were actual members of the C.P., but many simply supported "leftist" causes like desegregation and unionization. In L.A. the movie industry was terrorized by HUAC and the studio bosses, mostly Jews, who opposed anything to do with workers' rights. Thus, the Blacklist grew. Many lost their families, careers, and lives.

For my family, the ultimate horror came with the arrest, conviction, and execution of Julius and Ethel Rosenberg. By all accounts, Ethel played a very small roll in the conducting of information to Russia. Julius did give them some information, but did not divulge the secrets of atomic fission, allowing the Soviets to build the Bomb. They were both executed, making their sons orphans, and sending a message to us leftie Jews. The entire trial was conducted, on both sides, by Jews. As if to say, look, here are the real American Jews and there are the traitor Jews.

Watch your step, yids!

My mother, very far from being unpatriotic or communistic, wept heartbroken for the Rosenbergs. She regarded America as the *goldene medineh*, the golden land, as did most immigrants. Not for the wealth to be had, but for the treasury of freedoms we all enjoyed, especially when compared with the Old Country. But, the Rosenberg children!

My father railed against capitalism in general, and against Harry Truman, for his anti-union stance. We came by our suspicion of power and government with good reason. Our young people were looking for something better.

Boyle Heights – My Mama Told Me...

My mother told me once of an incident that occurred when I was very young. Our little community had a small business area on nearby Wabash Avenue. It was all Jewish. One very seldom saw "Mexicans" on Wabash ("Chicano" was unknown at the time), even though that community was rapidly expanding, and one never saw "Negroes".

I had never seen a Black person as a youngster. But there were Black residents of Boyle Heights, no doubt in a restricted area. I learned many years later that our "Heights" was known as "Jew Town" among Blacks. It was shocking to hear.

My mother told me that she was shopping, I think at Block's Bakery, with me in her arms.

Bernie Pearl At Age 22 Months

Courtesy: Bernie Pearl

A Black man came in, he was near enough for me to say "Ooh, dirty", and to try and wipe the black off his face. Needless to say, she was totally embarrassed and apologized profusely. She said that he smiled at my childish confusion, and said "It's alright". I have often wondered if I took to heart his benign and understanding response. I can say maybe, but not dismiss it. Messages like that tend to go deep.

The shared backyard of the duplex we rented from the Weinsteins had a large wooden structure we used as a playhouse. Many fantasies played out there. Next door was a little old English lady, named Mrs. Littlefield. A little house adorned with lace, porcelain knick-knacks, and a portrait of King Edward, who abdicated the throne for love of American divorcee', Wallis Simpson, that hussy! We respected Mrs. Littlefield, but constantly raided her fig tree, and invaded her backyard. Not to do damage, but for the adventure. Shame on us, she was a kind person.

At some point we were evicted from the duplex at 2611 Ganahl St – times were tough after the war and Mrs Weinstein's brother needed a place to live. We stayed temporarily in a house with friends of my parents down the block, and then moved into my Uncle Louie's duplex, from which, I presume, he had evicted some other poor soul. One summer day I saw our street being repaired by a black worker. His son was on hand and he and I shared a good part of the day hanging out. He later suggested we meet at the nearby activity center which had lately opened, the   Variety Boy's Club – I can only conjecture how many lives were changed by this open-to-all facility where one could learn to box, play pool, see movies for free.

Variety Boys Club, Boyle Heights, Founded 1949

Courtesy: Variety Boys and Girls Club

I readily agreed, but later I thought, "How will I recognize him?" Mind you, there was never any racial epithets or prejudiced ideas expressed in my house, or in our neighborhood. Joe Louis, Paul Robeson, Marian Anderson, Jackie Robinson were icons of the sort of America we wanted. Where did my idea come from? I think now that it was just in the air. Somehow, in America – even in Jewish Boyle Heights – these ideas were pervasive. As you can predict, I went there, spotted him right away, and we spent the, and had a very nice time together. A good lesson learned.

My grammar school was Evergreen Elementary. It was largely Jewish and secular.

Evergreen Avenue Elementary School (after remodel)

As I recall there were some Hispanics, no Blacks, some white non-Jews, and no ethnic prejudice ever expressed. It seemed a pretty calm and happy place.

Then came Hollenbeck Jr. High School. I was terrified going in. It was a couple of miles away from my house. As I recall, about a week into the semester, there was a killing in the neighborhood. I forget whether it was a Mexican or a black kid killed, but the result was visible tension between the two groups. The blacks walked to and from school on one side of the block, the Mexicans on the other. A chilling sight. I don't recall how long this lasted. The blacks were by far the smaller number. I do recall that I made one black friend, and we used to hang together at recess. Other free times I connected to the dwindling group from Evergreen Ave. I was told later by one of my classmates that he felt shunned by me.

Hollenbeck Junior High School

I stayed there for about a year and a half, did not thrive in the near-reformatory atmosphere. Getting swatted for infractions was the norm, and as I good as I tried to be, received that punishment on occasion. Those were the times, but they were much more rigid times, and the more I learned of reality, the less connected to common mores and attitudes I became.

I was quite small at the time, not athletic, and thus the subject of some derision by the super-macho white gym teachers.

There was some bullying. One incident stays with me. There was a Mexican kid who didn't like me, or thought I was an easy target. One day before school, he cornered me at the nearby candy store and tossed a couple of punches. I was startled, but easily parried the blows. He was shocked and stopped and never tried it again. One good thing was that I learned that I had good reflexes, which I still possess and use on the tennis courts for net play. I had no idea of how to throw a punch. I have never been a street fighter, and avoid trouble if I can. In the 1970's I took some karate lessons, but I still don't think much is worth getting into a fight over, except in self-defense. With one exception. I will protect my territory when performing.

I have a policy of no soap when a stranger comes up and wants to sit in with the band on a gig. Even people I know, decent musicians, I say no to. The reason is that we have worked to get the right sound, and I consider the thousands of hours I've put in to get the material the way I want, and what it took to hook up the gig. If it's someone I know whose playing would enhance the show, sure. Other than that, they're looking to do their own thing on my time. Oh no, baby. I mean red-faced, white-knuckled piss-off doesn't change my mind. On jam night, everyone gets to play. If I'm a side-man, I defer to the leader. But, on my own show....territorial.

Boyle Heights Legacy

I was glad to get away from Hollenbeck. I found my new school, Mt. Vernon Jr. High more amenable. Although it was not problem-free, there was a more relaxed and education-oriented atmosphere, and daily anxiety abated.

I cherish many aspects of my Boyle Heights upbringing, and was very happy to see the kids I grew up with on occasion. Fairly often I would bump into Leona (Lessikin) Sugar and her husband at McCabe's, where I taught in the 1970's. Her dad had a small neighborhood grocery, and she was one of the leaders of the class. We kept in loose touch, and several years later she invited me to a gathering of those who had stayed in The Heights and graduated from Roosevelt High.

What was special was that they had located our beloved 6th grade teacher, Mr. Gerber, and he would attend. I couldn't miss that. Mr. (or Dr.) Gerber was one of those remarkable educators who inspired kids to be their best through genuine concern and interest. He had an almost Mr. Rogers-like gentility and ability to communicate. The 5th grade teacher, Ms Azadian, was the heart's desire of all the boys, and an excellent teacher. We all suspected, or hoped, that they had something going on. I wasn't about to ask him, but after he left the gathering, we all buzzed about that real or imagined relationship as if we were the pre-teens of more than 5 decades prior instead of graying adults with many grandchildren amongst us. We all giggled and roared with delight. As great an educator as he was, he had been Blacklisted and dismissed from teaching Public School shortly after we left Evergreen. A further verification of the stupidity and harm to our society caused by jingoism and political malice. Not my America.

The Best Things in Life…

Money was always an issue in our house. It led to stress and emotional insecurity in all of us. I was an oops baby, born 5 years after what my parents thought would be their final addition. I think that I blamed myself for adding to my parents' woes. I tried to be as good and pleasing as I could be, but it was a load for a child to carry. But, I was also a normal kid with ups and downs, good and bad behavior. I just think that my "bad" behavior created guilt, held inside me. It has taken a while to realize this and to unburden myself of it.

Before I came along, Morris, my father, had tried to make a go of selling day-old bakery goods from a truck. He was nice-looking, honest, intelligent, affable, and a hard-working man. But, at some point in the early 1940's, Helms Bakery's truck fleet expanded and drove him out of business. He then learned the tool and die making trade. He was in his 40's and had 5 children to support, and had not been eligible for the Draft. My mother once inferred that she had to really pressure him to get his citizenship papers during the 1930's.

Without citizenship he would have been subject to deportation, to face the horrors looming in Europe.

His work was not consistent; paychecks, then layoffs, then new jobs. After the end of WWII the country was in a recession, many struggled, others prospered. We lived in Uncle Louie's duplex in one bedroom for my parents, a Murphy bed in the living room for me and my brother Sherman, and a couple beds in the garage for brothers Stan and Ed, next to Uncle Louie's vegetable truck. For me and, I think, for my brothers, it wasn't all that bad. We were young and full of life. My parents would have been another matter. Our sister Bernice, the oldest, had been stricken by polio as a youngster. Caring for her as much as she required was too much for my mother, who had two other children and one on the way at the time. I was to come later. My sister was living with my mother's older sister nearby. She took her to her frequent doctors' appointments, massaged and exercised her.

I'm sure that it was physically the right thing, but inside my mother felt guilt, as one would expect, for giving up her child. My sister, who passed away in recent years in her early 80's, bore lifelong emotional scars and resentment. She wanted to be with her own family. She got to do so periodically as she healed and grew stronger over the years, sleeping happily, I think, on a hospital bed in the living room. She was beautiful and loving, and had a profound influence on my life. She, who had suffered much, was the family go-to person for all of my generation, because she understood so much. This can be a mean old world, can it not?

Family life was not all gloomy and stressful by any means. One of my favorite things to do was to go to Venice Beach, where we had cousins with a little house. We'd meet other family, aunts, uncles, older and younger cousins, romp in the surf and dig in the sand, and picnic on cheese sandwiches. Shower at the cousins.

We had other cousins who lived in the "country", El Monte, 20 miles east of us. A long Sunday drive to another world, before freeways and suburbs. They had chickens and goats, a neighbor who had cows, a swing, and lots of trees and space. They built things out of stone and wood and metal. My father was very comfortable with cousins Jack and Eva, also immigrants from Russia, who worked with their hands, as he did. As I do, in my own way. Not to make too much of it, but I'm sure it is one of his principles that took root in me. I recall loving to fall asleep in the back seat on the drive home. I play occasionally nowadays at the Fret House in a very developed and urbanized El Monte, and I reminisce on the 40 freeway miles from Long Beach.

We move to West Adams 1952

Mama's sister Anne (we called her Tante – aunt) had moved to the fairly posh Carthay Circle area, near Olympic & Fairfax, with her daughter's family around 1950. Tante had become a mother to her since her parents passed away, and she missed the almost daily contact. For that reason, more than any other I can imagine, our family moved to the "West Side", although to the more working-class West Adams area. Otherwise, I would have joined my siblings as a proud graduate of Roosevelt High. But, I was not unhappy about the move and the change of schools. Ultimately, we settled at 2609 West Blvd.

2609 West Blvd

West Adams had been a smaller version of Boyle Heights, but like the Heights, the Jewish population was leaving there as well. African-Americans were moving in, rather than Mexicans, but the dynamic was the same. Our new neighborhood had its requisite nearby bakery, grocery, barber shop, plus a synagogue around the corner.

Henry and Ruth Stibelman had the grocery store around the corner to the west. I worked there for a while in high school.

As I was nearly 13, I was enrolled in a class of one to study for my Bar Mitzvah. I loved my teacher, Mr. Shapiro, and attended services fairly regularly.

**Bernie Pearl, Bar Mitzvah, Age 13
With Sara Pearl and Morris Pearl
Courtesy: Bernie Pearl**

However, my Jewish education was now being supplemented by joining the Labor Zionist youth group called Habonim – the Builders. This group was based in the Beverly-Fairfax area, a substantially middle-class area just east of Beverly Hills. I attended regular weekly meetings during the year and a summer camp.

Habonim was founded in 1929 in the United Kingdom to connect young Jews via Jewish culture. Particular emphasis was placed on Jewish development in Palestine (now Israel). By the time I joined Habonim, Israel had been established. Making Aliyah ("rising up" or resettling in Israel) , preferably on a Kibbutz collective, was the ideal goal. Several of my Habonim chaverin(comrades)/friends) made the choice to actually resettle permanently to Israel.

Over a period of years, the Habonim movement spread to all English-speaking countries. Each country developed its own independent version of the original movement. Yet, each country shared the core ideology of being a Jewish Zionist-socialist cultural youth movement.[37]

Organized Zionist activity in the US began in NYC. A large group of young Zionist supporters became members of the Hoshomer Hatzair youth movement which was active in the city. Amid growing tensions in the group, a large number of members launched a new Zionist initiative to be known as Habonim. David and Minna Yaroslavsky were original founding members of this group in NYC.[38]

Habonim in North America (HDNA) was founded on May 12, 1935 by Young Poale (Workers') Zion, the youth arm of the Poale Zion Party, at a convention in Buffalo, NY. Habonim's North American branch is based on five so-called *"pillars"*: Judaism, Labor Zionism, socialism, social justice, and Hagshama—commonly translated as actualization—by embodying and fulfilling the movements values through action.[39]

On the day of formation, Habonim North America conducted a ceremony to welcome its first 100 members. Minna Yaroslavsky was the MC at this ceremony. David came to the ceremony from a farm in New Jersey, where he was helping members to prepare for an agricultural life in Palestine.[40] In 1937, David and Minna Yaroslavsky moved to Los Angeles, helping to grow the Habonim Los Angeles Chapter.[41] Ater moving to Los Angeles, David helped organize the Los Angeles Hebrew Teachers Union. Minna helped organize anti-fascist marches and pro-Israel demonstrations.[42]

Son Zev Yaroslavsky was born in Los Angeles in 1949. Zev would himself become an avid member of Habonim Los Angeles. As an adult, Zev was elected to local government positions, including the Los Angeles City Council and the LA County Board of Supervisors. At the weekly meetings held on the weekends, Bernie Pearl met **Shimona Yaroslavsy, older sister of Zev**. Ultimately, Zev and Bernie Pearl would become friends through sister Shimona and the Habonim activities.

Camp Gilboa is one of six North American summer camps (machanot) associated with Habonim Dror North America (HDNA). Camp Gilboa was originally formed in the Los Angeles area in 1936 with the name Habonim Camp Kvutza (Collective)

Naame.[43] Naame was the name of the original Arabic town that was depopulated upon the formation of Israel. The town of Naame was later renamed Kibbutz Kfar Blum. Habonim Camp Naame was renamed Camp Gilboa when the camp was relocated from Saugus to Big Bear Lake. David Yaraslovsky was the business manager of Camp Naame during the 1950's.[44]

This camp began in Saugus and is currently located near Big Bear Lake. The summer camp runs for 6 weeks. Campers have the option of staying for the full summer or for shorter sessions. Each session has approximately 140 campers. Young campers (entering 3rd or 4th grade) have the option of a 4-day camp experience called seedlings (nitzanimot).

As with other Habonim camps, Gilboa instills the community-minded values of the Kibbutz movement, but in an American Jewish context.[45] Campers participate in traditional camp activities, such as hiking, kayaking, arts and crafts, and archery; there is also an emphasis is on "Israel, Hebrew, understanding current events and, most importantly, making campers personally responsible for the success of their Gilboa experience.[46]

I was introduced to the organization by my brother Ed, who somehow arranged for my attendance at the summer camp. We did not have money for such things. It was far from fancy, and all shared work and maintenance responsibilities. Lots of hiking, sports, a swimming pool – where I learned how not to drown, if not to swim. We discussed Israel, Jewish history, philosophy, politics, and idealism.

Every evening after dinner there was folk dancing, and we sang all kinds of songs. I especially loved the late-night "folk" music records: singers like Pete Seeger and the Weavers, Harry Belafonte, Josh White, Burl Ives. In those times, the "McCarthy Era", when the nation continued to conduct witch hunts and congressional inquisitions, seeking to expose and destroy the domestic "Red Menace" and "Fellow-Travelers", it was fairly risky and brave to be part of the dissident counter-culture that sang folksongs and played guitars. It was also meaningfully delicious to be part of the opposition. Music was integral to that identity.

I was not aware of the extent of the glorious music that was being made at that time in the rural areas of the Deep South, and in pockets of most urban areas. Guitars, banjos, harmonicas, fiddles were the accompaniment to magnificent singing and poetry originating in isolated communities in the Mississippi Delta, the Appalachians, the Brazos River, the Ozarks. The real traditional American folk music had yet to cast its spell on me. I should have guessed.

After Mt. Vernon Jr. High, I attended Dorsey High School. This high school opened in 1937.

Dorsey High School, 1939
Courtesy: Los Angeles Public Library[47]

I continued to attend the Friday evening and Sunday afternoon gatherings of my Habonim group. Singing and dancing along with discussions and social activities. I did not go to the regular gym dances with my classmates, else I might have become more aware of the Rock and R&B so beloved of my generation.

Hootenanny at Bernice's early 1950's

In the early 1950's, my brother Ed was part of the UCLA Folksong Club, an informal group which had embraced the music of what was generally considered the counterculture. This was the era when a carrying a guitar case marked one as at least a "pinko", if not an out-

and-out Commie! Identified with music that was not heard on radio, television, or in the movies: "We're Gonna Roll The Union On", English ballads like "Barbara Allen", Negro folk music like "Take This Hammer", anti-nuclear pro-peace songs like "The Strangest Dream", American folk songs like "The Streets of Laredo". And if a tune like Leadbelly's "Goodnight, Irene", sung by Pete Seeger and the Weavers, received airplay, sold records, and made the charts, it was an anomaly, and it didn't prevent the reactionaries from barring those artists from many studios and concert halls.

My sister Bernice, the oldest of the five Pearl siblings, was married, just starting her family, and she and her husband Bob had a house on the Westside.

Bernice Pearl

Courtesy: Bernie Pearl

The home folksong get-togethers were called Hootenannies, and Bernice hosted many of the first ones in her living room. 20 or 30 people would gather on a weekend night bringing nylon-string guitars, a banjo or two, and maybe an autoharp to sing the songs that most everyone knew. Not a high instrumental skill level for most, but tons of enthusiasm. Hoots were fun.

I Get My First Guitar

Ed's folksong friends had arranged for the purchase of a dozen guitars from Mexico at a special price, perhaps $25 each, but only if they bought the full dozen. They had eleven buyers including Bernice. He asked me if I'd like to join in. At the time I was around 13 or 14.

Bernie Pearl, Age 14

Courtesy: Bernie Pearl

I earned just a little selling newspapers on our street corner. I didn't have $25. I don't recall who put up the bucks, but I had my first guitar, metal strings with little colorful "caterpillars" on the ends that connected to the bridge. One of several things for which I am grateful to Ed.

At any rate, I was able to join in at the Hoots. I practiced, and quickly learned the chords to many songs from the Burl Ives songbook. Though the youngest at the Hoots, I fit right in. But, I wanted to learn more.

Advisor to the group, and the true "mother" of the L.A. folksong movement was Bess Lomax Hawes.

Bess Lomax Hawes

Courtesy: Library of Congress

Daughter of seminal folklorist John A. Lomax, and sister of the equally renown Alan Lomax, Bess had been working as a folklorist for several years, and was part of the historic and profoundly important group in New York which was pointing the way to new music and to new ways of thinking: Pete Seeger, the Weavers, the Almanac Singers, Leadbelly, Woody Guthrie, Brownie & Sonny, Cisco Houston, and more. She had written a hit song about a poor soul who got lost on a Metropolitan Transit Authority train, but realized that her future lay in other directions. She moved to L.A. to teach classes, continue to study American folklore, to guide the energy of the young people starting to explore this music, and to raise a family with her musician husband, Butch.

She could play some guitar, and I asked her for a lesson or two. She consented reluctantly, saying that she didn't play very well. But, she surely knew more than I. These sessions, among the few formal lessons I have ever taken, became the foundation for a friendship that I cherish to this day. Guitar, yes, but her vision of, and insight into America's real folk music remain with me. More on Mrs. Hawes as my story unfolds.

West Adams Nights

At 13 I became an active member of a Labor Zionist youth group called Habonim – the Builders. We were affiliated with the Labor party in Israel which was led, at that time, by iconic politician David Ben Gurion. It was left-leaning, and oriented towards introducing us to the agrarian communal lifestyle as practiced in Israel on the kibbutz. We would meet Friday evenings to celebrate in a secular way the coming of the Sabbath. We engaged in story-telling, discussions, singing and folk dancing. I used to hitch-hike from West Adams to the meetings near La Cienega and 3rd Street, near where the upscale Beverly Center is now located. Most of the group lived in the area. I would thumb a ride back home – I did have the key to the highway.

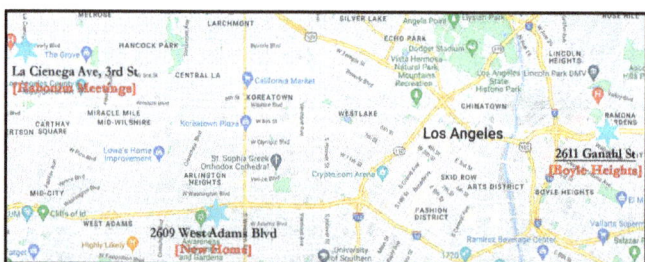

Traveling To Habonim Meetings From West Adams

Sometimes when I lay in bed I heard dance music being played live just across the street at the Jewish War Veterans Hall. JMV Hall was above the barber shop and cleaners across the street.

> **B'nai Emunah Stages Comedy**
>
> Young Women's Council of B'nai Emunah congregation, 4200 South Grand avenue, will hold a spring dance and Yiddish comedy show Saturday evening at 8 o'clock in Jewish War Veterans' hall, 2604 West boulevard. Profits will be used for an oxygen tent for Israel.
>
> Zena Bear will give impersonations; Estair Koplin will sing. Others in the cast will be Sam Peskin and Irving Goldfarb (Yiddish minstrel), Ben Peskin, singer, and Betty Katz, comedienne. Blossom Klein will be master of ceremonies.

Jewish War Veterans Hall

2604 West Blvd

The Southwest Wave

Apr 20, 1950, p15

West Adams Jewish population had also begun to migrate elsewhere in vast L.A. County, and Black people were moving in. It would be some years before I would go to a live electric blues dance, but I'm sure that was my introduction to the contemporary blues of that time.

By the early 1950's L.A. had great numbers of southern immigrants, and they were expanding out of south L.A., bringing the music with them. I have asked some of the older musicians I know if they remembered those dances, and none did. But, given the era, I might have been hearing T-Bone or Big Joe or Pee-Wee or Lowell Fulson before I knew what I was hearing. All I know is that I loved it. I never could have imagined meeting those greats, playing with many of them. I could not have envisioned being a part of that music, but I was already on that path, I just didn't know it.

Just a couple of years later I would enroll in Dorsey High School. Most of my friends were going to Fairfax High, and I wanted to go there, but I was out of that district, and to Dorsey I went.

Once, when I was a freshman, there was an assembly called to listen to a student band led by a senior at the school. The all-Black group rocked and rolled and played the Blues. I joined the other students in really loving it. I smile just thinking of it. The star of the show was a guitarist/vocalist who has earned a deserved renown. His name was Bobby Parker.

I don't recall what pieces they played, but it was smack dab in the middle of the R&B and Rock that kids were starting to make the new music of America. Music not so far from aspects of the Folk Music I was listening to as I perceived it to be. Irrespective of the genre, it was as lively and exciting as hell, and I never forgot about it and likewise never forgot his name.

A few decades elapsed, and I started to hear of a Blues artist who was attracting some notice, someone also named Bobby Parker. In a conversation with my niece Marnie Hoyt, brother Ed's daughter-by-marriage who lived in D.C., she mentioned she knew a musician of that name. I asked her to find out if he had gone to Dorsey in L.A. It turns out that it was the same Bobby Parker I remembered. I got his number and we talked.

A friendly and lengthy conversation, as he knew many of the people I came to know from the 1960's on: Etta James, Richard "Louie, Louie" Berry, Johnny Otis, Big J. McNeely, and the list goes on. I was determined to put him on stage somewhere if and when he came west. Unfortunately, it was not to be. He passed away in 2013, October 31 -Hallowe'en, in his 70's.

There were occasions when a couple of the older students at Dorsey High would scat what I can only recall as bee-bop riffs in the locker room. There was music around and, although I had begun learning "folk Blues" songs like "See See Rider", and "Midnight Special", I didn't see how it might connect to what I was hearing around me. But that awakening was just a couple of years away.

Hoots Become Concerts

I would practice my guitar and play at the hoots. I had learned to play the union songs, ballads, and protest songs prevalent at the hoots. But I also felt very drawn to the black artists who had recorded for Folkways and other underground labels were singing. Of course, Leadbelly, Josh White, Harry Belafonte were known to me, but Brownie McGhee especially drew my attention. By 16 I graduated from nylon to steel strings – when Ed upgraded his guitar to a Martin 000-28, he sold me his mahogany 1952 Martin 00-17. That has been the guitar of my life. I perform with it still today, and it sounds and plays better than ever.

1952 Martin 00-17

One evening, perhaps in 1956, the hoot had a guest artist. Brownie McGhee stood in Bernice's living room and sang the Blues. My first time seeing a real live Blues guitarist right in front of my dazzled eyes. There would be more to come that year, but I wouldn't get to participate because, despite my father's unbending objection, I was determined to go and spend a year in Israel working on a kibbutz after my impending High School graduation. I would be bringing my Martin along.

The Kibbutz Years (1957-1958)

Off to Israel 1957

My Habonim group sponsored an annual work-study program to newly-independent Israel, and I had been thinking of going for three years. My father objected. His signature would have been necessary to permit me to go because I was only 17. My father was not one to change his mind – period. I graduated Dorsey High in February of 1957.

Bernie Pearl, Graduation, Age 17

Courtesy: Bernie Pearl

Daddy had suffered a heart attack a few months prior, and was unable to attend, sadly. A couple of months later, in April, 1957, he suffered another heart attack., this one fatal. I grieved with the family. Understandably, Mama was distraught.

Time passed and I again asked to be allowed to go on the Workshop. Mama felt it would be disloyal to her husband's wishes to sign over his objections. I will be forever grateful to my siblings, Bernice, Stan and Ed for rallying behind me and convincing her to assent.

Bernice, Ed and Stan argued for the importance to me of my going. I now see that her objection was based not only on honoring my father's wishes but on fears for my safety, although I had no fears. Mama had the basic human feeling that she had already lost enough with the death of my Daddy. But, she relented because she realized how important the trip was to me. I love you, Mama.

Sherman, nearest in age to me, had completed his Army service and had gone adventuring in Europe, later to travel to Israel, where we were able to spend a little time together.

My family did not have the money to pay transportation costs, which was mainly what we needed to pay for the trip as we would be doing a fair amount of farm work, which would cover our room and board. Once there, other travel expenses were, I assume, to be largely covered by the Labor Zionist movement, the Jewish Agency, and other benefactors interested in our development and education. There would be times when we were free from our jobs to explore on our own or to just relax on the kibbutz. For free-time costs we were on our own.

I had worked a several part-time jobs while in High School, some arranged through the school. After graduation I had a couple of jobs, and then went to work full-time at what probably was a start-up aerospace company at which my brother-in-law, Bob, held a key position. It was on Jefferson Blvd in the Crenshaw district.

It was while going to get a burger at the local drive-in that I first heard and loved, the music of Fats Domino. "I Found My Thrill…", thrilled me. I don't know why, but it did resonate. "Folk music" of that time included songs of Black origin. But, I was yet to make the connection. Fats was talking to me, but I had yet to "hear" him.

It wasn't until many years later that I finally got to see Fats Domino live – he was wonderful. Once, while I was on the air, I called him in New Orleans – my drummer Albert Trepagnier, who used to be his neighbor, got me his number - to wish him a very happy birthday. He was gracious and friendly, and invited me to visit and stay at his place. Albert assured me that it was meant sincerely.

Before traveling to Israel, I had to obtain a passport and maybe a visa to Israel. I went to the building to apply for my passport and had an unsettling experience. I was shown a long list of Zionist and/or Jewish organizations that were considered subversive. It included a fairly left wing group called "Hashomer Ha Tzair" (Young Watchmen). I didn't know any of them but they were also kibbutz and labor affiliates. I was asked to sign an oath declaring that I was not a member of any of these groups. I signed. These were scary times.

This aerospace job helped me raise the money needed for the trip, and I was Israel-bound the coming September. There were four of us from L.A. We flew to New York via St Louis on a non-scheduled airline which took forever, for a pre-Workshop orientation at a camp in Poughkeepsie.

This flight was my first time in the air. There, we joined some 35 other recent HS graduates from around the US and Canada to prepare for our adventure. It would turn out to be the trip of a lifetime for many of us.

September 1957 – To The Kibbutz

After a few days of orientation at the camp near Poughkeepsie, we sailed from New York Harbor aboard an 23,400 ton cruise ship SS Independence in early September, before the High Holidays.

SS Independence, Photo In 1951

There were over three dozen of us, members of the youth organization Habonim (The Builders) from several cities in the U.S., mainly East coast and Midwest, four of us from L.A., and three from Canada. We sailed on the SS Independence to Genoa.

It took me a couple of days to get my sea legs and start to enjoy what was to be a memorable first-time experience on the ocean. We spent about 8 days crossing the Atlantic in what was really fair weather and relatively calm seas, passing through the Gibraltar Straits, and docked at Cannes. After another day's sail, we arrived at Genoa. We then sailed on the smaller Israeli vessel Zion from Genoa to the port of Haifa, Israel. Three days later we saw Haifa.

We were thrilled to finally see Israel. We from L.A. were met at the dock by the emissaries from Israel who had been our group leaders in the US. Ruth and Gid'on Tsur had made the trip from their farm in the south, close to Gaza, to welcome their "kids". What a special thing. What special, warm people. I was able to visit them at their home just once during the year, and they saw us off at the end of the year. I was not to see them again for 40 years. And when I did come to stay with them for a few days, it was as if no time had passed. Family, once again. Remarkable. What a gift they gave me. They are both gone now, deeply missed.

Our 11-month work-study program would be based on a collective farm in the Upper Galilee called Kfar Blum. This kibbutz is about 7 miles from the border of Lebanon in the west and about 5 miles from the border of Syria. Just a few kilometers to the east are the foothills of the Golan Heights, which was the Syrian border at the time. This border remained until 1967.

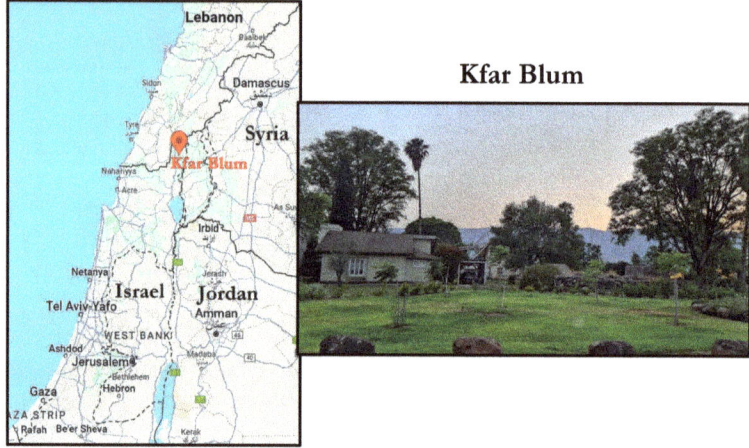

Kfar Blum

From Haifa, we then rode buses to our home for the next 11 months, Kibbutz Kfar Blum (named after Leon Blum, the Jewish Prime Minister of France in the late 1930's) located in the Upper Galilee by the Jordan River, which ran through the kibbutz. This part of the river was our "swimming hole" We were housed in small cabins, four to a room. There was a shower, a toilet, and a small closet for each of us. I was still 17, but would shortly turn 18 and have to take the bus back to Haifa to register for the draft at the U.S. Consulate, as was required by the law of the day.

Our group leader for the year was a little lady from New York named Ettie Skidell. How fortunate we were to have this firecracker to mentor us. Before we collapsed on our cots, we had enough time to look east to Syria and the Golan Heights, north to snow-capped Mt.

Hermon, west to the Lebanese mountains, and south to the wetlands of the Huleh swamp and the Jordan River.

September, 1957 – The First Potato Harvest

We were told that we would gradually join in part-time farm work after a month of adjustment and light labor. But, as life turns out to be a series of surprises, we were soon asked to "volunteer" our help with the impending potato harvest which, as all agricultural work, has to be done when the crop is ready. It was ready, but, were we? We'd soon find out. Our day would start when still dark, perhaps getting a little food in the communal dining room, then out to the fields. Soon, I started to eat copious quantities of American surplus hot oatmeal with lots of surplus butter.

Potatoes grow underground and have to be unearthed to be harvested. This was done by a special blade attached to a tractor. They grow in rows, so the tractor would precede us down a row and we would bend to the task. And I do mean bend. We dragged a burlap sack mounted on a square frame behind us and between our legs. When a sack was full we set it on the side and attached another one and started all over. We needed to move apace as the tractor was relentless, noisily approaching from behind to turn the adjoining row.

Work fast or risk being run down by the tractor, driven by a kibbutz member, who, I'm sure, enjoyed our panic. "Weak Americans" was kind of a standard but good-natured gibe for a couple of months. We then broke for a real breakfast, which generally included local foodstuffs: heads of catfish freshly pulled out of the Jordan River that morning, lots of home-grown, fresh vegetables, eggs from the kibbutz chicken coops. We hardly ever had any meat at any meal. But, we physically thrived. After breakfast, we returned to work, then a break during the hottest hours, then back to finish the day. This went on for about two weeks, with only an early quitting time on Friday, and Saturday (Shabbat) completely off. Sunday, back to work. It is called, in Hebrew, The First Day, Friday is "The Sixth Day".

I went to sleep each night during the potato harvest exhausted and invariably had waking nightmares featuring the sound of the tractor approaching from behind. Thus began my appreciation of what farm work really was, and greatly added to my appreciation of what lives many of the Blues men I met had lived. I worked under much kinder bosses, snide as they might have been. They knew we would grow stronger, unlike the bosses of the Blues men who simply did not care if the Black workers survived.

In retrospect, the work I did that year gave me real appreciation for farming in general, and in particular for what the words "…from kin to kaint " implied – work from sunup to sundown. Although chided by the strong and more fit kibbutz kids as "soft Americans", I had no taskmasters with whips over me, and was respected for my efforts. I had adequate food, lodging, rest periods, and free time in the evenings. I started to understand some of what I had heard Leadbelly sing about in his work songs on those Stinson/Folkways LPs.

1957 – 1958 -- Life On The Kibbutz

I did make one mistake as a newbie on the farm in Israel. In America water from the outdoor spigot was as safe as water from our faucet. Not so a mere 9 ½ years after the founding of the state. Things were still fairly primitive, if colorful: like we would ride to the fields on a horse-drawn wagon. I made the mistake of drinking from a sprinkler in the fields, or some other unsafe water source, In any event I contracted what would be later identified as Amoebic dysentery. Led to a fair amount of misery before diagnosis and treatment. Live and maybe learn.

We had several trained pianists in the group, a couple of guitars, and seemingly endless energy for singing and dancing after work. Music was a big part of our group interaction. I had bought my brother Ed's mahogany Martin 00-17 from him the previous year, and had made real progress in my playing. My first steel-stringed guitar, and I had it with me.

I was playing songs from the general folk song bag and some Israeli songs. My friend from L.A., Jerry, a wonderful concert pianist, also had brought his guitar. We were very popular. We also showed what we knew to a few others of the group. In recent years I have received words of thanks from those we helped get started playing. I had forgotten about that aspect our activities. But they hadn't and, to this day, they credit Jerry and me for giving them their start playing the guitar. I'm moved by this.

At first we had a variety of half-day jobs, and had study half a day. Later on we took on full-time regular work assignments. We took trips together in the back of a rickety old truck to go trekking through the southern wastelands; to climb steep hills to the Lebanese border; to ascend the Masada bastion by the Dead Sea; to look at the Old City of Jerusalem from afar, while being carefully inspected by a Jordanian Army machine-gunner behind his sandbag.

We also had time to go exploring on our own. My brother Sherman, after being discharged from the US Army, went traveling in Europe, and we found ourselves in Israel at the same time.

Sherman (L), Bernie (R) Pearl

Israel, 1958

Courtesy: Bernie Pearl

I took the bus to the Jezreel Valley, met him and he took me to Tel Aviv. Then we went south to see Ruth and Gid'on. My first time away from home, a phenomenal year.

Late spring 1958 – I Graduate to Sugar Beets

I had done all manner of agricultural work, including another potato harvest, and return to the U.S. was in sight. I was selected to be a truck loader for the sugar beet harvest. I was much stronger than when I first faced the potatoes, and I had to be as sugar beets were a lot heavier than spuds, and I had to toss them high over the sides of a large-bed truck. The sun was shining and I felt strong and did indeed enjoy the hard and sweaty job. Snow-capped, majestic Mt. Hermon, which was then occupied by the Syrian army, stood at the north, the Huleh swamp at the south, and I felt I belonged there. All that said, I was also eager to return to my family in L.A. and begin the next chapter of my journey.

July - August 1958 – From The Kibbutz

I had been corresponding with my mother. After several months she told me that everyone in the family was helping Ed get a coffee house/night club started. Ed had put on a few shows before I went to Israel, featuring some prominent local folk artists: Frank Hamilton, Guy Carawan, Ramblin' Jack Elliot, Odetta, as I recall. They were successful. At one point, I loaned Ed $20 of my savings to travel to Israel to help with a show. I never asked for it back. Ed never offered it back either. I was well-compensated in other ways over the years.

The new club opened in July of 1958. It was named after a Robert Burns poem, "The Ash Grove". When I first heard of the plans for the club, I was getting ready to start working on the spring potato harvest. By that time I was much stronger and was assigned to lift the potato sacks onto the wagon and stack them. It was fun, but I wished that I could also be in Los Angeles for the excitement.

We were due to sail back to the US in August. It seemed that every one was college-bound, and needed to get back in time to register for school. I loved being in Israel and had the opportunity arisen to stay longer, I imagine I would have done so. We sailed, waving goodbye to Ruth and Gid'on standing on the dock. I never thought that it would take me 40 years to see their farm again.

"Once We Were Slaves Unto Pharoah"…. My Bond With The Country Blues

Almost every year I can remember, and even before I can remember, I have celebrated the holiday of Passover (in Hebrew, Pesach: skip over). It commemorates the Hebrew people's leaving slavery in Egypt, under the leadership of Moses. To reach the point that

Pharoah agreed to "let my people go", the Almighty had to bring down 10 plagues on the Egyptians, including the final plague, death to all first-born males. This was conducted by the Angel of Death who skipped over the homes of the Hebrews who had marked their doorposts with blood. Hardly a light-hearted exit, considering the fact that Pharoah changed his mind and sent his chariots after the escapees, fomenting further death in his army.

Each celebration, called a "Seder" in Hebrew, which translates to "order", is guided by a text called the "Hagaddah", which means "the telling". In the Hagaddah there are numerous prayers and blessings over wine and symbolic foods. The actual "telling" begins with "Once we were slaves unto Pharoah in Egypt, but now we are free people", and we sing a song to that effect. When I was growing up the Seder was conducted solely in Hebrew, which most of the adults could read, but few understood, save my erudite cousin Leo who did know the language. Ultimately we adopted a Hagaddah which had the Hebrew text, but included phonetic pronunciation of Hebrew, and English translation.

Several times, I did not celebrate Passover. One year, I was feeling petulant – for what reason I can't recall. I declined to attend the family Seder at cousin Lil's. I remain embarrassed and rueful about it these many years later. Another failure to celebrate occurred when I was in Israel in 1958. The kibbutz was socialist and determinedly secular. Jewish holidays were not observed. Whether some observed Jewish holidays, including the Sabbath, in their rooms, I don't know. I do know that this "policy" changed over the years. By the time I revisited in 1998, the kibbutz had built a synagogue for worship. I asked about it and was told that many had come to settle on Kfar Blum. These settlers brought their parents, who were older and traditionally more observant. Who is to tell Mama and Daddy that they are not allowed to pray?

In later years, once the extended family, mainly my mother's, broke up into its different branches, I began to conduct my own seder with those friends and my close family who could attend. A large enough contingent. The Hagaddah I use has most of the traditional Hebrew elements, phonetics, and translations, but it also has a portion devoted to the Holocaust. Victims are honored and resistors are praised, many of those died as well. This has become common in American Seders. My Hagaddah also reflects a progressive and humanistic outlook.

Acknowledging that our ancestors were slaves goes only so far, our reading admonishes us to regard ourselves, personally, as if we were slaves who have found freedom. And, further, we are called on to act to aid others who are experiencing oppression, brutality, prejudice. As I see it, this is very much in keeping with the somber annual Day of Atonement – Yom Kippur – a day of fasting, introspection, and confession of sins, or transgressions against another. It is not enough to ask the Almighty for forgiveness, but one must also seek to correct the transgression and seek the pardon of those who were transgressed against. In plain English, actions speak louder than words.

I believe that there exists prejudice of one type or another around the world, and that it is taken in as naturally and unconsciously as we breathe the air. Whether it's misunderstanding, or mistrusting, or just plain hatred of people of differing religions, national origin, race, or even philosophies, it is endemic to the human race.

The remedy is to identify these harmful impulses and control our behavior, all the while attempting to understand and accept others. I honestly believe that my 11 months of hard work of many sorts on the kibbutz helped me understand and appreciate the outlook and experience of my blues mentors and heroes, many of whom endured fiendish brutality and inhuman hours in the fields, often in childhood, just to stay alive. That they were, to a person, mainly outgoing, generous, kind, and generally in a good mood is still a source of wonderment.

Furthermore, Blacks and Jews have some important historical experiences in common. Both groups were slaves, both groups were persecuted, both groups were targets of segregation and racism from ancient times to the present. This kind of history incorporates into your DNA. As a Jew, I respond to the deep seated emotions incorporated into the Blues. These emotions express the effects of emotional and physical slavery, persecution, and segregation and racism.

My love of the Blues is visceral and beyond intellect, and my bond with several artists is life-long. While I too carry whispers of false notions, I try to identify them, admit to them, then I ignore them and try to act on my healthier impulses. In Yiddish we call that being a "mensch". In my relationship with the many artists I have had the honor of meeting and befriending, the human contact, the life stories and guidance they provided, and the wisdom they shared have enriched and guided my life. Learning the notes takes a back seat to the feeling of the music.

The Ash Grove, 1959
Courtesy: Phil Melnick

Early Years At The Ash Grove (1958 – 1961)

August, 1958 I Get to the Ash Grove

On my return from Israel, I enrolled in Los Angeles City College, took up residence in my mother's two-bedroom apartment, from which I left for Israel a year earlier, My older brother Ed Pearl had founded the club earlier that summer of 1958 while I was on the K'far Blum Kibbutz in Israel.

Ed Pearl, Founder of The Ash Grove

Courtesy: Bernie Pearl

The club was in a former furniture factory at 8162 Melrose Avenue, close to Fairfax High, in a predominantly Jewish neighborhood, between Fairfax and La Cienega Avenues. Fairfax High was nearby. Rafters could be seen plainly from the floor seats.

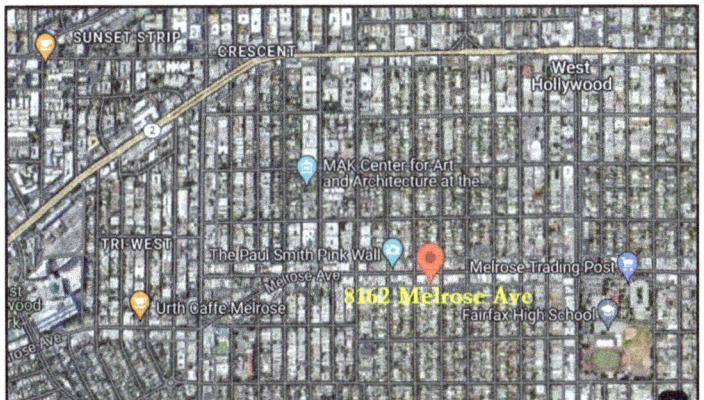

Location of The Ash Grove in Los Angeles

It was officially called "The Ash Grove & Galleries". It was a post-Beat coffeehouse, with art on the walls, poetry readings, and regular folk music concerts in the back room, which had about a 150 seat capacity with tables.

No alcohol was served yet, but there was an assortment of coffees (cappuchinos, espresso, and the like) and other non-alcoholic beverages offered, along with cheese plates, desserts, and probably some other food. One of the really unique things I recall was that the chandeliers were made by Tiffany. My brother Ed's significant other, later to become his wife, Kate (Hughes) Hoyt came from old East Coast money and had supplied these gorgeous lighting fixtures. The place had a clean, plain, and simple décor, which really worked to offset the overhead elegance.

But, my concern was the music. When I left the previous year, I was probably the most advanced guitarist in my young folkie circle. Things had changed in a year. My friends Lonnie Feiner and especially David Cohen, who were a year or two younger than I, had made great musical strides. Folk music had moved beyond Pete Seeger, Woody Guthrie, Cisco Houston, and their circle of socially-conscious pioneering songsters of the 40's.

America was re-defining folk music in a more commercial, less political way. The Kingston Trio was a version of folk music acceptable to America's tastes. Other groups along similar lines were forming almost daily. Dylan and Baez etc. were yet to emerge to turn folk on its head. Leadbelly was dead, but there were other African-American artists presenting tradition-based music to the new urban folk crowd.

Pre-eminent among the coffee-house, college campus Blues artists were Brownie McGhee & Sonny Terry. They were veterans of the New York scene, When "folk" became a thing, the country became rife with coffee houses and other venues featuring "folk music". Colleges and universities began folk concerts, McGhee and Terry became the most travelled "minstrels" of the day. This pair was especially in demand because they offered rare and authentic "Negro" folk music

There were others: Josh White among them.

Josh White

He was a veteran blues and gospel guitarist and singer when he got to New York in the 1940's. He applied professional polish and personal charm to a variety of material – the Irish song "Molly Malone" comes to mind – and became very popular, becoming the first artist to integrate the NYC Club scene.

White was working all of the time in NYC, despite the fact that the NYC club scene was still segregated at the time. Brownie McGhee and Sonny Terry were having trouble finding gigs. McGhee asked Josh White, *why can you get gigs all the time?* White responded, *Because I play white.* Brownie asked White, *how do I play white?* Presumably, McGhee took the unknown advice of White to heart, because Sonny Terry and Brownie McGhee became widely popular, but kept playing the Blues.

Rev.Gary Davis had recorded for Moses Asch's Folkways/Stinson label, and was also known to the NY folk audience. An extraordinarily skilled ragtime guitarist, he devoted himself to religious songs and the ministry in the 1930's. He set the bar for finger style guitar playing that has seldom, if ever, been surpassed.

Rev Gary Davis and Blind Blake (Arthur Phelps) are the two most prominent Piedmont style folk/Blues guitar stylists. Each was different from the other but equally brilliant in my mind. I was shortly to befriend Rev Gary Davis and he tried to show me how to play his music, to little avail. Several years later, I was to give it another go, with better results. But, by then, the original source was gone.

But, the undoubted kings of the blues in the coffee house, college circuit were guitarist Brownie McGhee and harmonica man Sonny Terry. They met in Durham N.C. in the late 1930's playing with recording star Blind Boy Fuller (Fulton Allen). When Fuller died unexpectedly, they joined forces. By the late 1950's they had almost 20 years experience adapting the country blues for urban white audiences.

Enormously entertaining, they were scheduled to play the Ash Grove opening in July, 1958. Sonny got ill, so Brownie did it solo, as he did at my sister's house earlier. I returned to the States in August, and it was to be another couple of months until I could get to hear them together. By then I would be washing dishes nightly, and by then I had also been smitten by the Blues.

Lone Cat Epiphany

It was late August or early September, 1958. I had just returned from Israel and had not yet started working at the club. I went in one night to see a show with my friends Lonnie and David.

Headlining the bill were a locally popular folk duo, Bud (Dashiell) & Travis (Edmondson). I was not familiar with them, but they were causing a lot of excitement. They were on their way up.

**Travis Edmondson
and
Bud Dashiell**

One of the unique aspects of their repertoire was the traditional Mexican songs they sang. Both Anglos, they were deeply into the culture and sang the music beautifully and with authenticity. They both played guitars well and had a marvelous gitarron player whose first name was Charlie (Carlos). I'm not sure, but his last name was possibly Gomez, and he was referred to as "Papa Charlie". He was also an officer in Musician's Local 47.

Jesse Fuller

Also appearing was a man named Jesse Fuller, who called himself the "Lone Cat". I knew nothing of him, except that he was black, from Oakland and, as I anticipated, played the blues. He had written a song called "The San Francisco Bay Blues". The place was full of the generally well-dressed and educated young folk audience of the day, there to see Bud and Travis.

We got a table towards the back, ordered coffee or a flavored soda, chatting and enjoying the scene until the show started. Fuller was announced. He was a one-man band, full of energy and rhythm, and when he began playing I began to come unglued. Lonnie and David reacted in the same way. Laughing and pounding my feet on the concrete floor, I had never heard anything so joyous and rhythmic in my life. I had never experienced that level of response to music.

I looked around at the audience, expecting to see the same general reaction. I was stunned. Everyone else seemed to be talking to each other, sipping their drinks, and ignoring what was going on onstage. If there was ever a moment when I started marching to a different drummer, that was it. The folk crowd couldn't wait for Bud & Travis, and I didn't want the music to stop. And, in truth, it never has. I didn't realize it at the time, but my blues journey had begun.

Getting to Know the Lone Cat

Jesse Fuller was a delightful entertainer. He had designed a unique bass instrument that he sat behind and played with one shoeless foot. Kind of like the pedals on a piano. The other foot triggered a cymbal attached to the side of the bass. He called the instrument his "FotDella" (my spelling), because his wife's name was Della, and he played it with his Fo(o)t, he laughingly explained.

He played an amplified 12-string guitar with his hands, and on a rack around his neck he had a harmonica and a kazoo. His repertoire included ragtime, railroad work songs, blues, show tunes, endlessly interesting stories, and bits of philosophy learned from living. Another of the blessings that he bestowed on us was that at the end of his set he would stand up and dance, while simultaneously playing his guitar, his harmonica rack, and singing.

Some people, I'm sure, were made uncomfortable by this, but Jesse wasn't. It was the type of dancing that was no less a part of his cultural heritage than his music. He had large taps on his shoes, and would sing and dance the way he did at the tent shows in the South, performing for largely African-American audiences. The "Buck and Wing" was my favorite. It wasn't very long after this time that tap-dancing was revived, popularized, and made it to the Broadway stage.

Jesse said that he was from Georgia, and had to leave because he stood up for himself, which didn't go down very well with the white folks. He did all manner of work, including railroads. He rode those rails, played in tent shows of all kinds, and found his way to Oakland well before WWII. He was a frequent and welcome performer. I would get him to the stage, making sure that things were the way he wanted them.

One time he asked me to string his guitar, and I asked what tuning he wanted it in. He said "Vastopol". He might as well been speaking Russian. I knew standard tuning, and open E, but Vastopol was a name I once read in a book. If I remember correctly, when inexpensive guitars first became available for order through the Sears (and other?) catalogues around the turn of the 19th-, they would arrive on the farm with an instruction booklet. That's how basic formal chording information was passed on to the farmers and laborers who were been used to home-made instruments and traditional music.

"Sebastopol" was a popular instrumental in the late 19th century. It was played in an open E or D tuning and was often included in the instruction manuals that came with guitars. The other tuning, "Spanish", corresponds to open G. Those became the dominant tunings of the MS Delta blues.

Thank goodness that all the notions of "proper" playing were not taken to heart by those who were born to play the blues. Adaptation is the rule.

Speaking of uncomfortable realities, Jesse would be hosted by local fans on occasion, but he would also sleep in his bag on the Ash Grove stage. He was used to making do with whatever situation presented itself, I'm sure, but one had to wonder why. There were no nearby commercial lodgings, and the closest ones would not accept black patrons at the time. Both of those conditions were to change subsequently. Learning this about my hometown was a shock to me. I hadn't ever thought of L.A. as segregated, but the truth was dawning on me. Times were getting ready to change, and all of us would soon enough have our notions and illusions challenged. The Ash Grove was an oasis for both the emergence of true American Folk music and real American multiculturalism. A great educational opportunity was unfolding.

Musical Environment at the Ash Grove

It was in the nature of my brother Ed's approach to "folk" music to include the music of all the folk. Scottish pipers, Caribbean songsters, red-neck banjoists, blind gospel guitarists...you get the picture.

The club was home to a very wide range of musicians and musical styles. And, yes, we all did get along.

This meeting of the musics was exemplified by two groups of brothers which, ultimately, would each achieve great renown and influence. They were each enormously gifted, and each occupied a very different part of the musical forest.

The White Brothers (originally LeBlanc, French Canadian, Arcadian) were a bluegrass/gospel group who came to be known as the Kentucky Colonels.

The Kentucky Colonels

Front, Left to Right
Roland White (mandolin), Eric White (bass),
Clarence White (acoustic guitar), Billy Ray Lathum (banjo)
Rear: LeRoy Mack(dobro)

All would sing harmonies on their gospel tunes. Yes, gospel tunes, for they were the first band on stage to play Bluegrass music, and bluegrass bands always featured a segment of sacred songs in their shows.

The Chambers Brothers group, just four of many Chambers brothers and sisters who sang gospel, came from Mississippi.

**Chambers Brothers
Young Gospel Singers**

Courtesy: Phil Melnick

<u>Left to Right</u>

Joseph, Lester, Willie, George

When I first saw them, they sang a capella, with only Willie strumming the guitar, and they were spellbinding. George, Joseph, Lester, and Willie Chambers used to sing a song that often closed a set, "I Got It!" They sure did.

Dressing Funky

A little digression is called for. Universally, and without exception, black and white, Southern/Real Folk performers were quite meticulous about their appearance on stage. Some were true fashion plates, some had bling to show, some had costumes, and even the plain-dressing rural "authentic discoveries" were always dressed immaculately. Contrast that with the ethos of us new folkies and bluesers. It was quite a contrast how we'd get up there, dressed any old kinda way, truly a kind of social protest, whereas the real folk were of a more meticulous mind in that regard, neat and buttoned down, and ready to tear the world a new a-hole. There's a lesson there somewhere.

A Portrait in Black and White

The Kentucky Colonels

While the Ash Grove was the Southern California portal for artists who were to revolutionize American popular music tastes – both Pete Seeger and Brownie McGhee were opening-night performers – it was also welcoming to talented lesser-knowns who were not following the generally accepted paths to wider popularity. In those early club days, two groups of musical brothers cut their professional teeth there, one Black, one White.

In fact, the Whites were the White Brothers. Roland on mandolin and main vocalist, Clarence on guitar, and Eric on upright bass. They were augmented by 5-string banjoist Billy Ray Lathum. All would sing harmonies on their gospel tunes. Yes, gospel tunes, for they were the first band on stage to play Bluegrass music, and bluegrass bands always featured a segment of sacred songs in their shows. A surprise to the mainly Jewish folk crowd, who were expecting more conventional folk concert material. But, the younger folks, Jewish or not, were absolutely wild about the music of The Country Boys. They had many female fans.

The White brothers were all teenagers, but they were playing in a much more polished and elegant manner than one expected. A special light radiated from Clarence's flat-picked (plectrum) Martin D-18 style. A level far higher than anyone would expect from the fairly small-statured and handsome mid-teen player. In fact, their involvement with this traditionally Southern style of play, composed of a mixture of traditional mountain music and the Blues, was surprising. Their family name was Le Blanc, and they were of French-Canadian heritage. I recall that their father spoke English with a very heavy French accent. How they first heard, learned, and mastered this post-WW11 deep Southern-fried music at such a young age is an open question to me. I suspect that they would have been great at any musical expression they chose, but they were totally professional by the time they came to the club.

They created an interest in Bluegrass music, and drew many fans of the form to their shows, which no doubt led to their fans' exposure to other artists who performed there. They talked about their heroes, Bill Monroe, the Stanley Brothers, Flatt and Scruggs, and many more, all of whom eventually came to L.A., some for the first time, to play the Ash Grove. Local Bluegrass groups formed there, and other young professionals like the Golden Gate Boys and the Dillards auditioned and worked there. In the following years they made a couple of personnel changes and re-named the group the Kentucky Colonels. In my opinion, they opened the door for Bluegrass in this area, and on a strictly musical basis have earned a deserved place alongside their heroes. The Colonels are legendary. Clarence was to reshape flat-picked guitar in this land. He was killed by a drunk driver while walking to his car after a gig. This gig was a musical reunion with his brother in Palmdale in later years. Roland was also hit but survived, but never to play together again.

Roland White came to perform at the 2008, 50th Anniversary of the Ash Grove at UCLA. He had booked a later show with my friend Phil Boroff at a place in San Diego, to which I also was invited. I had brought my guitar in case Phil wanted me to open the show. I had never played with Roland, and was not in any way a bluegrass player. I came to see an old friend whom I hadn't heard play in decades. The show went forward, I was not asked to play…until Roland invited me up. I demurred, reminding him that I only played the blues. He said, "Sure, come on up." I started on Lightnin's "Mojo Hand", a Blues shuffle. His mandolin and Phil's guitar came in right on time and in the groove. I was reminded that a healthy part of Bluegrass is the Blues, and that he and his brother came around when the Blues guys were playing, especially Lightnin' Sam, and sopped up some more of it. What goes around comes around. I had a ball that night in San Diego. His wife of many years thanked me for playing. Doesn't get any better than that. Roland White passed away in 2022.

The Chambers Brothers: Right on Time

I was honored to have been called on to stand up in the South L.A. church at the homegoing service of George Chambers, bassist and eldest of the Chambers Brothers. I was asked to stand as the brother of Ed Pearl who gave the Brothers their first gig, at the Ash Grove. I smiled and appreciated on his behalf the many applauding standees. But, I was also sad, not only for George's passing, but my brother had just been hospitalized and placed in a rehab facility with a poor chance of recovery. He passed several months later. But, that day was a day I was able to share with him when I visited. It made him happy to hear. He sadly remembered George.

The church was full of family and friends, many of whom had also been to the club decades earlier and recognized his work. No one more than the three remaining Brothers, guitarist Willie Mack, Joseph, also guitar, and Lester, harmonica man, in attendance with dozens of family members and hundreds of friends packing the sanctuary. George had been a long-time devout member and elder of that church. Joseph Chambers passed away in August, 2022.

As Ed had passed during the first state-wide lockdown due to Covid, our family decided to hold a memorial on Zoom. Among the invitees who spoke were Willie and Joseph Chambers. We heard about their first gig, a paid audition. They were then singing only Gospel tunes, but they brought all the vitality and depth of their church upbringing to the stage and absolutely brought everyone to their feet. The audience went wild. After the show they asked Ed how he liked it and if he'd want to offer another booking. Ed said he loved it, but couldn't bring them back. Shocked, they asked why. He replied, "Because people would get out of hand and destroy the place!" It was a perfect fit, and it led to dozens of appearances over several years.

Fairly quickly, they drew the attention and criticism of gospel icon Mahalia Jackson. In an L.A. Times article she objected to their presenting the Lord's music in a venue that served alcohol (the club had obtained a beer and wine license to supplement its non-alcoholic drinks and light menu).

In time the Brothers added secular material, overcoming George's reluctance, and developed into one of the most compelling acts in the nation. Ranging from jug band tunes, to contemporary blues, to R&B ballads, they had no musical barriers and always excited with their other-worldly harmonies and smooth musicianship.

They were invited to the Newport Folk Festival in 1965, where Dylan went electric and a new era for American popular music was born. They were there at the birth, they impressed and never looked back. I was speaking about them with Lightnin' and he commented, *Them boys doin' good*, and added that they should be cautious. He knew whereof he spoke.

One of the aspects of the Chambers Brothers growing success impacted my musical life directly. Lightnin' Hopkins had a disciple of sorts living in L.A. He had made an impression when he recorded a couple of very down-home duets with Lightnin' back in Houston in 1959 ("Country Blues" Tradition Records – TLP 1035, Mack McCormick producer). Luke Miles, whom Lightnin' dubbed "Long Gone" for his tall, lanky stature, would often join him for a song or two when he began playing the Ash Grove. There he met the Brothers and teamed up in a duo with Willie playing guitar. When the Brothers started to take off, Long Gone ("like a turkey through the corn" – L.H.) was without a guitarist, and I got the gig. We did some work together and availed ourselves of a slight possibility of playing at the 1966 Newport Folk Festival. But, that's a story I'll tell later. Back to the Brothers.

They became notable figures on the national scene, and had a very busy career through the 60's and early 70's. Their recording of "Time" is a perennial favorite every New Years. As in all things in show business, styles, tastes, and personnel change, and artists adjust if they can.

In the late 1960's, I originated the first all-blues program on FM radio in L.A. on KPPC-FM (not to be confused with the later KPCC-FM, also in Pasadena). I called it "Nothin' but the Blues", after a favorite Lightnin' Hopkins tune. I did it for a couple of years, and found the opportunity to revive it in 1980 on KLON-FM shortly after I moved to Long Beach. I will describe this new beginning in more detail later, but suffice it to say that the later show became very popular, raising lots of money, and that led to my proposing to KLON management that we do an outdoor Blues Festival, something I had long wanted to see in L.A. Long Beach looked like a good place to do just that.

The proposal was accepted, a miniscule budget was devised.

I had to find a venue. I met with Henry Zimmerman of the Long Beach Parks Department. He showed me Blair Field, a small baseball stadium at Recreation Park, near Wilson High. He offered it as a venue for the Festival. Having no idea how we could make it work, I agreed. Shortly, the Long Beach Summer Lleague baseball organization threw a fit. It would disrupt their summer league play. Henry then offered Veteran Stadium, a much larger and easier to manage site for a Festival. I accepted.

Booking the artists was among my tasks. Long and interesting story made short, I went about it vigorously and had it pretty much done when I saw that I still needed a headliner. I can't recall exactly how I arrived at the Brothers doorstep, and don't know how I had the boldness to ask them to play for the pittance I could offer, but I did ask and they did accept. They did play, and knocked it out of Veteran's Stadium, the site of the First Annual (optimistically named) KLON Blues and Gospel Festival. Their performance closed a long and magnificent concert, and started to answer the question on many people's minds that day, "What in hell is a KLON?"

The station was tiny, low-powered, and a totally obscure destination on the low-end of the radio dial at 88.1 FM, offering educational programming during the week, and music only on weekends. My spot was late on Sunday nights.

The stadium was not packed, we got almost no press coverage, including the Long Beach Press-Telegram, but anyone who was not totally deaf, numb, and tasteless would have realized that we had tapped a well bursting with enthusiasm. The Chambers Brothers appearance and stirring closing performance helped spark the revival of the music we all loved and had missed for so long in Southern California.

People I Met At The Ash Grove

Mutt Cohen (1959)

It was the end of the 1950's, I was working in the kitchen at the Ash Grove, washing dishes, preparing cheese plates, mixing non-alcoholic Italian fizz drinks, brewing espressos, and hearing a wide range music all the while.

The era of the "beatniks" and dark coffeehouses featuring black-clad poets and bongo players was giving way to artists who grew up musically listening to the often left-leaning folk singers of the 40's and early 50's, like Woody Guthrie, Pete Seeger, the Weavers. Something called Folk Music was arising, much of it counter-cultural and kind of daring, often seen as threatening by "the establishment". It was exciting to be a part of it. It was the place to be.

The club was quite popular and often very crowded. The biggest draws were the up and coming folk artists, including Peter Yarrow (before the formation of PP&M), Lou Gottlieb (before the Limelighters), and many others whose names I cannot recall. My brother Ed, the middle child of five, and my senior by some seven years, started the Ash Grove with a grand vision of presenting many forms of art, but the focus was on music.

The kitchen was run by Martin Cohen. His nickname, "Mutt", was based on his Yiddish nickname, "Mottel", itself an affectionate version of a more formal Hebrew name, possibly Mordechai. He was soon to leave to open his own club with his brother Herb, the Unicorn, which itself occupies a significant place in L.A. cultural history.......Mutt was tough and funny and often expressed cynicism about the social significance of the emerging music He became a lawyer, quite prominent and successful in the Hollywood entertainment field, including movies. Herb Cohen, who I had only heard of but never met, managed the career of Frank Zappa, among others.

Barbara Dane (1961)

Barbara Dane was a young veteran vocalist, amazingly tuned into the women's blues of the classic era: Ma Rainey, Bessie Smith, et al.

**Barbara Dane At The Ash Grove
Courtesy: Gerth Archives, Special Collections
Cal State University, Dominguez Hills**

I imagine that, though young, she had a lot of professional stage experience and in her heart she loved the blues. Not a slip-of-a-thing with flowing hair and a guitar, Barbara was confident, womanly and very sexy. She did strum the guitar, but most often appeared with two veteran accompanists, bassist Wellman Braud, and pianist/trumpeter Kenny Whitson.

Braud was an accomplished musician. He was from New Orleans with tons of credits, including Duke Ellington. He was in the musicians union (local 47) and was known as "Papa" Wellman Braud.

Whitson was also an accomplished musician. He always did some playing one-handed piano and blowing his trumpet. He also sang. He was billed as Kenny "Good News" Whitson.

People I Met At LACC

While working nights at the Ash Grove those first couple of years back from the kibbutz, I attended Los Angeles City College, preparatory to moving over to UCLA. That actually took me three years. But, while at LACC I met some memorable people. I had a circle of several old friends, and was generally quite comfortable socially. I was a general Liberal Arts major, and was entering academia at a time of transition for the US.

The times were, indeed, starting to change, McCarthyism was fading, "folk singers" like Pete Seeger, were exerting larger influence on the youth. While carrying a guitar around still had the more or less welcome stigma of "leftie" about it. It was becoming less unusual. "Folk" as a viable commercial music was emerging – I could not foresee how totally I would reject the genre in a fairly short time. The pent-up hopes of a great number of Americans was soon to find an outlet in the Kennedy era.

LACC, the original site of UCLA, was just west of downtown L.A., and had what was, if I recall correctly, quite a varied population. Many foreign students, whites, Hispanics, Jews, Arabs, blacks. Its music department faculty was crème de la crème of working musicians and composers. But, I was not in that department. I took English, History, Psychology, Sociology, flirted with Theater Arts, and both Hebrew and Arabic. I wanted to bring peace to the Middle East. Although I had played the guitar for several years by then, I had no professional musical ambitions that I admitted to. Those took a long time to emerge and to be fully recognized by me.

But there were the people I met. Of course there were the inevitable flirtations several of the multitude of gorgeous and intelligent women I encountered: An actress, a body-builder, a handicapped Eurasian beauty, another actress, a ravishing Mexican-American with mixed-race children, a red-hot African American who sat across from me in English. Oh, Lord, so many women....It was heaven and hell. None came to fruition, but all were interesting and lovely people. I was shy and slow to act. Besides, I had some other fish to fry back at the club.

Among the men was a body-builder actor who, as it turned out, had the hots for me – no thanks. Nice guy, though. I struck up a friendship with a Palestinian Christian fellow, Sam'an (Simon), with whom I discussed the Middle East endlessly. We remained friends throughout LACC. When I moved on to UCLA I did not keep in touch, regretfully. I heard later that he was very hurt by this, and rightly so. Apologies, sah'bi (my good friend).

There were several overt members of the Nation of Islam – the Black Muslims of the time. There was discourse and leaflets, but never any confrontations or violence. Late 1950's, different times. I made friends with a young black man in my Arabic class, Ted, and helped him get a job at the Ash Grove. I found out later that he was a practicing Muslim – made no difference.

Karenga (1961)

Perhaps the most interesting new friend I made, and certainly the one who was to achieve renown and even notoriety in some circles, was someone we might term nowadays as a student activist. Ron Everrett was black, extremely intelligent, very outspoken about racism, and always willing to discuss ideas on pretty much anything. I was fresh off the kibbutz, and shared my experiences with him. He was interested. He ran for student body office once. The student paper ran photos of the candidates and mis-identified his picture with the name of another black candidate whose first name was Everrett.

Ron Everrett

Maulana Karenga

What I saw was a student typo, but what Ron saw was an example of racism – along the lines of "nobody knows my name". I argued briefly that it was an understandable mistake, but he saw it as just another example "they all look alike". I had not and would not ever walk in his shoes, and couldn't possibly know what his experience had sensitized him to. When people tell me, "this happens all the time", I listen. Even though to me it might seem like an absurdity or an exaggeration, every time I've checked into it more thoroughly, I've found that it does happen all the time.

As it happened, Ron had transferred to UCLA around the same time I did, around 1961. We occasionally ran into each other and exchanged a friendly "jambo bwana". I was taking an optional Swahili class and Ron "Everrett", who by them was calling himself Ron "Karenga", was mastering the language.

Always articulate, informed, and outspoken, never belligerent or garrulous, Mr. Karenga went on confronting American racism. He challenged the system in many ways and spent time in prison for doing so. He took the first name of Maulana (learned one). Maulana Karenga, who now heads the African-American Studies program at California State University Long Beach (as of 2025. according to https://maulanakarenga.org/bio-sketch/), along his journey founded Kwanzaa, the seasonal holiday that celebrates the cultural heritage of those of African descent, observed around the world.

I have no idea if discussion of my experiences and ideas made an impact on young Ron Everrett in the late 1950's at City College, but my feeling and identity as a Jew, an outsider, certainly helped me understand Maulana Karenga's dynamism, and sympathize with his beliefs.

Bernie Pearl with Mance Lipscomb
Royce Hall, UCLA, 1964 Folk Festival
Courtesy: Phil Melnick

Studying With The Masters (1958 – 1968)

For an aspiring musician that wanted to play the Blues, I was at the right place and at the right time. During the next decade, I would have the opportunity to closely study the playing of a number of masters of country Blues.

Lightnin' Hopkins	East Texas Blues
Mance Lipscomb	East Texas Blues
MS Fred McDowall	Hill Country Blues
Rev Gary Davis	Piedmont Blues
Sonny Terry, Brownie McGhee	Piedmont Blues

Most of my Blues education came from casual conversation with these musicians and other artists. These conversations put flesh and blood on the structural bodies of the music.

For the most part, I did not ask for or obtain lessons. I would sit next to the musician on stage. Under the circumstances, my goal was to keep in tune and on time with the musician. I really did not have the time and luxury to study the playing techniques, to stop, to observe and to test. I would try to replicate the sound and the feel from what I heard and from the audience reactions.

Very occasionally, I was able to obtain specific lessons. Mostly, I spent long hours listening to their recordings and trying to replicate their sounds. I would listen to a recording, drop the needle, and try to play what I had heard. I would repeat this play/test approach until I could accurately reproduce the sound that I heard on the recording. My needle dropping grew more accurate over time.

In the following reminiscences, I give unique perspectives into the musicians above as well as others not listed. My perspectives provide insights into the musicians as people, their behaviors, their relationships with other musicians, unknown aspects of their histories and elements of their playing styles.

Brownie McGhee and Sonny Terry

Beginnings for Brownie and Sonny

By late 1958, I had begun working in the kitchen washing dishes, and flirting with the waitresses. I can't recall just sitting and listening initially, but rather hearing them from the kitchen and having to run out to see who was making this wonderful sound and creating this delightful energy. I was hooked again.

Sonny Terry and Brownie McGhee

One branch of "folk music", which had been earlier defined by Pete Seeger and the Weavers, Woody Guthrie, Leadbelly, Burl Ives and several others had begun morphing into a form of popular song. More for entertainment than for political statement and societal comment, groups like the Kingston Trio, Bud & Travis, and subsequently the Limelighters, and Peter, Paul, and Mary, had begun to hold sway.

This new Folk Music was becoming big. Tennessee-born guitarist Walter Brown McGhee and his "harp" blowing partner from Georgia, Saunders Terrell, had met playing on the streets of Durham, N.C. Tobacco was king, and there was steady work, active street life and, consequently, money was to be had. Brownie described his arrival in "Bull City" in the late 1930's, seeing blind Reverend Gary Davis on one corner, and across the street was popular recording guitarist Blind Boy Fuller (Fulton Allen). Accompanying Fuller was a blind harmonica player who was by then known as Sonny Terry. They all became friends and playing partners.

When Fuller passed away not long after, Brownie and Sonny became a team. They moved to NYC and eventually became part of the folk music scene. They played many traditional blues songs and wrote lots of their own, developing a riveting and joyous stage show to go with their irrepressible beat. They were among those artists who challenged and broke racial barriers in the New York club scene in the 1940's. Their recordings for ethnic recording pioneer Moses Asch, help slake a growing awareness and thirst among young folk fans for real American roots music.

That's where I came in. Brownie & Sonny were veteran showmen of the blues by the time I saw them.

First Encounter With Brownie and Sonny

Soon after I returned from Israel I enrolled in Los Angeles City College and began a Liberal Arts program, and I started washing dishes at the Ash Grove.

I worked for Mutt Cohen in the kitchen with a very hip, funny and wise Black man named Carroll Peery, who was on the "welcoming committee", as I was soon to be, when the club began to bring in its astounding array of blues artists. One evening early on I was washing dishes when my attention was grabbed by the music on stage, just a curtain away. This night it was guitarist Brownie McGhee and harmonica master Sonny Terry.

I stopped washing, parted the curtains and beheld another magical sight. They were holding the audience in their palms as they sang powerful tales of real life, all with a compelling rhythm. Both were seated as they rocked the house. I was especially drawn to Sonny who was rocking side to side as he played his harp. It was in that moment, for the first time, I perceived the importance of rhythm and keeping the beat with your body. I can't say when I integrated that lesson fully, but I can't recall a time, whether performing seated or standing, when I didn't keep the beat with my feet.

Brownie, who limped noticeably from childhood polio, and Sonny, mostly blind in both eyes from two separate accidents as a child, would often start singing and playing from the back of the house. Brownie in the lead, playing a D-size Martin guitar strapped to his shoulder, Sonny's left hand on his partner's shoulder, his right holding the harp to his mouth, doing his country blues whoops as they gained the stage,. An astounding spectacle, incredibly joyous, and poignant enough to bring tears to my eyes. They would sometimes leave the stage that same way, singing *Walk On* or *Packin' Up Gettin' Ready To Go*. I loved this last song especially. I never heard anyone else do it, even in church. Audiences adored them, and I was a shameless worshipper.

Prior to going to Israel, I had abandoned my nylon stringed guitar for a steel-string Martin 00-17, which I had purchased from my brother Ed for $50. I now had a guitar on which I could play the Blues. It remains my primary acoustic Blues instrument to this day.

Brownie played a dreadnought-sized, acoustic Martin., I think it was a D-18, a standard model for Bluegrass guitarists. He used both thumb pick and finger picks. I don't recall if he amplified it at that time, but for sure in later years he played it with an electrical pickup set across the sound hole. Whatever the set up, that big box delivered a thumping, solid beat that provided an ideal backup for his rich baritone and Sonny's exciting country blues squalls and bends, blown directly through the house system.

Blues Roll on with Brownie & Sonny

In the early days, I washed dishes. Sometimes I also helped with seating. Later, I learned to run sound and lights from the upstairs booth, also announcing the acts.

I would often go to the upstairs sound and light booth to hear Brownie and Sonny play their sets. I would thrill as I heard them introduced from the upstairs sound and light booth, their music getting gradually louder as they played their way down the main aisle toward the stage. Brownie taking the lead, Sonny following, one hand holding his harp, the other resting on Brownie's shoulder, their rhythm glorious, their vocals rich, proceeding regally to their thrones through the haze of the room. An indelible image.

Brownie had polio as a youngster and walked with a pronounced limp. Sonny had lost almost all his vision in two separate childhood accidents. It was, in the most positive and moving way, the lame leading the blind, with loving support from the crowd.

Fairly soon after I saw Brownie & Sonny together the first time, which was probably in early 1959, I asked Ed if he thought Brownie would give me lessons and he told me to ask him, which I did. Brownie said OK, and we agreed on a $20 fee. Mind you, at the time one could rent a decent little living space somewhere for $40-50 a month, so $20 was not to be sneezed at. I can't recall how much (or little) I was paid for my part-time dish-washing job, but it seemed like a bargain to me, and it turned out to be just that and more.

Brownie and Sonny were staying at a large house in the Hollywood Hills owned by my brother's wife-to-be, Kate (Hughes) Hoyt. Kate was a modern dancer who came from a old and monied East Coast family, and she helped the club financially at times. She was a modern dancer and very supportive of Ed's social and cultural vision. They were actually a couple, but both would have resented such a bourgeois designation. They married a few years later.

Chief Justice Charles Evans Hughes was Kate's ancestor. The family owned an island off the Massachusetts coast, where I was later invited to stay while traveling East with my blues partner Long Gone Miles. But, that tale is for later.

I met Brownie at Kate's house and we sat in the kitchen for lessons, right by the refrigerator. He and Sonny were staying upstairs. I had my little Martin, but I really didn't know the first thing about playing blues guitar. I could strum a few chords. He began and we went somewhere. I comprehended little but got a few notes and we proceeded. Meanwhile Sonny, hearing what was going on, came downstairs and sat nearby listening. At a certain point very quietly began doing those little "whoops and hollers' for which he was famous. After a short while, he put harp to lips and quietly accompanied us, gently letting out a few of his country whoops.

Was I in heaven? Does it get better than that? Brownie showed me the same riffs that I was later to learn he had shown to everyone who ever took lessons from him. But, I tell you, that doesn't matter at all. It was all-inspiring. I took several more lessons over time as they were frequent Ash Grove performers, especially in those early days.

I don't know how much guitar technique I understood or retained at the time from the several sessions we had, but I hear a lot of

Brownie in my playing now. But the thing I appreciated most was the feeling of being that close to the music.

I took only a few lessons from Brownie, but drew closer to them both as time went on. I was on hand for dozens and dozens of performances over the next several years, looking forward to their return to the Ash Grove stage. Their sound helped shape my concept of the Blues. It was glorious music for most of their partnership,

At one point a couple of years later, while housed at the Hollywood YMCA, Sonny asked me if I would write his biography. I was stunned and flattered. I had no experience writing, and the thought never occurred to me. But, I had access to a small, portable reel-to-reel tape recorder, and with the encouragement and prodding of friends, I agreed. I met him in their shared room and recorded what we talked about. He spoke of his origins in rural Georgia, and how he lost his sight.

I commented that he must have had a very rough time during the Depression. His response educated me. He said, on the contrary we had plenty to eat in the country. They grew their own food and, I imagine, had poultry and perhaps a goat or cow for milk. I also asked about Segregation and how Black folks were treated, and got a typical Sonny optimistic response. He said, and I paraphrase, that things weren't as bad as people say. Now, Sonny was no fool, and I know he endured some tough times, but his generally optimistic personality and outlook allowed him to not dwell on the negative. One of their signature songs said, "The sun's gonna shine in my back door someday."

Brownie was forthright and outspoken. He would have had a different answer. I asked Sonny about meeting Brownie in Durham, North Carolina, and he painted this picture. He was playing on the streets of Durham with Fulton Allen i.e. Blind Boy Fuller, a recording star of the time.. The "Bull City" was a center of tobacco product manufacture. Plenty of jobs, and workers had some money to put into the cups of the street performers, most of whom were blind.

Perhaps it is my imagination, but I believe he said that he and Fuller were on one corner, Rev Gary Davis was on another, and Blind Willie McTell was on a third. I tremble to think who might have had the fourth. Nevertheless, Brownie arrived, played with Sonny and Fuller for a while. When Fuller passed away suddenly, Brownie was recorded as Blind Boy Fuller II, which he didn't care for, as close to Fuller musically as he was. He was always his own man.

Sonny told me an anecdote from his Durham days. He was living with his girlfriend. One time he arrived home earlier than expected. The lady was with a man, who started to jump out the rear window. Sonny said he grabbed his gun and fired a couple of shots but, luckily, missed. We would have been cheated out of decades of great music had he been able to see what he was shooting at. I never did complete my interviews and, much to my regret, didn't write his life story. My bad. It hurts me to this day that I can not find that precious tape!

Brownie McGhee and Sonny Terry went to New York and soon became prime players in the burgeoning folk scene, recording, and playing in clubs, and in Broadway shows. Sonny told a memorable story about auditioning for a major Broadway production, "Finian's Rainbow". They liked his country blues harmonica playing - trains rolling down the track, hounds on the hunt for rabbits, lively and audience-pleasing all. They wanted him to open the show. He played the audition, and the music director praised him and added that he wanted Sonny to play it just that way every night.

Sonny responded that he couldn't do that as he changed it every time he played. The director insisted that was what he wanted, and Sonny insisted that he couldn't do it. Finally Sonny thought to ask what he would get paid. When told of his salary, Sonny says, "Oh, yes I can do it". And do it he did. Brownie and Sonny were hired to perform in Tennessee Williams' play, "Cat on a Hot Tine Roof", and did it so well that they also appeared in the subsequent film.

Brownie & Sonny recorded for Folkways Records and others, but each maintained a certain degree of musical autonomy. Together they toured the U.S. and Europe. Doing traditional tunes,, and some of their own songs and instrumentals. A warm, inclusive, and energetic show.

They played together for several decades, the landmark acoustic duo blues artists in the land. One night at the Ash Grove someone in the audience shouted out, "How long have you been playing together?" Brownie didn't skip a beat and replied, "We've been together 40 years…(pause)…that's a long time to be with a man." The audience broke up! So it was.

And Then, Disaster Struck

Things began to come unglued after they released an album in 1973 (33 1/3 RPM vinyl, in case you're too young to remember albums) on A&M Records, a major player. They sang mostly fresh material and had some very fine studio musicians to back them, bass, drums, piano, some on electric instruments. Songs by Randy Newman, Michael Franks and pianist "Mighty" Mo Rodgers, and their dynamic mastery of story-telling all mixed together to make it their most popular recording. It introduced them to a new generation and potentially larger audience. To use an old term, it was simply bitchin'. Titled, "Sonny & Brownie", the cover featured a black & white photo of the two of them casually sitting in the Ash Grove's very modest dressing room getting ready for a set.

It was fresh and modern. It could have begun a new chapter in their partnership, introducing them to a new audience. I really loved it. It was not classic McGhee and Terry, but it worked for them big time.

Based on that success, Brownie told me, he proposed that they start travelling with a bassist to fill out their sound and be more appealing to a younger, larger, more general audience. Sonny flatly refused, and continue to refuse over time. He wanted to keep things as they were, after all they had made a living doing what they had done for decades. Brownie had a different vision. Their stage shows began to noticeably reflect the tension between them. Their onstage presence saddened me. There was bickering and animosity, and they hardly played songs together, and it broke my heart. I loved them both.

It got to the point where they took the stage and, essentially, did solo sets with very little support from their partner. It was terribly sad to witness. They ultimately broke up the duo, each performing separately. Sonny recorded a wonderful album with Texas guitarist Johnny Winter, released by Alligator Records. I spun it happily on my radio show, but with an edge of melancholy. Bless them both. I loved them both.

Shortly after I got the LP, I went into that same dressing room and Brownie was there. I told him how terrific I thought the record was, and I asked whose idea it was. He said, "mine". He had been after Sonny for a while to modernize their stage show and to start using a bass and maybe a drummer. Sonny refused to consider it, on the basis that it would cost too much to carry a band. Brownie was of the notion that it would allow them to cast a broader shadow and allow them to play more and larger venues for more money. That was one very obvious bone of contention and, while there may have been other areas of friction between them, that would have been enough to cause the alienation one and all could see on stage.

Brownie was an assertive person. He could come off as gruff at times, but whatever the subject, he'd let you know how he felt. I found him to be very intelligent and informed, and a straight shooter. He was a poet of the blues and a fine finger style guitarist. I found it kind of upsetting that as the sixties came on that the new wave of blues aficionados who had been listening to the pre-war country showed a lack of respect for his playing.

I guess that he was too polished for them, nowhere near as "authentic" or rough as Charlie Patton. They judged Brownie & Sonny as pandering to a white middle-class audience and not playing the real nitty gritty blues. There's some justice in that, but they were professionals who had developed an approach to the blues by living the blues which allowed them to make their way for decades. They introduced the blues to an audience totally unfamiliar with that music. And, they both could really play and sing.

Sonny was a more laid-back personality. Always willing to talk to you, or to "sign" an autograph with his "Yours Truly, Sonny

Terry" stamp. He appeared easy going and generally had a smile for everyone. I don't think it was put-on.

Very different personalities, McGhee & Terry, but it worked for a long time, and they made a lot of people happy.

One fantasy I, and others, had was that one day Brownie or Sonny would call and ask me to play because their partner couldn't make the gig. Never happened. I did manage to play onstage with many blues artists in my career, but not with Brownie. Sonny, on the other hand, did come up once and played when I began working with Louisiana Blues singer Long Gone Miles. He wanted to help us get started. It was unexpected and flattering.

I was invited to play at Brownie's 80th Birthday celebration at Yoshi's in Oakland. I asked him to sign my treasured copy of his solo 1955 10" LP on Folkways, Brownie McGhee Blues. He did.

Lone Cat Fuller had set me up with a jab to my consciousness. Brownie & Sonny delivered an uppercut that spun my world.

The haymaker was yet to come.

Who Was Sonny Terry?

48

Sonny Terry

Sonny Terry was a virtuoso Blues harmonica player. His signature *whoopin'* harmonica style incorporated energetic, intense, high-pitched vocal yawps and often featured uncanny train and animal imitations.

Alan Lomax called Terry that greatest of harp blowers. I once filmed him in slow motion lifting quarter tones off the back of his harmonica with his fingertips. He would beat his cupped hands and make blatting trumpet notes. Most of all, by muting the harp, he could make it sing the blues, the harp taking up the phrase just as the singer leaves off and moaning right on for him.[49]

Terry used a "*cross-note*" technique, playing in a key other than the key of the diatonic harmonica. He was especially talented in creating special effects, including train whistles, animal cries, and vocal moans. He sometimes sang while he played. By controlling his breath and cupping his hands over the harmonica, Terry was able to modulate from key to key, blending the musical pitch and slurring notes.[50]

Sonny Terry was born Saunders Terry Terrell on October 24, 1912 (some say 1911) to Reuben Terrel and Minnie Terry. His family nicknamed him Sonny, as in young son. When he became a performer, he adopted his nickname and his middle name as his musical name.

Reuben Terrell, a farmer, played harmonica at social functions. Each night he put the instrument away on a high shelf, well out of reach of young Sonny. But when he left for work for the day, Sonny climbed up and got the harmonica down to try it out. One day, Sonny placed the harmonica differently from his father. When his father noticed, he asked Sonny if he'd been playing. Sonny's mother told his father that he played a tune for her every day. His father decided to teach him how to "really play." Terry was age 5 or 6 when he learned to play Blues from his father. He soon taught himself to mimic the sounds of far-away trains and the baying of hounds on the harmonica.[51]

When he was 11, Sonny had an accident that resulted in the loss of vision in one of his eyes. Sonny Terry had another accident when he was 16 years old which further worsened his eyesight. After the second accident, Terry started playing harmonica in local churches and dance halls.

Prevented from making a living from farming by his poor eyesight, Terry began working the streets as a Blues singer in Shelby, NC. *In them days I just as soon died — except for my harmonica. It was like a friend who didn't give a damn if I could see or not.*

At age 19, Terry began to tour with traveling medicine shows, moving from town to town, supporting himself as best he could.[52]

After a stint in one of the medicine shows, Terry decided to take to the road, playing for tips on the streets[53] and playing at dinners and dances in tobacco belt cities (Winston-Salem, Greensboro, and Durham) of NC. He also worked briefly at a factory for the blind and occasionally sold liquor.

In 1934, Sonny Terry met Blind Boy Fuller, a popular Blues guitarist and singer. Fuller convinced Terry to relocate to Durham, NC, which was the hometown of Fuller. Durham had a lively musical street scene outside its tobacco auction warehouses. Terry played at tobacco warehouses, fish fries, and house parties. In Durham, Fuller and Terry would perform together. Fuller and Terry became a local attraction.[54] On the streets of Durham, Terry also met and played with Rev Gary Davis. All three musicians were blind!

In 1937 Fuller and Terry traveled to New York to record for Vocalion. A year later in 1938, John Hammond of Columbia Records contacted Long. Hammond wanted to book Fuller for his upcoming *Spirituals to Swing* concert at Carnegie Hall. He intended to present *Negro music from its raw beginnings to the latest jazz*.

Hammond arrived in Durham accompanied by future Columbia Records president Goddard Lieberson,. Unfortunately, Fuller was in jail for shooting his wife. However, Hammond did not come away empty handed, *next door lived a blind harmonica player named Sonny Terry, and, as soon as we heard him play and shout his unique song, we decided he was a far superior performer. He definitely should be brought to New York for the concert.*[55] Thus Terry became the first artist to be signed up for the legendary event.

On Dec 23, 1938, Sonny Terry performed in *Spirituals to Swing* at Carnegie Hall. Carnegie Hall was completely sold out for the show. On the very next day, Alan Lomax recorded Terry at Havers Studio in New York City for the Library of Congress. Two days later,

Terry made his first solo commercial recording, *Train Whistle Blues* and *New Love Blues*. This single was issued by Columbia in its classical series.

Upon his return to Durham, Sonny Terry continued to perform with Fuller. In 1939, Terry met his future partner, Brownie McGhee, while performing in Durham. Terry and McGhee performed together from time to time in Durham.[56]

Who Was Brownie McGhee?[57]

Brownie McGhee

Walter Brown McGhee was born on November 30, 1915 in Knoxville, TN. His parents were George Duffield "Duff" and Zelda Evans. Shortly afterwards the family moved to Kingsport, TN. In 1918, at 3 years old, Brownie contracted polio. As he grew older, he got around in a cart, which was pushed and navigated with a pole by his younger brother Granville.

Granville "Stick" McGhee

Granville was born in 1918. He became a fine guitarist in his own right. For his own efforts, Granville earned the sobriquet "Stick." Stick had a big nationwide hit in 1947 entitled *Drinkin' Wine Spo-Dee-O-Dee*.

Duff McGhee often teamed up with his brother-in-law, John Evans, a fiddler, to play for local dances and parties. When Brownie was seven years of age, Uncle John Evans built a five-string banjo for Brownie. The banjo was his first instrument. Within a year, McGhee also began learning to play the piano and the guitar. He recalled his father's telling him never to strum the guitar, but to pick it as he did, using his bare fingers: *My daddy forbade me to play with a straight pick, and he was absolutely against me playing with a slide.*[58]

Following his father's directive, McGhee developed his own style, characterized by picking patterns and syncopated melodies played over a thumb-picked bass. *My thumb is another hand. My father always told me something should be happening on the guitar all the time I was 14 or 15 before anybody knew I could play the guitar. But my daddy knew I was foolin' with his guitar, because I'd get it out of tune.*[59]

Another influence was family friend Lesley (or "Esley") Riddle. Riddle accompanied A. P. Carter of the Carter Family on song collecting trips. His style influenced the style of Maybelle Carter.

McGhee's family moved several times while he was growing up. He attended elementary school in Lenoir City, TN, near Knoxville. In Lenior City, McGhee sometimes played the organ at the Solomon Temple Baptist Church. Later, he sang in the choir at the Sanctified Baptist Church. A few years later, the family relocated to Marysville, TN. Here, McGhee started high school. During the summer after his freshman year, Brownie McGhee quit to become an itinerant musician. He entertained at resorts in the Smoky Mountains. Then McGhee earned a living traveling throughout TN. He played and sang with the Hagg Carnival and in medicine and minstrel shows.[60]

As a result of the ongoing Depression, in the early 1930s, McGhee rejoined his family on their farm in Kingsport. He stayed there for a few years helping with farmwork. In his spare time, McGhee sang with The Golden Voices, a gospel quartet. As pressures of the Depression began to ease, he moved to Knoxville. Over the next few years, Brownie McGhee formed a series of small bands to play at local affairs in and around the city.[61]

In 1937 a successful operation sponsored by the March of Dimes led to greater mobility for Brownie McGhee. He was in the hospital for nine months. While in the hospital, McGhee made up his mind to walk without a crutch. *I just wanted to pick up my guitar and start walking. And that's just what I did.* [62] Despite the successful surgery, Brownie McGhee walked with a noticeable limp for the rest of his life.

This greater mobility enabled Brownie to move about the Southeast with tent shows and perform with his father's gospel group. In 1939, McGhee started traveling again. He made his way through NC as a street performer. In Winston-Salem, McGhee formed a group with harmonica player Jordan Webb.[63] McGhee, Webb and this group made their home base in Knoxville.[64]

This group didn't stay together long. McGhee and Webb crossed the state line into NC, eventually ending up in Burlington. Here, Webb introduced Brownie to the albino George "Bull City Red" Washington. 'Bull City Red' was the washboard player for Blind Boy Fuller.

McGhee and Webb moved to Durham, NC, in 1939. Brownie wanted to move to Durham, NC, in hopes of meeting Blind Boy Fuller. McGhee was inspired by the musical form of Fuller and wanted to learn from him. "Bull City Red" Washington introduced Brownie McGhee to Blind Boy Fuller and to Sonny Terry. Washington, Fuller, and Terry were performing as a trio in the Durham area.

Through "Bull City Red" Washington, Brownie gained an introduction to both Blind Boy Fuller and talent scout James. B. Long of Okeh Records. After hearing Brownie McGhee play, Long felt the similarity of style between Brownie and Blind Boy Fuller. At that time, Fuller was in poor health. Worse yet, Fuller wasn't getting any better. In 1940, Long recorded Brownie singing in a carbon-copy Blind Boy Fuller style for Okeh Records.[65]

Who Were Sonny Terry and Brownie McGhee[66]

**Sonny Terry and Brownie McGhee
In the Upstairs Dressing Room at the Ash Grove, Los Angeles**[67]

Sonny Terry was a great harmonica player. Brownie McGhee was a great guitar player. Together, Sonny and Brownie were a force in the Blues music world. This pair represented the Blues music world in the growing folk music scene in the early 1960s. As a result, Sonny and Brownie were one of the first, if not the first, Black Blues groups to perform regularly in Europe.

Blind Boy Fuller died in February 1941 at the age of 33. Three months later, Brownie was recalled to the Chicago studios of Okeh Records to record more songs. One of these songs was called *The Death Of Blind Boy Fuller* which was credited to "Blind Boy Fuller No. 2".

On October 22, 1941, Brownie was back in the New York studios of Okeh Records to record more Blues. Sonny Terry was n the studio at the same time, due to record after Brownie. Brownie had brought Jordan Webb, his own harmonica player, to the studio. Nevertheless. Brownie invited Sonny to play second harmonica on one song. Then, Brownie let Sonny take over the harmonica role completely on another song.[68]

In May of 1942, Sonny Terry was invited to sing at a concert in Washington, D.C., James Long sent Brownie McGhee along to look after Sonny and back to him up at the performance. *I was just going along for the ride. But I introduced myself to the Library of Congress people and made some records under the supervision of Alan Lomax. From then on in, me and Sonny started making records. My first records, Sonny was backing me up. Sonny wasn't singing natural at the time; he was singing falsetto.*[69]

Lomax recorded the pair in the Coolidge Auditorium. He is heard on these recordings announcing that Terry and McGhee were appearing courtesy of J. B. Long and John Hammond.[70]

Later in 1942, Millard Lampell of the Almanac Singers invited the pair to make New York City their base of operations. Sonny Terry and Brownie McGhee moved to NYC, settling in an apartment on downtown Sixth Avenue. The pair appeared frequently with Woody Guthrie and the Almanacs.

In 1942, McGhee opened the Home of the Blues Music School in New York City, where he taught young musicians the intricacies of fingerpicked blues guitar. He operated the school until 1950, but also continued his recording career.[71]

During the years of World War II, Sonny Terry and Brownie McGhee were very busy.

Terry and McGhee performed on programs broadcast on Armed Forces Radio, including *This Train is Bound for Glory*, *Hootenanny* and *Your Ballad Man*. These shows later aired in the US on the Mutual Broadcasting System. All of these programs were produced by Alan Lomax.

"Ballad operas" were produced in 1944 by Roy Lockwood for the radio home service of the BBC. Sonny and Brownie appeared in some of these operas, including Langston Hughes' *The Man Who Went to War*, *The Chisholm Trail*, written by Elizabeth Lomax and *The Martins and the Coys*. Elizabeth Lomax was the wife of Alan Lomax, the famed Blues field recording folklorist. Unfortunately, these shows were never broadcast in the USA.

After the War, Terry and McGhee were seen and heard playing with Woody Guthrie in the film *Hear Your Banjo Play* (1947). This film was narrated by Pete Seeger and written by Alan Lomax.

In early 1947, Sonny Terry was approached by Milton Rosenstock, the Musical Director of the Broadway play *Finian's Rainbow*. Rosenstock wanted Sonny Terry to be a part of the musical accompaniment to the play. He gave Terry a specific music set. Furthermore, he told Terry that the music had to be played exactly the same way every night of the performance. Sonny Terry refused, explaining that he had to play what he felt and how he felt at the time he was playing. But, Terry asked Rosenstock how much he would be paid. When Sonny Terry heard how much he would be paid, Terry responded enthusiastically, claiming *I can do it!*. Apparently, the amount was substantial![72]

During 1947 – 1948, Sonny Terry provided musical accompaniment for the Broadway show *Finian's Rainbow*.[73]

As well as performing for folk revival audiences, the duo also formed a " jump-blues" combo with saxophone, called, alternately, Sonny Terry and his Buckshot Five or Brownie McGhee and his Jail House Rockers.

McGhee also recorded regularly on his own while teamed with Sonny Terry. He released a number of R&B singles including *My Fault*,, an R&B hit in 1948, with Hal "Cornbread" Singer on tenor sax, *Robbie Doby Boogie* in 1948, and *New Baseball Boogie* in 1949, with Brownie fronting a full band.[74]

During the late 1940s through the mid 1950s, Sonny Terry and Brownie McGhee attained considerable success. The pair recorded prolifically and entertained at private parties, on radio programs and in stage shows.

In 1958, just before the explosion of the urban folk boom, Brownie McGhee issued *Living with the Blues* on the Savoy label. On this recording, Roy Gaines and Carl Lynch blasted away on lead guitars. This sound was light years removed from the folk world.[75] McGhee also recorded a number of gospel sides. He used the pseudonyms of Big Tom Collins, Blind Boy Williams, and Spider Sam in order to steer clear of contractual conflicts.[76]

In the late 1950s, Sonny Terry and Brownie McGhee became part of *the folk revival*. This revival was a catch-all for both folk music and rural Blues. The pair was often invited to participate in numerous European tours. For a time, Terry lived in an old loft building where Woody Guthrie, Burl Ives, and other popular folk singers stayed.

Their popularity continued to grow. During the 1950s and the 1960s, Terry and McGhee played in clubs, folk festivals and rock shows throughout the US and the world.

In 1973, the pair released *Sonny and Brownie* on A&M Records. This record was a major departure from their normal recordings. Normally, Sonny played the harmonica, Brownie played the acoustic guitar. For the most part, no other musicians performed on the earlier records. Eight of the songs on this album were written by other musicians and were more timely. On this album, Brownie McGhee played an electric guitar on some of the songs. John Mayall played an electric 12-string guitar and an electric piano on some songs. A Moog synthesizer was even played on one song. Furthermore, a complete band, including drums, played on every song on the album.[77] More contemporary songs, written by other musicians, were play on this album. This album was the most popular album released by the pair.

Ironically, the popularity of this album lead to the split between Sonny Terry and Brownie McGhee. Brownie recognized that the musical world was heading towards electric instruments. He wanted to continue with using a band and electric instruments. Sonny was adamantly against this musical evolution, preferring to continue as a pair with only an acoustic guitar. This fundamental difference in their future musical style caused the rift between the two musicians. Each musician began to resent the other musician for refusing to cooperate in their future musical style. Both musicians became angry and bitter towards each other.[78]

As this acrimony became greater, Terry and McGhee preferred not to share a stage with one another, let alone communicate.[79] When actually appearing together on stage, Terry would play with another guitarist while Brownie sat silently and listened. When Sonny completed his song, then McGhee would perform a solo. While McGhee performed, Sonny Terry sat silently and listened. When the pair did talk, the conversation was generally bitter and contentious.[80]

Around 1975, Terry and McGhee split up over personality conflicts and tensions related to their respective musical careers.

However, on different occasions over the years, the pair did reunite for shows. Sonny Terry began playing solo harmonica. For a brief period, he led his own small band.[81]

Brownie McGhee maintained a busy and diverse performing schedule into the 1970s. He recorded the soundtrack for the film *Buck and the Preacher* and appeared in two French films, *Blues Under the Skin* and *Out of the Blacks and Into the Blues*. In the early 1970s, McGhee moved to CA. In CA, he built his own home in Oakland in 1974. Brownie McGhee continued to perform across the United States and abroad until his death.[82]

Sonny Terry died on March 11, 1986, in Mineola, NY. He was 74 years old. His death was attributed to natural causes. Brownie McGhee made one of his last concert appearances at the 1995 Chicago Blues Festival. Brownie McGhee died on February 16, 1996, in Oakland, CA. He was 80 years old and died of stomach cancer.

Who Was Blind Boy Fuller?

Blind Boy Fuller

Blind Boy Fuller (born Fulton Allen) was the preeminent exponent of Piedmont-style guitar picking. In this style, the thumb plays the bass line while one, two or three fingers play the melody and harmony. Using combined fingers in this way gives an effect that imitates ragtime piano and scat singing.[83]

Fuller was an expressive vocalist and a masterful guitar player who possessed a formidable fingerpicking guitar style. He played a steel-bodied National guitar that was a natural resonator before amplification. Fuller fused together elements of traditional and contemporary songs and reformulated them into his own performances. This fusing and reformulating attracted a broad audience.[84].

Much of his material was culled from traditional folk and Blues songs. Fuller is best remembered for his up-tempo ragtime hits, such as *Step It Up and Go*. At the same time, Fuller was capable of deeper material. His versions of *Lost Lover Blues*, *Rattlesnakin' Daddy* and *Mamie* are as deep as most Delta blues.[85]

A number of popular double-entendre "hokum" songs were in the repertoire of Blind Boy Fuller., such as *I Want Some of Your Pie*, *Truckin' My Blues Away*. Other well-known titles included "*Let Me Squeeze Your Lemon*" and "*Get Your Yas Yas Out*".[86] These songs reflected the lifestyles of Bluesmen and their clientele. According to Fuller himself:

> *Ninety percent of em' back in that day was a backdoor man!*[87]

Fulton Allen was born on July 10, 1904,[88] in Wadesboro, NC.[89] He was one of ten children born to Calvin Allen and Mary Jane Walker. After the death of his mother, Calvin, Fulton and the other children moved to Rockingham, NC. As a boy, he learned to play the guitar. Older singers taught him the field hollers, country rags, traditional songs and Blues that were popular in poor rural areas.

Fuller began to lose his eyesight when he was in his mid-teens.[90]

> *While he was living in Rockingham, he began to have trouble with his eyes. He went to see a doctor in Charlotte who allegedly told him that he had ulcers behind his eyes, the original damage having been caused by some form of snow-blindness.*

Only the first part of this diagnosis was correct. A 1937 eye examination attributed his vision loss to the long-term effects of untreated neonatal conjunctivitis.[91]

He married Cora Allen when he was young, working as a laborer to support his wife. By 1928 he was completely blind. He turned to whatever employment he could find as a singer and entertainer, often playing in the streets.[92] Fuller became a formidable guitarist, playing on street corners and at house parties in Winston-Salem, NC; Danville, VA; and then Durham, NC.[93] In Durham, playing around the tobacco warehouses, he developed a local following. This following included guitarists Floyd Council and Richard Trice, harmonica player Sonny Terry, and washboard player and guitarist George "Bull City Red" Washington.

Fuller generally played the guitar with a bottleneck in his early years. In 1935, Blind Boy Fuller met Rev Gary Davis in Durham, NC. Davis worked with Fuller to help Fuller develop his playing into a non-bottleneck style that became extremely successful. Davis also introduced Fuller to a number of the themes that he recorded later in his career.[94]

James Baxter Long was a record store manager and talent scout in Burlington, NC. In 1935, Long secured a recording session for Fuller with the American Recording Company (ARC).[95] Fuller, Rev Gary Davis and Bull City Red Washington recorded several tracks in New York City. These tracks included the traditional *Rag, Mama,*

Rag. For purposes of promoting sales of the records, Long credited Allen as Blind Boy Fuller and Washington as Bull City Red.[96]

From 1935 until 1940, Fuller recorded over 120 songs, which were released by several labels.

> *His style of singing was rough and direct. His lyrics were explicit and uninhibited, drawing on every aspect of his experience as an underprivileged, blind Black man on the streets with an honesty that lacked sentimentality. Topics included pawnshops, jailhouses, sickness, and death. Although unsophisticated, his artistry as a folk singer lay in the honesty and integrity of his self-expression. His songs expressed desire, love, jealousy, disappointment, menace and humor.*[97]

In April 1936, Fuller recorded ten solo performances Early in 1937, he recorded for Decca Records, but then reverted to ARC. Later in 1937, Blind Boy Fuller made his first recordings with Sonny Terry.[98]

Fuller was known to have a fiery temper.[99] In 1938, he was imprisoned for shooting a pistol at his wife, wounding her in the leg. His imprisonment prevented him from performing in "*From Spirituals to Swing*", a concert produced by John Hammond in New York City that year. Sonny Terry performed in his place. This performance was the beginning of the career of Sonny Terry in folk music. After Fuller was released from prison, he held his last two recording sessions, in New York City in June 1940. By then, Fuller was becoming physically weaker and weaker. Much of the material produced during this period failed to match the quality and energy of his earlier recordings.[100]

Fuller underwent a suprapubic cystostomy in July 1940, probably due to the urethral stricture noted on Fuller's death certificate. This structure is a narrowing or blockage of the urethra which can be caused by syphilitic chancres, infections from gonorrhea, or chlamydia.[101] Regular and continuing medical treatment is required.

Blind Boy Fuller died on Feb 13, 1941, at his home in Durham, NC. Cause of death was pyemia, due to an infected bladder, gastrointestinal tract and perineum, plus kidney failure.[102]

On his deathbed, Fuller made a religious confession. *My sickness is heavenly retribution for playing the Blues.*[103]

Performing At The Ash Grove (1964)

As he became increasingly exposed to the Blues and Blues musicians, Bernie had the urge to perform live music.

Even White Boys Get The Blues[104]

With this motivation, Bernie Pearl actually formed a Blues band with guitarist friend David Cohen, King David and the Parables. This band was the first white Blues band in Southern California.[105]

**King David and The Parables, several months in 1964
Courtesy: Bernie Pearl**

This was a group that played primarily for the sheer fun of playing, with no commercial considerations involved. Mainly Blues but also some folk, blues, R&B, and surf music, or whatever was called for on any given night. King David & the Parables was heard by few, but fondly remembered by all who did hear the group live.[106]

Several recordings exist of live performances at the Ash Gove, These performances were recorded on Aug 25, 1964, Set 1, Set 2, and Aug 28, 1964.[107] The recording on Aug 28, 1964 especially manages to capture the spirited fun of this band onstage.

The set begins with some fine picking on one of Jesse Fuller's more obscure songs, *Hanging 'Round a Skin Game*. This selection sets the tone for a set that places heavy emphasis on traditional blues styles. The band continues with a pair of Brownie McGhee numbers, *I'm A Stranger Here* followed by *You Don't Know My Mind*. Both feature tasty guitar interplay between Cohen and Pearl, with its nice relaxed groove.

The Parables only entered into a recording studio once. Jay Jay Cameron, a pop singer, recruited the group to add a bluesy backing track to a song called "Short Dresses".

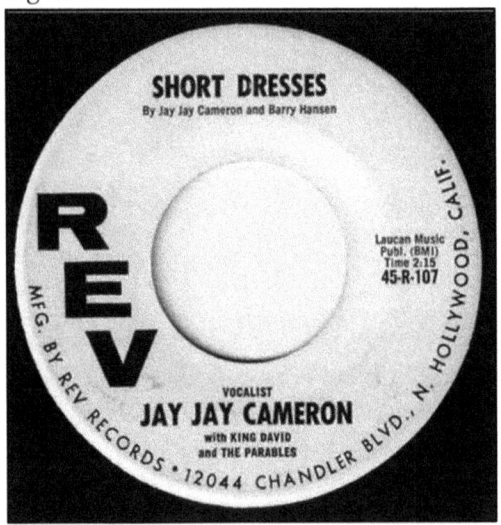

This song was promoted as the A side of the recording. "Miss Missile" was the side B of this recording.

A few hundred copies of the single were distributed to radio stations. Few ever played either side. No orders were ever received. This lack of response ended the not-so-illustrious recording career of the group.

The group only existed for several months. All of the members of the band went on to successful musical careers.

David Cohen became a highly in-demand studio musician.

Cohen began his musical career as a finger-pickin' folk guitarist, studying the Blues with Brownie McGhee. Cohen performed regularly at the Ash Grove in Los Angeles. His musical career evolved considerably after that period.

While playing at the Ash Grove, David Cohen became close friends with fellow guitarist Ry Cooder. Cohen and Cooder played together regularly at other small venues like the Ash Grove. At some point, Cohen and Cooder had a major disagreement. Cohen and Cooder separated and permanently lost contact with each other.[108]

In 1965 Cohen met his mentor, composer/guitarist Don Peake.

David Cohen and Don Peake[109]

Don Peake encountered David Cohen when Cohen played at the Ash Grove in Los Angeles. Peake arranged for Cohen to play at the recording session for *If I Were A Carpenter* with Bobby Darin. This session was the first session in which Cohen participated as a studio musician.[110]

Cohen then became a Los Angeles studio musician. *Being a studio musician was an incredible education. Listening to great players like drummer Hal Blaine taught me to feel music, not just hear it.*[111]

In the late 1960s, David Cohen joined a band named The Wrecking Crew.[112] This band was a loose group of high-level

American session musicians based in Los Angeles who played on many studio recordings. In the early 1960's, the band became the de facto house band for producer Phil Spector. Using this band, Spector created his signature Wall of Sound production style. By the late 1960s, the Crew became the most requested session musicians in Los Angeles.[113]

One member of the band was Los Angeles keyboard player Don Randi. Randi and Cohen became lifelong friends as a result of their participation in The Wrecking Crew.

David Cohen

And

Don Randi[114]

Cohen formed a folk music group by the name The Great Awakening in 1969. This group performed at the 1969 Isle of Wight Festival at Wooten Creek on the Isle of Wight in England. *Amazing Grace*, performed by the group, became the theme song of the concert.

The Great Awakening Performs Amazing Grace
Source: https://www.youtube.com/watch?v=pfHuJxTzRlw

The Great Awakening consisted of David Cohen on the guitars, Jim Gordon on drums and Joe Osborn on the bass guitar.[115] *The mantra-like fuzz guitar provided by David Cohen added a spiritual quality that was missing from later versions.*[116]

As a studio musician, Cohen soloed on albums in musical styles that ranged from folk to electric, dobro and Motown. Solo performances by Cohen accompanied Bobby Darin, "If I Were A Carpenter", Kenny Rogers and the First Edition, "But You Know I Love You", and The Jackson 5's "I Am Love."[117]

David Cohen also collaborated with musicians in other genres, such as Larry Carlton, the famed electric jazz musician.

…and when I first started in the early 70s, there were two other guitar players. … they were more rock sounding. So, when producers wanted something a bit more edgy or maybe for that time a bit more contemporary, they would call these guys. You had David Cohen and Mike Deasy. Deasy was a real Hendrix-influenced kind of player. He didn't read a note, but they would just have him come in and play whatever he felt like playing because it sounded more contemporary. They were very busy at the time, and David Cohen was a folk guitar player, so he was a really good finger picker. Those guys were still busy, but as the, shall you say, the level of musicianship got higher, meaning guys who could play AND read the music, their work started to diminish. They had a wonderful 6-8 year run, but the industry was changing.[118]

Cohen served as a studio musician with Carlton on a number of recordings by major musicians. Cohen and Carlton played guitars on the Barbara Streisand album *Stoney End* released on Jan 1, 1970.[119] In Oct-Dec, 1973, Phil Spector and John Lennon produced the first half of John Lennon album eventually entitled *Rock 'N' Roll*. Recording sessions were held at the Record Plant Studio, 8456 West Third Street near La Cienega Boulevard, in Los Angeles. Cohen and Carlton, among others, are credited with guitar work on the album.[120]

When Lennon arrived, David eagerly approached Lennon, saying *how ya doin'?* Lennon curtly responded *same as you* and kept walking. David recalled Spector bringing guns to the session and refused to work with Spector again.[121]

After 5-6 years in the studio scene, I began to feel restless ... in the studio scene. I had gone as far as I could playing other people's music. I wanted to find my own.[122] Cohen spread his musical wings. by playing with country and rhythm & blues bands. When at UCLA, he had majored in music studying film scoring, arranging and orchestrating, and voice. His teacher in modal counterpoint and composition was Roy Harris. Cohen studied classical guitar with Celedonio Romero.

Eventually, David Cohen moved into classical music. Cohen wrote a chamber orchestra piece that was performed by the Topanga Symphony. He was experimenting with writing other works. During his experimentation, a neighbor complained to him about noise. This complaint led Cohen toward New Age music.[123]

To assist with his classical compositions, Cohen purchased a Korg music workstation; he found the orchestral sounds disappointing, but was intrigued with the 400 built-in sounds with names like *Air Castles* and *Blue Moon*. Soon he was composing for these unique voices and reorchestrating his classical compositions for these evocative new age sounds. In 1996, he released *Circadian Symphony*, a rhythmic yet melodic album bristling with brisk electronic sounds. *Octagonal Ballet* followed in mid-2000.[124]

Stuart Brotman gained a reputation as a leading Klezmer bass guitarist.

Stu Brotman had Jewish music in the family. His maternal grandfather, Cantor Louis Itkiss, was European-born of a dynasty of cantors. Brotman used to practice at home in Atlantic City and sang in temple for the High Holidays.

Brotman holds a B.A. in music with a concentration in Ethnomusicology from *UCLA – go Bruins*.

After the Parables, Stu was the bassist for Kaleidoscope. **Kaleidoscope** was an American psychedelic folk group which recorded four albums and several singles between 1966 and

1970.[125] This band also included renowned, late string-master David Lindley, who was also an Ash Grove regular.

Following a year of fieldwork recording folk music in Eastern Europe, Bratman moved to Woodstock. Here, he recorded with Geoff and Maria Muldaur.

Brotman then moved on to Klezmer music. He gained a reputation as a leading Klezmer double bassist.

Klezmer is an instrumental musical tradition of the Ashkenazi Jews of Central and Eastern Europe.[126] The term *klezmer*, as used in the Yiddish language, has a Hebrew etymology: *klei*, meaning "tools, utensils or instruments of" and *zemer*, "song, tune"; leading to *k'lei zemer*, meaning "musical instruments".[127] Generally klezmer music is primarily instrumental and can be divided into two broad categories: music for specific dances, and music for listening (at the table, in processions, ceremonial, etc.).[128] In the US, vocals began to be added to Klezmer music.

Melody in klezmer music is generally assigned to the lead violin, although occasionally the flute and eventually clarinet.[129] Clarinet based Klezmer music became an element of jazz played by Klezmer musicians who transitioned into jazz during the swing era in the US. The opening clarinet solo in George Gershwin's "Rhapsody in Blue" has a flavor of Klezmer. Strains of Klezmer can be heard in the old Benny Goodman recording "And the Angels Sing." About the last third of the song, Goodman and his big band switch to a syncopated rhythm, staccato trumpet, and wailing clarinet. This combination is a "frailich," klezmer music with a German flavor.[130]

Generally, the prevailing Klezmer style is the pizzicato style that involves plucking the strings of the bass with the fingers. However, Brotman had observed the upright bass being played with a bow in Eastern Europe. Stu became committed to spreading use of a bow to play the bass for klezmer in his performing and teaching. Thus the nickname Klezbow.

Stu has been recording, performing and teaching with world class ensembles Brave Old World since 1989, and Veretski Pass (2002).

He is featured in the PBS Great Performances film and CD, *Itzhak Perlman, in the Fiddler's House*, and in the 2010 documentary, *Song of the Lodz Ghetto*. Stu also performs and records with Khevrisa, Stempanyu's Dream, Andy Statman, Klezmer Conservatory Band, The Klezmorim, Klex-X, Klezmatics, Red Hot Chachkas.

Brotman has taught at KlezKamp, Buffalo on the Roof, the Balkan Music and Dance Workshops, KlezKanada, KlezCalifornia, and numerous European festivals and institutes, including Oxford University, Klezfest London, Yiddish Summer Weimar, Klezmer Festival Fürth, and the Krakow Jewish Festival.[131]

<u>Dr. Craig Woodson</u> became a well-known ethnomusicologist. Craig Woodson earned a Ph.D. from <u>UCLA</u> in music with a specialization in ethnomusicology, music education and musical instrument technology. He has presented student programs for over 30 years, and professional development workshops for over 25 years.

In 1976, Craig founded Ethnomusic, Inc., a world music education consultancy that presents multicultural instrument making, educational concerts, school programs and professional development.

He has presented for the Los Angeles Music Center, Kronos Quartet, Rock and Roll Hall of Fame and Museum, Cleveland Museum of Art, the National Symphony Orchestra, Carnegie Hall, Kent State and Xavier Universities, as well as in Ghana, Iraq and Indonesia.

Woodson is author and Director of the industry-sponsored, free, online world drumming professional development curriculum, *Roots of Rhythm*.

Dr. Woodson has been a percussionist, music educator, and consultant in the percussion industry for over 40 years.[132]

Barry Hansen years later became the well-known Dr. Demento.

Barry is an American radio broadcaster and record collector specializing in novelty songs, comedy, and strange or unusual recordings dating from the early days of phonograph records to the present.

Hansen created the Demento persona in 1970 while working at radio station KPPC-FM, in Pasadena, California. After he once played "Transfusion" by Nervous Norvus on the radio, fellow DJ "The Obscene" Steven Clean said that Hansen had to be "demented" to play the song. This event inspired his stage name. His weekly show went into syndication in 1974 and was syndicated by the Westwood One Radio Network from 1978 to 1992. Broadcast syndication of the show ended on June 6, 2010. However, the show continues to be produced weekly in an online version.

Hansen holds a master's degree in ethnomusicology from *UCLA* and has written magazine articles and liner notes on recording artists outside of the novelty genre. He is credited with introducing new generations of listeners to artists of the early and middle 20th century whom they might not have otherwise discovered. This list of artists includes Harry McClintock, Spike Jones, Jimmy Durante, Benny Bell, Rusty Warren, Yogi Yorgesson, Nervous Norvus, Allan Sherman, Ray Stevens, Candy Candido, Stan Freberg, and Tom Lehrer. Hansen is credited with helping to bring "Weird Al" Yankovic to national attention.[133]

Encounters With Lightnin' Hopkins

Mr. Hopkins Delivers a Haymaker To Bernie

I was tuned into the blues. I regularly saw Jesse Fuller, Brownie & Sonny, Barbara Dane with Kenny Whitson on piano, and Wellman Braud on upright bass.

Most of the acts around that time were of the Folk variety, largely white, some original "folk" material – this was just around the time that Dylan appeared. Some groups which became very well-known later: Lou Gottlieb as a single and then with Glenn Yarborough and the Limelighters, Peter Yarrow solo, later to join with Paul & Mary. I had had a few promising sessions with Brownie, when Barbara Dane arranged for Sam "Lightnin'" Hopkins to play the Ash Grove. He was just a name to me.

I can never forget the moment when I was smitten by his performance. Acoustic Gibson in hand, back-lit, rings and watch reflecting stage lights, front teeth of gold gleaming.

Lightnin' Hopkins
Source: Wikipedia Creative Commons

Hopkins was seated on a stool he raised his right arm in a gesture of pure stage magic, matching the emotion of the song he let loose with a sound that came from somewhere I couldn't identify, but wanted to find out about. I got hooked on the country blues in that instant. I loved everything I heard and saw. The exploration has never waned, the interest has never faded.

The Process

My brother Ed tells of how when Lightnin' Hopkins first came to play the Ash Grove, before he would appear on stage he needed his hair seen to. Suit could be pressed, rings and medallions could be glistening, and gold front teeth all aglitter, but the process needed attention before the spotlight shone on Mrs. Hopkins' son.

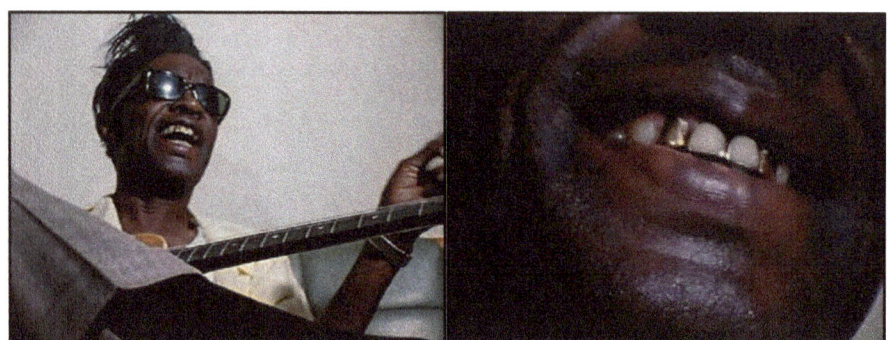

Lightnin' and His Perfect Gold Teeth

The Ash Grove was in the overwhelmingly Jewish Fairfax neighborhood and the barber shops were strictly snip and clip, and definitely didn't stock what was needed to tend a process. Joseph Chambers, who knew about hair-dressing was on hand, and knew what was needed, but South L.A. salons were at a great distance, and time was short. Then Ed remembered that when we moved from Boyle Heights, we lived above an African American beauty shop. West Adams was not that far away, haste was made, and the day was saved. An impeccably dressed, beautifully adorned, and sleekly groomed Sam Hopkins took the stage that evening and once-again dazzled an unexpecting new audience.

I believe that Lightnin' was brought to the Ash Grove by Barbara Dane.

Struck by Lightnin'

I met Lightnin' Hopkins when he first came to the Ash Grove, around 1960. I believe he came through contact with vocalist Barbara Dane, who ran a club in the San Francisco area. I had been fascinated by the rhythms of Jesse Fuller, and the warm and charming songs of Brownie & Sonny. I didn't know what to expect from this "new guy". Lord have mercy, I was in no way prepared for Sam "Lightnin'" Hopkins.

He sat on a stool dressed to a T, shoes buffed, shades on his eyes, hair "conked", Gibson acoustic guitar in hand, rings glistening on his long elegant fingers. He began singing and cast a spell, which is the only way I can put it. Blues of a much different and deeper sort than I had ever heard. A performer of a sort I was totally unfamiliar with. He hit his notes, gestured with his right hand expressively, and let his gold front tooth catch the spot light and reflect from it a dazzling, glowing beam. We were all captivated. The magic never abated through his entire set of mostly original tunes. He was comfortable and at ease wherever he played. Where do I sign up?

I got an answer to that question when my friends Barry Hansen and David Cohen suggested we three set up a private lesson with him. Barry was a student in UCLA's folklore department and wanted to interview him for a class paper he would write. The other two of us would try and learn just what he did with that guitar. Tutoring spell casting cost extra. I believe we offered him $20 each which in that day was a substantial, if not princely, wage for an hour of putting up with our questions. He agreed and told us where he was staying. I don't recall much about the location other that it was in South L.A.

Barry brought his tape recorder (advanced technology in 1960), Dave and I brought our guitars. A note about Dave Cohen. He had been a friend before Israel adventure. He played a little guitar previously, but had increased his knowledge prodigiously in the year I was gone. Being a very quick study and having a good ear had led him to a major in music. He was generally very bright and excelled at whatever he did. I greatly needed to learn those basics that led to good Blues playing. It has been my life-long preoccupation. The lesson was enriching.

Barry wrote his paper, continued to study, and graduated. He got involved in producing recordings and, bolstered by his enormous record collection, and his thorough knowledge of many forms of American music and their history, he became involved in hosting radio programs, eventually adopting the moniker "Dr. Demento", and becoming world-famous and a great factor in the re-setting of America's musical taste..

Dave Cohen and I opened a school at the Ash Grove, which lasted for several years. He had developed "studio chops", could read music fluently, and became the go-to guitarist for folk and related music recording sessions for several years. He played on many recordings, including "If I Was a Carpenter" by Bobby Darin, and became his guitarist for some time. Cohen also recorded with Larry Coryell, Barbara Striesand and John Lennon, among a long list of other musicians. David Cohen eventually left the studio world for work in the computer field.

I continued my relationship with Lightnin' and we became friends. When he came to town, which was fairly frequently, I would meet him wherever he was staying, bring him a half-pint of Gordon's Gin (all I could afford), and we would talk.

**Bernie Pearl and Lightnin' Hopkins At The Ash Grove
Courtesy: Phil Melnick**

Eventually Lightnin' Hopkins began inviting me to play with him at the Ash Grove. Not every set, not every night – Ash Grove bookings were for several days. An artist could settle in, and a young aspiring player could learn something.

Three Compliments

Everyone likes compliments for the meritorious things they do. Musicians are no exception. Compliments are welcome and needed, especially if one is walking on the students' path. Three instances stand out in my memory.

The Ash Grove was honored to have football great Roosevelt Greer in attendance at times. You may recall his position as part of the L.A. Rams' "Fearsome Foursome", the renowned defensive linemen regarded as the NFL's best. He was sizable and very congenial and loved the blues. One evening he showed up with the Rams' phenomenal halfback Dick Bass to see Lightnin' play. Bass wasn't that large a man, but was very fast, muscular and elusive, and was extremely hard to bring down. They sat at the section attached to the stage, immediately to my right. By then I had played with Lightnin' several times and was gaining some comfort. We did the set, and I heard part of the conversation between the two, and I distinctly heard Bass comment, *"He got good time"*. Now, I assumed that was about me as Lightnin's time was beyond questioning. To have that star athlete who made his living by having great timing comment that this young (white) guy playing with a blues giant passed the most critical test of all was something I've held dear my whole life.

On another occasion both Mance Lipscomb and Lightnin' were on the bill. As we took the stage I saw Mance sit down at a ringside table. When the set ended I passed by him and stopped to chat a bit. He commented, as closely as I can remember, *Well, Bahney* (he had his own charming way with words) he continued, *I reckon you'n me's the only ones who can keep up with ol' Lightnin'*, referencing his renown habit of changing chords *when Lightnin' want to change* (Lightnin's assessment of that inclination).

Once, after a run at the Ash Grove, Lightnin' told me he was going up to Carroll's place. Carroll Peery, my friend from the Ash Grove kitchen, was now running a coffee house in Berkeley called the Cabal. I asked if he minded if I showed up and played a couple of sets with him. He was OK with the idea, and I drove up and sat in with him. Lightnin' had relatives in both L.A. and the Bay area, and some of his family was at the show. I was on stage while Lightnin' was talking to his family nearby. In response to their question as to who I was, he replied, *"That's me up there"*. Does it get any better than that? I've never confused myself with him, nor have I ever thought I was his peer. But, I have studied his music and taken his words, his advice, his thoughts about living, as well as his encouragement to heart. He gave me the most important instruction of all. He said, *"Be yourself"*. That has been the watchword in my approach to this music, at once old and new, ancient and modern, this wisdom of life called the Blues.

A Fourth Compliment and Lightnin'

I was catching up on things with Brownie McGhee when he posed this question, "When you seen Sam last?" He was referring to Lightnin' the way he spoke to him, "Sam". I never thought of myself as a peer of any of the genre-defining giants I had met. I never addressed or thought of Lightnin' as "Sam". But, there was something in it that I didn't quite grasp. I was wont to think, perhaps overthink, when I heard a puzzling utterance from one of the definers of the genre. I didn't roll and tumble all night long, but I did come to the astounding conclusion that I was someone, in Brownie's eyes, who had earned a certain status in that elite company. Let me sit down. Welcome to the club?

A Night to Remember

Lightnin' had brought his wife Antoinette, whom he called 'Nette, with him, and they were continuing on to Berkeley, where I joined them. They had been booked into a small motel, and offered to put me up on their couch as I had not made other sleeping arrangements. I recall that there was a big music event in nearby Altamont that weekend, but no one was nervous about attendance at Lightnin's performance. He always drew well. Lightnin' took time to visit with his relatives, had put on his usually fine performance, and we retired to the motel after the show. A quick glance around the room showed that there was no couch, just a large bed with a wooden chair at a desk. I didn't know what to do, other than sleep on the floor. Lightnin' and 'Nette told me sleep across the foot of their bed, and handed me a pillow as they went to sleep. It was an act of graciousness and generosity that I'll never forget. The next day we heard reports of a killing at the Altamont festival. In retrospect, that event is seen as ending the days of flowerchild naivete', which began with the totally peaceful mammoth Woodstock festival. Viet Nam loomed larger and more ominously daily.

Chris Strachwitz, Austrian-born founder of Arhoolie Records, wanted to cut a new LP with Lightnin' while he was in town. Chris asked me if I'd like to play on it. He had heard me play with Lightnin' at the Ash Grove and at the Berkeley show. I was honored and flattered, but there was a problem. That was Sunday night, the session was Monday evening. I had an obligation on Monday nights teaching a class for an arts organization in Altadena. No way I could do both. I was not only torn, I was frustrated and insulted. If he had said something even one day earlier I could have called and postponed the session. To be on a recording with this great blues man would have been fantastic. But, damaging my reputation on the circuit where I was actually making some regular money was at stake. I opted for responsibility and paying my rent.

Let me now digress – I promise it will be relevant. My brother Ed had recorded many performances on tape, and, unlike the films that were destroyed in one of the Ash Grove fires, the tapes survived. Years after the club closed Ed was setting up a non-profit foundation and trying to reopen the club in a new location. He needed money. He sold many, if not all, tapes, to Wolfgang's Vault, an online purveyor.

The singular recordings were then archived and offered to the public, as were historic club photos by Phillip Melnick. I looked at the list of recordings, and my name was mentioned several times as playing with Lightnin' Hopkins. I was pleased, but I was afraid to listen to how inadequately I had played in those days. After a couple of years, "It's no joke", I screwed up the courage to listen on-line and, guess what, it not only sounded good to my ears, but it was very close to how I would play it today, several decades later!

So, getting back to Berkeley and Chris Strachwitz, the recording would have been truly bitchin', to revive an old cliché. On my behalf, and to underscore what Mance Lipscomb said, I never missed a chord change or a shift of time while playing with the great Mr. Hopkins. The reason is I paid very close attention to him, had him on my radar, and stayed tuned to his nuances. He could neither vip nor vop without me being on his tail. I was riveted to the right side of his blues.

Scars

Lightnin' came to play the Ash Grove several times a year. I had become accustomed to visiting him when he first arrived wherever he was staying, bringing him a celebratory half-pint of Gordon's gin. My income demanded moderation in all purchases. I'm reminded of his song, *You Better Watch Yourself, Sonny Boy*, a caution to his wine-loving nephew or cousin. He continued, *You drink that ol' wine, it's going to kill you*, followed by the remedy, *You better start to drinkin' that gin*. Sound advice. He usually travelled from Texas on a Greyhound bus, and liked to take it easy when he got here. I greeted him and we sat down and unscrewed the top. He offered me the first crack at it, and I sipped a little bit, not being that much of a drinker anyway. He admonished me to take a good swallow, to no avail, then took a solid belt.

Then he glanced around the room, reached into the cuff of his pants and pulled out a decent-sized joint. He fired it up and offered me a toke. Being modest in my use of any drugs I took one and passed it back. We talked for a while, and somehow the subject of prison came up. He said that he once had been on a chain gang, and started to pull up his pant leg to show me the scars. I was hurt and horrified and passed on a closer, more painful look. I later found out that he had been in the wrong Texas town at the wrong time. The county was looking for a press gang to do some road work. He was picked up for vagrancy, tried, and received time on a chain gang. His oft-repeated musical cry of "Lord have mercy" came from a place well beyond my experience.

An Affair

 A young college coed used to come to he club to see Lightnin'. It soon became clear that there was more than musical interest involved. Jane Phillips came from a Creole family of education, social status, and wealth in the Bay Area. She was very light-skinned and could have "passed" had she chosen to. But, she did not. She fully embraced her Blackness and Black culture generally, and she loved the Blues. She was an English major at prominent Catholic Mt. St. Mary's College, near the UCLA campus. She also became close with the Chambers brothers and Long Gone Miles, who nick-named her Skinny Minnie, for her slender figure. All in fun and love. How her relationship with Lightnin' evolved and expressed itself I have no details about or interest in finding out. At one point she did follow him to Houston and, after a time, was confronted by Lightnin's wife and eventually returned to her studies here.

As a writing class assignment she wrote a fictionalized account of a young woman, light-skinned of Creole descent, who falls in love with a Blues singer, Blacksnake Brown, and, pretty much follows her real-life relationship with Lightnin'. She titled the novel, "Mojo Hand: an Orphic Tale" (1966), and in it gave life to a series of characters based on her experience, and breathed reality into the language, words, and society she encountered on her journey into the Blues world. It was an extraordinary work that received honors at school and immediate publication. Fine reviews and widespread distribution followed. It is regarded as one of the earliest works of a new Black literature. This novel was titled after the Lightnin' recording entitled *Mojo Hand*.

Who Was Lightnin' Hopkins?

134

<u>Sam Lightnin' Hopkins</u>

(1912-1982) Centreville, Texas

Sam Lightnin' Hopkins had a knack for writing songs impromptu, and frequently wove legends around a core of truth. His often autobiographical songs made him a spokesman for the southern Black community that had no voice in the White mainstream at the time.[135]

Sitting on stage with his gold front teeth flashing, Hopkins tapped his feet enthusiastically and sometimes danced in his seat. Instrumentally, his dynamics were unmatched. Lightnin' went from soft bass accompaniment of his vocals to loud, screaming treble riffs up the neck of his amplified acoustic guitar in a seamless, and seemingly effortless display. Hand gestures, facial expressions ranging from sorrow to wry grins, and other body language added to the expressiveness of his act. His instrumental virtuosity was in the service of his art, which was simply, the Blues.

In addition to his standard songs, Hopkins' often composed impromptu lyrics and melodic variations. No two of his sets were ever the same. He was a fluent stage performer whose banter disarmed audiences. His songs were often humorous and self-deprecating but also bespoke the suffering that typifies the blues. Hopkins strongly felt that anyone could have the Blues, not just the poor or and the Blacks. *If you've ever had a sad feeling, you can tell the whole round world you ain't got nothing but the Blues.*[136]

Lightnin' Hopkins was the son of Abe and Frances (Sims) Hopkins. After his father died in 1915, the family (Sam, his mother and five brothers and sisters) moved to Leona. At age eight he made his first instrument, a cigar-box guitar with chicken-wire strings.[137]

As a child, Hopkins was immersed in the sounds of the Blues. He developed a deep appreciation for the music at the age of eight (8). Sam met Blind Lemon Jefferson at a church picnic in Buffalo, TX. He began accompanying Jefferson on guitar at informal church gatherings around Leona County.[138] Sam later learned from his distant older cousin, Alger "Texas" Alexander, the country Blues singer.[139] Another cousin, Frankie Lee Sims, the Texas electric blues guitarist, later recorded with Hopkins.[140]

By the mid-1920s Sam had started jumping trains, shooting dice, and playing the blues anywhere he could.[141] In the mid-1930s, Hopkins was sent to Houston County Prison Farm.[142] In the late 1930s, he moved to Houston with cousin Alexander in an unsuccessful attempt to break into the music scene. By the early 1940s, Sam was back in Centerville, working as a farm hand.

Hopkins took a second shot at Houston in 1946. While singing on Dowling Street in Houston's Third Ward, Hopkins was discovered by Lola Anne Cullum of Aladdin Records, based in Los Angeles.[143] Cullom convinced Hopkins to travel to Los Angeles, where he recorded, accompanied by the pianist Wilson Smith. The duo recorded twelve (12) tracks in their first sessions in 1946. An Aladdin executive decided the pair needed more dynamism in their names .He dubbed Hopkins "Lightnin'" and Wilson "Thunder". These names stuck.[144]

In the late 1940s and 1950s, Lightnin' rarely performed outside Texas, occasionally traveling to the Midwest and the East for recording sessions and concert appearances. He performed regularly at nightclubs in and around Houston, particularly on Dowling Street in the Third Ward where he lived and on West Dallas Street.[145]. By the mid- to late 1950s, his prodigious output of high-quality recordings had gained him a following among African Americans and blues aficionados.[146]

In 1959, the blues researcher Robert "Mack" McCormick contacted Hopkins, hoping to bring him to the attention of a broader musical audience engaged in the folk revival.[147] McCormack presented Hopkins to integrated audiences first in Houston and then in California. **One of the locations at which Hopkins performed regularly during this period was the Ash Grove, owned by Ed Pearl.** Lightnin' Hopkins made his debut at Carnegie Hall on October 14, 1960, alongside Joan Baez and Pete Seeger.

Through the 1960s and into the 1970s, Hopkins released one or sometimes two albums a year and toured. He played at major folk music festivals and at folk clubs and on college campuses in the U.S. and internationally. Lightnin' toured extensively in the United States. After a 1970 car crash, many of the concerts he performed were on his front porch or at a bar near his house in Houston.[148] He played a six-city tour of Japan in 1978.[149]

Wolf

Lightnin' was asked to join a tour of Europe, the "American Folk Blues", with many other blues notables, including Howlin' Wolf.

He had never flown before, but it was good money and he accepted. Numerous concerts in different cities and countries. It was hailed as a great success. I saw him shortly after he returned and asked how the tour was. He said it was fine, but I detected something less than enthusiasm in his tone, and asked about it. Lightnin', while fairly quiet and somewhat reserved, was nonetheless the center of attention in a group situation. When he talked, people listened.

Howlin' Wolf

(Chester Burnett)

Contrast that to the more gregarious and boisterous personality of Howlin' Wolf, who made himself the center of attention. Though each on the tour had separate rooms, and maybe separate dressing rooms and curtain times, there had to be times when the artists had to be together. Lightnin' related that he was irritated by Wolf's loud boasting that "he could eat more chicken than any man seen". Rubbed him the wrong way, a lot. He decided to be cool, thank the lord. I have thought about this over time and concluded that the whole thing could have turned very ugly if the wrong words were uttered.

Wolf, who notoriously would resort to physical violence if provoked, was a very large man who looked exceedingly powerful. Lightnin', lanky, wouldn't put up with stuff either. I speculated that one or both might have been packing. In those days passengers were not screened that carefully at boarding. Given the tough culture and circumstances they each grew up in, it was likely that a tragedy had been averted by Lightnin' choosing not to confront the braggart. A "Lord Have Mercy" moment for all of us.

Who Was Howlin' Wolf[50]

Chester Arthur Burnett, known as Howlin' Wolf, was one of the most influential musicians of the post–World War II era. His electric Blues guitar and harp blowing, backing his powerful, howling voice, helped shape rock and roll.

Chester Burnett was born on June 10, 1910, in White Station, Mississippi, four miles northeast of West Point, Mississippi. His parents were Leon "Dock" Burnett, a sharecropper, and Gertrude Jones. His parents separated when he was one year old; his father moved to the Mississippi Delta to farm. Burnett and his mother moved to Monroe County, Mississippi. Gertrude became an eccentric religious singer who performed and sold self-penned spirituals on the street.

Burnett got the nickname "Wolf" because his grandfather would scare the youngster by telling him that the wolf in the woods would get him if he misbehaved. The rest of the family would then call him "Wolf" and howl at him.

When he was still a child, Burnett's mother sent him away to live with his uncle, who was particularly hard on him, whipping him with a bullwhip and making him eat separately from the rest of the family. At age thirteen, he ran away from home and moved to the Mississippi Delta. He eventually found his father and his father's new family on a plantation near Ruleville, Mississippi, and he began working on the plantation.

While there, Charlie Patton, the most popular musician in the Delta, showed him a few chords on the guitar. In January 1928, Burnett's father bought him a guitar, and he began to play regularly, eventually teaming with Patton, who taught him many tricks of showmanship.

Preferring the life of a blues musician to the harsh life of sharecropping, Burnett began wandering the delta regions of Mississippi and Arkansas, playing music anywhere he could make money. He was a giant of a man, standing over six feet three inches and weighing some 275 pounds, and he became well known in the region as a blues performer, not only for his showmanship but also for his large size and loud, howling voice.

In 1933, the Burnett family left Mississippi and moved to a large Arkansas plantation in Wilson (Mississippi County). In early 1934, they moved to the Nat Phillips Plantation on the St. Francis River approximately fifteen miles north of Parkin (Cross County). Despite his commitment to his music, Burnett faithfully returned each spring to plow his father's land.

Burnett began traveling in Oklahoma and all over the south, but Arkansas remained his main stomping ground. He learned to play harmonica from blues legend Sonny Boy Williamson and added it to his performing arsenal. Along with Williamson, Burnett also performed in the 1930s alongside Robert Johnson, Son House, Johnny Shines, Willie Brown, and Robert Jr. Lockwood.

Burnett enlisted in the army, for which he was not well suited. After serving in the army, Burnett returned home to farm on the Phillips Plantation. Then he went to Penton, Mississippi, to farm for two years, farming by day and playing music by night. In Penton, he met Katie Mae Johnson, and they were married on May 3, 1947.

In 1948, Burnett moved to West Memphis (Crittenden County). He took a job in a factory there, but the area's blues clubs were the real draw for him. West Memphis, then a town bustling with blues clubs and gambling, was at the forefront of the newly amplified blues music, and Burnett adapted quickly. He assembled a blues band in the area called the House Rockers and made a commitment to make music his career. While Muddy Waters was giving birth to electric blues in Chicago, Illinois, Burnett was doing the same thing in West Memphis.

Beginning in 1948, Burnett was performing on local radio station KWEM in West Memphis (he both produced and sold advertising for his program), where he attracted the attention of record producer Sam Phillips in Memphis, Tennessee. Phillips's recordings of *Moanin' At Midnight*"\ and "*How Many More Years*"\ were leased to Chess Records and became a double-sided hit, making *Billboard* magazine's R&B top ten.

In September 1951, Burnett signed with the Chess label. The Chess brothers convinced him to move to Chicago in the winter of 1952. His wife refused to follow him, and their rocky marriage ended. Upon arriving in Chicago, Burnett broke into the scene quickly. He assembled a band in the West Memphis style. Among his band members was a young guitarist from West Memphis, Hubert Sumlin, who would stay with Burnett for the remainder of Burnett's career, except for a short absence.

In 1954, he recorded "Evil," his biggest hit to that point, which landed on the *Cash Box* magazine Hot Chart. This tune was the first of many tunes that Willie Dixon wrote for Burnett. As his audience grew, he toured more widely. 1955, he played New York's Apollo Theater. That year Burnett made *Cash Box* magazine's list of the top twenty-five male R&B vocalists. By that time, only Muddy Waters rivaled his popularity in the blues arena.

In 1956, Burnett recorded his masterpiece work, "Smokestack Lightnin'." The hit peaked at number eleven on both the *Cash Box* Hot Chart and Billboard's R&B chart. Over the next five years, Burnett recorded many hits. In 1959, Burnett released his first album on Chess, *Moaning in the Moonlight*, which was followed in January 1962 by *Howlin' Wolf*, sometimes referred to as the "Rocking Chair" album. Greil Marcus of *Rolling Stone* magazine called it "the finest of all Chicago blues albums."

On March 14, 1964, Burnett married Lillie Handley Jones, who was from Alabama. She was a property owner and a smart money manager, and they settled in south Chicago. She would remain with him until his death.

Burnett garnered wider exposure through the folk movement and British Invasion remakes of his classic blues songs. In 1965, he appeared on the ABC TV show *Shindig* with the Rolling Stones, who had a number-one hit in England with "Red Rooster." Over the next several years, he played the prestigious Newport Folk Festival, the Berkeley Folk Festival, and the Ann Arbor Blues Festival. In 1968, he released *Howlin' Wolf*, often referred to as the "electric" Howlin' Wolf album.

Despite failing health, including a 1969 heart attack, high blood pressure, and kidney problems, Burnett continued to tour and record. In May 1971, Burnett had a second heart attack, and doctors discovered that his kidneys were failing. He began to get hemodialysis treatments and was ordered by doctors to stop performing. But Burnett would not quit. Three months later, he was the opening night headliner at the Ann Arbor Blues Festival.

On January 7, 1976, Burnett was diagnosed with a brain tumor. He underwent surgery from which he never recovered. He was removed from life support and died on January 10, 1976. He is buried at Oak Ridge Cemetery in Chicago.

Hubert Told Bernie

Hubert Sumlin, Wolf's signature guitarist for years, told me this story. Hubert was a nice-looking man, and a great, significant player.

Hubert Sumlin

When he smiled, which was often, one could see that he was missing his front teeth. It was known that Wolf had knocked them out with his Derringer pistol, purportedly because his protege' was fixin' to leave him to go play with Muddy Waters. What I had never heard was that there was a part two. I asked Hubert about the incident. They were driving to a gig and Wolf pulled the car over to the side of the road. Angry, he had simply walked up to Hubert, pulled his pistol "his *durnger*, as called by Hubert", and knocked his front teeth out with it. Hubert did nothing to retaliate, and they all walked back to the car and drove on. End of incident. They went on playing together.

Later, perhaps even years later, the hens did come home to roost. They were again riding together to a gig and stopped at a place to buy sodas, which were still being bottled in those days. Hubert thought that the time had come, and took the occasion to hit Wolf in the mouth with his bottle, hard. He might have said that he knocked out a tooth or two, but at a minimum he proved that payback was indeed a bitch. They got back in the car and continued playing together until Wolf's passing.

Who Was Hubert Sumlin?[151]

Hubert Sumlin was a Chicago blues guitarist and singer, best known for his wrenched, shattering bursts of notes, sudden cliff-hanger silences and daring rhythmic suspensions.[152]

Sumlin was born in Greenwood, Mississippi on November 16, 1931, and raised in Hughes, Arkansas. He got his first guitar when he was eight years old. As a boy, he met Howlin' Wolf by sneaking into a performance.

When Wolf relocated from Memphis to Chicago in 1953, his longtime guitarist Willie Johnson chose not to join him. In Chicago, Wolf hired the guitarist Jody Williams. In 1954, Wolf invited Sumlin to move to Chicago to play second guitar in his band. Williams left the band in 1955, leaving Sumlin as the primary guitarist. Sumlin held this position almost continuously for the remainder of Wolf's career., except for a brief spell playing with Muddy Waters around 1956.

Howlin' Wolf sent Sumlin to a classical guitar instructor at the Chicago Conservatory of Music to learn keyboards and scales. Sumlin played on the album *Howlin' Wolf* (called the "rocking chair album", with reference to its cover illustration), which was named the third greatest guitar album of all time by Mojo magazine in 2004.

Upon Wolf's death in 1976, Sumlin continued playing with several other members of Wolf's band, as the Wolf Gang, until about 1980. His last solo album was About Them Shoes, released in 2004 by Tone-Cool Records. He underwent lung removal surgery the same year, but he continued performing until just before his death.

His final recording, just days before his death, was tracks for an album by Stephen Dale Petit, Cracking The Code (333 Records).

Sumlin lived in Totowa, New Jersey for 10 years before his death.] He died of heart failure on December 4, 2011, at the age of 80, in a hospital in Wayne, New Jersey.

Encounters With Mance Lipscomb

Ol' Man' Lipkins, Lightnin' Hopkins Called Him

My brother handed me an LP from a new blues label, Arhoolie Records. It was their first release (1960) and it's cover showed a rural man in a hat, sitting on his porch playing a Harmony guitar. It said, "Mance Lipscomb Texas Sharecropper and Songster". He said to listen to it and tell him what I thought. This was perhaps 1961. I thought I knew something. After all, I had studied with Brownie McGhee, and had become familiar enough with Lightnin' Hopkins to begin playing with him a little. What I heard didn't knock my socks off, and thought he was OK (please forgive me, please), and I told Ed so.

**Mance Lipscomb, Texas Sharecropper
Courtesy: Bernie Pearl**

Fortunately he had already decided to book Mance, and was I in for a surprise once I saw him play. His style was not in any overt way sensational, but, Lord have mercy, was it ever profoundly baffling. He sat up there in his clean khaki trousers, and immaculate shirt, wearing his hat at a slightly rakish angle, and proceeded to effortlessly wave his right (picking) hand around in a way I've never seen before, while his left hand never stopped moving. He sang songs I had never heard before, as he drew much of his repertoire from pre-blues era tunes. He was humble and charming and, as it turned out, very open and eager to meet people, and talk about anything they wanted to.

I can't say that "I got it" right away. It gradually dawned on me that his style was the Texas predecessor of what Lightnin' innovations were based on. As it turned out, it was in fact Lightnin' who was responsible for his "discovery" and recording.

As I recall the story, Lightnin' was friends in Houston with Mance's nephew T. Lipscomb. Mance had met Lightnin' years earlier when he, according to Mance, began singing a song about wealthy land owner Tom Moore, who was a major mover in the area. Mr. Moore employed many workers, who were, in effect, serfs, indebted to Moore, and operating under his say so in their lives. Mance's song was about how good Moore was to "his" men, but with a noticeable underlayer of sarcasm and pain. Moore got word of it and got a message to Mance to cease or else. He exercised his discretion and fled to Houston where his nephew was, to "let things cool down", as he expressed it. Eventually he returned to a safer and calmer Navasota.

A few years passed, and Chris Strachwitz, an Austrian reputedly of noble lineage, asked Texas folklorist Mack McCormick if there were any players back in the country still playing the old-time blues. Mack asked Lightnin' who, by then had also started playing for largely young white "folk" audiences, if he knew of any. I can imagine that Lightnin' didn't immediately respond, but maybe made a bit of a show about it. He ultimately said something like, *Well, there's this ol' boy back in Navasota who plays like that, "Man' Lipkins.* Honestly, that's how he pronounced it, I've heard him.

McCormick got the drift and the two folklorists found Mance and recorded him at his home on his front porch. He had by then stopped farming and sharecropping and had gone to work for the county building roads. He got injured and received a modest settlement. To the best of my knowledge, he used that money to buy his house and a little land in Navasota, where he did a bit of farming, had a couple of cows, and raised greyhounds. Then came more recording and more traveling around the folk circuit for money. From that he, very proudly, was able to buy a modest house for his son, Mance Jr., and his large family and have it moved to his lot. Cost $500 he said. He said, *I ain't got but one son, but lots of grands*. They called him *Daddy Mance*.

Magic Hands Picking

It took me a while to understand that what I was seeing Mance do with the guitar was nothing short of magical. The right hand, which appeared to be strumming the strings casually was, in actuality, picking riffs, melodies, and chords, all the while keeping a steady rhythm on the bass strings. Huh? The moment I really perceived the complexity and sophistication of what he was doing is captured clearly on the photo of the two of us jamming backstage in UCLA's Royce Hall at the 1964 Folk Festival, which my brother Ed put together.

The dumb-founded look on my face says it all. Easily worth a thousand words. I had accompanied him at the Ash Grove a few times, fairly competently and without major embarrassment, but this was the face-to-face moment when I better understood with whom I was playing. I usually sat on his right, to get a clear view of his left hand.

He had named himself Mance rather than using his birth name, Beau De Glen. A friend of his brother's had re-named himself after the Emancipation Proclamation. This appealed to him. An early indication of his awareness of, and interest in, freedom of thought and action for all people.

He was born near the end of the 19th century, and aside from working with his fiddler father, Charles, in the fields, also accompanied him on guitar when he played out. He recounted that as he and his father were ploughing to get ready for planting, they would dig up human bones. He said that they were prisoners who had died or had been killed and were buried where they fell. Brazos River true horror stories. Apparently, it was a regular occurrence.

Over the decades he had amassed a huge repertoire of pieces from the many eras he lived through, field songs, reels, WWI pop tunes, traditional songs, church songs, and Blues of different types, including slide pieces played with his pocket knife. Each arrangement unique and rhythmic, suitable for the many parties and jukes he played regularly for decades. Also suitable to driving guitarists hoping to understand how it was done to distraction. All headway is hard-won, and deeply satisfying.

The key element is the right hand thumb, on which he wore a pick. He kept up a relentless beat on the bass strings while his index and middle fingers picked out melodies, riffs, and chords. This is challenging enough. But, to make it sound like Mance one had to go further and hit the bass note clearly and then mute it, providing a pulse. I call it the "Open/Close" technique. All the while the two fingers relentlessly picked out the arrangement.

It took me a while to figure that out, but I put in the time, and now have the satisfaction of watching numerous live performances and videos of acoustic guitarists playing Mance's tunes note perfect, but missing the thumb element. It's all in how you hold your hand. Most of the signature country blues players have that going too. Notably, for me, MS John Hurt, who used his his thumb without a pick and with two fingers, like Manc. The great difference between the two was that Hurt alternated his bass notes, mostly between the sixth and fourth strings, but maintained the same Open/Closed technique on both. Also MS Fred McDowell, who played with a thumb pick and one pick on his forefinger, employs the same technique. I think it was integral to having people dance to solo acoustic guitars in the juke joints and porch parties before electricity. Works today too.

A note on learning the music. In almost no cases did I ask for or receive guitar instruction. We talked a lot about life, history, music. I studied the riffs and techniques, as well as I could perceive them, by the needle-drop method on my home record player. Much guesswork, lots of fun and frustration. Another note – even had I received more face-to-face guitar guidance, it wouldn't have benefitted me much. Shocking? Not really. Neither Brownie McGhee nor any of the other artists I sat with thought about the centrality of the right/rhythm/picking hand. It was just what they did. It was the notes they played that folks were interested in. But, without it you have notes, positions, and scales, but no pulse. Valuable as they are to performing the music, it is the rhythm that provides the basis of the feel. Took a while to get the style and settle on the right side of the blues.

Who Was Mance Lipscomb[153]

<u>**Mance Lipscomb**</u>

(1895-1976) Navasota, Texas

<u>Recommended Track</u>
"Mama Don't Dog Me", 1965

Mance Lipscomb represented one of the last remnants of the 19th-century songster tradition. This tradition predated the development of the Blues. Songsters might incorporate Blues into their repertoires, as did Lipscomb. However, a wide variety of material in diverse styles was incorporated into their musical repertoires, much of it common to both Black and White traditions in the South.

Styles included ballads, rags, dance pieces (breakdowns, waltzes, one and two steps, slow drags, reels, ballin' the jack, the buzzard lope, hop scop, buck and wing, heel and toe polka), and popular, sacred, and secular songs. Lipscomb himself insisted that he was a songster, not a guitarist or "Blues singer," since he played "all kinds of music." His eclectic repertoire has been reported to have contained 350 pieces spanning two centuries.

Lipscomb's Blues music was characterized by his unique musical style. This style incorporated elements of ragtime, country, and Blues. His lyrics often told stories of life on the farm and the struggles of everyday people. Lipscomb songs were both entertaining and thought-provoking.[154]

Mance himself described his guitar playing technique. *"Most of the young singers have to have a band behind them, but I don't need no band 'cause I can play my own bass. If you listen when I play, you can hear two guitars — my thumb plays the bass part and these two fingers [index and middle fingers] do the rest."*[155]

Usage of the right arm and right hand were important elements of Mance's playing style. Mance used his right arm as if the arm were a pendulum, hinged at his elbox. His right arm was in a continuous up-down motion. As he moved the arm down, Mance struck a low tone string to create a beat. As he brought the right arm back upwards, Mance used the heel of his right hand to mute the string. Muting the string terminated the beat by completely stopping the vibration of the low tone string.

Mance Lipscomb was born Beau De Glen Lipscomb, in the Brazos Bottoms near Navasota, Texas, on April 9, 1895. Mance was the son of Charles and Jane Lipscomb. His father was an Alabama slave who acquired the surname Lipscomb when he was sold to a Texas family of that name. His mother was half Black and half Indian.[156] Lipscomb dropped his given name and named himself Mance when a friend, an old man called Emancipation, died.

Mance joined his mother in the fields in 1905 when he was 10 years old, picking fifty pounds of cotton each day. When he joined his mother in August of 1915, temperatures were usually approaching 100° F. Within a year, Mance was picking 100 pounds of cotton each day. In that year, Mance started plowing, although the 11-year-old could barely reach the plow handles. By the time he was 18, Mance could pick 300 to 350 pounds each day. When he was 16, Mance picked 500 pounds of cotton on one day. *That liked to killed me.*[157]

Lipscomb was born into a musical family and began playing at an early age. His father was a fiddler, his uncle played the banjo, and his brothers were guitarists. Jane Lipscomb bought her son's first guitar when he was around 12 years old, on credit, for $1.50. This amount was a lot of money when the family was barely surviving on 50 cents a day. The guitar had only three strings. The guitar wood was so thin that the sunlight could pass through the wood. Mance took to the instrument, played it every spare moment. By the time he was 14, Mance had passed his brothers *like a pay car passin' a tramp*. One of the first songs that that Mance learned to play was *Sugar Babe*.[158]

Mance was soon accompanying his father Charles at suppers and Saturday night dances around the County. Father Charles deserted his family when Mance was about 15. After his father deserted, Mance began entertaining alone.

Mance honed his skills by playing with a blind musician, Sam Rogers, in nearby Brenham, Texas.[159]

During the 1940s and 1950s, Mance had some contact with such early recording artists as fellow Texans Blind Lemon Jefferson and Blind Willie Johnson and early country star Jimmie Rodgers,. However, Lipscomb did not make recordings until his "discovery" by whites during the folk-song revival of the 1960s.

Between 1905 and 1956, Mance farmed as a tenant for a series of landlords in and around Grimes County, including the notorious Tom Moore, subject of a local ballad. Lipscomb left Moore's employ abruptly and went into hiding after he struck a foreman for abusing his mother and wife. His rendition of "Tom Moore's

Farm" was taped at his first session in 1960 but released anonymously (Arhoolie LP 1017, Texas Blues, Volume 2), presumably to protect the singer.

Between 1956 and 1958 Lipscomb lived in Houston, working for a lumber company during the day and playing at night in bars where he vied for audiences with Texas Blues great Lightnin' Hopkins, whom Lipscomb had first met in Galveston in 1938.

In Houston, Mance was badly injured while working for a lumber company. He received a $3500 settlement, half of which went to his lawyer. With the remainder, Mance was able to have a house built on a three-acre lot in Navasota in Grimes County, a town just across the Navasota River from the bottomlands,. He owned the property free and clear. *You just try to live right. One of these days a little right come comin' to ya.*[160]

Mance Lipscomb was working as foreman of a highway-mowing crew in Grimes County when Blues researchers Chris Strachwitz of Arhoolie Records and Mack McCormick of Houston found and recorded him in 1960.

Lipscomb's encounter with Strachwitz and McCormick marked the beginning of over a decade of involvement in the folk-song revival. During the 1960s, Mance Lipscomb won wide acclaim and emulation from young White audiences and performers for his virtuosity as a guitarist and the breadth of his repertoire. Admirers enjoyed his lengthy reminiscences and eloquent observations regarding music and life.

One day short of a year after being discovered by Strachwitz and McCormick. Mance Lipscomb performed at the Berkeley Folk Festival of 1961. At this Festival, Mance played before a crowd of more than 40,000.

For the remainder of his life, Mance Lipscomb performed in small venues and large concerts. Performances by Mance Lipscomb were always well received.

Lipscomb died in Grimes Memorial Hospital, Navasota, on January 30, 1976, and was buried at Rest Haven Cemetery.

Encounters With MS Fred McDowell

Drinkin' Water Out a Hollow Log

Texas-based folklorist John Lomax had travelled the rural South in the 1930's with his son Alan. Toting a huge wire recorder in their trunk, they recorded all manner of traditional songs for the Library of Congress. Thank you President Roosevelt, we all owe you. White and Black singers and musicians, secular and religious songs, fiddles guitars, banjos and more. A compendium of a huge range of orally transmitted (i.e. Folk) music treasures.

In the early 40's Alan returned to Mississippi to find, among others, a near-legendary recording artist named Eddie "Son" House in Robinsonville.

Eddie "Son" House

For my money, House's rendition of "County Farm Blues" is as moving and damning a portrait of Southern justice as we have. Later, in the early '60's, the Blues-singing former minister was found living with his daughter in Rochester, N.Y. After a period of musical rehabilitation led by Canned Heat guitarist Alan Wilson, he resumed performing his Delta blues and religious songs at festivals and clubs, until he felt that he couldn't continue. A true inspiration to every blues lover who heard him. He passed away in 1988 at age 86.

Lomax also inquired around the Delta during this trip if there were any good blues singers around. He was directed, according to his sister, L.A.-based Bess Lomax Hawes, to Stovall's Plantation, and told to look for a young man who went by the name of Muddy Waters.

Muddy Waters Home, Stoval Plantation
Courtesy: MS Blues Trail Commission

As he was driving there he spotted a man walking down the road carrying a guitar. He stopped and offered a ride. As they drove he asked the passenger if he played the Blues. "Yes, sir". "Well, what is your name". "McKinley Morganfield...but, folks 'round here call me Muddy Waters". The rest is history.

Alan Lomax returned to Mississippi in the late 1950's partly to see how many of the older players he had recorded with his dad two decades earlier. He did find some still alive and playing. He also went there to see if there were any new developments. He found several fine new artists he had not met earlier, and released several volumes of recordings of a wide range of traditional music on the Prestige label under the title "Southern Journey". Staggering, really.

A couple of the "newer" artists were to come west and play the Ash Grove. Among them was a slide guitarist playing in a style not recorded previously, who called himself Mississippi Fred McDowell. He was of mixed African and Native American blood, and was quite striking. His repertoire differed greatly from the ones offered by other local artists, in that his songs had mostly never been heard outside the area. Most everyone else offered re-dos of John Lee Hooker, Jimmy Reed, B.B. King. One of the songs that struck me was a slow love lament that went "Lord, I Been Drinking Water Out a Hollow Log". I had no idea that I would meet him and play with him. I had no idea that I would teach this song to a great young vocalist who was in a play I was part of, Ms

Barbara Morrison. We were to work closely together for many years. We had connected through the Hollow Log Blues.

Take Your Time

When Fred McDowell, originally from Rossville, Tennessee, moved to nearby Como, he added "Mississippi" to his name. Locally recognized as the best in his area, he was unknown to the rest of the world until recorded by Alan Lomax. Farmer, laborer and weekend musician, he had an unique style of play, and a large repertoire of traditional and "original" blues, and moving religious songs.

Mississippi Fred McDowell
Courtesy: Bernie Pearl

Fred mostly played with a slide in open guitar tuning and using infrequent chord changes. Open tuning means that the six strings are tuned to a chord, rather than the standard EADGBE, associated with most other world guitar genres. Often the originality came by singing traditional verses, adding some new, and combining them spontaneously to a rhythmic slide guitar riff, familiar or original. That mix of is true of most traditional country blues, regardless of region.

But, Como is in Mississippi's northern hill country, and their dance tunes were played with a different beat than the classic Delta Blues, as exemplified by Charlie Patton, Tommy Johnson, Son House, and Robert Johnson. Hill country Blues artists who have gained fame beyond the region include John Lee Hooker, R.L. Burnside, and Mississippi Fred. Their music tended toward few chord changes and hypnotic, danceable rhythms.

Fred was an outgoing person and was easy to talk to, and he enjoyed playing in public. Very much reminded me of Mance Lipscomb, who also had been unknown to the outside world. Neither had recorded until being "discovered" by young white city folks. They were not on the radar and commanding attention as were Skip James, Son House, Mississippi John Hurt, Bukka White, and others. All of them had recorded in the pre-WWII era, and had been presumed "lost". Mance and Fred were the once-anonymous bearers of rich musical traditions who fulfilled a craving we didn't know we had.

I had no idea of how Fred did what he did. I was not interested, at that time, in learning slide, but I loved what I heard him doing and sat in with him at times. Just playing the blues. Like most of the country blues men who played the Ash Grove and like venues, he was encouraged to include religious songs on his sets. I don't recall any of these musicians rejecting the idea of including sacred songs along with the secular. We were all the richer for it and appreciative, even though a good proportion of Ash Grove attendees were Jewish, especially in the first years it was open. I must have played "You Got to Move" with him sometime. A tune familiar to many Christian congregations, it became his best-known song, covered by the Rolling Stones.

One of the things he used to say on stage when he played a fairly slow tempo at the start of a piece, to me as well as being a general comment, was "take your time". Indeed, wise words. Ironically, and it's something that I still haven't completely come to terms with. Neither he nor Mance Lipscomb felt obliged to keep one steady tempo throughout a tune. They both had impeccable senses of rhythm. They would both speed up tunes deliberately, it seemed to me. Never missing a note, never in a panic or a hurry, just a gradual acceleration. My only reasonable thought is that they were very used to playing for dancing, and in their world the dancers expected the music to pick up tempo and excitement. I'd like to consult them about that next time we meet.

In truth, I did not have a great deal of interest in digging into the details of his slide style during the period I knew him, though I nibbled around the edges. I took it more seriously in later years when I was offered a teaching position at McCabe's Guitars contingent on teaching a slide class. I dug in, and have stayed dug in for decades. I seldom perform a concert of any duration nowadays without including a Fred piece or two.

Fred came west one memorable time. He came not as often as Lightnin' or Mance who were quite a bit closer in Texas. But, he would be here often enough. Most of the time the musicians were offered space in homes. I was reticent to make the offer because most of the time I lived in places that were sub-par and, frankly, embarrassing. But, I once made the offer to Fred and he accepted, for one night. I apologized for the roaches who were endemic, and he said, "That's alright, we got them at home too." Made me feel better.

During the next day he stepped outside for a few minutes. One of my neighbors asked if that was Fred McDowell? I said yes, and he rushed to meet him. Word got around and there were several who gathered and asked him to play. He agreed and held forth in my most humble abode to everyone's delight. I backed him up, and we had a party. I did take my time.

"I do not play no rock'n'roll" (a tale of two Freddies)

That statement by Mississippi Fred McDowell was also used as the title of his most widely heard recording. It was followed by his disclaimer, *..unless you rock me in the bed, y'understand.* Issued on Capitol Records in 1969 and recorded in Jackson, Mississippi, it was produced by Malaco Records' Tommy Couch. It was to introduce Fred to a much broader audience than any of his previous recordings. Sadly, he did not live long enough to reap the rewards of his musical gift to us as was his due. He died in 1972, at the age of 68.

Around 1969 I had done a little recording work for the Bihari Brothers of Kent, Modern, and other labels (known as the record company by the tracks –the rails running down Slauson Ave.). I played on a Big Joe Turner session, and even recorded a few of my own pieces, which went nowhere. The Bihari Bros. (Sephardic Jews) had collaborated with the Chess Brothers (Ashkenazic Jews) in the early years of both of their legendary Blues labels and then, apparently, parted ways as their individual interests diverged.

I got a call one day from a young man who was working with the Biharis in their "studio across the tracks". In their building they recorded the music, produced their own vinyl discs, and created their own art work, as well as their own liner notes.*

The young man, named Freddie DeMann, asked me to come in and listen to the recording, an anthology of notable blues artists, John Lee Hooker, Jimmy Reed, Elmore James, Howlin' Wolf among them. I talked with him about the "Underground Blues" LP and agreed to do it. At the end of this conversation he asked me if I knew Fred McDowell. I said I did, I didn't ask how he knew about him. He was impressed enough to ask about recording him and if I could get in touch with him. I did have a number and called him. The ring was answered by a woman who said, "Stuckey's Gas Station". I asked if Fred McDowell was there. I was asked to hold on, and soon Fred picked up. I had never given a thought as to him having to work outside of music again. He had played around the country, and in Europe, and I wrongly imagined that touring provided enough for him and his family. Reality check.

Fred was friendly, as always, and I asked him if he was interested in coming to L.A. to record. His answer surprised me. He said I'd have to talk to Mr. so and so because he was getting ready to do a recording for Capitol Records. Now, that was good news for him, though I was somewhat disappointed. I had once recorded some back up guitar with him when he recorded a couple of tunes for a well-known English rocker, whose name I cannot remember. Maybe get a chance to do another? However, I was glad for him. Capitol was a major label and while he had recorded notable tunes for Alan Lomax and later for Chris Strachwitz on Arhoolie Records, this had greater potential. Indeed, it has lived up to the potential. His name is much better known and his musical uniqueness has achieved some renown.

A few years later, I had business in a building in Hollywood which housed many high-level music industry offices. I parked in the underground lot and was walking to the elevator when I noticed a very, very sleek and expensive looking car parked in a space which had a plaque posted above, "Reserved for Freddie DeMann". The sign also indicated that Mr. DeMann was Madonna's manager. A guy who had made a humble start in the blues end of the industry had gone all the way. Further research revealed that he later managed Michael Jackson. Mazal Tov my man.

A personal take on liner notes: I used not only history books to prepare my various radio shows over the years, but found most liner notes, printed in legible fonts on the back cover or in a booklet inside, very informative. They came in especially handy when you needed information while on the air, sometimes even when the mic was live. CDs, while more compact, were hard to read under pressure and, truth be told, the vinyl sounded better too.

Who Was MS Fred McDowell?

MS Fred McDowell

Early 1920s – 1959:   developed and locally played Hill Country Blues
1959 – 1972:   recorded 26 albums, 2 singles and participated in 16 compilations by multiple artists

I Do Not Play No Rock and Roll. In 1969, MS Fred McDowell released an album clearly stating that his music was different. At the time, Blues based rock and roll was hugely popular. McDowell distinguished his music from Blues based rock and roll.

As introduction to the recordings, Fred McDowell describes his style of music. *I'd make the guitar say what I say … If I say "Our*

Father", it say "Our Father". If I give out a hymn, it'll say it. If I play "Amazing Grace", it'll sing that too." And, my type of blue, I play it with a bottleneck ... I play it on my ring finger ... you get more clear sound out of it.[161]

These statements give real insight into the playing style of MS Fred McDowell. McDowell used a glass bottleneck on the ring finger to play the melody with a single string. Bending the string with the bottleneck enabled McDowell to obtain a very wide range of tones. In comparison, most guitarists move the finger across multiple strings which limits the tones to the tuning of the strings.

McDowell went even further. He added an intensity to the music by using his thumb and the slide to play a rhythm that sounds like a moving freight train.[162] This rhythm created a hypnotic, pounding beat to the music.[163]

Using his right hand, Fred simultaneously played a repetitive beat with his thumb. By simultaneously using the slide on his left hand to bend a string, Fred created a rattling sound that added a rhythmic charge to the beat. This combined repetitive beat and rhythmic charge gave a distinctive feel to the music played by Fred.

MS Fred McDowell was born on Jan 12, 1904, in Rossville, TN.[164] Jimmy McDowell and Ida Cureay, his parents, were both farmers. Orphaned early in life, McDowell was raised by an older, married sister from Mississippi who moved to his father's farm.[165] McDowell spent his early years working on the farm in Rossville.[166]

When I was a boy, the first blues record I ever heard was Blind Lemon Jefferson singing 'Black Snake Moan.' 'O-oh ain't got no mama, now.' Man, I tell you, I thought that was the prettiest little thing I'd ever heard.[167]

At the age of 14, in 1918, Fred McDowell began learning to play the guitar.[168] *I was just a young man when I started playing guitar. In my teens, I was. I used to go to dances. I used to sing to the music whilst others was playing. When they'd quit, I'd always grab the guitar, go to doing something with it.*[169]

"Big Fat Mama (With the Meat Shakin ' On Your Bones)" by Tommy Johnson was the first real song that Fred learned at age 14.

I learned it on one string, then two, note by note. Man, I worried that first string to death trying to learn that song.[170] Fred used that one string approach throughout his playing and recording future.

In 1926,[171] Fred moved to Memphis because *I just got tired of plowing.* In Memphis, Fred spent three years working in the Buck-Eye feed mill which processed cotton into oil.[172] He stacked sacks of yellow corn bigger than himself.[173] After this job, Fred worked at a number of casual jobs, such as picking cotton, building railroad freight cars and general labor.[174] Fred McDowell moved to MS in 1929, after this short, unsuccessful period in Memphis. He found work picking cotton in locations in northern MS.[175]

In the late 1920's the young McDowell spent a great deal of time with his uncle Gene Shields.[176] Shields was the first guitarist he ever saw playing in the bottleneck style. Shields played in a trio with a harmonica player named Cal Payne, who introduced McDowell to the blues classic "John Henry." Payne's son Raymond was a good guitar player.[177]

McDowell tried to learn to play from Raymond but Raymond prevented Fred from learning. *If you would walk into the room he'd put the guitar down so you couldn't see what he was doing. Then he'd make some sort of excuse like 'I'm tired now' or 'My fingers hurt'.*[178]

Fred learned from everyone he could, but ... *Even if you'd be showing me, I'd have to go off on my own and get it my way. They'd all be playing ball or something and I'd be practicing on Booster Green's guitar.*[179] McDowell's progress as a musician was seriously hindered by the fact that he didn't actually own his own guitar until he received one as a gift in 1941.

Around 1940, Fred McDowell finally settled in Como, MS. He worked as a full-time farmer for many years while continuing to play music on weekends at dances and picnics.[180] Here, Fred McDowell met and mentored R L Burnside, who later became a well known player of the Hill Country Blues. At one party, Fred invited Burnside to play in public before an audience, for the first time ever.[181] During this time, McDowall regularly performed at parties with Othar Turner, master of the fife. Fred and Othar were best friends.[182]

In 1959 folklorist Alan Lomax traveled around the southern United States recording rural music. Lomax was the first to capture Fred McDowell on tape.[183] Lomax captured 6 songs by McDowell and 2 songs in which McDowell played guitar for other vocalists. Three of the songs by McDowell were published on 3 compilation albums. Both of the vocalist recordings featuring Fred on guitar were published, on a separate collaboration album. All of these compilation albums were published in 1960 by Atlantic Records.[184]

These recordings introduced McDowell's sound to a huge audience. Suddenly, at age 55, Fred McDowell was lauded as a great "new" discovery in the Blues world.[185]

From 1963 until his death in 1972, Fred McDowell began extensive recording and playing festivals and concerts in the United States and abroad.[186] Yet, with all his success, Fred maintained his job as a gas pump attendant at the Stucky's located at the Como exit at the intersection of I-55 north and Mississippi 310. Letters, phone calls, contracts and plane tickets were all sent to MS Fred McDowell in care of the Stuckey's Restaurant.[187]

Encounters with Doc Watson and Ravi Shankar

"I'm the Onliest Man...."

When blues guys get together to shoot the breeze – i.e. brag to each other – someone (with tongue in cheek) will claim, "I'm the onliest man who…", whatever. While I would state this differently, I do have a couple of brags to share with the reader. Neither one tongue-in-cheek. The first one I have shared sometimes with audiences who might have been familiar with both artists I cite. I never found someone who doubted or could contradict my boast, which is that I am the only person on the face of the Earth who can state that he had private paid guitar lessons from both blues icon Sam 'Lightnin'' Hopkins, and superb country guitarist Arthel 'Doc' Watson.

Arthel "Doc" Watson

I have already spoken of the lesson with Mr. Hopkins, shared with guitarist David Cohen and an academic interviewer around 1960. Doc was a complete surprise when he hit the stage at the Ash Grove for the first time, around 1962, as one of two guitarists in a group from Appalachia backing old-time banjoist, recording artist, and medicine-show performer Clarence 'Tom' Ashley. This represented the dive into White traditional music also sparked by the "Folk" revival, as was the Blues revival.

Principals in this newfound old music were an East Coast trio called The New Lost City Ramblers. John Cohen, Tom Paley, and Mike Seeger, Pete's half-brother. They researched the field of "Old-Timey" music and breathed life into it. Of course, there were others, notably The Greenbriar Boys, with Ralph Rinzler, Eric Weissberg, and John Herald. They went a'lookin' and kept a'findin'. They came west with Mr. Ashley & Co.

**Clarence "Tom" Ashley and Group at the Ash Grove
Courtesy: Ash Grove Archive
CA State Univ, Dominguez Hills**

Tom Ashley's band: Lead guitarist Doc, fiddler Fred Price, and second guitarist Clint Howard had been recorded by Folkways Records (Moses Asch, owner) and released their first LP album in 1962. The recorded music I heard did not raise great expectations, but were a nice addition to the burgeoning traditional music scene. A giant underestimation. I expected to be pleasantly pleased, not shaken to my very foundations, just as I had been by Jesse Fuller a couple of years earlier.

That we had no clue as to what "Tom" Ashley and company were bringing to us, is evidenced by the fact they were co-billed with Jean Ritchie, the fine and well-known folk singer of Appalachian ballads, and a noted dulcimer player. All well and good, except that they were second-billed and preceded Ms Richie's solo show that opening night. She didn't stand a chance. The audience had been lifted high in spirits, and to have to simmer down far enough to pay much attention to a low-key, detailed and lovely presentation of mountain ballads was asking too much.

This was a several-day run, and she was informed that she would be opening the show on the remaining dates. She was in tears, but understood the reasoning, it really was the right thing. She went forward, often joining the band for some precious old religious tunes. Notably, they performed a version of the old church standard, "Amazing Grace", which had never before had been done that way. Their rendition became the oft-performed version universally sung – even by the President of the United States.

Ed said, "They're here. Go in and meet them". I went into the small dressing room on the ground floor and greeted the four men. I don't know if they drove or took the bus, but they were fresh off the road from Appalachia. They were all friendly, and as we chatted I noticed that each of the four had something noticeable about their eyes. The eldest, Clarence Ashley had strabismus, one somewhat cocked eye. Guitarist Clint Howard's eyes were kind of popped out, what we would describe as thyroid eyes. Fiddler Fred Price's eyes were the kind of red you get when you've lost a lot of sleep. But, the biggest surprise of all was when I realized that the big guy depicted on the cover of their first recording (Old Time Music at Clarence Ashley's – Folkways Records), Arthel "Doc" Watson, was blind.

Ashley sang humorously and with authenticity and was backed with verve and toe-tapping rhythm. The band really rocked. Each of the others also had featured spots in the set. Clint sang with real country twang, loud and piercing. Fred fiddled and revealed his great debt to the Blues, which he acknowledged. Then Doc took the mic and stunned. Safe to say that flat-pick guitar was never the same again. He revealed a mastery of the music, a fine voice, and an absolutely winning personality. He also played finger-picking style, laced with authentic blues influences. It was immediately clear that we were looking at a star. Blind from birth, Doc had been playing all his life, whatever style or opportunity came his way. This was not Bluegrass style, this music both pre-dated and post-dated Bluegrass. Older and newer at once. Among the pieces that Doc played that night was one called "Little Sadie". He used a nifty blues riff as its theme, and played a lot of blue notes on his solos.

I wanted to learn about that from him, and I approached him offering the same fee as I had paid Brownie and Lightnin', $20. At first he demurred, saying that he didn't give lessons. John Herald, bless his heart, was also on the bill, and encouraged Doc to accept, saying, "It's good money, Doc, you ought to do it." Doc relented, and I met him where they were staying, at my brother's rented small house on the beach in Malibu. I learned what I could but, most important, I established a personal relationship with Doc, ongoing.

That's the background to my first boast. The second is even more involved and farther-fetched, but it's true.

Meeting Ravi Shankar

I had met and played with Fred McDowell, and had some good conversations with him. Aside from running the Ash Grove, my brother Ed would also book and promote concerts at other locations. He had worked with record producer Richard Bock (Pacific Jazz) previously, and had booked noted Indian sitar master Ravi Shankar through him.

Ravi was not yet the "discovery" by John Lennon and the Beatles, which was to bring him richly deserved world-wide fame and attention. But, in the early '60's, he was fairly obscure except among Indian audiences. Ed booked him for a concert at the Santa Monica Civic Auditorium. To promote the show, a press conference was held at Dick's studio. David Cohen, my partner in a school we were running at the club, and I were invited to attend. Ravi and tabla master drummer Ustad Alla Rakha performed.

Ustad Alla Rakha (drums) and Ravi Shankar (sitar)

Shankar then took questions as people reverently filed by him, seated on his performing platform.

I approached and asked if I could look at his picking hand, as he seemed to be wearing a pick. He showed it to me. The right forefinger was deeply calloused and indented from the pick he wore, which reminded me of a clothespin spring, Differed from the metal finger pick that Fred wore. I thanked him and shook his hand. He was very gracious. I didn't get to the concert, I may have been working or, as I was still enrolled at UCLA, I might have actually had some studying to do.

It occurred to me later that I had shaken hands with both men, stylistic paragons of very different styles, or so I thought. Now, that doesn't cause the earth to tremble, but what I realized in more recent times was that their musical styles also were not worlds apart as I once thought.

The event was focused on Ravi Shankar, ignoring the fact that Alla Rakha was an equally prominent musician in India. Alla commented on that lack of attention to my brother, who related that he commented, "I know that Ravi is the star, but I'm not his son either." Now, that's a pro with a sense of humor.

Fred and Ravi

Fred McDowell, as I have said, played both secular and sacred music. When he played his religious melodies, he modified his picking to where he played almost all his melodies on the single high E string with his forefinger, while his thumb retained the rhythmic E bass string in response, seldom striking the strings at the same time. This is also characteristic of John Lee Hooker's playing – think: *Boogie Chillun*. He also glided his slide through the melody with a steady motion, inferring rather than stopping at each scale note. That's part of the magic and an indication of the sophistication of his music, simple as it sounds. OK. So what?

In recent times I took a moment to look at a Ravi Shankar video and was dumbstruck. I had never observed that the raga lead phrases Ravi played on the sitar were played on one string, like Fred McDowell's gospel. Ragas are also a form of prayer. I didn't realize that the multiple strings on a sitar were not involved in the melody line, but were sympathetic tones only. This conclusion rocked my world. While Ravi Shankar's playing was in many ways more varied and complex than Fred's style, both nonetheless employed basically the same technique. I shared this with my friend Phil Boroff. Phil astutely pointed out that Shankar also just used thumb and forefinger, like Fred.

Now, this new found knowledge would have been enough to leave me in awe and wonderment. But, I had a another log to put on the fire.

Encounters With Rev Gary Davis

If I Had My Way (I'd play just like Gary Davis)

In 1962 I went back East, as we used to say, and stayed with my "girlfriend" from Israel, Janet, (we remain friends and have stayed in touch) and her family in Queens. Her half sister Flora was a prominent theatrical agent (Stephen Sondheim was a client), she got us tickets to a hit off-Broadway show, "The Princess and the Pea". The star was a sensational newcomer from Hollywood, California named Carol Burnett. Safe to say she tore the house down.

Young Carol Burnett

We also went to the movies at Radio City to see "North by Northwest", memorable in itself. The showing opened with the sensational and dazzling Rockettes. Gulp, "country boy in the Apple" kind of reaction to it all.

Then she took me to a record store just to look around. I was struck by an album called "American Street Songs".

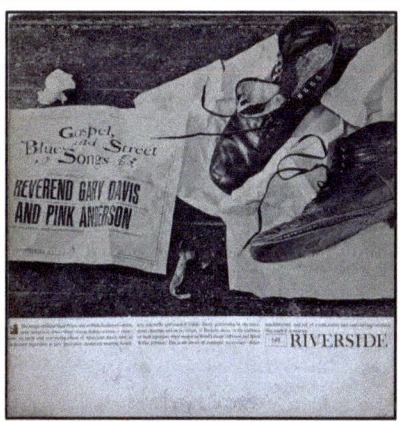

American Street Songs

This album featured two guitarists I had not heard of, Pink Anderson and Rev Gary Davis. I had already been exposed to Jesse Fuller, Brownie McGhee, and Lightnin' Hopkins, but I hadn't heard of these two. It mentioned Blues and Gospel tunes, but I was mainly snared by the allure of them both being guitarists.

One side was mainly ragtime and lively picking from Mr. Anderson.

Pink Anderson

But, when I flipped it over (you could listen to a record before purchase in those days), I was spell-bound. Rev. Davis was doing the impossible on the instrument and singing in a passionate way which did remind me of those I had seen at the club, but with an occasional growling fervor. I snapped it up.

Rev Gary Davis

Turns out it had been recorded in Charlottesville in 1950 by a man named Paul Clayton. Another unrecognized hero and guide on my journey to whom I must be deeply grateful. I had no idea that the Rev. Davis had by then moved to New York and was an established figure on the NY folk scene, as well as preaching on the street and having his own little congregation. I also had no idea that I would soon meet him, see him perform, and become friends.

When I returned from the trip, I asked Brownie and Sonny about him, which drew a laugh.

"Of course!" Rev Gary Davis had played for tips on one of the street corners across from Blind Boy Fuller and Sonny Terry.

It may be that in those days, the late 1930's, Davis was still playing blues and ragtime pieces. At a certain point, he decided to become an ordained minister, leaving the Blues and secular music behind. This change in orientation did not entail abandoning his approach to the guitar, he just devoted his skills to a higher purpose. Notably, after we started spending time together, Gary made the statement that he "wasn't playing the guitar, he was playing the piano". His picking style (thumb and index finger only) and his harmonies were complex and rhythmically akin to ragtime, and was regarded by his peers as the best guitarist among them. I never herd a serious rebuttal.

The nearly-evangelical guitar teacher in me compels me to cite the numerous people I've seen announcing that they're going to play a Gary Davis piece and start picking with three fingers. It never sounds right. It moves from a misdemeanor to a felony when the perp is also a guitar teacher. To the best of my knowledge, and humbly so, not having studied his playing deeply, I'd say that the greatest ragtime guitarist, Blind Blake, also used just two fingers. So sue me.

A disturbing lesson in racism

I had a car and, as a UCLA undergrad, at times could provide rides to the artists. Gary was staying with my brother, and when Ed went into the club to work, he was at the club sitting and playing. I picked him up there one time because he had mentioned that he needed to get to a barber to get a shave. We drove east on Melrose and near LACC I spotted a barber pole and pulled over. We got out and entered. The barber seemed friendly enough when he asked if he could help me. I told him that Rev. Davis was a visiting musician and needed a shave. He responded, "We don't do that here." That seemed impossible. I questioned him naively about this. It was an honest naivete', I didn't pick up on the implications. "Nope, we don't do shaves." I was sort of embarrassed, and we left. I apologized to Gary, it had begun to dawn on me that this was a racial insult. I was hurt for Rev. Davis, but was not prepared go back in there and do battle. Rev. Davis had no comment that I recall. It was another instance of awakening to the existence of the many forms of bigotry, even in my home town.

I play with Gary, sort of

The evening after one day of the 1964 UCLA Folk Festival, some of us went back to the Ash Grove, which was at a fair distance from the campus. We straggled in, and a few of us took to the stage and started playing our acoustics. Listeners straggled in as well. I believe that Ash Grove regular Taj Mahal, who was a fine artist but not yet a star, was among us up there. Then someone leads Rev. Davis in, he hears the music and guitar in hand heads for the stage. I made up a couple of song lines welcoming him, and he partied with us for a while. He did love a good time.

I never dreamt of playing with him on stage, though he did take the time, unasked, to show me some things on the guitar. Not that I didn't want to learn, but his complexity was intimidating. He didn't care about that, he wanted to pass on his art. Once he made me learn a ragtime piece he called, "Getting Away From the Law" (he hadn't absolutely abandoned secular themes). I struggled with it, but he seemed pleased that I tried. In more recent years I've calmed down, studied, and have integrated some of his ideas in my arrangements. Most all of the older blues generation were concerned with passing their knowledge along. Just carry on when we are gone.

Rev. Blows the harp

One afternoon I sat with Gary in my small, shared house in Echo Park, with a nice view of the little green gully on which it sat. We were just talking, when he pulled a harmonica out of his pocket and began playing. I had begun taping some of my own guitar and writing, and had the machine already set up. I turned it on and recorded the several tunes he played. I intend to get the decades-old recording rehabilitated (there's a technical procedure necessary to keep the tape from falling apart) and listenable. He had recorded a piece or two on harp that was released, but this may fill out the picture of another side of the genius of Rev. Gary Davis.

If I Had My Way

The song made popular by Peter, Paul, and Mary "If I Had My Way" (I'd tear this old building down) originated with Rev. Gary Davis. It was the story of Samson and Delilah retold. It resonated hugely with the nation's anti-Vietnam War, anti-Government oppression spirit. They recorded a rousing version and, I'm sure, did it with all respect for the Reverend Davis. You owe it to yourselves to listen to him singing it. It'll send chills down your spine, and send you out to battle the bad guys. We still have them, you know.

Who Was Rev Gary Davis?

Rev Gary Davis

Reverend (Blind) Gary Davis was a powerful gospel and folk Blues singer and a masterful acoustic guitarist. Davis was *truly, one of the supreme talents to emerge from the Piedmont tradition.*[188]

Unlike some of his contemporaries, Davis could play in any key. He was one of the few Blues guitar artists to explore minor keys, *creating works of deep pathos such as 'Death Don't Have No Mercy', 'Children of Zion', and 'I Heard the Angels Singing'.*[189]

Davis produced a polyphonic style with the use of only his thumb and index finger.

> *You've got three hands to play a guitar and only two for a piano. Well, your forefinger and your thumb — that's the striking hand, and your left hand is the leading hand. Your left hand tells the right hand what strings to touch, what changes to make. One hand can't do without the other.*[190]

In particular Davis was known for his chord positions, playing five chords where other guitarists managed only one.[191]

His repertoire was comprised of Medicine Show tunes, white ballads, military marches, country instrumentals, the emergent ragtime piano, a virtuosic Piedmont Blues guitar style, old church hymns, revival meeting and Gospel songs, popular tunes, and original compositions based on all the above. Davis also played an archaic harmonica style rarely heard elsewhere.[192]

Primarily a street musician, Davis made relatively few recordings in his early career. However, his virtuosic finger picking was an important influence on other regional musicians. His most notable influence was on Blind Boy Fuller, the prime exponent of the Piedmont guitar style in the 1930s. In the 1950s and 60s Davis taught and played concerts in New York City. He became a beloved mentor to urban folk and rock legends Ramblin' Jack Elliot, Dave Van Ronk, and Bob Dylan, to name a few.[193]

Gary Davis was born on April 30, 1896.[194] His parents were John Davis and Evelina Martin.[195] Davis was born on a farm in Laurens County SC.[196] This farm was *way down in the sticks, so far you couldn't hear a train whistle blow unless it was on a cloudy day.*[197]

Evelina Martin Davis, his mother, bore eight children. Gary and one other child survived to adulthood.[198]. Gary Davis became blind as an infant.

> *My grandmother said I taken blind when I was three weeks old. The doctor had something put in my eyes that was too strong and that was what caused me to go blind.*[199]

Evelina Martin Davis treated her son extremely poorly, even to the point of being highly emotionally abusive. She outright rejected Gary emotionally, although she remained in his life. This emotional abandonment had a profound effect on Davis.

> *I felt horrible about it 'cause I felt like I was throwed away. In fact, my mother never had cared as much about me as she did my younger brother. He was her heart. Because of the way she talk in' to me, she'd wish that I were dead. She tell me that a heap of times.*[200]

As a result, John Davis placed Gary Davis in the care of his paternal grandmother.

> *My father gave me to my grandmother when I was a child because he knowed that there was no confidem:e to be put into my mother. She was always from one place to another, going from different towns and dances. Things like that. So my father gave me to my grand-mother.*[201]

A traveling musician came through the area toting a guitar around 1903 when Gary Davis was just 7 years old.

> *The first time I ever heard a guitar played, I thought it was a brass band coming through. I was a small kid and I asked my mother what was it, and she said that was a guitar. I said, 'Ain't you going to get me one of those when I get large enough?'*[202]

The first Bluesman Davis heard was Porter Irving, a South Carolinian, and his song *Delia*.[203]

Once infected by this early exposure to the guitar, Gary Davis just had to have one. So, Davis quickly built himself a guitar from a pie pan after hearing the itinerant Bluesman. *I drove me a hole in each end of the pie-pan, run me up a stick through there, that's the way I made it.*[204]

Davis taught himself to play guitar, banjo, and harmonica. He began playing local dances for the white folks while still a child.[205]

Young Gary Davis took to the guitar and assumed a unique multi-voice guitar style produced solely with his thumb and index finger. Using this style, Davis played gospel, ragtime, and Blues tunes along with traditional and original tunes in four-part harmony. At ten years old,[206] Davis publicly sang for the first time at the Center Raven Baptist Church in Gray Court, SC.[207]

John Davis, his father, was killed in Birmingham, AL, in 1906, when Gary Davis was 10 years old. Rumor held that his father was shot by the Birmingham sheriff.[208] Evelina Davis, his mother, re-married and gave birth to a boy.[209]

In 1910 or 1911 Davis joined a string band in Greenville, SC. A string band was generally the only source of income for blind southern Blacks. This band included Willie Walker, the blind guitarist who was to become a legend during the folk-music revival. Walker taught Davis the famous Piedmont guitar style.

Gary Davis wrote a gospel called *There Was a Time When I Went Blind* in 1911. This song was one of his first songs. Davis was only 15 years old.[210]

In 1914, at age 18, Gary Davis applied to and was speedily granted a scholarship to attend the South Carolina Institution for the Education for the Deaf and Blind at Cedar Springs, Spartanburg. At this school, Davis learned to read Braille. After six months, Davis left the school behind. Apparently, he didn't like the food.[211]

Soldier's Drill, an instrumental based on Sousa marches, was written by Davis in 1918. This instrumental became part of his standard repertoire.[212]

Davis married Mary Hendrix, a woman five years his senior, in 1919.[213]

In the 1920s, Davis played music on the streets to earn a living. He again joined a local string band in Greenville in the early 1920s,. By this time, Greenville, SC, had become a center of the Piedmont Blues style.

During the mid 1920s, Davis and his wife Mary, traveled around SC, NC, and TN, performing in the streets and teaching guitar to earn a living.[214] Davis played on the streets of each town until the police ran him off. Many cities had vagrancy laws. Blues musicians were lumped in with all of the other vagrants.

By 1925 Davis was frequently visiting Durham, NC. He visited Durham to be near his mother, despite her abusive treatment.[215] Davis left his wife Mary when he found that she already had a husband, and numerous lovers besides. She *wasn't my wife but everybody else's.*[216]

After the separation from Mary, Gary Davis wandered around NC acting recklessly. He began drinking heavily for the first time in his life at age 29. *I never knowed what a drop of whiskey was until I got tangled up with Mary.* Davis moved from one town to another, staying only long enough to fill his tin cup, then moving on. He played anywhere a buck could be made: barrelhouses, dance halls, country jukes, any place where alcohol flowed. By the end of the night tempers often flared. *I been in places where men got killed. Didn't shake me a bit more than nothin'*.[217]

Now completely sightless, Davis was playing spirituals, ragtime, Blues, and dance music. Interspersing his Blues and ragtime with gospel music held off the police who harassed the street musicians. By the late 1920s Gary Davis was considered one of the best ragtime guitarists on the east coast.[218]

In 1931, Davis returned permanently to Durham, NC, a major center of Black culture at the time. He moved into an area called Hayti, again to be near the house of his mother. After moving permanently to Durham, Davis began collecting welfare.[219]

Crime was a big problem in Hayti. A blind street singer who ventured out at all hours and preferred not to be led around faced great danger. Davis had already begun carrying a .38 special revolver and a knife for protection. *I carried a pistol all [the] time I was in North Carolina. I didn't ever shoot nobody.*[220]

According to legend he once repeatedly stabbed an acquaintance with a large pocket knife. As a joke, this man had snatched away a dollar bill that a listener had given Davis. Davis retaliated by stabbing the jokester.[221]

In Durham, Gary Davis taught Blind Boy Fuller and collaborated with a number of other artists in the Piedmont blues scene, including Bull City Red.[222]

> *When I first run across him [Blind Boy Fuller] he didn't know how to play but one piece and that was with a knife. He wanted to take some of my training. I'd sit down and he'd come up to my house everyday and sit down and play. I taught him how to play.*[223]

J. B. Long, a store manager with a reputation for supporting local artists, introduced Davis, Fuller, and Red to the American Record Company in 1935. ARC conducted several recording sessions with the trio. These recording sessions marked the beginning of the musical career of Rev Gary Davis.

Davis was paid only $40 for the recordings. He decided that Long had cheated him. Davis also had a major disagreement with Long over the music. Davis wanted to record only gospel music. Long insisted that the public wanted Blues. As a result of the cheating and the disagreement, Rev Gary Davis would not enter a recording studio for another 19 years.[224]

From this time, Davis began to prefer inspirational gospel music. He didn't entirely abandon secular music, until his ordination as a minister in 1937.[225] In 1937 Davis was ordained in the Free Will Baptist Connection Church in Washington, NC.[226] He became a singing preacher, playing lumber camps and traveling the revival circuit.[227]

In the latter part of 1942, Gary Davis met Annie Belle Hicks in Durham. Hicks was as deeply spiritual as Davis.[228] On Nov 14, 1943, Gary and Annie were married by justice of peace William O'Kelly in Durham. Annie looked after Davis devotedly until his death.[229]

In 1943, the Blues became less popular in Durham. So, Davis and Annie moved to Mamaroneck, NY, in Jan, 1944.[230] Mamaroneck is a small town about 20 miles NE of NYC. Here, Annie found work as a housekeeper. Later that same year, the pair moved to 169th Street in Harlem. Gary Davis and Annie lived at this address for the next 16 years.[231]

Living conditions in Harlem for Davis and wife Annie were dismal. This area was extremely run down. Davis made money by walking the streets of Harlem, playing gospel music and collecting tips. Annie had various low-paying menial jobs. Their apartment at 169th St was a shoebox with only two rooms. A tiny kitchen allowed Annie to cook meals. A main room, about ten feet by ten feet, served as both living room and main bedroom. The building itself was just plain run-down. Frankly, the couple lived in complete squalor.[232]

During these years, Davis became an ordained minister of the Missionary Baptist Connection Church in the Bronx. This church was about 7 miles away from his home in Harlem. However, he remained primarily an itinerant circuit minister who preached and sang at various churches around the city. These churches were mostly tiny storefront Baptist churches with poor Black congregations of southern migrants like the Davises.[233]

In February, 1948, Gary Davis traveled back to Durham by train. Davis wanted to attend a revival meeting and to see an uncle who was seriously ill. On this trip, Davis broke his left wrist after slipping on the snow.

> *I was carrying on at a revival and I slipped down. I was going along one night and there was snow on the ground. When I stepped up on a bank of snow and my foot slipped and to keep from falling I was shuffling around. I struck my hand on an iron-water dog. I didn't know it was broken until I went to the doctor the next morning. He told me it was broke. I thought I wasn't ever going to be able to play no more, but I did.*[234]

His left wrist was set out of position (left of axis). Speculations exist that this angled wrist accounted for his ability to play some unusual chord patterns. These patterns were not possible for a normal wrist. Davis later denied having altered his playing in any way as a result of his incorrect wrist repair.[235]

During the late 1940s, Davis spent much of his time preaching at churches and performing on the street in Harlem. At one time, Harlem had been a multi-ethnic enclave. However, by this time, central Harlem had become almost entirely Black. Hundreds of thousands of Jews, Irish, and Italians had departed from Harlem during the previous decade.

Harlem was a dangerous and unforgiving place in the late 1940s. Housing was overcrowded. Drugs like heroin ravaged neighborhoods. Homicides were routine. The vast majority of buildings had few working windows, were without heat or hot water, and housed huge mice or rat infestations. After dark, streets were filled with illegal activity.[236]

> *Every time somebody walk up close to you, you think they're gonna kill you.*[237]

Davis would stay away from home more than a week at a time during his early years in New York. He would not sleep much out on the street, for fear of being robbed. Cat naps were the order of the day. These naps were taken wherever he could, in restaurants or the basements of Harlem tenements, if necessary.

Bathing was not on the top of the priority list. Sometimes, fellow ministers found Davis on the street looking disheveled and dirty. These ministers brought Davis home to Harlem to get cleaned up. Annie, his wife, was distressed by his condition. *I used to go in Harlem sometimes and he was so dirty I wouldn't know him. I'd almost scream. Because I wasn't around to make him keep himself clean.*[238]

In January 1950, Rev. Gary Davis appeared at the Lead Belly Memorial at Town Hall in NYC. His performance completely stunned the audience. This performance represented his debut as a New York performer on the big stage. A rousing notice of the performance appeared in the *New York Times*.[239] On July 1-2, 1950, Gary Davis performed at the *Song Festival of American Ballads* in the Berkshires of MA. Davis performed along with folk music superstars Pete Seeger and Woody Guthrie. Gary Davis was now officially a part of the royalty of folk music.[240]

Obviously, Gary Davis was not a folk musician. Davis was a gospel and Blues musician. However, performing rural music with an acoustic guitar attracted the folk musicians. That approach aligned with their own approach. Thus, the folk musicians adopted Gary Davis into the fold of folk musicians.

The folk revival of the 1960s invigorated the career of Gary Davis. He was considered a superstar in the folk world by this time. Davis performed at the Newport Folk Festival in 1965. Eleven songs from those performances were released on the 1967 album entitled *At Newport*.[241]

Davis toured Europe and played at numerous folk festivals in the US. Major folk festivals included the Cambridge Folk Festival of 1968 and the Newport Folk Festival of 1968. Davis experienced the peak of his career as a result of his performances at Newport and the recording of his song *Samson and Delilah* by Peter, Paul, and Mary.[242]

Samson and Delilah was retitled as *If I Had My Way*. Peter, Paul, and Mary used *If I Had My Way* on a number of their most successful albums. These albums made the trio extremely wealthy. Prior to its usage, the song had been copyrighted as *words and music by Rev Gary*

Davis. So, Davis received regular and extremely large royalty checks for the usage of this song by the trio.[243] These royalties allowed Davis to live comfortably for the rest of his life without having to perform musically.[244]

In 1968 Davis bought a house in Jamaica, Queens, financed by royalties. Davis referred to the house as *the house that Peter, Paul and Mary built*.[245] While he did not have to work, Davis continued to perform locally in the New York and New Jersey area.[246]

John Townley, a former student and driver for Gary Davis, had established Apostolic Recording Studio. In March 1969, Townley persuaded Davis to participate in his first recording studio session in five years. *O, Glory – The Apostolic Studio Sessions* was the final studio album recorded by Rev Gary Davis.[247]

Other musicians and groups recorded songs credited to Rev Gary Davis. Bob Dylan covered *Baby, Let Me Follow You Down* on *Bob Dylan* his self-titled debut album for Columbia Records in 1962. Eric Von Schmidt, who wrote the song, credited Davis with three-quarters of the song. In 1971, The Rolling Stones released the album *Sticky Fingers. You Gotta Move* is performed on that album. Both Rev Gary Davis and MS Fred McDowell are credited for this song. Davis regularly received royalty checks from these recordings and from music recorded by other musicians.

Davis died of a massive heart attack on May 5, 1972 in Hammonton, New Jersey.

> *Early on the morning of May 5, Annie decided to travel down to the Davises' second house in Newtonville, New Jersey, where contractors were trying to fix a broken well, and Gary agreed to accompany her. Along for the trip was Mose, a tall, skinny young man about twenty-one years old who lived a few doors down from the Davises, sometimes worked as a bill collector, and drove occasionally for the Reverend. He took the wheel of the Davises' white Ford Galaxie, with Gary in the passenger seat and Brezer and Annie in the back. It was a bracing morning, in the mid-fifties, as they set out for the Verrazano Bridge.*
>
> *Two hours outside New York, they had just gotten off the New Jersey Turnpike at exit 7 in Bordentown when Davis suddenly made several*

jolts. Annie reached over the seat to comfort him, and Davis said, "Sweetheart, I'm leavin' you this morning!" Then he collapsed. "We did everything we could to find a hospital;' Brezer says. About a half hour went by before they reached William B. Kessler Memorial Hospital in Hammonton, New Jersey.

Davis had had a massive heart attack. Doctors took him inside and tried to revive him, shocking his heart with a defibrillator, to no avail. Decades of living hand to mouth, standing on street corners singing for twelve hours a day, had finally taken their toll. "We couldn't save him," the doctor told Annie. Davis was pronounced dead at 11:47 a.m. Annie took the news hard and had to be sedated.

Later, she provided her husband's details for the death certificate, giving his occupation as "Minister" and his business as "Church." **She made no mention of the music that had rescued them from threadbare poverty.**[248]

O, Glory – The Apostolic Studio Sessions, that final studio recording by Rev Gary Davis, was released posthumously in 1973.[249]

Encounters With Some Other Notables

Bukka White – Sky Singer

Booker T. Washington White was born on his grandfather's farm near Houston, Mississippi near Tupelo. Fellow admirer and follower of blues icon Charlie Patton, Chester Arthur Burnett, known as the Howlin' Wolf, came from nearby West Point. Both growled their Blues when they wanted to, just like their idol. His grand dad played fiddle, his father guitar, and he played the slide, just like Charlie.

Bukka White

He recorded under the name "Bukka White" just before the outbreak of WWII and America's rationing of products that made records possible. He was among the final great interpreters of the Mississippi country blues to record. He was among the first to be rediscovered when interest in the Blues took hold of young white aficionados in the days leading up to the U.S. war in Viet Nam. He was living and working in Memphis and was still young enough to remember his material and was in fine enough vocal and guitar-playing shape to get out and play for a new audience. He remained creative and never stopped "pulling messages from the sky". "They just come to me" he said of his new material, which he called "Sky Songs". He said he wanted to record everything that came to him lest it vanish.

A large, outgoing and good-humored man, when young he had travelled and performed and was recorded by Victor Records which paid him fairly well. He even came to the attention of noted guitarist Big Bill Broonzy, who offered to bring him up to Chicago to record for Lester Melrose (Bluebird label).

Along his travels he had a problem with a man, who he "had to burn a little", and got sent to Parchman Farm. He said he didn't have too hard a time there (I'm sure he could take care of himself). But, when his time was up, he still was angry about it. He recorded for a Mr. Lomax – presumably Alan – and spent a little time on the West coast. He didn't care for it and returned to Mississippi, married, and settled into working a job. His cousin Riley (Riley B King – BB) came to Memphis and stayed with him. Bukka said he bought him his first electric guitar. It is a fact that B.B.'s signature hand vibrato was his attempt to sound like Bukka's slide. He said so himself.

A few years later John Fahey and Ed Denson were to look and find him and enable a West Coast tour, which is where my story begins.

While I did not attempt to learn his style – at the time I was not very interested in slide – I really liked his friendly, outgoing personality, and spent as much time with him as I could. I was still enrolled at UCLA. One day I dropped by the Ash Grove to visit with him and found him sitting on a crate next-door, sipping a beer, talking to the mechanics whose repair shop was adjacent to the club. The owners of Raleigh & Granberry were Black men from Kentucky and Mississippi. Very kind and capable, they were the go-to guys for repairs.

It turns out that "Barry", Mr. Granberry, and Bukka were family. They were also cousins of Riley B. King, the famous Blues Boy from Indianola! In fact, on one occasion I recall seeing B.B. King's tour bus parked there for a servicing. I knew who he was, but hadn't yet met him or heard him live, but regularly listened to and tried to learn from his LP's. I asked if I could go aboard and look. I was allowed to. Once on the bus I saw B.B.'s guitar case, clearly marked "Lucille". I asked if I could look at it. I was given permission, and opened the case, and there she was! I also noticed when I opened the little internal box where you could store your picks, spare strings and such, he was using Black Diamond strings, the same as I was using on my acoustic box. Shock. In retrospect, those were the opening days of a guitar-mania that is yet to subside, and the sophistication of the guitar accessories that abound nowadays was still in the future.

But, back to Bukka. He had come back to L.A. a couple times in succeeding years, and I spent more time talking with him and driving him places he wanted to go. He was in town in 1965, staying at my brother's wife's home in the Hollywood Hills when Watts exploded and burned. We were looking out the windows of his room, watching the flames not that far south of where we were, speechless. All he could do was shake his head, and say "Lord have mercy". No other words sufficed for this calamity.

In more recent times I had been invited to play the King Biscuit Festival in West Helena and the Aberdeen Bukka White Festival (his home town on the Tombigbee River). I had time in between them to stop and play a show at the B.B. King Museum in Indianola and do a Blues in Schools concert. While there I inquired if the name Granberry rang a bell locally. No recognition. The Museum personnel inquired of several local folks who came by. Nothing. I went on to Aberdeen and asked the same question, got the same answer. By then Raleigh & Granberry had long been closed, and I couldn't find Barry.

I know that he was connected, because when we were getting ready to do the first Long Beach Blues Festival in 1980 (then called the KLON Blues & Gospel Festival, that one time only). I wanted to inform B.B., with pride, that good things would be coming his way from Long Beach. He was on the road, but Barry had his number and shared it with me. I called, B.B. answered, and I got my message out. He responded, "Look here man, you're gonna make me late, we're just leaving". Didn't make my heart swell, but I was able to fulfill that promise in 1984.

Who Was Bukka White?[250]

Booker T Washington "Bukka" White

Booker T. Washington White was one of the most expressive vocalists and powerful slide guitarists in the Blues. White was also a remarkable lyricist as well. Between 1930 and 1940, he recorded such classics as *"Shake 'Em On Down"* and *"Fixin' to Die Blues"*. These songs were released under the names Washington White or Bukka White. Bukka White was an important influence on his cousin B. B. King. Beginning in 1963, White enjoyed a second career as a performer and recording artist.

Bukka White was born about five miles south of Houston, MS, on the farm of Willie Harrington on Nov 12, 1904. John White, his father, was a multi-instrumentalist who performed at local gatherings.

Bukka was named after Booker T Washington, the famous Black scientist. With its southern accent, the family pronounced the name Booker as *Booka*. This accented version of the name stuck. Booker was called *Booka* by everyone.

John gave Bukka his first guitar. Other local musicians taught White his signature bottleneck slide technique. Stays in Tallahatchie County. MS, (in the Delta) and in St. Louis further developed his skills on guitar and piano. At sixteen White married for the first of several times. However, White was soon back to rambling across the South and Midwest.

Recording agent Ralph Lembo of Itta Bena, MS, arranged for White to record his first Blues and gospel songs. These recordings were performed in Memphis in 1930. In 1937, White recorded a *Shake 'Em On Down"* in Chicago. This song became a minor hit.

But that same year, 1937, White was sentenced to Parchman Penitentiary in MS for a shooting incident. In 1939, John Lomax of the Library of Congress recorded White at Parchman. After his release, White recorded twelve of his best-known songs at a Chicago session in 1940.

During World War II, Bukka White settled in Memphis. White worked at a defense plant. In Memphis he also performed with Blues legend Frank Stokes, among others. His cousin B.B. King came to live with Bukka White in Memphis. Bukka White gave BB King his first guitar. Using this guitar, BB King established himself on the local music scene.

In the 1960s Bukka White began to tour and record again. White was still a skilled and energetic performer. He became a popular figure on the folk music circuit, performing as far as Mexico and Europe.

On May 27, 1976, White returned to Houston, MS, as the featured artist at the bicentennial celebration of the city.

Bukka White died in Memphis on February 26, 1977.

Robert Pete Williams: Inmate #4-6506

When I met him, Robert Pete Williams had been released not only from Louisiana State Penitentiary in Angola but also from the slavery-like servitude he had to provide a local farmer to get out of prison on parole. As I recall, he explained, "It was a case of mistaken identity. I went to the grocery and a guy came up and accused me of (something), and I told him he got the wrong man. He kept on and I denied it again. The guy pulled a knife and came at me, and I pulled my gun and shot him." He was sent to Angola.

In 1959 Dr. Harry Oster and Richard B. Allen, academics at Louisiana Universities, went to Angola to find blues artists who may well have carried on older musical traditions. They found three unique artists of interest and recorded them, "Guitar" Welch, "Hogman" Maxey, and Robert Pete Williams. The first two, though very interesting, played 12-bar Blues in a mostly conventional style. Robert was different.

One night after an evening performance at the Ash Grove, he and I took our guitars and sat at the back of the house to play. But, we talked first. He spoke about his servitude, and having gone to play at a festival accompanied by a prison guard. He spoke quite softly and gently about things. He said that he had "brain fever" as a child, and that made him more spiritual than many around him. While he was drawn to religion, he was also followed by secular music, which wouldn't let him go no matter how hard he tried. He sang in a quiet and reflective manner, about things he had on his mind, very much like John Lee Hooker. The words didn't have to rhyme or fit a particular chord scheme, because he never changed chords. He was pretty free-form. His notes were rhythmic and bluesy, played with foot-tapping rhythms that wove in and out. I had heard that folklorists regarded him as the most African vocalist then performing. That coincided with my fairly limited listening to traditional West African music. One needed to let his music and feeling wash over you. He was not out to impress, but rather to express.

Then we began to play, he might have sung as well. As we played, he began picking in his style, unlike no one else's, and I was spellbound. Single note blues runs in every position. I can't account for it, but I had the thought, "This is where Rock and Roll comes from". The notion of not playing chord changes, only melodic riffs stayed with me. By and large, nowadays when I come up with an instrumental piece it is generally done without changing chords. A session of instruction that influenced me beyond my conscious understanding. A brain-fever by proxy.

I don't know what happened to Robert. He returned to his home in Scotlandville, near Baton Rouge and I had no further contact with him. Years later I went to play in Baton Rouge with Harmonica Fats, and we did a Blues in Schools gig in Scotlandville. I asked around, no one had ever heard of him, let alone knew where he lived, or even if he lived. Lives on in my understanding of the Blues. That's the best I can do.

Encounters with Phillip Walker & Little Walter

Electric K.O.

By 1962 I was enrolled at UCLA and had moved from the apartment I had shared with my mother to the first of many cozy (i.e. tiny) hovels I was to occupy, this one in Venice. One of my Venice neighbors was Barrett "Barry" Hansen. One day in late 1963 or early 1964, Barry said, "There's a very famous harmonica player from Chicago playing at the Knights of Columbus Hall in Venice tonight, do you want to go?" I quickly said yes.

You need to know that by then Barry had established himself as the go-to guy for blues history for us all. He conducted weekly talks at his somewhat larger hovel on recorded blues history. There I first heard the name of Robert Johnson, there I was exposed to rootsiest of all, Charlie Patton. Barry didn't charge admission, but he did sell us some Red Mountain wine out of a gallon jug for 25 cents a paper cup full. There could be a dozen or more crowded around him. His talks were well-prepared and scholarly, with note cards and records (78 RPMs). His floors sagged with their weight, I kid you not. Those were the days.

So, Barry and I and Mark Levine, another friend from the Ash Grove, a fine vocalist, went that night to the Knights of Columbus Hall near Ocean Park Blvd and 20th St in Venice to see Little Walter and a couple of other acts, playing for dancing.

We walked up to the door, paid the fee (I'm sure it was very affordable) and entered a hall full of Black folks sitting at tables, talking, laughing, and getting ready for a good time. We were escorted to a table and felt immediately welcome, no room for uptightness at being almost the only white faces in the room. Later I saw and smiled at two white women who were with black men, they smiled back. *It's a party, y'all.*

Showtime! The M.C. brought to the stage a band headed by a guitarist and singer named Johnny Success. As stunned as I had been by Jesse Fuller's performance, this one equaled and in a way even surpassed that previous shock and involvement. He and the band were playing electric instruments with a drummer! I had no idea…. and, they were good too. It was the blues of a kind I had never heard before. That night I had to put my socks back on several times. Diverging a little, I wondered at his name for a long time after. One day I was driving through Watts and I spotted a street sign that said Success St. (or Ave.) Mystery solved. Later, I looked for his name but never saw him or heard of him playing in subsequent years. My grinning face never left the stage the whole set..

Next was a guitarist named Phillip Walker with his band. His show was a little tighter and generally a cut above the previous act, but equally involving and appreciated by the crowd and we three.

Phillip Walker

As I recall, there weren't that many people on the dance floor at any given time, but the toe-tapping and shouts of understood responses never let up. Phillip was great. I was to become friends with him, and booked him on several shows.

The breath-holding could relent, Little Walter was up next. While it may be surprising that I had never heard his name or his music, but the fact is that his recordings had sold better to Black audiences than his one-time boss's, Muddy Waters. They both remained largely unknown to white audiences in the early 60's. Barry had expressed some doubt that Little Walter would actually be there., but his name was announced and he took the stage strongly. He didn't look that small to me.

In fact he was a fairly tall man. Given that sometime large people are nicknamed "Tiny", I was accepting. I kept asking Barry if it really was who it was supposed to be and he commented, "He plays just like him." As it turned out, indeed he did. But, it was not Little Walter at all, but L.A.'s own George "Harmonica" Smith.

 **George "Harmonica" Smith**

George could play like anyone and had his own style and wonderful stage show to boot. Born, depending on whichever version he told, in the Delta or in Cairo, Illinois. He played with them all in Chicago, including Muddy and Wolf. He was one of the all-time Blues harp masters, and almost every harmonica player of prominence on the West Coast learned to play the Walter style and the chromatic harp by his example. Just ask 'em, those who are still here.

I saw him again just a few years later when Big Mama Thornton brought him on stage during her Ash Grove debut in 1966, during which I had the honor of playing as a band member. George was to play a significant role when I started working on the first year of the event which was later named the Long Beach Blues Festival, some 14 years in the future.

Learning to Laugh to keep from Cryin' (1964)

There were times when my brother would put on concerts elsewhere than the Ash Grove. Sometimes in conjunction with another promoter. In 1964 he got together with Chris Strachwitz, founder of Arhoolie Records, and they decided to produce "Blues '64", one in the Bay Area (Strachwitz's turf) and one in Santa Monica. Each bill would be there same, both focused on the re-appearance after a period in prison of the famed Chuck Berry. The Rock n' Roll great had enough blues roots to call it a blues show, and younger folk/blues lovers were becoming hip to rock roots. The return of Chuck Berry to the stage was not a world-wide event, but was of importance to aficionados.

Also on the bill, was an artist of considerable standing in the blues, Big Mama Thornton, known largely to Black audiences in this pre-Joplin period, appearing almost as debut to an entirely new whiter audience. To fill out the program were the Chambers Brothers, doing largely blues and gospel material at the time, and gaining a young following, even before Newport '65, and Mississippi Fred MacDowell. MacDowell was "discovered" not long before by Alan Lomax playing in a previously un-recorded blues style, as opposed to being one of several re-discovered Mississippi artists with pre-war recording history, such as Son House and Skip James.

I had been dating a young woman of considerable beauty and charm. I committed the grave error of taking her somewhat for granted. Uh-uh. Everybody knows that won't work. I was beyond stupid. The Blues '64 concert was around the corner, and I simply expected her to go with me. Didn't ask. WHAT??? YOU DIDN'T ASK HER? That old line about another mule keeps kicking in my head. Sure enough, someone else did, and I was stag.

Ed asked me to M.C. the show. Lump in throat, knowing that she was out there in the Santa Monica Civic dark with some other guy, I took to the stage to make some upbeat announcements and crack a little wise (never my forte anyway), hurting all the while. The image of Pagliacci comes to mind – Clown suit, over-wide grin, tears leaking down one cheek. Oh, Lord, the world had that one right, and I just walked into it. Mmm….mmm…mmm,

Like a Turkey Through the Corn

My first recollection of Luke "Long Gone" Miles was when Lightnin' called him up to sing with him one evening at the Ash Grove. Probably dressed in a suit, complementing Hopkins' attire, the very dark-skinned, tall, and lanky man languorously made his way to the stage. I can think of no better description of his gait than *languorous*. In fact, I never saw him move at any other pace for any reason whatsoever in the 30 or so years that I knew him.

Long Gone Miles
Courtesy:
Northwestern University Libraries[251]

Long Gone Miles
Courtesy: Bernie Pearl

Long Gone had recorded a couple of tunes in Texas for Mack McCormick around 1959 singing behind Lightnin'. Powerful field hollers behind Hopkins evocations of a prison song, for one. An impressive country blues voice. But, I must have seen him just a couple of years after that, and was unaware of his vocal prowess. Almost self-effacing, the apprentice opened his mouth and let loose with the real thing. Not in competition, but he did himself proud.

I had always believed that he came to California with Lightnin', but I learned later that he had come on his own and came to the club to re-connect with his blues *sensei*. He became a club regular, and in general he sang with the Chambers Brothers. Luke and Willie often became partners on stage, and were just terrific together. Long Gone took his time singing everything, and Willie was in no hurry to get there either.

His ability to simply go with the flow was a remarkable and attractive personality trait. I always felt at home with Willie. Even many years later, when I was doing a gig with Harmonica Fats and Papa Creach at a club in the Pico-Robertson area, Willie Chambers – who had long since left the blues for the church – and his son happened by. It was, as ever, old home week. Genuine smiles and friendship. Though I did not hang out very much with "The Brothers", as we referred to them, I socialized around music with them very easily. Lightnin' and Long Gone were two strong points of mutual respect.

By the time the Chambers Brothers went to play the Newport Folk festival in 1965, they had moved their musical identity from a purely Gospel one, to mostly Gospel, to a lot more Blues, and even a period doing Jug Band music, a la Jim Kweskin and company. They were going to, as far as I was concerned, knock everyone's socks off in Rhode Island, with their magnificent voices, elegant stature, and rock-solid understanding of the Blues. And so they did, to a degree.

That year was the turn-around year for American Folk music and Rock. It was the Paul Butterfield Band stunning with their rocking Chicago Blues, and Bob Dylan taking the music electric in a moment, often employing the Chicago blues guys. The Brothers emerged as stars though, and went on to what seemed a too short career on top of the heap, as Rock crested, changed, and fell in a few short years. "Time" is their enduring identifying "hit", and it makes me cringe every time I hear it. Made lots of money for them, or some of them, I guess. Though, nothing like the four statuesque brothers singing the lights out of "I Got It!"

What Happened to the Turkey Through the Corn?

As the Brothers became more popular, the duo of Willie and Long Gone took a back seat. I began doing sets at the Ash Grove with him, and they were well-received. He, a natural-voiced country bluesman, and me….well, I used everything I had learned backing Lightnin' and Mance and others to try and cover the gig.

Long Gone Miles was very tall, and very thin, and took his time doing everything, including singing. A true rural stylist, he started and finished his lines regardless as to when the formal music said he should. He had that in common with greats like Muddy Waters and, I've been told, a young Riley King. I heard that directly from pianist Lloyd Glenn, who was in a position to know. I was doing a little trio with him and bassist Billy Hadnott in a little place on the Sunset Strip. Glenn was the premier studio pianist for the blues in L.A. in the 40's & 50's, and is the pianist on T-Bone's all-time classic, "Call It Stormy Monday Blues". Hadnott was the bassist. But, I digress.

Long Gone had a totally believable authenticity. Sometimes, however, it worked against him. When you sing something like Tampa Red's, *Play With Your Poodle*, written with a certain chord structure and tempo, the listener (who might also be trying to dance to the music) has an expectation that the beat will be steady and the chord changes will be more or less regular. The choice, it seems to me, is to either learn to at least keep time, or find material more suitable to your style. After all, John Lee Hooker took his songs wherever the hell he wanted to and made it work – he did keep a steady beat and real good time, though.

Often Black musicians use *time* to mean *a good sense of rhythm*, which Long Gone did not have it all. I'd say John Lee Hooker had good *time*, with the meaning of a *good sense of rhythm*. Hooker also played loose when it came to *time* meaning *to make the right changes according to convention*. He started and ended lines irregularly.

Long Gone was undisturbed by such conventions, and he took his time getting from one musical place to another. He was an affable and charming stage presence, gifted with a magnificent baritone designed to holler the blues with the best. Keeping time was beyond a challenge.

A crowd favorite was *Long Gone, Like a Turkey Through the Corn*" Luke was dubbed "Long Gone" when Lightnin' took a gander at the tall, slender young Louisianan from Nackatosh (Natchitoches) when he appeared on the Houston blues scene. One way or another, Luke Miles was often on hand to sing with Lightnin' at the Ash Grove. He had a small apartment in South L.A., which still had totally segregated housing in the early 60's, with his lady, Miss Hazel Mae. Long Gone and the Chambers Brothers worked many shows around town for a while, but with the Brothers' growing renown, Luke had lost his band. I began playing gigs with him, Ash Grove and a few other places, as an acoustic duo. We were actually a pretty good team.

Mike Seeger, half-brother of Pete, and member of the *New Lost City Ramblers*, the ultimate Old-Time (a recognized musical genre which was counterpoint to Country Blues) trio revivalist group, liked what he heard and asked if we'd be interested in playing at the 1966 Newport Folk Festival. I was ready to jump on a Greyhound tomorrow. Long Gone, to his credit, wanted to know what the financial deal was, and other technicalities. Truth was, Mike still had to submit our names to the Newport "committee" for approval.

At one point he asked me if Long Gone did anything other than the "Deep Blues". I wasn't quite sure what the term meant, but was pretty sure that described what he sang. He would try other songs, like "Play With Your Poodle", "Hello, Josephine", but his versions were way slower and more rural in outlook and timing than a coffeehouse crowd would expect. He was a true singer of the deep blues, one of the best, but was not very versatile. He had an engaging stage personality, matching his musical orientation. I was a bushy-headed Jewish young man with a beard and lots of enthusiasm. Might work better today than in yesteryear.

Ultimately, we were rejected by Newport. Undaunted, I said let's go anyway. Mike and my brother Ed said that they'd do what they could to get us onstage.

I had a beautiful white '57 (?) Cadillac two-door (oh, that I had that beauty now!) and it was in good mechanical and physical shape, so I said that we'll get some gigs and split the costs. Long Gone agreed. The Brothers said they'd put us in touch with a couple of gigs. I must have been working regularly and saving money, else we wouldn't have made it to Arizona. Summer of '66 we were on our way cross country, California to Rhode Island.

On The Road With Long Gone (Summer, 1966)

On the Road with Long Gone – Summer of '66

I picked up Long Gone one day at the start of summer, the exact date eludes me. He was staying at Chambers Brothers' rental – a once-elegant mansion – on Crenshaw Boulevard, and off we went. The Brothers saying they'll get in touch with some folks for us. I don't remember much about the trip itself, except that we drove from L.A. across the land to Rhode Island, stopping only for gas, rest rooms, and infrequent food stops. Long Gone didn't eat much, period, and I probably had some kind of sustenance in bags until I really needed a meal.

I recall Long Gone being more road-wise than I expected, especially when it came to road speed, crossing lanes, and especially fuel awareness. I tended to let the tank run down to the one quarter mark, as I did at home, but he started asking me about it shortly after we passed the half-tank mark. He was right. I later learned that lesson a couple of years later driving a friend in a rental van moving back to L.A. from Berkeley through the night on the newly-opened I-5. Spent a bit of time hitchhiking for gas near Coalinga.

We arrived in Rhode Island, got scolded by a traffic cop for making a U-turn in the middle of the street. He didn't care that I headed into and backed out of a driveway to do so. It was against the law. No ticket, however. I apologized and went on our way. Brother Ed had found lodging for us with a private family which rented rooms during festival season.

There was lots of blues that year, several of the re-discovered pre-war blues legends were to play: Bukka White, whom I knew fairly well, Son House, Skip James, and probably others. Joseph Spence, the Bahamian genius guitarist was on hand. I got to talk to him there. Later that year, he came to play at the Ash Grove. Of course, especially following the cultural explosion there the previous year, when Dylan established electric folk rock, and Butterfield upset everyone's notion of the blues, there were folk, rock and hybrids aplenty. I most recall the crowd's adulation of the Lovin' Spoonful when they took the stage.

But, my focus, as always, was on the Blues. I recall standing with Ed and Long Gone, and perhaps Mike Seeger and Ralph Rinzler, he of the Greenbriar Boys, later to become a major figure with the Smithsonian Institute. We were by the housing for many of the blues men, when a car pulled up and out popped the enormous figure of Howlin' Wolf. The Wolf had arrived, and no Muddy to diminish the glow. He was large, full life and humor. He took one look at me, I may have been carrying my guitar, and seeing that I was connected to a blues man, threw his right arm over my shoulders and bellowed *I WANT HIM!!*

Lest there be any misunderstanding, he was joking about me playing with him. Rounds of laughter. He had never heard me play a note. Besides, his guitar man was the superb Hubert Sumlin. I was a year or two later to have the honor of booking him at the Ash Grove. To call him a character is was too small a descriptive. He was a dominant figure everywhere. This was his introduction to a major predominantly white audience in the USA, and he made the most of it with a smashing daytime performance, and an unforgettable night time romp on the main stage. The band struck up "Dust My Broom", and after a few choruses, from stage right out comes Wolf, dressed in blue coveralls, wielding a broom to sweep his way to the microphone and into everyone's gleeful hearts.

My good friend from St. Simon's Island, the late Mable Hillery, also on hand, told me a story about Wolf that would now be appropriate to tell, long after both have gone from the scene.

Mable Hillery

Mable said that when she was introduced to Wolf at Newport, he had eyes for her, and immediately began the sweet-talk. She was a grown woman of some experience, and was not overwhelmed by his attention. He kept at it for a while, and then popped the question, and asked her to sleep with him. Always on top of the situation, Mable replied that she thought he was sharing a dorm-like room with his band. He said he was, but said that all she had to do was come into the room when they were all asleep and just tap him on the arm, third bed from the right!

One for the books. We laughed about it for years.

The Newport Saga Continues – Mrs. Fanny Lou Hamer

The Newport Folk Festival, summer of '66 featured a hefty roster of noted blues artists, Son House, and Howlin' Wolf amongst them, many up-and comers, like the Lovin' Spoonful, plus some very unique performers.

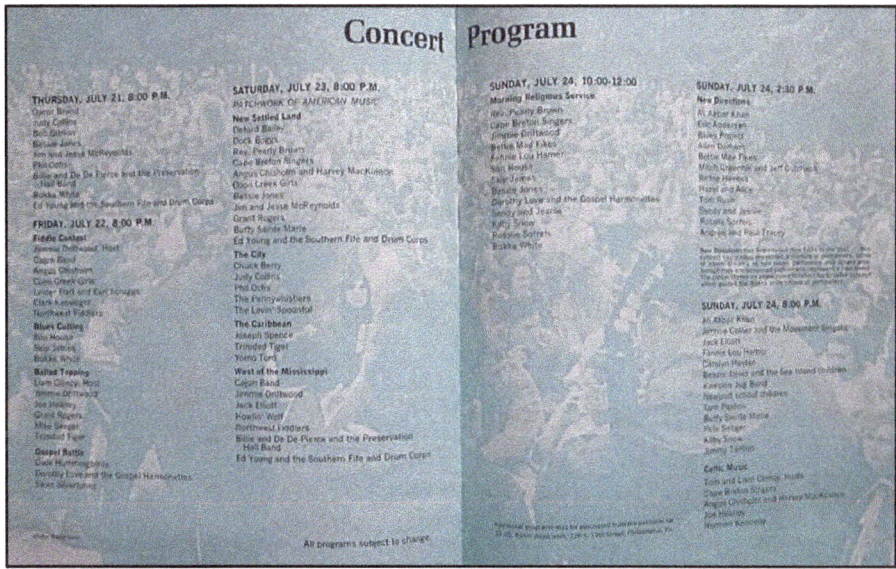

Concert Program, Newport Folk Festival, 1966

Among these was the embattled but undaunted civil rights activist from Mississippi, who was two years later to lead the Mississippi Freedom Democratic Party in an attempt to unseat the segregationist and ultra-conservative official Democratic delegation at the notorious 1968 Democratic Convention in Chicago: Mrs Fannie Lou Hamer.

Fannie Lou Hamer

Nowadays Fannie Lou is rightfully recognized as a towering figure in the fight to force America's turn towards a legally desegregated and more just society. In 1966 she was not so well known, leading the "troops" in her state in the war against Jim Crow. She was also a great and impassioned singer. Known for her Gospel renditions, she was invited to perform on the main stage one afternoon. She came alone, and they were looking for an accompanist.

My brother Ed said, "Wait, I'll get my brother Bernie". I was asked and I agreed to try it out with her backstage. But, I must admit I was intimidated, both by playing with someone I had never seen and by the unfamiliar setting. I sort of knew who she was, and considered it an honor to be asked. She was as gracious and kind as almost all the blues people I had met, and so I felt more relaxed as we talked.

One could sense her power and comfort with herself. She wanted to sing *12 Gates to the City*. This was a song I learned from a Rev Gary Davis recording, and was somewhat familiar with playing his arrangement. She began singing, and I found the key and began playing, as close to Davis-style as I could. As we went on, it became more comfortable, and I was ready to at least play in time with the right chords. A singer of that caliber pretty much carries the show, and all you have to do is not make too many glaring errors and get in the way. She commanded attention. As I recall, she was satisfied, and we were ready to go.

Gradually I could sense a change in the mood. Either Mike Seeger or Ralph Rinzler came up and said that the contingent of Black activists, no names mentioned, was not comfortable with such an iconic figure singing with a white guitarist, and they wanted someone else. I could have retorted, *Hey, why doesn't one of them do it?* I could make more of this than I did, but chose not to. I can understand their feeling, but it was not only a lost opportunity for a young bluesman (think if I could list Fannie Lou Hamer as one of those I performed with), but a lost opportunity to express, at least symbolically, the unity of the forces for justice, regardless of race, creed, etc. I still thank Ed for trying, and I'm still a little pissed.

Newport, We get to Play

While the powers that be at Newport did not offer us a main stage spot, Long Gone and I were invited to perform on a smaller showcase stage.

**Long Gone Miles, Bernie Pearl, Newport, 1966
Courtesy: David Gahr Estate**

As I recall, it was a windy day, and although I was playing my beautiful new Guild Navarre, it was strictly acoustic, and I didn't hear very much of what I sounded like. But, Long Gone seemed happy with the brief set, and we had actually played Newport. However, after the performance he began complaining that we should have been paid. I said, well, we weren't hired or contracted to play, it was a courtesy that probably Mike Seeger arranged. He would not be pacified and, though not an aggressive person, he was persistent, and I think eventually he managed to wring a few dollars out of someone.

When we left L.A. we knew we had no invitation, we were coming on our own and taking our chances. I could live with that, he couldn't. I later encountered similar difficulties with Harmonica Fats, in that once he thought things should be a certain way, that was that. He called it *standing flat-footed.* I later wrote a song about it, singing, *Standing flat-footed like a Lou'siana mule!* Fats was from McDade, Louisiana.

While being on the scene near the performers' housing (Long Gone and I stayed at a nearby private home that rented beds at festival time) I did get a chance to meet and talk with the great Bahamian musician Joseph Spence.

Joseph Spence

I had loved his first recording, Music from the Bahamas-Volume I on Folkways. I had tried to learn some of what he was doing, to little avail. At the Ash Grove, my friend David Cohen, and partner in the School of Traditional Folk Music we ran at the Ash Grove, was able to learn from the recording, a great accomplishment.

But, he was to be eclipsed by young Ryland Cooder, a teen at the time, who had stayed at it day and night for Lord knows how long, and came away having all but mastered it. It was a blow to Dave, who had begun getting serious competition from Ry for acoustic folk gigs in the Hollywood studios.

Ry Cooder

Dave had been very successful, working studio dates for some of the hottest "folk" stars of the early '60's, working in super-producer Phil Spector's "wall of sound", and on several Bobby Darin hits. But, the times were a'changin', and he began losing work, and after a while dropped out of the scene entirely, going into the growing computer field. He was an extremely intelligent guy. His older brother, Norm, was in fact a rocket scientist. Dave was also very competitive, and unless he could be first he chose not to stay in that arena. I almost completely lost touch with him by the end of the 60's, and our school closed. One of two partnerships that started promisingly, but which had to end when the partners went in different directions.

However, I really enjoyed Newport, meeting Spence and sitting right in front of him as he performed one of his magical rhythmic pieces for me in private recital. He was due to go to L.A. to start his West Coast tour at the Ash Grove, but I wouldn't see him there as Miles and I were going to spend a few days along with brother Ed at a private island off the Massachusetts coast which was owned by the Hughes family, of which his wife, Kate, was a member.

The Island

As I recall, we drove my spacious 1956 Cadillac coupe onto the ferry, and parked it where we docked. We never used it again until we left the island a few days later. It is possible that we parked it in a lot on the land side. But, in any case, our few days on the island were spent walking from house to house, to dock and back. Ed and his wife Kate were in the house we stayed in, presumably a guest house. It had full facilities, and I drew an upstairs bedroom which I had to myself. It was very cold at night, but I had plenty of blankets.

Another house guest was a former member of the Greenbriar Boys, a fine revivalist band of East Coast guys, which included John Herald on guitar, and Bob Yellin on banjo, and mandolinist Ralph Rinzler, the other house guest. I was surprised and pleased many years later to see Bob's credit as composer of the score for a Woody Allen movie. I believe that he was also the banjoist heard on the sound track of "Deliverance". Rinzler was a very nice guy, and easy to room with. He had continued his trajectory as a traditional musician and folklorist, and had attained a position of influence with the Smithsonian Institute. Ralph was occupied much of the time practicing his weaving technique on a quaint hand loom.

It was on the Island that I read the autobiography of Malcolm X (Muhammad el-Shabazz, if memory serves). I had heard him speak at UCLA a few years previous, in a fairly small lecture hall. On hand was a squad of formidable bow-tied Fruit of Islam guards, This being prior to his split with Elijah Muhammad and the Nation of Islam. He was very witty and challenging and, although I understood the concept, he brought the term "Black" to a fuller meaning and since that time have used it in the sense that he presented it, as a cultural designation having little to do with shades of skin color. He was a brilliant and powerful speaker. I can easily see his becoming more and more open and universal, never abandoning his principals, but broadening his understanding of the forces of freedom. I can also see the threat he posed to the doctrines of the movement he formerly embraced. His killing was a great American loss, and coupled with the assassination of Dr. King, it allowed the forces of reaction to turn the tide back. Together they would have been unstoppable.

I remember those few days as a time of relaxation, and of a growing awareness of just how little I knew about the power of great wealth. The family was cordial, in a formal way, and we even got a chance to go boating on a wind-blown inlet. But we were definitely not in down-home territory.

Subsequent to this sojourn, I was to learn that my brother's wife Kate was going to leave him for Ralph. They did divorce, and Kate and Ralph remained a married couple until his untimely death a few years ago. I was sorry to hear of it.

After we left the island, Long Gone and I headed to Boston to play a gig.

On to Boston

Through the Chambers Brothers, Luke and I got a one-nighter at a club in Boston. The Brothers were a big hit at the 1965 Newport event, and had made many new friends on their way to popularity in the Rock area. I don't recall the name of the club, but remember that the man who ran it was George Papadopoulis – which Long Gone in his best Louisianese called Papadappa. It was a nice night as I recall, not particularly memorable, but it went well. We stayed in a house owned by a fellow whose last name was Lincoln. He was indeed a descendant of Abraham, and was most gracious in his reception.

One unpleasant memory of that two or three day stay was that Long Gone and I were not seeing eye to eye on much. It was, by and large, an adventure to me, but he wanted to get gigs and make money, and that was not happening. There was frustration on both sides, and our discourse with each other became fairly contentious. Our host let us know that it bothered him as well. We canned it. I recall that Ed and possibly Ralph Rinzler were in Boston at that time, and we all went to see the Muddy Waters Band at a (Club 47?) one evening.

Muddy Waters

(McKinley Morganfield)

Prior to then, Long Gone had shocked me when he stated that Muddy, and not Lightnin', was his favorite bluesman. I don't remember if he was along that night, but judging from his opinion of Waters I can't imagine that he'd not go.

215

It was my first time seeing Muddy and I was very impressed. I had judged him, with no information to judge by, to be a Rhythm & Blues artist who played loud electric guitar, like Rock & Roll. Embarrassing to admit to, but so. He had Buddy Guy and Jr. Wells in the band at the time, and it was great.

Buddy Guy (guitar)

Junior Wells (harp)

It wouldn't be long before he's be appearing at the Ash Grove. Buddy was the young guitar burner of the Chicago Blues, was very aware of it, and had plenty of 'tude to spare. I have to laugh remembering how absolutely casually he smoked a cigarette during the set, and in his nonchalant manner held the glowing nail between the third and fourth fingers of his picking hand while he tore off magnificent riffs and solos one after the other. The young prince of cool. The confidence was astounding.

The sojourn in Beantown came to an end, and we drove to Queens to stay with my sister's family and to explore the Village.

New York – First, a little Family History

After Boston, Long Gone and I drove to New York – Queens, to be exact – to stay with my sister Bernice's family, while we looked into playing in Greenwich Village, where much of the "action" was supposed to be. We found that it was so.

We managed to find the ground-floor apartment where my sister, her four kids, and her new man had landed when she left her husband and father of her children, Bob Wolfe.

Bob was from the neighborhood in Boyle Heights. He had served in the US Air Force as an underage volunteer during WWII. He and Bernice got married when they were both quite young, and with some push back from both families. He had three sisters and parents who had what appeared to be an unhappy open relationship. Our family was poor but "respectable". Bernice and Bob produced five children in fairly short order. Tragedy struck when their first-born, Mark, died of a brain tumor before his third birthday. Bernice suffered greatly and really never recovered from this blow.

Combined with her childhood polio and her having been raised by a very strict aunt physically nearby, but at an emotional distance from her parents and four brothers, caused her to have to fight depression all her life. We could all bring our troubles to Bernice and receive loving therapy, but she could not give voice to her innermost feelings.

Bernice Pearl

Bernice was talented, intelligent, and very beautiful. She loved music and liveliness, and people loved her for it. Bob had very little formal education, sometimes acting in a crude and insensitive manner, and in many ways did not belong with my sister, but he was quite bright and motivated to succeed.

This he did. He taught himself engineering, later proving himself to be quite astute in real estate. He began his "career" by assisting his father for a while with a carnival attraction traveling arms display across the US, Bernice in tow. He did provide well for his family, very quickly moving from rental to home ownership. Then came children and, as a veteran, qualified for a home in the brand new development in Lakewood, California. After the passing of young Mark, there was a move to New Jersey, but eventually they moved back to L.A. Their house became a center of folk hootenannies. There was lots of music and their second child, Randy, showed musical talent early on. But, Bernice was looking for something else. This continued into the 1960's. Teen Randy had become a very good guitarist, and began playing with a group of young musicians at the Ash Grove. Young, save for the drummer Ed Cassidy, who was conspicuously older than any one in the band – and considerably more experienced. He helped guide the group, called the "Red Roosters", in the show business aspects of the growing Rock music.

It came to pass that "Cass" began offering rides home from Rooster performances in L.A. to the (San Fernando) Valley, where Bernice and Bob had bought a home. One thing led to another, and the next thing the family heard is that Bernice had left Bob for Cass. I wasn't particularly fond of Cass from the beginning, but Bernice was the sister I loved and wanted to support. I was fond of Bob with whom I had a different relationship than I had with my three older brothers. I did feel for him, and offered a mattress on the floor of my tiny basement apartment in Ocean Park, which he accepted.

I had all that background in mind when we arrived in Queens for what turned out to be a very interesting Summer of '66.

The Village and Jimi

Long Gone and I found my sister's apartment in Queens. Two bedrooms, or was it three, afforded us a place to sleep. She was living with drummer Ed Cassidy, called Cass, and her four kids, Randy, Andrea, Janet, and the "baby" Marla. Cass had been sitting in on various Jazz sessions, and Randy, a fine guitarist in his mid-teens at the time, had begun exploring the Greenwich Village music scene.

Long Gone and I went to the Village, talked to a couple of clubs recommended by the Chambers Brothers, and got us a gig at the Gaslight. It was downstairs and small, as were many of the venues in the area.

The Gaslight Café, Greenwich Village, NYC

As you walked in, there were photos of some of those who got their starts there. The most recognizable one was of Bill Cosby, at the height of his early TV popularity on "I Spy", as I recall, who had inscribed his autograph with a loving thank you to "Pops", owner Clarence Hood, who had given him a break into the "business".

I recall playing my big, recently purchased Guild F-50 "Navarre", a top of the line Guild. We got a warm reception, but to be honest, Mr. Hood didn't seem impressed with my playing. Still, it was a good learning experience.

My nephew Randy had been talking about this guy he was playing with named Jimmy James. I didn't care that much for Rock Music, but thought it would be a good idea to check them out. Long Gone and I walked over to the Café' Wha, another small, below-the-street venue, where the band was holding forth to a small but appreciative crowd and....Holy Cow!

Café Wha?, Greenwich Village, NYC

There was my nephew Randy, a bassist, and a drummer, playing behind this tall, left-handed Black guitarist who was ripping the hide off the guitar, in a style I had never heard before. While I generally prefer the Blues over most other material, "Jimmy" was beyond impressive on his axe.

It was Jimi Hendrix, who had met Randy at Manny's Music Store, heard him play, and invited him to become part of his "Blue Flames". A couple of days later, they got a gig backing John Hammond at Howard Solomon's Café Au Gogo, a larger, nicer venue than the Wha.

After my nephew Randy Wolfe became a member of the Blue Flames, Hendrix renamed the two Randy's. Randy Wolfe, my nephew, became Randy California. Randy Palmer became Randy Texas. These names indicated the state of origin of the band members.

Problem was that Jimi's Fender amp was being worked on, and he needed an amp to play the gig. I told him that I would lend him the Gibson amp I had brought along in my Cadillac (sigh, I wish I still had that car). As one must know, there is no parking in New York generally but you could double that in the Village. So, I hauled the Gibson, comparable to a Fender Twin in size and weight, but without casters, on the subway from Queens to the Village, just in time for their set. At the same time, Jimi's Fender was brought in, much to his relief. He couldn't get the sound he wanted from the Gibson.

Later that evening, Long Gone and I did a short, well-received set. Paul Butterfield's band was also featured that show, and Mike Bloomfield came running up to us saying how much he enjoyed the set. I had heard him live in L.A. earlier that year and was very flattered. A footnote to that meeting was that I didn't meet Butterfield until many years later, when he asked to sit in with my band backing Linda Hopkins at a festival in Topanga Canyon. He was very nice, and played beautifully, with great tone and taste, and thanked me afterwards for letting him play. He died not long after that.

At one point during the NY sojourn, Randy asked me to hold onto a hand-painted Fender guitar case which said "Jimmy James and the Blue Flames". I returned it to him several months later upon his request.

Sittin' in with John Lee

Another place I was told to check out in the Village was Gerde's Folk City. It was the nesting place of burgeoning folksters like Bob Dylan before they had a dime to their name. I saw that John Lee Hooker was playing there, and decided to bring my guitar. I did, and when I introduced myself to him, he recognized me from the Ash Grove and knew that I played with Lightnin'.

Gerde's Folk City, Greenwich Village, NYC

He invited me to sit in. He was amplified, and I was strictly acoustic, but we had a good time together. So much so that he invited me back for a second night.

John Lee Hooker

What struck me was that the place was nearly empty both nights. That underscores the ephemeral nature of popularity. In a couple of years, due largely to Canned Heat's popularity, Hooker became iconized, and was never out of the public view from that time. He had popular recordings in the early 1950's, playing that stomp kind of blues that emerged from his North Mississippi blues culture, and his unremitting deep Southern vocals. By the time of his passing he had achieved a great deal of national recognition and was earning thousands per appearance. While it was not all smooth sailing for him from the late '60's on, he kept to what did and triumphed.

At one point, John lee asked me to drive him back to Detroit. I can kick myself for not doing it. I had the wheels, would have enjoyed the company – he was a nice guy – and would have gained a friend. But, I was expecting to drive us back to L.A. soon, possibly with my sister's family. But, that didn't happen either.

Back to L.A. w/ Ms Hazel Mae

Long Gone had taken to upon himself to send for his wife, Ms Hazel Mae. He and she were not married, but lived together in apparent harmony in L.A. She was tall, dark, and elegant, and a very friendly person. However, her arrival by Greyhound was totally unexpected. My sister moved her daughters out of their bedroom to accommodate the couple, but was not happy about it, as could have been expected. Within a couple of days Cass asked them to leave, politely and reasonably, and so they did, in my Cadillac. I asked Long Gone to change the oil and have it lubed and drop it off at my mother's apartment, as we had put thousands of miles on it during this trip. I thought that a reasonable request. The other option was to put them both on the bus, but that never occurred to me as I considered them both friends.

Back to L.A. with the Family

My sister and her three daughters, her son, and Cass and me piled into their station wagon at the end of Summer of '66. We made our way to L.A. without any memorable problems. My friend Lonnie had rented a little hut up in the hills above the Echo Park-Silverlake area, near Dodger Stadium, and he invited me to be his roommate. I had given up my little below ground-level studio flat in Ocean Park before going to Newport. My landlords had begged me to come back there, even offering to waive the rent for the time I'd be gone. But, as in many situations in my life, I ignored the practical and opted for the unknown and sometimes illusory path.

I spent some very memorable times at the studio flat in Ocean Park through my early 20's. I remember lying on my bed listening to the Cassius Clay-Sonny Liston fight – I didn't get a TV until several years forward – thinking that these are times to remember, times of change. There I courted my beautiful Elizabeth, actress and school teacher, and several others. There I gave temporary bed and board to my dear friend and sometimes lover Sandy, fleeing a disastrous second marriage to a nice guy in New York who she claimed was impotent and probably bi.

Her earlier marriage had been to attorney Mitch Geffen, brother of the now-famous David. The day after she arrived I was informed by my graduate advisor Dr. Malcolm Kerr – I was slogging through courses in a Master's program in Middle East Studies at UCLA – who informed me that President Kennedy had been shot. I went back to my apartment and got Sandy and then went to my mother's. I knew that she would be distraught, as well all were. I recall that some two decades earlier she stood crying at the ironing board when the radio announced the death of President Franklin Roosevelt.

The moment in 1963 changed everything in America. Kennedy embodied hope. He had emerged from being the conservative scion of ill-gotten wealth, staunch cold warrior, and one indifferent to segregation and poverty, to being an entity surrounded by light and hope. The powers that were and still are could not tolerate this. We have suffered as a nation for this travesty.

Big Mama's in Town (Sept, 1966)

After having discovered that my car was not at my mother's place. I tracked Long Gone down – he wasn't in hiding – at the Chambers brothers house on Crenshaw Blvd. Car was filthy with road grime and had not been lubed or oiled. I was not happy, but it was still running fine and it didn't take long to get over my huff. I liked Long Gone (I never called him Luke) and just accepted that that was the way he rolled. He was a nice, friendly guy, but I wouldn't ever do that again.

I showed up at the Ash Grove during the day shortly after my return from New York, and there in the dressing room was Willie Mae "Big Mama" Thornton, due to open at the club that night.

Mama had fired her guitarist that day and needed one for her opening that night. My brother asked me, "Who plays better electric blues, you or David (Cohen)?" I didn't hesitate, "Me". I went home, got my Telecaster and returned to audition for her and her band leader, bassist Curtis Tillman.

Big Mama Thornton (Willie Mae Thornton)
(baritone sax on left, upright bass in rear: both unknown)

I played the few B.B. King riffs I had learned from record, and got the gig. A scary prospect, but I was going to play Big Mama's debut at the club. "What songs, what keys" I asked Curtis. I heard back, *It ain't nothin' but the Blues*. I had seen her show before, but that gave me little to go on.

A couple of years earlier, I had driven up to Berkeley with my friend and co-director of our Folk Music School, David Cohen, and my brother Ed. We had been invited up by Carroll Peery to see Big Mama Thornton at his little club, the Cabale, at 2504 San Pablo Ave.

Carroll had been my co-worker at the Ash Grove. He had managed the kitchen after the departure of Martin "Mutt" Cohen (not related to David), who had gotten his law degree and had opened the Unicorn Club with his brother Herb at 8907 Sunset Blvd on the Sunset Strip.

The Unicorn Club

8907 Sunset Blvd

Herb became a major player on the emerging music scene, managing Frank Zappa, Linda Ronstadt, Tom Waits and others. Mutt became a major legal figure in the entertainment industry. Both now deceased.

Herb Cohen

Carroll Peery was a Black man with deep political sensibilities and a great sense of humor.

Carroll Peery

I believe he had been a card-carrying Communist at one point. By no means a rigid doctrinaire ideologue, he was a natural raconteur and had great rapport with all artists. But his presence was an especial asset with all of the Blues people who came through the Cabale.

The Cabale, at 2504 San Pablo Avenue (at Dwight) in Berkeley, was a folk club founded in late 1962 by Rolf Cahn and Debbie Green (two Cambridge, MA folkies) along with Howard Ziehm and Red Dog alum Chandler A. Laughlin III (later known as Travus T. Hipp). Cahn had previously owned the Blind Lemon at 2362 San Pablo.

The Cabale opened to the public on January 4, 1963. By 1964, Carroll Peery, manager of the Chambers Brothers and Big Mama Thornton, happened to acquire a majority interest in the Cabale. Jesse Cahn, son of Cabale founder Rolf Cahn and folksinger Barbara Dane, recalls *I was the one who cleaned the johns and swept up and practically lived there until 1965*. The name of the venue was changed from the Cabale to the Cabale Creamery in August of 1964.

This club operated until mid-1965, when the folk action in Berkely moved from the Cabale to the Jabberwock.

Cabale Program

Brownie McGhee and Sonny Terry played at Cabale quite regularly in the beginning years. One-man band Jesse Fuller, out of Oakland, played frequently also. Barbara Dane, a white woman who was a powerful vocalist who could credibly cover Bessie Smith, Ma Rainey and, it seemed, the entire Classic women's songbook, was probably responsible for bringing Jesse in. They were all incredibly important and eye-opening to me in my late teens.

But, for sure Barbara was responsible for introducing us to Lightnin' Hopkins, a life-changing encounter for me. Carroll and Lightnin' had a warm and hilarious relationship from the get-go. Carroll Peery told me that he would regularly banter with Lighnin'. Once Lightnin' called Peery a *short som' bitch*. I cracked up. The appelation stuck! Alan Govenar's excellent biography, *Lightnin' Hopkins – His Life and Blues* has several of Peery's Lightnin' anecdotes[253].

We rolled in to Berkeley at night and found the Cabale at 2504 San Pablo Ave in Berkeley. I don't remember much about the night save for the fact that Big Mama was big and a powerful presence who filled the tiny stage and small room with her voice. It was a kind of blues I was unused to. Loud, electric guitar, bass, drums, and a trombone played by, as I remember, a man in medical scrubs. I didn't quite know how to react, but I liked it.

Who Was "Big Mama" Thornton?[254]

Willie Mae "Big Mama" Thornton (1926-1984) was an influential Blues singer and songwriter whose career extended from the 1940s to the early 1980s. Thornton was called "Big Mama" for both her size, as much as 200 pounds, and her robust, powerful voice. She is best known for her gutsy 1953 blues recording of "Hound Dog," later covered by Elvis Presley, and for her original song "Ball and Chain," made famous by Janis Joplin.[255]

Big Mama could play the drums and the harmonica. She could belt out those Blues songs with amazing sexuality and feeling. And, Willie Mae Thornton entertained when she performed. Thornton carried her harmonica in her brassiere. Right in the middle of a song, she would reach into her brassiere and withdraw that harmonica. Then, she would start playing that harmonica.[256]

Elvis made a lot of money recording and playing *Hound Dog*, originally made a hit by Big Mama Thornton. Janis Joplin also made a lot of money recording and playing *Ball and Chain*, originally written and performed by Big Mama. **And, yet, Big Mama Thornton died broke and was buried in a pauper's grave in Los Angeles, CA.**

Willie Mae Thornton was born December 11, 1926, in the rural outskirts of Montgomery, AL. This area is in the unincorporated community of Ariton in Dale County. Her parents were Thomas H. Thornton and Edna M. Richardson Thornton. Willie Mae was one of at least four siblings. Thomas Thornton was a minister. Edna Thornton sang in the church choir.

Willie Mae grew up singing in church. She learned drums on her own. When she was 8 years old, Thornton learned to play the harmonica from her brother Calliope "Harp" Thornton. Harp was apparently an outstanding harmonica player.²⁵⁷

Willie Mae "Big Mama" Thornton Plays The Harmonica

Thornton's musical talent and skills were self-taught.

*My singing comes from my experience... My own experience. I never had no one teach me nothin'. I never went to school for music or nothin'. I taught myself to sing and to blow harmonica and even to play drums by watchin' other people! I can't read music, but I know what I'm singing! I don't sing like nobody but myself".*²⁵⁸ *I was a young type of youngster always running around the house humming the blues and my daddy wanted to get me with the razor strop, but I hit the door."*²⁵⁹

Edna Thornton, Willie Mae's mother, contracted tuberculosis in 1939. Thornton cared for her mother until her death in the Montgomery Tuberculosis Sanatorium. Edna Thornton died a short time later in 1939 when Willie Mae was 14. At the time Thornton was still in the third grade, even though she was 14 years old. After losing her mother, Willie Mae was unable to continue to attend school. She had to earn money to help support the family. Thornton left school and got a job washing and cleaning spittoons in a local tavern.²⁶⁰ One night, the regular vocalist become so drunk that she could not perform. Willie Mae convinced the tavern owner to allow her to substitute. After that first performance, Thornton became the regular vocalist.[261]

In 1941, Atlanta music promoter Sammy Green was in Lauderdale County with The Hot Harlem Revue, his Georgia-based show. Willie Mae auditioned for Green.

> *I did an audition on this show when they were playing a little theater there in the home town. They didn't have a singer, and so I asked him, I said, 'Give me an audition, let me sing'. I said, 'I've been singing all the little talent shows around here'. He said, 'Oh, little 'ole girl, you can't sing'. I said, 'Will you give me a try?' He said, 'Yeah, well, when the show start, say we gonna give a little audition for singers, 'cause I'm looking for a singer'. And so he give auditions. So I was there, he wrote my name down, and several people they sung, and then he said, 'Well, I, I want to see what you can do'. So I got up there, I had an old pair of jeans, one leg rolled up, I got up and I started singing one of Louis Jordan's song called "G.I. Jive", and I sung that song, and I sang this blues by Big Maceo, "Worried Life Blues" and he hired me. Out of 25 people, I was the 26th but then he hired me"*[262]

Thornton joined the show then and there. *I left with the show. We went to Atlanta, Birmingham, and back home to Montgomery, Columbus, Georgia, Macon, Georgia, South Carolina, Florida.*[263] Willie Mae sang and danced as part of the Revue. She became known as the new Bessie Smith. Thornton later acknowledged the influence of artists she heard during these years. She included Smith, Ma Rainey, Junior Parker, and Memphis Minnie. Thornton remained with Green and the Revue for seven years until 1948.

In 1948, Thornton left the Revue and moved to Houston. She immediately started singing at the Eldorado Ballroom at Elgin and Dowling.Streets for $50 a night.

Eldorado Ballroom, 1939
Courtesy: Houston Press

In 1950, Thornton recorded her first record, *All Right Baby* and *Bad Luck Got My Man*. These songs were credited to the "Harlem All Stars". Vinyl releases were on the E&W Recording Studio record label, a Houston company. Thornton was credited as songwriter on both songs.

Producer/promoter Don Robey of Houston heard Willie May Thornton playing at the Eldorado Ballroom.[264]

Don Robey

Robey was impressed with her ability to play multiple instruments, rare for a female singer. In 1950, Robey signed Thornton to a five-year contract with Peacock Records, his record company. Peacock, was known for gritty rhythm and blues and gospel and was an important influence on soul music and rock. Featured artists included Marie Adams, Johnny Ace, and a young Little Richard.

Her first Peacock record was *No Jody For Me / Let Your Tears Fall Baby*. These recordings were local hits in the Houston area. However, the recordings did not fare well outside Houston.. Thornton needed additional income to live. She started shining shoes to survive.[265]

Willie Mae Thornton was an open lesbian. Her openness caused some tension with Robey. Despite the tension, Robey produced her first recordings. He also gave Thornton a regular performance schedule at The Bronze Peacock, a Houston club owned by Robey.

Bronze Peacock

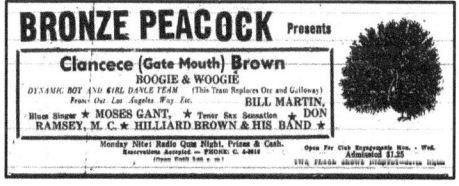

Robey also scheduled tours for Thornton on the Chitlin' Circuit. This string of Black owned and operated clubs, venues and juke joints covered the eastern and southern US.

In 1952, Thornton was working around Houston at different small night clubs. Johnny Otis came to Houston on tour with his band, the California Rhythm and Blues Caravan.

L to R: Mario Delegarde, Pete Williams, Lady Dee Williams, Don Johnson, Johnny Otis, Lorenzo Holden, Walter Henry, Lee Graves

Otis saw Willie Mae perform and asked her to audition with his band. Willie Mae did a song with the Band. Otis liked the way Thornton performed on stage. As a result, Johnny Otis, signed a contract with Don Robey allowing Peacock Records artists to travel with Otis' California Rhythm and Blues Caravan to gain experience and exposure. This deal included recording the artists in Los Angeles and giving the recordings to Robey for distribution. Thornton was one of the artists Otis selected.[266] After this contract was signed, Willie Mae Thornton left Houston for Los Angeles.[267]

Johnny Otis, Don Robey

In August, 1952, at a recording session in southwest Los Angeles, Thornton was approached by the young songwriting team of Mike Stoller and Jerry Lieber.

Mike Stoller and Jerry Lieber
Photo: *What's My Line* Television Appearance

This pair of songsters were soon to become rock & roll legends. Stoller and Lieber offered Thornton a 12-bar blues vocal entitled *Hound Dog*. She liked this song and paired the song on a single with her own *They Call Me Big Mama* on the B-side.

Otis and Thornton went on tour from Los Angeles throughout California in the Fall of 1952.

Johnny Otis

Big Mama Thornton

Venues included Sweets Ballroom in San Francisco and The Fillmore Auditorium. After a short return to Los Angeles, the tour headed east towards Houston. In Houston, shows included *Battling the Blues* with "Gatemouth" Brown.

Clarence "Gatemouth" Brown

After leaving Houston, the tour headed east through Florida and then up the East Coast coming into New York.[268]

In Dec, 1952, as part of the tour, Otis and Thornton played the famed Apollo Theatre in Harlem. The Apollo Theatre was considered the most prestigious performance venue for Black artists throughout the US.

The Apollo Theatre
Courtesy: Wikipedia Commons

Initially, Thornton served as the opening act for R&B artists "Little" Esther Phillips and Mel Walker. However, Willie Mae was shortly promoted to headliner.

During the appearance of the show at the Apollo, Thornton did not have a hit single of her own to sing. She sang a version of *Have Mercy Baby*, the hit by Billy Ward and his Dominoes. The audience went wild for Thornton. Audience reaction did not stop until the stage manager brought the curtain down in order to get the show moving again.

> ...*that's where they made their mistake. They put me on first. I wasn't out there to put no one off stage. I was out there to get known and I did!... They had to put the curtain down. That's when they put my name in lights. Mr. Frank Shiffman, the manager came back stage hollerin' to Johnny Otis... 'You said you had a star and you got a star. You got to put her on to close the show!*'[269]

From the next night onward, the Apollo marquee was changed to read "Big Mama Thornton".

At this time, Thornton was given her nickname "Big Mama" by Frank Schiffman, the manager of the Apollo Theater. Shiffman gave her this nickname because of her strong voice, size, and personality. *I was louder than any microphone and did not want a microphone to ever be as loud as I was.*

After the Apollo shows, the tour went through all of the New England states. Tour dates included Providence, RI, all the New England states; Boston, and venues all around this area.[270]

> *I wanted to go home. I was kind of home sick. So, I wanted to see the whole gang. I caught a train, I leave New York and come back to Houston. I got there just a little before Christmas. Don Robey put me on a show in his night club. I worked that Christmas and that New Year at his club. It was called* The Bronze Peacock.[271]

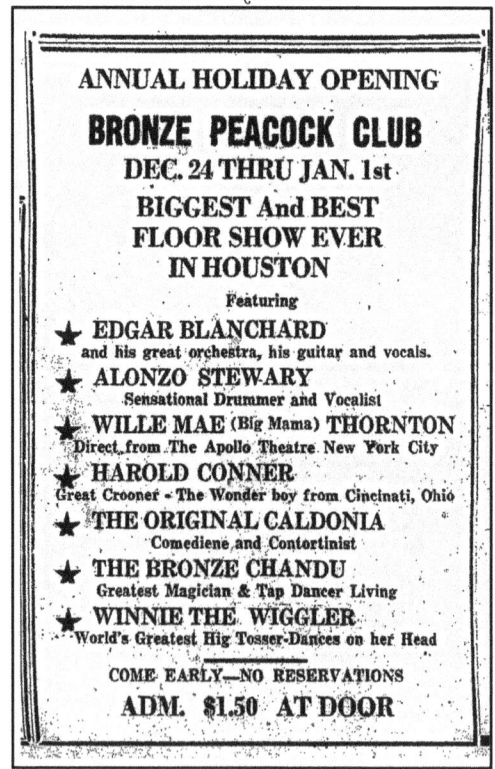

Hound Dog by Big Mama Thornton was released in February, 1953. Thornton's exuberant delivery, laden with open sexual references, whoops, and barks was addictive.

In 1953, Big Mama Thornton met piano player Johnny Ace.

Johnny Ace

Don Robey sent Thornton to Dayton, OH. to join Johnny Ace playing at a theater in Dayton.

Buffalo Booking Agency

(Don Robey Owned)

Promotional Poster

On her way to the theatre, Thornton heard her song being played on the radio.

> *I was going to the theater, and I just turned the radio on in the car. And the man said, "Here's a record that's going nationwide! Hound Dog by*

Willie Mae Thornton." I said, "That's me!" [laughter] I hadn't heard the record in so long. When we get to the theater, they were blasting it. You could hear it from the theater on the loud speaker on the outdoor. They were just playing Hound Dog all over the theater. I go up in the operating room and I said, "You mind playing that again?" The man held the record in so long, I had forgotten the words myself.

I stood there while he was playing it, listening to it. So, that evening, I sang it on the show, and everybody went for it. Hound Dog just took off like a jet.[272]

Hound Dog sold more than 500,000 copies. Her recording spent 14 weeks on the 1953 *Billboard* R&B chart., including seven weeks at number one.[273]

Although the record made her a star, Thornton received little of the recording royalties.[274] She received just one royalty check for $500 from her version *Didn't get no money from them at all. Everybody livin' in a house but me. I'm just livin'.*[275] In contrast, Elvis Presley's 1956 version was heavily refined for mainstream audiences. This release brought Presley both fame and considerable financial reward.

Elvis Presley Sings Hound Dog On The Ed Sullivan Show

Thornton continued with Johnny Otis's band until 1954. During the period 1951 – 1954, Thornton made 30 recordings for the Peacock label. These recordings are considered *remarkable for the vocal presence and total cohesiveness.*[276]

On Christmas Day 1954 at the City Auditorium in Houston, TX, Thornton was performing at a show with pianist Johnny Ace. Ace was in the backstage dressing room playing with a new .22 caliber. revolver

> *I looked over at Johnny and noticed he had a pistol in his hand. It was a pistol that he bought somewhere in Florida. It was a .22 cal. revolver. Johnny was pointing this pistol at Mary Carter and Joe Hamilton. He was kind of waving it around. I asked Johnny to let me see the gun. He gave it to me and when I turned the chamber a .22 cal. bullet fell out in my hand. Johnny told me to put it back in where it wouldn't fall out. I put it back and gave it to him. I told him not to snap it at nobody. After he got the pistol back, Johnny pointed the pistol at Mary Carter and pulled the trigger. It snapped... I told Johnny again not to snap the pistol at anybody. Johnny then put the pistol to Olivia's head and pulled the trigger. It snapped. Johnny said 'I'll show you that it won't shoot'. He held the pistol up and looked at it first and then put it to his head. I started toward the door and I heard the pistol go off. I turned around and saw Johnny falling to the floor. I saw that he was shot and I run on stage and told the people in the band about it. I stayed there until the officers arrived*[277]

Thornton returned to the Apollo Theater in February of 1955. After performing at the Apollo this time, Big Mama toured around that part of the country. When that tour ended, Thornton drove back down through Alabama and Georgia stopping to see old friends *I didn't have anything else to do.* After visiting friends across the south, Thornton returned to Houston. During the first part of 1956, Thornton went on a tour with Gatemouth Brown. She spent the remainder of 1956 performing in small clubs around Houston. Around Thanksgiving 1956, Big Mama Thornton returned to CA for good.[278]

Blues and rhythm and blues were soon eclipsed by the growth of rock and roll. As a result, Thornton's career slowed in the mid-1950s, although she was only in her thirties.

Her agreements with both Robey and Otis had expired in 1955. Thornton performed in R&B package tours with Junior Parker and Esther Phillips and continued to record for Peacock until 1957. Thornton did not have another hit record that she recorded.

In the late 1950s, Thornton moved to San Francisco to perform with her old friend Clarence "Gatemouth" Brown, a former Duke-Peacock artist. She had no contract or regular band. During her residence in San Francisco, Big Mama mostly played in local clubs. She endured a number of difficult years.

In 1956, Thornton and Gatemouth Brown went on a tour together. After this tour ended, Thornton settled in Los Angeles.[279]

Thornton wrote, *Ball And Chain*, another signature song, in 1961. This song relates the feelings of a woman who has been mistreated by her partner. Thornton assigned her copyrights to Bay-Tone Records, a small, independent record company in San Francisco. Bay-Tone released three of Thornton's singles, including "*You Did Me Wrong / Big Mama's Blues*". However, the label chose not to release her recording of *Ball And Chain*. Instead, the recording label retained the copyrights.

Fortunately, traditional Blues were revived by the mid-1960s. Rock and Roll artists such as Bob Dylan, Eric Clapton, and the Rolling Stones, embraced the Blues. The Bay Area became a center of Blues activity. Although still drifting along playing club dates, Thornton was always invited to the Monterey Jazz Festival. In 1965, she toured Europe with the American Folk Blues Festival, an unusual honor for a female artist.

In the late 1960s, Big Mama Thornton made several seminal recordings for Chris Strachwitz, producer of Arhoolie Records. On *Big Mama Thornton: In Europe* (1966), Thornton was backed by Buddy Guy, Walter Horton, and Freddy Below. *Big Mama Thornton with the Chicago Blues Band* (1966), included Muddy Waters, Sam "Lightnin'" Hopkins, and Otis Spann. *Ball & Chain* (1969) was a compilation of original work by Thornton, Hopkins, and Larry Williams. Rock artists took note of these powerful recordings.

On May 22, 1966, Big Mama Thornton performed at the Both/And Club at 350 Divisadero Street in San Francisco. This show was one of her many performances at the club.

Big Mama Thornton

Promotion Poster

Both/And Club

Big Brother and the Holding Company heard Thornton perform *Ball and Chain* at this show. [280] Vocalist Janis Joplin and guitarist James Gurley approached Thornton and asked permission to record *Ball And Chain*.[281] Thornton agreed. Gurley slowed the Blues song, using a minor key.[282]

Joplin and Big Brother performed their version of *Ball And Chain* at the 1967 Monterey Pop Festival. The crowd was stunned. Band guitarist Sam Andrew joked, *This was no 'wear flowers in your hair' song*.[283]

Subsequently, Joplin and Big Brother released their version of the song on their album *Cheap Thrills* in August 1968. The album remained at the top spot of the Billboard Hot 200 charts for two months. Joplin's interpretation of the song renewed interest in Thornton, boosting her career.[284]

Big Brother and The Holding Company, circa 1967
Source: Public Domain
(L->R) David Getz, Janis Joplin, Sam Andrew,
James Gurley, Peter Albin

Unfortunately, Thornton once again received small publishing royalties when *Ball and Chain* became a hit. Bay-Tone Records held the copyrights and were entitled to all the royalties. During her later efforts to secure the royalties from the song, Thornton described how she had written the song 9 years before she recorded it, saying: *"I was singing that way before I recorded it."*

Ultimately, Thornton acknowledged receiving some royalty payments after the release by Joplin. *I gave her the right and the permission to make 'Ball 'n' Chain' . . . It's all right, it made me money. At least I got paid for it, and I'm still drawing royalties.*[285] With the success of Big Brother's *Cheap Thrills* album, Arhoolie Records released Thornton's recording of *Ball And Chain*. This release was a way to capitalize on the success of Joplin's cover.[286]

The Ash Grove was the center of Blues in Los Angeles in the late 1960s. Big Mama Thornton played a number of shows at this very popular venue. In 1966, Big Mama and band leader Curtis Tillman hired Bernie Pearl to play guitar for the first Ash Grove show by Big Mama and her band..[287] Another performance at the Ash Grove was from April 28-30, 1967.[288] Additional performances at the Ash Grove were in January, 1968 and from May 25-30, 1968.[289]

Big Mama Thornton At The Ash Grove, May 25-30, 1968

**Big Mama Thornton and Her Band, Circa 1968
(L->R): Terry "Big T" DeRouen, Unknown, Big Mama
Thornton, Everett Minor (called "E Minor")
Courtesy: collection of Terry DeRouen**

Later in 1968, Big Mama Thornton made some changes in her band. Edward "Bee" Houston replaced Terry "Big T" DeRouen on the lead guitar. Curtis Tillman re-joined the band to play the bass guitar. Terry DeRouen became a member of the Bernie Pearl Blues Band in the 1990s. Bee Houston also eventually became a major recording Blues musician in the Los Angeles area.

Curtis Tillman   "Bee" Houston

In September 1968, Thornton appeared at the Sky River Rock Festival with a lineup that included the Grateful Dead, James Cotton, and Santana.

During the 1970s, Big Mama continued to record more of her songs such as *She's Back* (Backbeat) and *Jail* and *Sassy Mama!* (Vanguard). She also toured extensively through the United States and Canada.

In 1973, Thornton was diagnosed with cancer. Shortly after her cancer diagnosis, Big Mama was involved in a serious auto accident. This car accident left Big Mama Thornton fighting for her life, confined to a hospital bed for six long months. Most people assumed that she would never perform again, due to the pain and uncertainty of her recovery. These setbacks tested her resolve. But Willie Mae Thornton was familiar with pain and suffering.

Willie Mae Thornton fought back. Her miraculous recovery left everyone stunned. Thornton rallied to perform at the 1973 Newport Jazz Festival with Muddy Waters, B. B. King, and Eddie "Cleanhead" Vinson. This performance resulted in a live recording, *The Blues—A Real Summit Meeting* (Buddha Records).

Thornton spent most of 1976 performing at The Rubaiyat Room, at 2022 West Adams Blvd. This club was located in the Hotel Watkins in the Crenshaw District of Los Angeles.

Rubaiyat Room

Courtesy: Tom Reed

Eddie "Cleanhead" Vinson and Dan Papaila were regular performers at this club. Thornton would perform regularly, mostly singing *Hound Dog*. Papaila observed, *By this time she was quite frail, but she had a great impact on the audience.*[290]

However, cancer and the years of heavy drinking began to affect Thornton's health. Big Mama had to be led to the bandstand at the 1979 San Francisco Blues Festival. Despite her illness, Willie Mae Thornton gave a stunning performance.

Thornton performed at the Newport Jazz Festival on July 2, 1980. She also performed in the "*Blues Is a Woman*" concert that year, alongside Sippie Wallace. Thornton sported a man's three-piece suit, straw hat, and a gold watch. She sat at center stage and played pieces she wanted to play, which were not on the program.[291]

One of her notable performances was at the 1981 Juneteenth Blues Fest in Houston, sharing the bill with John Lee Hooker.[292]

Despite her poor health, Willie Mae Thornton continued to perform. She would often make unannounced guest appearances at clubs in south central Los Angeles. At those small clubs such as the Tiki Lounge on Western Ave, a thin and weak Willie Mae Thornton had just enough strength to perform a single song. Despite her waning health, Willie Mae always delivered those songs with the gusto and fire of her youthful days.[293]

Willie Mae "Big Mama" Thornton was found dead at age 57 by medical personnel in a Los Angeles boarding house on July 25, 1984.[294] Thornton died of heart and liver disorders due to her longstanding alcohol abuse. She had lost 105 pounds in a short time as a result of illness. Her weight had dropped from 200 pounds to 95 pounds.[295]

A funeral was held for Willie Mae Thornton at Conner Johnson Mortuary at 4700 Avalon Blvd in Los Angeles. Rev Johnny Otis, her old friend, conducted the funeral. Two hundred friends attended the funeral. Blues singers Jimmy Witherspoon and Margie Evans sung at the funeral. Tina Mayfield, wife of Blues singer/composer Percy Mayfield read a short obituary.[296]

Sadly, Percy Mayfield himself would die a few days later on August 12, 1984.[297]

Thornton was buried in Inglewood Park Cemetery in Los Angeles County, California. Pall bearers for the funeral were Terry DeRouen, Jeremiah Wright, Eldridge Hall, and OB Wright.[298]

Her pauper's grave features a small granite marker with two additional name. These markers indicate that her body was buried along with two strangers.[299]

Big Mama Thornton summarized her life.

> *I've been happy. There have been dull moments, but you have to take as worse as you going to get it or else you are never going to see it. And I've been happy and I'd like to stay that way.*[300]

Thornton's final compilation, *Quit Snoopin' Round My Door*, was released posthumously by Ace Records (U.K.).

Visiting Mance and Lightnin' (Xmas, 1973)

Xmas in Texas '73

On November 11, 1973, the Ash Grove was burned to the ground. I never heard if there was an investigation of the cause of the fire, or any result. My brother had been very active politically, and it has been speculated that his activism prompted the arson. I had been working outside the club for several years and was not directly involved in bookings or other functions, but I was concerned that the Ash Grove seemed to be waning. Lightnin' Hopkins, on one of his last runs there, commented that the place seemed "haunted". His word.

It was obvious that my mentors would not be coming to "my house" again, but there were other places in L.A. where they would be welcome. I had long thought of going to Texas to visit Mance in Navasota, and Lightnin' in Houston. I thought that going around Christmas time would work, and I called them both at home, and both said, "come on". I can't recall where I was working at the time, or was "at liberty" to just pick up and go. Plane fare and auto rental was beyond my financial reach, so it was "go Greyhound", and leave the driving to them.

I had checked details by phone and drove to the Downtown station, or so I thought. I saw a big Greyhound sign and went in. I arranged for my ticket, to only discover later on the trip that they had made an error in my routing. A bump in my road, in a couple of ways.

I packed a minimal clothes bag, encased my mahogany Martin 0017 guitar, and headed East. I became friendly with my seatmate, a young man about my age of Mexican heritage, and we chatted all the way to Arizona. Once in Arizona, the game changed. At one point during the night, the bus was pulled over by the police. Whatever agency it was, they pulled off all Latin-looking people and questioned them. When they were finally released back, my buddy sat down (his name was possibly Phillipe) and commented something like, "Welcome to America. This is what they do." I was shocked and outraged. We discussed it and rolled on.

There was a dusting of snow on the ground as we continued on into Texas. That was surprising to me too. It was a long trip and we stopped at a café in the morning. A welcome break. It was also a place to pick up new riders. Official. I glanced at the roof of the building and saw some lettering that had been chipped away, but was still quite legible. It said "colored entrance".

Bus Station Waiting Room Sign **Door Entrance Sign**[301]
Source: *Library of Congres*

My jaw dropped. This was 1973, this was a national transportation business, and there were laws. On June 3, 1946, the US Supreme Court ruled in Morgan vs Virginia that racial segregation on interstate bases was a violation of the interstate commerce clause.[302] On December 5, 1960, the Supreme Court ruled in Boynton vs Virginia that segregation was prohibited in waiting rooms, lunch counters, and restroom facilities associated with interstate travel. Both rulings were largely ignored in the southeastern, southern, and southwestern areas of the US.[303]

Or were there? It seemed obvious that there had been a perfunctory attempt to comply with the letter, but not the spirit. The reminder was, "You're still in Texas, remember that." Left a bad taste in my mouth, to this day. Those folks are still around, in heavy numbers.

We re-boarded and continued on until we stopped at where I was supposed to change buses. I showed my ticket, and a very nice bus driver informed me that my ticket wouldn't get me to Navasota. We were discussing how to correct it, when a second driver, who turned out be my next driver, started jawing about it being a phony ticket and was about to deny me passage. The first driver remained calm and straightened the route out, the second one grumbling.

While I was as polite as I could be, the guy just didn't approve of my beard and semi-long hair. In fact, when I went to board, he told me not to play any damned guitar on the trip. In fact, we loaded my guitar in the general baggage compartment under the bus. I kept my mouth shut.

A Typical Small TX Town Bus Station

We rolled peacefully into the Navasota station a while later. It was a good riddance, and I had no further unpleasantness in Texas.

With Mance and Family

Once in Navasota, I went to a pay phone (you remember those, don't you?) and called Mance. He said he'd be right there. There was a florist nearby, and I bought some flowers for Mrs. Lipscomb. Mance soon drove up, hat cocked over one eye, and greeted me.

Mance Lipscomb

Hat Cocked

1973

It was an old car, I don't recall the model, but it ran well. I went to go to the passenger side, but he asked me if I could drive. I had my license and was pretty reliable behind the wheel. Essentially, he gave me the car for the duration of the visit. He directed me to his house at 907 Washington Ave.

Mance Lipscomb At 907 Washington Ave In 1972
Source: 'Le Blues Entre Les Dents'
(The Blues Between the Teeth), 1973

It was a modest building, which he was able to purchase using settlement money from a work accident. I'm sure that the money he earned from playing helped later on, but he had bought this on his own. It was on the outskirts of town, and had retained its rural quality. He had some room to plant, raise his greyhounds, have a couple of milk cows, and enough space to buy a small home for his son, Mance Jr. and his large family, and have it placed on his property. He was proud of being able to do that.

I entered and met Elnora Lipscomb, his wife. Friendly and welcoming, she wore slippers because she had some leg trouble that hindered her from lifting her feet.

Elnora Libscomb, 1972

Source: 'Le Blues Entre Les Dents'

I had seen her in the Les Blank film on Mance, "A Well-Spent Life". She was featured frying chicken for Mance's dinner, a mouth-watering scene. I experienced her cooking first-hand, delicious. One other thing stood out about the scene. She said that she never ate with Mance. She said that once she prepared a meal for him and, he didn't show up. She told him that from then on "everyone's got to eat for himself". He looks a little sheepish when he makes a joke of it. I always wondered about the incident. She stuck to her word the rest of their lives. If one needed further evidence of the resolution and problem-solving abilities of Texas women, the film presents it.

There is footage of a neighbor of the Lipscombs who had just one leg, full of joviality, riding a spirited horse. Mance explains that he used to mistreat his wife, drank, and generally carried on. A Navasota no-goodnick. One day, after he had abused her once too often, she took her shotgun out to the fields where he was working, and blew his leg off. They stayed together. Mance comments, "He's a good man now!" The man laughs.

I had no idea where I was going to sleep, but assumed I'd have me a pallet on the floor in the house. It was Christmas week and the house was full of kids. Mance said that he'd made arrangements with a local guy who had a motel. To be truthful, I wondered if there was some reluctance to having a white man sleeping in their place, even if only to avert talk among his neighbors. Nonetheless, we drove to the motel. It was seedy as could be, and would not have passed a rodent-control inspection, but the bed was clean, and I was exhausted. Looked like home to me, at least for a few days. I took all my meals with the Lipscombs.

The day after I arrived, Mance wanted to show me around town. At the top of his agenda was to show me downtown Navasota, the spot where the final lynching took place. On March 7, 1908, John Campbell was taken from the Navasota County Jail by a mob. Campbell was taken across the street to the Farquhar Meat Market. He was hanged from a telephone pole. Frank Hamer was hired after this event to prevent future lynchings.[304]

As we looked around, referring to the several white men sitting nearby, Mance commented, "Some of these old boys was there." He went on to say that Texas Ranger Chief Frank Hamer, of Bonnie and Clyde fame, put an end to it, saying that "this will never happen no more". And it didn't.

Next stop was at a place (a nice barrelhouse) that he had played at for years, but had not played recently because he was told that his music was too old-fashioned. Ironically, he had agreed to come and play for a family reunion that afternoon. Elnora questioned him about that, and Mance replied, "I gave my word". End of discussion. He introduced me to the owner, a Black man, smiles all the way around. Mance said, "This is Mr. Pearl, come all the way from California to visit." I'm pretty sure that he had had occasion to present people who just "came to visit" in recent years. People from all over the world, where he had played his music and made friends. We did play the family reunion, and the family had folks from L.A.

Mance Jr. was taller than his dad, but he looked very similar to Mance Sr. And he could even play like him. Regretfully, I had no way to record the music. One of his local disciples came over and we had a session. Mance showed me around his property. No more cows, he explained, because none of the youngsters wanted to do farm work. I don't recall the exact number, but Mance Jr. had a lot of kids. Other family was visiting as well. I recall a phone call Elnora took where she was admonishing a relative who said he couldn't make it by saying, "You can make it if you try". The grands all referred to Mance as "Daddy Mance", a reference I use in my song "Sittin' on the Right Side of the Blues".

We stood on his porch, looking out into the distance and Mance told me that he was having some health issues, and he had engaged a "conjur woman" to come to his place and tell him what she could. He said she was an old blind lady, but she could sense things and pointed out where everything was. He felt she had helped him. Mance Lipscomb lived another three years.

When I took my leave on my way to Houston a couple of days after Christmas I told the Lipscombs how much I would miss them. Elnora sent me off with, *I guess you gonna miss me from slidin' 'around the house.* A memorable adieu.

As to the separate eating question. It may have been answered by the appearance sometime after Mance's passing of another Lipscomb son (Mance only claimed one child) who proved his identity and was accepted by the family.

The 3rd Ward – Lightnin' at Home

I said my goodbyes to the Lipscomb family and boarded the Greyhound bus to Houston. At the station I saw a taxi and asked the Black woman driver if she was free. She was, and I put my guitar and bag in the trunk. She asked me where I wanted to go. When I told her the address at 3124 Gray St. in the 3rd Ward, she answered incredulously, "Are you sure you want to go THERE?"

I said yes, and she asked again. I responded that it was Lightnin' Hopkins' address, and her face brightened up and we were on our way. It wasn't a long drive. When we arrived, Lightnin' and his wife Antoinette were waiting outside the front door.

The cabbie jumped out of her seat, went up to him, and in short time he was signing an autograph.

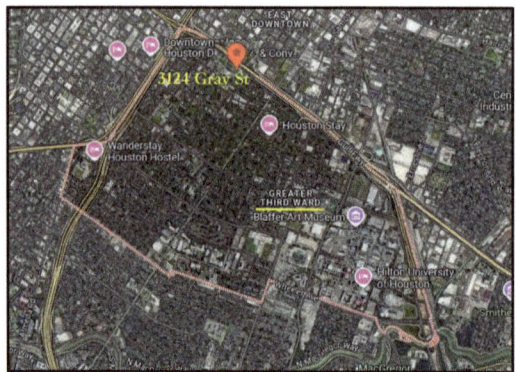

**3124 Gray Street
[dark red pointer]
3rd Ward Houston**

Houston established the 3rd Ward in 1839. After the Civil War ended former slaves from the areas surrounding Houston began to move into the 3rd Ward. Between 1910 and 1930 the Black population in the 3rd Ward exploded from 22,929 to 66,357. As a result of the rapid population growth, Black owned businesses increased along Dowling Street. As a result, Dowling Street became the center of Houston's blues movement. Blues clubs were lined up and down the street and became places where artists from throughout the South and Southwest went to experiment and perfect their craft.

By the early 1950s, with the demise of segregation, wealthy and middle-class Blacks started leaving the 3rd Ward as they integrated formerly all-white residential areas. That outward migration continued through the 1960s and 1970s and included business departures. Those businesses that remained began to fail, leaving the 3rd Ward a shell of its former prominence.[305]

At the time of the trip in 1974, the 3rd Ward was the most violent ward in the city of Houston. Gangs, drugs and prostitutes populated large areas of the 3rd Ward. Gang wars with extensive gunfire exchanges occurred on a regular basis.

The 3rd Ward is where Hopkins performed regularly at Irene's Bar, the Showboat Lounge, and the Sputnik Café. In this ward, he held court in front of Johnnie Lee's Chinese Grocery.

Lightnin' Hopkins In Front Of Lee's Grocery
Courtesy: Chris Strachwitz Collection/Arhoolie Foundation

In the back of Shorty Calloway's Auto Shop, Hopkins shot dice with his cronies. Lightnin' Hopkins drove through the streets of the 3rd ward in his black 1977 Cadillac Coup de Ville.[306]

Lightnin' Hopkins could be regularly seen walking through the streets in the 3rd Ward of Houston. In later years, Hopkins lived at 3405 Dowling Street in the 3rd Ward. As he grew in fame, he performed more at the high end clubs on West Dallas Street in the 3rd Ward than in the lower end bars above.

Lightnin' Hopkins Walking In The 3rd Ward With His Guitar

Hopkins and his wife Antoinette, lived in the Chateau Orleans Apartments, which were located at 3124 Gray Street.[307]

Chateau Orleans, 3124 Gray Street, Houston, TX

Chateau Orleans, 3124 Gray Street, Houston, TX

Lightnin' Hopkins and Antoinette Charles
Courtesy: Northwestern University Libraries[308]

It was a modest but modern apartment, two-bedrooms, neat and clean. I had no idea of what to expect, but was glad to see them living in a comfortable place. I felt very welcome. I put my things in the spare bedroom and we sat and talked. I'm sure there were delicious meals over the couple of days I spent there – we took all our meals in-house – but my strongest recollection is of the tranquility in their home. Lightnin' was about 6 foot tall and thin. I had observed that he ate sparingly on the road, as he didn't trust that his food had been prepared properly, and may not be healthy for him. I don't recall any reluctance to eat 'Nette's cooking.

He drove me around that first night to show me the neighborhood. Then he mentioned that his cousin 'Hop' Wilson lived nearby, and would I want to stop by there? Harding 'Hop' Wilson got his nickname because he started out playing the harmonica, and that was the way the 'harp' (Hop) was pronounced.

However, his fame, local as it was, came because of his lap-steel work. I was not into the instrument at the time, was exhausted, and I wasn't that excited. Big mistake. Nowadays, I am a devotee of the lap steel, working on both Blues and "Sacred Steel" playing. In fact, I play steel with the church band at the monthly "Gospel Brunch" at the Plain Truth Mission Center at 95th and Avalon in L.A. If I could kick my own butt, it'd be black and blue for having passed on a chance to meet Hop Wilson, one of the greats. Lesson learned, hopefully.

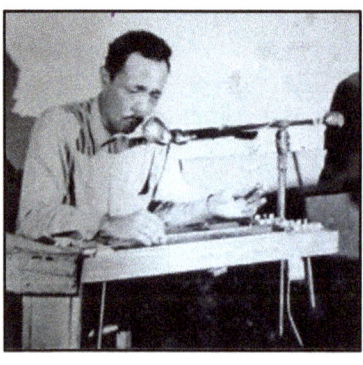

Hop Wilson

Playing

His Lap Steel Guitar

The couple of days spent with Lightnin' and 'Nette were not full of activity, but were really pleasant and relaxing. An opportunity to see him in another setting. Bonding, I'd say.

He had a New Year's Eve gig to drive to, and I had a bus to catch. I did have further chances to see Lightnin' again in L.A. but, as expected, it wasn't the same having him at the Ash Grove. When we started the Long Beach Blues Festival in 1980, I immediately called him. But, he had already been diagnosed with lung cancer and had stopped touring. Memories of seeing him at home, relaxing in his 4th Ward home made all the more precious.

The Greyhound trip back to L.A. was uneventful, but my bag of memories was quite full. It has endured over many years.

Dylan in the Afternoon (Mid 1970s)

In the mid-70's I was living upstairs in a modest duplex just off the end of the Glendale Freeway, they called it Frogtown. I got a call from a classical guitar friend of my pal Phil Boroff. I had met Morris Mizrahi a couple of times, but was surprised to hear from him. Morris lived in Malibu, where he had a successful printing business, and knew his way around town. He had met another Malibu resident, Bob Dylan, and had engaged with him about music and the guitar. He said that Dylan was interested in meeting a slide guitar player. Morris immediately thought of me, and wanted to know if I was interested in meeting with Dylan at his house that coming weekend. I said of course, and got the number to call. It was Bob's home number and he answered when I called. We talked and arranged a meeting for the coming Sunday.

The day arrived, I grabbed my Martin and a slide and drove across town to the coast and found the place without trouble. It was a large house on a large lot and, as I recall, I drove through the gate right to the front door.

Bob Dylan House, 29400 Bluewater Rd, Malibu, CA

I was surprised that there was no one at the gate or at the door when I knocked. Bob himself greeted me and we went and sat in what I remember as a modest kitchen nook – not very different than what I have in my house now.

We talked for a while about the Ash Grove, which he was familiar with, and the players I learned from, whom he was also familiar with:

Brownie & Sonny, Lightnin', Mance, Fred McDowell, Gary Davis, and , Bukka White. We might have talked about Israel too. After a while he offered up a joint, and we smoked a little. I soon played some slide songs, probably Fred McDowell tunes I had been working on. He seemed to enjoy it.

We got up, and in the adjoining spacious, largely unfurnished living room, he showed me a lap steel guitar on a stand. He asked if I knew anything about it. At that time I hadn't thought about playing lap steel at all. I strummed the strings a little and told him I really couldn't play it. Ironic, considering that nowadays I'm all but obsessed with lap steel for both Blues and Church music.

I look for places where I could do a number or two. Oddly, audiences have responded well enough to keep me enthused about learning more. I play with the house band in Lester Land's monthly Gospel Brunch/Music Service at a church in South L.A. It has been held sporadically due to pandemic concerns, but I play whenever possible.

The day was going on and I took my leave. Bob was friendly and congenial throughout our couple of hours together that afternoon. I enjoyed meeting him and expected nothing further from it. A nice afternoon memory.

Terminal Island (Late 1970s)

Meeting Edie

While I was teaching at McCabe's in the late 1970's I met a lovely lady named Edie and we got together.

**McCabes Guitar Shop, 3101 Pico Blvd, Santa Monica, CA
Courtesy: Cbl62, English Wikipedia, CC BY-SA 3.0**

I was single and looking, as was she, and we decided to set up house together. The question of where was solved practically and, if you will, romantically. Edie had been offered a job running a marina store in Wilmington. She had been a' sailing, knew the hardware, was familiar with life on a boat, even one tied to a slip. Fellows & Company had built small craft for the U.S. Navy during WWII, but now that the war was over, they downsized their nautical building side and ran two moderate-sized marinas, one in Wilmington and one on Terminal Island. Each had a moderate-sized store that served the needs of their tenants, many of whom lived on board, while some came and stayed weekends. They needed someone reliable who knew what was what on a boat. Edie was perfect.

Only problem was, she needed a nearby place to stay. As it happened, the Terminal Island marina had a small building on the dyke in which a night watchman used to sleep and cook. Terminal Island is an actual island in Long Beach harbor and needs built-up areas to keep the sea from swallowing it. Company management offered to refurbish the guard shack to the point of habitability as part of their employment offer to Edie, and, as it turned out, a guitar-playing landlubber from L.A.

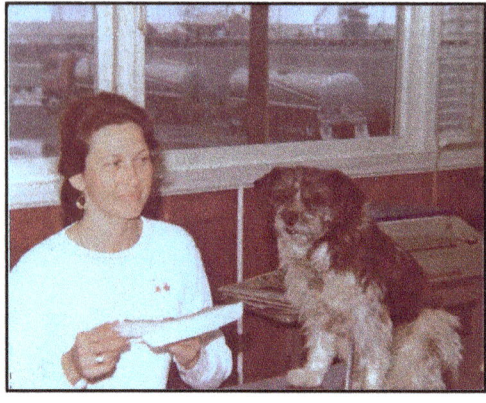

Edie And Knuckles

Courtesy:

Bernie Pearl

Temporary housing was not an issue as Edie had refurbished the interior of an International Harvester step-van to accommodate two campers, cozy and comfortable. We connected to Marina electricity and moved into a vacant lot which had been used to win the war in the Pacific.

We moved in around the time of the Iran hostage crisis, and the beginning of the Reagan presidency. Edie began work, driving daily over the drawbridge that connected Terminal Island and Wilmington. I continued teaching. I would go, on occasion, to Smokey Wilson's Pioneer Club to listen to the blues, Southern style. I had had grown close to Smokey, and had introduced Edie to him. We both adored him. He was, as was said at the time, "SOMEBODY". He was so great a player, and drew in other great players. Blues was alive in L.A. and something should be done about it.

Moving In

At a certain point, the guard shack had been declared ready, and indeed it was. A small kitchen, a working shower and sink, a small elevated double bed, drawers for clothes and bedding and, best of all, a small, window-enclosed living room from which we could look out and see many boats, tied to the floating docks, masts asway. The whole thing could fit in a fair-sized living room. Don't mention the front yard, an endless dyke, or the back yard, Long Beach harbor.

It was a lovely little place. But, it needed music. We didn't have a radio or phonograph, just a little TV, which we turned on as soon as we sat down after moving in. Much to my surprise the TV only had audio. In fact it was not broadcasting a TV show, but radio. I listened and was floored when it began playing Albert King! Was I interested. Listening on, more blues, and then an announcement that I was tuned into radio station KLON, from Long Beach City College. The announcer was named Dan Jacobson, his show was "Blues After Hours". I found the number and called.

Dan Jacobson, 2009

It was late Sunday night and was told that this was a taped show, but the host would be in the next day. I could hardly wait to talk to Dan. I called and spoke with him. He knew who I was. He had listened to "Nothin' But the Blues" on KPPC. Sounded like we had much to talk about, and we made an appointment to meet in person.

1st Annual KLON Long Beach Blues & Gospel Festival, 1980

The Smoke – Pioneer Club Blues (1978)

Bernie Pearl and The Pioneer Club

I was reading the L.A. Weekly, our local alternative paper at the time. I looked at the music pages and glanced at the ads. One jumped out at me. It welcomed everyone to come and listen to the blues at the Pioneer Club, 88th & Vermont, and listed a phone number with what had to be a South L.A. prefix. It may have also shown the name of the promoter, Smokey Wilson, a name I had never heard before. It spoke to me. It challenged me.

In all my years playing behind a who's who of the Blues, I had done almost all of it on the Ash Grove stage. I had not yet been South to play, and I had not been to any Black clubs in L.A. In fact, I wasn't aware of any Black clubs where you could hear the Blues. The Ash Grove had closed and I was a Blues orphan. I had been thinking about calling the Pioneer Club when I attended my nephew Steve's Bar Mitzvah ceremony (1978). I had a good time at the after-party, and even took my two left feet to the dance floor. I figured that I was ready to call Mr. Wilson. I got back home and dialed the number.

Robert Lee "Smokey" Wilson

I was tentative in discussing my background, but I was met with an outgoing personality who knew everyone I was talking about, including the local musicians I had played with, including George "Harmonica" Smith, and bassist Curtis Tillman. Smokey was welcoming and told me to come on down. It was a Saturday, and I couldn't have picked a better time to enjoy the unexpected riches that the Pioneer Club offered.

I found the pink Pioneer Club on the corner, parked on the street, and walked in looking for Smokey Wilson.

The Pioneer Club, 88th and Vermont, Los Angeles
Courtesy: Erik Lindahl

There he was, his trademark cowboy hat on, behind the bar, serving up ice-cold quart bottles of beer. They didn't pour at the Pioneer. He was as outgoing, friendly, and welcoming in person as he was on the phone. This was, essentially, a juke joint. Mismatched tables and chairs and a large place on the concrete floor for dancing. The joint was indeed jumpin'. The Blues was going on onstage, guitarist Joe Kincaid's band, and they were "gettin' it".

Joe Kincaid (left) and Smokey Wilson (right), Pioneer Club
Courtesy: Erik Lindahl

Have I found my new Blues home? Is this Paradise? Through the evening musicians would get up to play the Blues, the way it's supposed to be. There for the Blues, the crowd loved it. Most were from the Deep South, had grown up with the Blues, and knew what they were hearing. They were at home. Smokey continued serving from behind the bar as the non-stop music continued. Not until late in the evening did he get up with his guitar. And then, Lord have mercy, he played the Blues like I never heard in person. Outrageously loud, the band cranking, with a powerful, emotional vocal mastery, and an incredible guitar, Smokey embodied the demonic Blues man. I couldn't believe what he was doing. I couldn't give words to what I was experiencing.

Smokey Wilson Plays

Courtesy: Erik Lindahl

I had met my wife-to-be, but was still living in L.A. I told my friend Phil Boroff about the Pioneer Club, we went together one night. Though a Classical and Flamenco guitarist, he had nonetheless experienced the authentic blues at the Ash Grove and had a deep appreciation of musical mastery in any genre. He was similarly taken with Smokey.

I went to the club one day with my fiancé Edie to introduce her to Smokey and his wife Celia. It had been whispered to me that Celia was the deed-holder on the property. Edie told me that while I was talking with Smokey, a man had approached her, opened his coat and offered her drugs from the variety pinned to the lining. She declined. Neither of us spoke of this to Smokey.

Once while visiting during the day, the subject of gangs and gun violence came up. Smokey smiled and said he had no problems with gangs. He went on to say that every so often – I imagine that he had a sense of when to do it – he'd go outside the club, stand on the corner where he could be seen and open coat to display the .45 in his waist belt. He smiled and said, "Naw, they don't bother me".

I saw trouble in the Pioneer Club just one time. Two men were getting a little heated. One was Skip, a white guy who lived in south LA, the drummer in the band. Skip picked up some drum hardware and was threatening to use it on the other guy, who wasn't backing down. Smokey, standing behind the bar, said something like, "Cut it out", and knocked his large ring on the bar loudly and got their attention. Both men immediately broke it off and went their own ways. At the Pioneer Club Smokey ruled.

If you went into the backyard of the club, you were likely to see racks set up. These were used to display fruits and vegetables that Smokey would sell. "Where do you get them?" I asked. He responded that when the club closed he would get in his truck and drive up to Bakersfield (about 100 miles north of L.A., up Highway 5) buy them from the produce market, along with local vendors, and then head back to the Pioneer. Fresh vegetables and fruit were generally unavailable locally. He was providing a lacking service. He was an entrepreneur. He also ran what I would call an unlicensed pawn-broker business in musical equipment. I was offered needed equipment, but suspected it might be "hot", and declined. If I am mistaken, I beg his heavenly pardon. Life can be like that.

Hearing Smokey Wilson for the first time had a significant impact on my future and the future of the Blues in Los Angeles. As I listened, I imagined that demons were flying around the ceiling. The real deal Blues had come alive for me. Smokey and the Pioneer Club enhanced my imagination. I had attended outdoor Bluegrass festivals and asked *Why not the Blues?* I had the idea and now the inspiration. Smokey was living proof that the real Blues were alive and well in

Los Angeles! But, I didn't yet have the place. Then, I moved to Long Beach with Edie.

Smokey Wilson and His Music

Later in life, Smokey Wilson once described his style of Blues in an interview. *When it come down to that cornstalk, corn shuckin', 'tater diggin', hog killin', milken' them cows and churnin' the butter off that milk, you lookin' at this old man.*[309]

You only had to hear Smokey Wilson play once to know that you were in the presence of a real and unique Bluesman. Smokey had a powerful voice that could range from soft and velvety smooth to a rough growling Howling Wolf voice. His guitar playing was razor-sharp and stinging. He made every note count.[310]

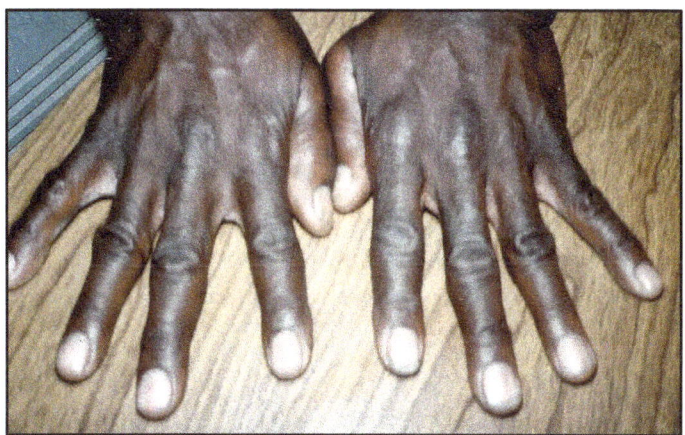

The Working Man's Hands of Smokey Wilson
Courtesy: Living Blues Magazine, Issue #240

Band members playing with Smokey quickly realized that Smokey was very demanding. You had to keep an eye on him at all times. Smokey constantly gave visual cues to bring the band down to a whisper or to bring the band back up to full roar. If the band member was looking away into the audience, missed a cue or played the wrong chord, Smokey would look at the band member over the top of his glasses. He gave a stare that actually would send shivers down the spine of the band member.[311]

Once Smokey hit the stage, nothing else mattered but playing and singing the Blues for his audience. Few musicians ever hit the level of intensity and emotion reached by Smokey when he was playing.[312] Smokey prowled and danced on and off the stage all night, despite his having lost a leg in a driving accident.[313]

Who Was Smokey Wilson?

Robert Lee "Smokey" Wilson was born on. July 11, 1936 in Glen Allan, MS. Glen Allen is a very small town (pop 250) in the heart of the MS Delta about 7 miles east of the Mississippi River.

Smokey was actually born on a plantation. His mother worked for the "boss man" caring for his home. Smokey had life relatively easy in those days. The boss accepted Smokey pretty much as part of the family. Smokey played with the children of the boss and went on trips to town with the children.

As a child, Smokey's burning desire to play the blues had to be satisfied on a homemade broom handle and bailing wire guitar until his mother bought him his first acoustic guitar at age thirteen.[314]

In his teens, Smokey regularly attended performances by Howling Wolf and BB King when these musicians came through town. His teenage years were spent developing his singing and playing skills.[315]

When he was a young man, Smokey worked as a truck driver on a local route which ended with physical consequences.

I was driving on the highway one day when I seen an automobile go out of control in front of me. I could see children inside. If I had driven straight ahead them kids would all die, so I made me a new right-of-way. I made me that new right-of-way through the trees linin' the road. After the dust cleared, I found I was pinned in the cab of the truck. The emergency crew was busy tryin' to free me.

My first memory after the accident was waking in the hospital and seein' my leg suspended from a sling. I thought somethin' felt strange and soon realized that my leg had been removed from jus' below the knee. I cried and cried, but cryin' didn' change anythin'. Afore I left the hospital, I decided I was not goin' to let the situation get me down or hold me back.[316]

Smokey began by teaching himself to play the bass and the 6-string guitar.[317] In 1961, Smokey became a member of his brother's band, Junior Green And His Soul Searchers. Smokey played drums and bass in his older brother's band until he could outplay his sibling on guitar.[318] The band was then renamed "Little Robert and the Soul Searchers" and toured Southern juke joints with Roosevelt "Booba" Barnes on harmonica.[319]

Nearby Greenville was a hotbed of blues activity and spawned a new generation of bluesmen. Artists such as Little Milton, Frank Frost, Sam Carr, Big Jack Johnson were nurtured in the juke joints around Greenville.[320]

Sometime in 1966, Smokey left the Soul Searchers along with Roosevelt 'Booba' Barnes.[321] After joining Barnes, Smokey and Barnes continued to play all over the MS Delta region on tours with Big Jack Johnson, Frank Frost, and Johnny Dyer.[322]

In 1970, Smokey's mother died. Smokey felt that he had no reason to remain in MS. He packed up his gear and moved to Los Angeles, hoping that his down-home style would be popular. To his surprise, Smokey checked around and found that local Blues groups were not playing the down-home style Blues that Smokey played.

When I first come to California, wasn't nobody playing no blues… That funk and disco, I didn' want to go out there and hear that. They said, "what you lookin' for?" I said, "I'm lookin' for some cotton field, pullin' corn, muleskinnin' blues." So they told me, "You better play 'em then."[323]

So, Smokey started to play his version of the MS Delta Blues in a number of local clubs. His style became very popular since many Los Angeles residents had grown up in the South. This music reminded the listeners of home.[324]

Smokey was so successful that he became half-owner of the Casino Club, where he worked on a regular basis. In 1972, Wilson sold his interest in the club and bought the Pioneer Club at 88th and Vermont in south central Los Angeles.[325] **Under the management of Smokey Wilson, the Pioneer Club became the center of Blues in south Central Los Angeles.** Artists such as Percy Mayfield,

George Smith, Lowell Fulson and Big Mama Thornton played alongside Wilson.[326]

For the next 5 years, Smokey never slept much. He fronted the house band at the Pioneer Club on weekends. He also sold vegetables from the back of the Club to the neighborhood. Finally, in 1977, he received a break that helped to bring him some regional recognition. Smokey was signed to a recording contract with Big Town Records in Los Angeles, owned by the Bihari Brothers. In 1977, Big Town released the album *Blowin' Smoke*. This album was followed in 1978 by the release of *Smokey Wilson Plays the Blues*.[327]

Throughout the 1980s, Smokey continued to play primarily at the Pioneer Club but was beginning to perform at other locations.

By 1990, Smokey was playing on tours all over the world. In 1990, he toured Europe along with the Bernie Pearl Blues Band, Floyd Dixon on the piano, and Joe Houston on the saxophone.

Sadly, Smokey Wilson closed the Pioneer Club in 1992. Smokey spent the rest of his career playing at clubs around Los Angeles and touring all over the world. In 1999, he participated in a tour in Japan with the "Andy T" Talmantez Band. Every night was a performance before a packed house. Smokey was on fire, in top form, and the Japanese fans loved him.[328]

Throughout the 1990s, Smokey recorded a number of other albums. These albums did not have much commercial success

In August, 2000, Smokey Wilson participated in a recording session with Andy Talamantez and the old Smokey Wilson band lineup. Smokey brought his family along to watch the recording session. He placed his family in the control booth. During the recording session, Smokey performed and danced just as if he were on stage in front of a 1000 fans.

After recording three songs, Andy suggested that Smokey could pack up and go home. Smokey responded, *I ain't done yet. You keep recordin'*. After 3 more hours of recording, an additional 7 songs had been recorded. Most of the songs were completed in one take. Smokey told Andy, *You better get it right, 'cause I ain't comin' back*.

Sadly, Smokey Wilson was correct. Nine (9) days after the recording session, Smokey Wilson suffered a major heart stroke. His days of performing and touring were over forever.[329]

On Sept 8, 2015, Smokey Wilson died in his sleep in Los Angeles.

Sam King and The Pioneer Club

In the 1970's, Sam King played drums behind Freddie King, his cousin, and the great Blues guitarist Albert King.

Ronnie McMillan, Bernie Pearl, Sam King
Courtesy: Sam King

About 1977, a young Sam King began to play the drums behind Smokey Wilson at the Pioneer Club. This Club was located at 88th and Vermont in south central Los Angeles.

Sam King, 1980

Playing With Smokey Wilson

1st KLON Long Beach Blues Festival

Sam really liked playing with Smokey Wilson at the Club. However, shortly after starting at the Pioneer Club, Sam King encountered a bad experience.

In 1977, I had just bought a Lincoln Continental Mark V. I had the car parked in the back lot of the Club. This parking lot was on the west side of the Pioneer Club. During the first break, I took the band out to the back to see the new Mark V.

While the band was admiring the car, I went across the street to the liquor store and purchased a Mountain Dew. I went back to the car where the band members were admiring the new car. Everyone returned to the club. I needed to close and lock the car. So I lowered the antenna to the car and raised the windows.

Then, I happened to look into the rear view mirror. I saw two Black guys walking east up 88th Street towards the back of the club. I locked my car, then headed east on 88th myself to enter the Pioneer Club. The two Black guys caught up with me. I greeted these two guys.

One grabbed me. The pair took me back to the rear of the Pioneer Club. The person holding me was choking me. The other person said, Hey, mutha' fucka', give me your money. I replied, I don't have any money. So, the partner went into his pants and pulled out a .38 revolver. Suddenly, the gun was pushed up under my throat. Hey, fucka', give my your money. I stayed calm but told the guy holding the pistol, I don't have any money. I'm just a musician trying to make some money. The guy holding me released me. But, the pistol holder whacked me really hard in the jaw with the barrel of the revolver. I was almost knocked off my feet, he hit me so hard.

Both the robbers looked at each other. Then, the one holding the revolver looked at me, Motha', fucka', next time have some money. Then, the pair casually walked off as if nothing had happened.

I was a trained boxer. If not for that gun, this whole incident would have turned out differently!

I was never bothered by the pair again. On the day after, I told my brother Lee and some fellow band members about the incident. At first, the group did not believe that this happened. But, my jaw had really begun to swell from being hit so hard with the pistol. After seeing my swollen jaw, my brother Lee, and my other bandmates realized that the story was true.[330]

Clearly, the location of the Pioneer Club at 88th and Vermont was in a really dangerous area – the hood. A Black band member was being robbed by two fellow Black residents of the area.

Despite this experience, Sam King played with Smokey Wilson until about 1990. At that time, Sam King and his brother Lee formed The King Brothers.

**The King Brothers: Sam King, Lee King
Courtesy: Sam King**

This band was one of the leading Blues bands in Los Angeles during the 1990s.

Bruce Krell and The Pioneer Club

In 1981, I was working full-time at Hughes, an aerospace company in El Segundo. I had began teaching Computer Science part-time at CA State University at Long Beach.

One day I arrived early and was sitting in the Math Dept office. I picked up a copy of the student newspaper. I found an ad for a radio show on KLON at CSULB. This show was *Nothin' But The Blues* hosted by Bernie Pearl. I was exposed to and have liked Blues and Black Gospel music since I was born.

Bruce Krell, 1983

Yep, This Was My Real Hair-Do

I started listening. Bernie kept talking about Smokey Wilson and live Blues shows at the Pioneer Club at 88th and Vermont. I had only been in Los Angeles for 4 years. So, I checked with friends. Everyone told me not to go into that area. But, I had lived in the hood in New Orleans and Houston for 10 years before moving to Los Angeles. So, neighborhoods like 88th and Vermont don't intimidate me.

I can still remember that first day that I went to the Pioneer Club. My first impression was *I'm home*. This place was like all the juke joints and clubs where I had spent lots of hours in MS (growing up) and in New Orleans and Houston (going to school). Back then, I listened to the same music and the environment and people were the same.. *This joint was jumpin'*, as stated by Fats Waller.

When Smokey Wilson and the band played, you could not sit still. You had to get off your butt and move. This music by Smokey and the band had a rhythm that infected your very soul. You just had to move.

.Smokey Wilson Performing At The Pioneer Club

(Joe Kincaid, Guitar, With Afro, At Left Of Smokey's Hat)
(Buddy Clemons, Trumpet, Vocals, In Upper Right)
D V Chatmon, Bass, Blind (Not Shown)
Courtesy: Erik Lindahl

Smokey Wilson was the real deal Bluesman. He came from Glenn Allen, MS, in the MS Delta. But, Smokey Wilson had his own unique brand of the Blues. Smokey had a voice and a beat to his guitar playing that just set the listener on fire. He had a wooden leg to replace a leg lost in a work accident. Smokey would sometimes hop around on this leg as he played. He would beat the guitar with the heel of his hand, play the guitar with his teeth, and play the guitar behind his back.

At the Pioneer Club, you could play pool for 25 cents a game. A quart of beer was $2.50. Lots of beautiful women were available to dance, drink and just have fun if you were alone. Some were just there to have a good time. Others were for sale, although I never participated in any of that activity. If I took a date, I was almost guaranteed to spend the night with my date. Something about the music would get under the skin and require intimacy and passion.

I had a bunch of interesting experiences at the Pioneer Club.

One time I took some friends to the Pioneer Club in an old beat up van I owned. While we were in the Club, someone stole the battery out of the van. I asked Smokey if I could use his phone to call a cab. *Sorry, we don't got no phone in the club.* Fortunately, Mogi, one of the customers, managed an apartment building across the street. He let me use his phone to call the cab company. When I called, the dispatcher told me, *Sorry, we don't go into that area at 2 am!* I told the dispatcher, *You have 4 of the whitest honkies in the world sitting an a street corner in south central Los Angeles. You can't leave us stranded.* He reluctantly agreed with a warning *The driver will slow and if he doesn't see you coming to the cab, he will leave immediately.*

We waited in the doorway of the Club. As the cab approached, we scrambled from the doorway, falling into the open door. The driver was a young Black kid in his 20s. His eyes were big and round, totally afraid. He looked at us like we were crazy. But, he did get us back to my house. We gave him a big tip.

Another time, I went to the Club by myself. I was sitting quietly at the bar drinking beer. A very pretty Black woman sat down beside me. I bought her a beer. We got to talking. After a bit, she gave me her name and number. I asked her where she worked. She said that she received child support from the five fathers of her five children. She was beautiful, but I did not want to be father number six.

Just as I was about to leave, Ms Smokey, (Celia Wilson) pulled a revolver from under the bar. She pointed the gun into the air and started firing. While she fired, she looked at the young woman next to me and started yelling, *You, bitch, get out a' here and stay away from my man.* And, then she fired some more into the ceiling. Apparently, Smokey had girlfriends. Maybe, these girlfriends were the reason that Smokey and Celia eventually divorced.

As the shooting started, I dove underneath one of the tables next to the bar. I looked out and saw a bunch of heavy bouncers dragging the young woman out of the bar. I came out from under the table. Everyone was simply sitting where they had been sitting before the shooting began. Just a normal night at the Pioneer Club, I guess.

And, then, …

My friend Dean Forbes came from Houston to visit for a weekend. On Saturday night, I suggested we go to the Pioneer Club for some real Blues. Dean liked the Blues. I told him about the area. Dean was a sworn Deputy Sherriff in Harris County where Houston was located. He had spent plenty of time in the hoods, like the 3rd Ward. Going to south central did not bother Dean. We went to 88th and Vermont.

About midnight, the band had taken one of its short breaks. I was always bringing groups to the Club. Smokey knew me by name. He always made a point to say hello and to individually thank my guests for coming. So, this night, Smokey came up to me and Dean. *Bruce, I have something I want to show you. Come out back with me.*

Dean and I went to the back parking lot with Smokey. He took us to the rear of his Continental Mark V and opened the trunk. Inside were mason jars of Mississippi moonshine. Now, I grew up in a small town in MS, Jewish in the middle of Klan country. And, I knew all about moonshine. If moonshine is yellow or smells or both, then the moonshine is bad. Copper from the metal tubing of the still has leached into the alcohol. Bad moonshine can blind you or kill you. This moonshine in the mason jars was crystal clear and had no smell, perfectly pure and probably about 90% alcohol. Dean and I drank moonshine with Smokey.

All I could think was, …

> *midnight, Saturday night, in the hood, south central Los Angeles, drinking moonshine from mason jars out of the trunk of a Continental Mark V with a Blues singer. Doesn't get any better.* **And, that's the Blues!!**

Playing The Blues (1979)

Boboquivari

Having spoken with Dan Jacobson at KLON on the phone, I felt like I was coming in as a known entity with credibility, as indeed I was. He had hinted at the possibility of returning to the air, which I desired, but wasn't on my mind when I called the station initially. I was just so happy to find that there was blues coming out of Long Beach. I had never heard of KLON. I had broadcast *Nothin' but the Blues* on KPPC for about two years. It ended, and I can't recall the circumstances, but around that time I began working outside of the Ash Grove, occasionally returning to back such notables as JB Hutto, Johnny Shines with Big Walter Horton, Koko Taylor, who constantly complained that I didn't back her like Robert Nighthawk did – a most reasonable plaint, and the great Freddie King.

Koko Taylor
Queen of the Blues

Freddie King
Texas Cannonball

Bernie Pearl Plays With Freddie King Live

On the other hand Freddie liked my backing and the band I brought in – largely the guys from the Big Mama Thornton days, bassist Curtis Tillman, pianist Nat Dove, and a drummer friend Bill Henderson. Freddie was asked to record a show at Public Television's studio on Melrose. The segment would be part of a series focused on Afro-American music called *Boboquivari*. I believe that Lightnin' and Mance Lipscomb had also recorded segments.

I learned a real important lesson there before the show. I had been under the very mistaken impression that blues guys were competitors who wouldn't hesitate to one-up one another if they could. I couldn't have been more wrong. Blues players tend more to community and helpfulness. Sure, there is competition in ways, but don't be an asshole, to speak bluntly.

Freddie had travelled west without an amplifier, and used one provided by the club. Apparently, that was not available for the time needed, and there was concern over what he would play for the program. No worries. In walks Albert Collins with his Fender amp for Freddie's use. They were fast friends from years of playing in Texas. Natural competitors, but friendly as all get-out. I took it all in, and took it seriously. Attitude don't go in these circles.

But, there was a bit more to it too. I had noticed that when you mentioned a Texas blues player you had "discovered" to Lightnin' Hopkins, he responded, "Yes, that's my cousin". Texas Alexander, Lil' Son Jackson, Smokey Hogg, and most almost every Texas Blues man you could name drew the same response, "Yes, that's my cousin." I asked about Blind Lemon Jefferson, and Lightnin' said, "No, but he was a family friend. Used to come for Sunday supper." Witness that Lightnin' in his pre-teen years used to travel with Jefferson to assist him.

I took this statement to mean that Lightnin' merely referred to the artists as "cuz'n" to denote a comradeship rather than a blood relationship. Wrong again. When I mentioned both Albert Collins and Freddie King and got the usual response from Mr. Hopkins, I took it to them both, and they both affirmed that Lightnin' was indeed their cousin, and went into how they were related. We recorded the *Boboquivari* segment, and it can be viewed on You Tube. Pretty darn good, if I may comment.

On Wed, Aug 4, 1971, Episode 1 of Season 1 of *Boboquivari* aired on PBS. Freddie King was the star of that episode.[331] I accompanied Freddie on that show.

Network writers and planners had Freddie King on Episode 1 of Season 1 because that the network felt that Freddie was the most important of the musicians. Having Freddie in that first episode of the series would spark great interest in the viewing audience.

Bernie Pearl and Freddie King, Boboquivari, 1970

Bernie Pearl, Freddie King, and Elton Something

Freddie re-hired us when he returned to the west coast shortly after his first engagement.

He was, by then, working on a recording with Leon Russell, who would come into the club with his band and do Freddie's second set with him, working out material for their recording. Friendly guys, fine musicians who came up with Freddie's classic "Goin' Down", and elevated Freddie's name to a much-deserved higher recognition.

Leon Russell was featured artist on a big show at the Anaheim Convention Center, Freddie was to open the show.

Freddie King and Leon Russell

It was an immense venue filled with people waiting for the fireworks. We opened, Freddie ablaze. I was totally at home as his rhythm guitarist, and we were takin' it to 'em. And then, out of nowhere, Freddie threw me a solo in the key of B flat. Instinctively, I found a position that worked, and scratched out something that actually had the crowd oohing and aahing….until I ran out of gas. Freddie picked it up and scored a touchdown. My jaw still drops, but I learned that I was not meant to be any kind of guitar idol. Getting a huge crowd roaring for you is heady stuff, but you really have to want it and love it enough to dedicate yourself to that purpose. My love of the blues lies elsewhere, and that is where I've put my passion.

Freddie absolutely won the audience over, as he always did, and then came the second act….a pianist/songwriter from England named Elton something, that the audience really liked – to say the least.

Freddie King kept a fairly high profile professionally for a while, then became ill and passed away on Dec 28, 1976, far too young at 42. I went to see Brownie & Sonny at the Lighthouse in Hermosa Beach one evening and ran into Freddie. He was friendly as always, but I felt that his energy was down and feared there was something going on with him. There was. A great loss.

Who Was Freddie King?

Freddie King was known as *The Texas Cannonball*. His music was a powerful fusion of the raw and gritty east Texas Blues and the sophisticated techniques of Chicago Blues with hints of R&B and rock. This unique combined style resonated with listeners worldwide.

Freddie King

King's guitar playing featured vibrant and explosive solos, haunting soulful bends, amazing fingerpicking skills, captivating rhythms, and heartfelt vocals.[332]

Fred Christian was born on Sept 3, 1934, in Gilmer, TX. His parents were John Tyler Christian and Ella Mae King. When Freddie was 6 years old, his mother and his uncle Leon King taught Freddie to play the guitar. As a youth, King purchased a Roger's acoustic guitar with money he had earned picking cotton.

In 1949, at age 15, Freddie and his family moved from Dallas to the South Side of Chicago. At age 16, shortly after moving to Chicago, King started sneaking into South Side nightclubs, where he heard blues performed by Muddy Waters, Howlin' Wolf, T-Bone Walker, Elmore James, and Sonny Boy Williamson.

In 1952, at age 18, King started working in a steel mill. In the same year he married Jessie Burnett, another Texas native. Freddie and Jessie had seven children together. In 1952, while employed at the steel mill, the 18 year-old King occasionally worked as a sideman with such bands as the Little Sonny Cooper Band and Earl Payton's Blues Cats.

King formed his first band, the Every Hour Blues Boys, towards the end of 1952. This trio included King, the guitarist Jimmie Lee Robinson and the drummer Frank "Sonny" Scott.

Every Day Blues Boys, circa 1953
(left to right) Sonny Scott, Jimmie Lee Robinson, Freddie King

In 1953 King recorded with the Blues Cats and Earl Payton for Parrot Records. These recordings were never released.

As the 1950s progressed, King played with several of Muddy Waters' sidemen and other Chicago mainstays, including the guitarists Jimmy

Rogers, Robert Lockwood Jr., Eddie Taylor, and Hound Dog Taylor; bassist Willie Dixon; pianist Memphis Slim; and harmonica player Little Walter.

In 1956 Freddie King cut his first record as band leader for El-Bee Records. *Country Boy*, on the A side, was a duet with Margaret Whitfield.[333] *That's What You Think*, a King vocal, was on the B-side. Both tracks feature the guitar of Robert Lockwood Jr. At the time, Lockwood was also adding rhythm backing and fills for records by Little Walter.[334]

Initially, King gave his first name as Freddy, ending with a "y". Some time later, he changed his first name to Freddie with an "ie".

King was repeatedly rejected in auditions for the Chess Records, the premier Blues label. This label which was the recording home of Muddy Waters, Howlin' Wolf, and Little Walter. Chess felt that Freddie King sang too much like B.B. King. However, a newer Blues scene was burgeoning on the West Side, lively with nightclubs and upstart record companies.

In the late 1950s, the bassist and producer Willie Dixon was undergoing a period of estrangement from Chess. Dixon was employed at Cobra Records. Dixon asked King to come to Cobra Records for a recording session. Those recordings have never been heard. Meanwhile, King established himself as perhaps the biggest musical force on the West Side of Chicago. He played along with Magic Sam and reputedly played backing guitar, uncredited, on some of Sam's tracks for Chief and Age labels owned by Mel London. King does not stand out on those recordings.

In 1959 King became friendly with Sonny Thompson, a pianist, producer, and A&R man for King Records of Cincinnati. Thompson recommended Freddie King to Syd Nathan, owner of King Records. Nathan signed King to Federal Records, a subsidiary of King Records. in 1960. King recorded his debut single for the label on August 26, 1960. King performed and Thompson produced *Have You Ever Loved a Woman* backed with *You've Got to Love Her with a Feeling*. Both recordings were credited to Freddy King. These two songs became perhaps the most famous of the songs released by Freddie King.

A Young Freddie King

During the 1960 recording session at the King Studios in Cincinnati, King cut the instrumental *Hide Away* along with *I Love the Woman*. *Hide Away* refers to Mel's Hide Away Lounge, a popular Blues club at the time located at 3945 S Indiana Ave on the West Side of

Chicago. Willie Dixon later claimed that he had recorded King performing *Hide Away* during that recording session at Cobra Records in the late 1950s. However, no such version has ever surfaced.[335]

From 1961 to 1963, Freddie King sold more records than any other Blues artist, including B.B. King. Freddie toured extensively in concert halls and nightclubs and performed at numerous jazz and Blues festivals throughout the US.[336]

In 1962, *Hide Away* reached number 5 on the R&B chart and number 29 on the Pop chart. Charting at these levels was an unprecedented accomplishment for a Blues instrumental at a time when the genre was still largely unknown to white audiences. *Hide Away* became a Blues standard.

After their success with *Hide Away*, King and Thompson recorded 30 instrumentals at King Records in Cincinnati. These recordings included *The Stumble, Just Pickin', Sen-Sa-Shun, Side Tracked, San-Ho-Zay, High Rise, and The Sad Nite Owl*.[337,338] Vocal tracks were recorded but these tunes were often released as instrumentals in an attempt to capitalize on the success of *Hide Away*. During this period, King also toured extensively with many notable R&B artists of the day, including Sam Cooke, Jackie Wilson, and James Brown.

Freddie was fond, perhaps overly fond, of the Chicago night life, *gambling 'til dawn in the backroom of Mike's cleaners*.[339] Jessie King wearied of her husband's gambling, carousing and his brutal recording and touring schedule. So, Jessie and their six children moved to Dallas in 1962.

Once in Dallas, Jessie called Syd Nathan, demanding that Syd send her some of the royalty money due to Freddie. To his credit, Syd sent Jessie $ 2,000. Jessie made a down payment on a house in Dallas with this money.[340]

After the house purchase, King realized that his family would not return to Chicago, So, King left Chicago and moved to Dallas to be with his family in spring 1963 at age 29. In Houston, King worked on perfecting his own soulful vocal style.[341]

King's contract with Federal expired in 1966. A first overseas tour followed for King in 1967. King Curtis, the producer and saxophonist at Atlantic Records noticed that Freddie King was not signed to any label. Curtis signed King to Atlantic in 1968. With Atlantic, Freddie King recorded two LPs: *Freddie King Is a Blues Master* (1969) and *My Feeling for the Blues* (1970). Both albums were produced by Curtis and released through Cotillion Records, a subsidiary of Atlantic Records.[342]

In 1969 King hired Jack Calmes as his manager. Calmes secured an appearance by King at the 1969 Texas International Pop Festival, alongside Led Zeppelin and others.[343]

Texas International Pop Festival, 1969, Freddy King
Source: Larry Willoughby Collection[344]

This performance led to a recording contract with Shelter Records. Shelter was a new label established by the rock pianist Leon Russell and the record producer Denny Cordell. Shelter Records treated King as an important artist. Shelter flew King to the former Chess studios in Chicago in 1971 to record the album *Getting Ready*. A lineup of top session musicians was provided during the recording, including Russell.[345] Three albums were made during this period. These albums included Blues classics and new songs, such as *Going Down*, written by Don Nix, released on the album *Getting Ready*.[346]

In 1971, King recorded the first major live album ever made in Austin, TX, at Armadillo World Headquarters. This Austin club/playhouse was sometimes known as *the House That Freddie King Built*. He regularly played at the club and returned periodically for fund-raisers.

In the early 1970s, King performed alongside the big rock acts of the day, such as Eric Clapton and Grand Funk Railroad. GFR even mentions King in the lyrics of its song *We're an American Band*.

> Out on the road for forty days
> Last night in Little Rock put me in a haze
> Sweet, sweet Connie, doin' her act
> She had the whole show and that's a natural fact
> **Up all night with Freddie King**
> **I got to tell you, poker's his thing**
> Booze and ladies, keep me right
> As long as we can make it to the show tonight
>
> We're an American band
> We're an American band
> We're comin' to your town
> We'll help you party it down
> We're an American band

1st Verse, *We're An American Band*, Brew Music Co

These performances were for young, mainly white audiences. These rock tours continued for about 3 years.[347] King had a multiracial backing band at these performances. Freddie King was one of the first Bluesmen to have a multiracial backing band, breaking barriers and setting new standards.[348]

Freddie King signed with RSO Records in 1974. During that same year, he recorded the album *Burglar*. Tom Dowd produced *Sugar Sweet*, a tune on the album, at Criteria Studios in Miami. Backing musicians on this track included guitarists Eric Clapton and George

Terry, drummer Jamie Oldaker and bassist Carl Radle. Mike Vernon produced the other tracks on the album.[349] Vernon also produced *Larger than Life*, a second album by King, for RSO Records. Vernon brought in other notable musicians for both albums, such as Bobby Tench of the Jeff Beck Group, to complement King.[350]

Freddie King was on the road almost 300 days out of the year. This nearly constant touring took its toll on King. In 1976 he began suffering from stomach ulcers. His health quickly deteriorated.

In Dec, 1976, King passed out in the middle of a solo while playing a club in New Orleans. He returned to Dallas, then played a gig in New York on Christmas Day. But he canceled a show scheduled for the next night. King immediately returned to Dallas and entered the hospital.[351]

Freddie King died of complications from this illness and acute pancreatitis on December 28, 1976. King was only 42 at the time of his death.

According to those who knew him, King's untimely death was due to stress, a legendary *hard-partying lifestyle*,[352] and a poor diet of consuming Bloody Marys. King claimed that he liked the Bloody Marys because *they've got food in them*.[353]

Freddie King is buried at Hillcrest Memorial Park in Dallas, Texas.

Bruce Krell Experiences Freddie King Live

On March 4, 1971, Liberty Hall opened at 1610 Chenevert, in a rapidly decaying area near downtown Houston.[354]

Liberty Hall, Houston, TX

Liberty Hall was relatively small, holding about 450 people. Stage and floors were wooden. This intimate setting allowed for good acoustics, different from very large, very open popular arena-style venues at the time.[355]

Inside Liberty Hall, circa 1975

This nightclub hosted musicians from the country, rock, zydeco, and Blues genres.[356] Soon after its opening, Liberty Hall had a six-week-long Blues show with musicians like Big Mama Thornton, Lightnin' Hopkins, John Lee Hooker and Freddie King.[357,358] Hopkins performed multiple times at Liberty Hall by himself and with Mance Lipscomb.[359]

Freddie King also played at Liberty Hall many times after the opening of the venue.

Live Music Performed At Liberty Hall, 1971

In addition to Blues, Liberty Hall was one of the first venues in the US to host the *cosmic cowboys*. These musicians emerged from the vibrant music scene in Austin, TX. Their music was influenced by Blues and Punk music. The cosmic cowboy movement represented a departure from the polished, formulaic approach of mainstream country music. Emphasis was placed on authenticity, creativity and a connection to the audience. Electric guitars were a primary instrument for these musicians resulting in a Blues rock sound.[360]

Jerry Jeff Walker, Michael Martin Murphey, Gary P. Nunn, Ray Wylie Hubbard, Doug Sahm (Sahm the Sham and the Pharaohs), Willis Alan Ramsey, Command Cody and the Lost Planet Airmen, Asleep at the Wheel, Kinky Friedman (the Texas Jewboy), Townes Van Zandt, Willie Nelson and Waylon Jennings. These guys changed country music by heavy dependence on the electrical guitar. At the time, producers in Nashville and Los Angeles laughed at these musicians. Now, most country music has electric guitars. These musicians were the pioneers of Blues based country rock music.[361]

All of these musicians performed thousands of performances at the Armadillo World Headquarters in Austin, TX. Freddie King was a regular performer at the Armadillo. He and the cosmic cowboys performed regularly at Liberty Hall in Houston. From 1974 to 1977, the Univ of Houston hosted live concerts on the quadrangle in front of the Student Union. All of the Cosmic Cowboys performed in those live concerts with free admission for students.

From 1973 until 1977, Bruce Krell was living in Houston, TX, working on his PhD at the Univ of Houston and Rice University. One day in the spring of 1976, Bruce was reading *The Cougar*, a newspaper for students at the University of Houston. Buried within the pages of The Cougar was the following advertisement.

These same posters were spread throughout the Student Union. Signs indicated the office where tickets could be purchased inside the building. No need to go downtown to purchase tickets.

I knew that Freddie King was a major Blues singer. I had a number of vinyl records (this was before CDs) by King. Liberty Hall was a well-known Houston performance venue at the time.

Tickets were actually being sold in the Student Union at the Univ of Houston. Bruce purchased 4 tickets for Sat, Apr 24, 1976, at that low price of $5 each ($ 28.19 in 2025), for himself, his wife, and another couple that were friends. Liberty Hall prided itself on keeping the cover charges low.

Two shows were scheduled for that Saturday night, as usual for Liberty Hall. One show was from 8-10 pm with a second show from 11 pm until 1 am. One ticket allowed you to watch both shows.

This small group went out for dinner that Sat night, April 24. After dinner, the group arrived at Liberty Hall around 7:00 pm. About a half hour after arrival, the doors opened.

We entered the venue around 7:40 pm. Shockingly, the venue was fairly empty. Seats were on a first-come, first-served basis. We took seats about the 3rd row from the front of the stage. Atlanta Rhythm Section played from 8pm until 8:45 pm. For us, this group was a big yawner. We had come to see Freddie King.

Immediately after ARS left the stage, Freddie King's band took the stage. This group played a number of solo songs. At 9pm, one of the band members spoke up. *Now, from Dallas, please welcome Freddie King.*

A hush fell over the sparse crowd. For a few minutes, the tension built. Then, a tall figure began walking out of the offstage shadows onto the stage. A collective gasp escaped the audience. Freddie King was walking onto the stage with a big grin on his face. And, King was just plain electric as he walked. We could feel the crackling in the air!

King was a tall man, 6' 5" tall with a wide girth. Freddie was just a big man physically Yet, he was wearing large high heeled shoes, increasing his height to over towering. He also wore a bright sequined rainbow colored suit. This guy walked with majesty and with electrical sparkle. Just breathtaking.

Freddie King, The Smart Dresser   **Rainbow Outfit**
                                                                                         High Heeled Shoes

Freddie walked out onto the stage. He plugged his guitar into his amplifier and slung the shoulder strap over his shoulder.

> *Freddie King struck a chord with his guitar. A thrill travelled down the spine of each member of the audience. The Texas Cannonball was about to treat us to some real Blues. ..., and, he did!*

Freddie King played a number of his great hits during the next hour.

> *Around 10 pm, Freddie finished his set and left the stage. He received a standing ovation from the somewhat sparse crowd. He returned to the stage and performed an encore song. He left the stage.*

Overhead lights came on. Our group began chatting. Shirley, my wife at the time (name disguised) said *OK, let's go now*. I asked, *why? That's barroom music*, she loftily replied. *You are damn right it is. I'm not leaving*. I simply was not going to miss another show by the Texas

Cannonball, one of my favorite Blues musicians. Shirley left in a cab. I stayed. So did the other couple.

As with many live events, the audience had further diminished in size as the hours grew late. And, like many live events, the second set was even better than the first set.

> *Atlantic Rhythm Section did not play at all during the second set. We were treated to two solid hours of Freddie King. And then we received a 2 song encore. All of us in the audience were just spellbound. Freddie King knew how to grab our attention and hold fast. This set was one of the best Blues shows I have ever attended, only surpassed by some of the live shows of Albert King.*

Sadly, this show on Sat, April 24, 1976, was the last show to be performed at Liberty Hall by Freddie King. He died 8 months later on Dec 28, 1976.

> *I was saddened to hear about the death of Freddie King. Freddie was a real musician and a real Bluesman. He likely had started to feel the effects of the cancers that were eating his body and killing him. Yet, that night, he gave one hell-of-a-performance. He could have dialed in the performance, just coasted through. Freddie King did not. He gave 100% to his performance, despite any sickness that might have weighed on him at the time.*

Keeping It In The Family

In the 1990s, The King Brothers, Lee King and Sam King, were the best known Blues band in Los Angeles. Lee and Sam were told that Freddie King was their cousin.

In around 1970, Jerry Combs, a director, invited Freddie to listen to Lee and Sam King play. Around 1972, Freddie King hired cousin Sam King to play in his band. Sam King played drums on tour for Freddie King for about 6 years until 1978.

Sam King and Lee King

In fact, the King Brothers were related to Freddie King through their father, Levester (Lee) King, Sr.

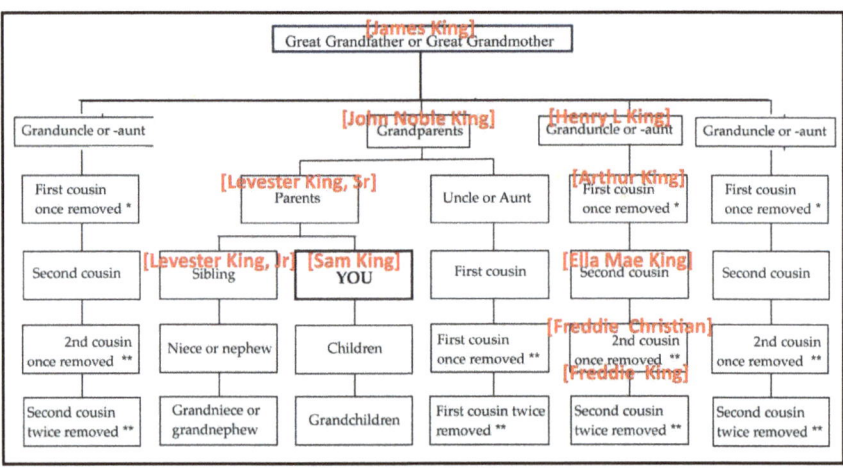

King Family Tree

Freddie King was the 2nd cousin, once removed, of Lee and Sam King! Lee and Sam are the descendants of grandfather John Noble King. Freddie King was the descendant of Henry L King, brother of John Noble King.

This King family was a musical family indeed.

Impact of KLON & the Blues Festivals

Bernie Pearl served as Artistic Director of the Long Beach Blues Festival from 1980 until 1990. Over that decade, a large number of Blues musicians from all over the US performed at the Festivals. Festivals extended into 2 and 3 days for much of that decade. Performers included the most well-known Blues musicians at the time. Each year, the crème de la crème of Black Blues artists appeared to larger and larger crowds of attendees.

The KLON Long Beach Blues Festival became the defining Blues event for southern CA. Demand for the Blues in affluent white areas lead to a large number of monthly Blues performances in West Los Angeles, Hollywood, West Hollywood and Chinatown. Blues performances were also extensively continued in west and south central Los Angeles and Watts as a result of *Nothin' But The Blues* hosted by Bernie Pearl and the annual Blues Festivals.

As the Festivals grew in attendance after 1980, Blues musicians from all over, including Chicago, appeared at the Festivals. In 1982, the Long Beach Blues Festival was broadcast on APR. These broadcasts helped create a nationwide interest in attending live Blues concerts. Headliners such as Albert King, Willie Dixon, Bobby Rush, and BB King enhanced the reputation of the KLON Long Beach Blues Festivals. Blues musicians from Chicago were performing at the Annual Long Beach Blues Festivals. Not surprisingly, in 1984, Chicago inaugurated its own series of Annual Blues Festivals.

By 1984, the Festival had grown to a 2-day event with 13000 attendees. After this peak, attendance settled in at about 8500 per year for the remaining years the radio show and Annual Festival were hosted by Bernie Pearl. After the departure of Bernie from KLON, annual attendance dropped dramatically.

At the time when Bernie began the *Nothin' But the Blues* radio show and the Blues Festivals, the only place to see the Blues in Los Angeles was the clubs in South Central Los Angeles. As a result of the radio show and the Festivals, a large number of venues in West Los Angeles and Hollywood began to host Blues performances.

Before 1980, Blues performances generally were not offered in the more affluent areas of Southern CA. Fans had to go into south central Los Angeles to hear the Blues. Then, from 1980 – 1990, Bernie Pearl hosted *Nothin' But The Blues* and conducted the Annual Blues Festivals.

After 10 years of these two activities, Blues had spread to more affluent areas in the Los Angeles area. In Jan, 1991, 16 Blues radio programs were broadcast from radio stations throughout southern CA **every week.**. These programs ran from 1 – 3 hours each. About 68 venues throughout the Los Angeles area had regular Blues performances. Venues ranged from Santa Monica to East Los Angeles (west to east) and Huntington Beach to Granada Hills (south to north).[362] During that same month, 43 Blues performances were given in these more affluent areas across southern CA. 26 days of the month had live Blues performances Many days had multiple performances, sometimes even on weekdays.[363]

By Jan 1995, 28 Blues radio programs were broadcast from radio stations throughout southern CA **every week**. These programs ran from 1 – 3 hours each. During That same month, 529 Blues performances were given in affluent areas across southern CA for that month of Jan, 1995. All 31 days of the month had live Blues performances at clubs in affluent areas. Even a weekday generally had 10 or more live performances at club venues. The Bernie Pearl Blues Band was among those performers.[364]

These statistics do not include ongoing Blues performances at locations throughout south central Los Angeles still continued. Locations like the Pioneer Club owned by Smokey Wilson, Babe's and Ricky's Inn, The Tiki Bar, the Parisian Room, The Spade owned by Phillip Walker and Club Safara owned by Shakey Jake Harris, among others.

Blues performances in the more affluent areas were financially beneficial to blues musicians. Fans in these areas could afford to pay cover charges and buy 2-drinks minimum. Big name Blues recording stars could often be seen these venues. Both BB King and Albert

King regularly performed at Concerts by the Sea in Redondo Beach. Memphis Slim and Albert Collins could be seen at the China Club in Hollywood.

Additionally, local Los Angeles Blues musicians were able to make reasonable incomes playing at these local venues. When a musician played at a local south central LA club, he/she might earn $25 for a 4 hour set. Most Blues musicians needed regular jobs to survive and to support families. At the clubs in the more affluent areas, these same musicians could sometimes make as much as $1000 for a 3 hour set. With all the clubs scrambling for Blues acts, a musician could often make a living playing the Blues.

Without Nothin' But the Blues on the radio and the growing Blues Festivals, Blues musicians would have still been earning $25 for a 4 hour set.

Joining KLON (1980)

Bernie Joins KLON-FM, some of 'em anyway

Terminal Island is adjacent to the city of Long Beach and its harbor in the west, and to San Pedro, which was part of L.A., and L.A. Harbor in the east.

The drive from T.I. to Long Beach was a piece of cake normally, with just one bridge to cross. It being a draw bridge, it regularly was raised for cross-channel sea traffic, and we motorists had to wait. Not a big deal, unless you were racing to get to Long Beach Memorial Hospital for the emergency Caesarian which delivered your first-born (it all worked out fine a couple of years later, by the way).

I went to the Pacific Coast Highway campus of Long Beach City College where the tiny facilities of KLON-FM were housed on the second floor. The station largely broadcast educational programming through the week, and had a music schedule on weekend nights: Polka, musical comedy, some Jazz, and late Sunday nights Dan Jacobson played the Blues.

Dan Jacobson

As it was a public station, it regularly held fund-raising campaigns on air. All this was explained to me by Dan, who hosted his "Blues After Hours" show. He explained that he was part of the governing board, was otherwise busy and had been looking to turn over his late Sunday radio spot to someone competent.

He had listened to my "Nothin' But the Blues" programs on KPPC-FM a few years earlier, and had caught a few shows I did on the LBCC student channel KSUL. I had been invited by my friend

Sharon "Cherry" Wood, a gifted graphic arts student at LB State, who had some connection there. I'd do the shows after I drove to LB after whatever day gig I had. I really loved being on the air. At any rate, Dan knew my work and was comfortable enough to invite me to co-host a couple of shows with him. I did so, and he offered the 2-hour slot to me – I accepted, and returned "Nothin' But the Blues" to the So Cal airwaves, late Sunday nights as it was.

**Nothin' But The Blues – During The First Few Months
Courtesy: Bernie Pearl**

There was an unexpected challenge to the return though. I was scheduled, but couldn't gain access to the second floor studios to do my broadcast. The host before me, Broadway show music, if I recall, would often neglect to pick up the phone when I called to identify myself, so that he could go unlock the door to the building. He knew when I was due there, but still did not answer. I often had to resort to throwing small stones at the studio windows to get his attention. Folks, this ain't no lie. Humble beginnings, indeed.

The First Fund-Raiser

I have no data to support this, but I felt a certain energy when I began doing my own show, and I felt that there was an audience gathering. A negative confirmation of this came from an essential cold-shoulder from the show tunes host and an icy-response when his show was reduced to give me a third hour, late as it was. Dan and his fellow board members seemed happy as we approached our first fund-raiser. I had not done one of these while at KPPC-FM. That was a commercial station, even though advertising was sparse.

I have to cast a small shadow on all this acceptance. I have never been convinced that all along, even through the years that followed, that radio Jazz hosts have real enthusiasm for blues music, or the seeming public embrace of various aspects of blues music. I contrast that with the attitude of acceptance, even reverence, of the core music that birthed Jazz among even the most polished musicians. Conversations over the years with renown artists such as John Collins (Nat Cole), Red Holloway, Plas Johnson (saxophonist on the "Pink Panther" theme, comments by Miles Davis, Wynton Marsalis and more recognize the importance of the roots.

KLON was public and a date was set. I was assigned to invite artists to the studio for a live broadcast. Dan had not been slow in the past in bringing blues musicians to the studio. In fact, he had some of the same guests I asked in. Even though there was no pay for musicians, the core of L.A.'s blues cats were ready. I was not quite integrated into the Long Beach scene in 1980 and cannot recall if I had invited the local great Blind Joe Hill for that show. I didn't miss having him at the first festival though.

I had kept contact with some key blues buds through this period, primarily George "Harmonica" Smith, Smokey Wilson, Marjorie Evans.

George "Harmonica" Smith   **Smokey Wilson**

Margie was not only working with the Johnny Otis Band, but was also an outspoken proponent of Black participation in Blues events. While I could not agree with her more, I sometimes thought she carried it to the stage a little more than was necessary.

Marjorie Evans

Nonetheless, she was an important guide and bellwether as things developed.

I called George Smith and he agreed to participate. He asked for William Clarke to back him - a local young white student of his I had not heard of.

William Clarke

George has been cited by almost every harmonica player of note on the West Coast as being their entre' into the Chicago style blues, particularly the playing of Little Walter. No better interpreter existed. I asked Smokey to play, and he accepted. I can't recall all who did that late-night fund-raiser on a tiny, low-powered, and almost unknown educational station on the second floor of Long Beach City College, but history was made that night.

During the show, I looked at Dan and commented, *Wouldn't it be great if we could do this for a live audience!* Dan had the same thought. I came from L.A. which had a large, outdoor old-time banjo and fiddle contest in Topanga Canyon, which also sported two competing major outdoor Bluegrass Festivals, but no outdoor Blues event. It seemed a natural to me. Odd that no one had yet tried one in L.A. (numerous subsequent failures perhaps pointed to trying other locations). Long Beach seemed open, fresh, and even ripe for a gathering of the Blues community – if even one existed. I though it did, and Long Beach looked like the place to raise the flag and see if anyone saluted.

My first call was to Smokey Wilson to see if he'd appear and play a tune or two for the fund-raiser. He agreed, as did several others, including George "Harmonica" Smith, and possibly Blind Joe Hill.

William Clarke backed George, but I'm unclear on who backed Smokey. You'd think I'd remember if it was me.

Blind Joe Hill

Although the station signal was very weak, and the audience was relatively tiny, the fund-raiser was a success. It led to adding a third hour to my show fairly soon after. Of even greater importance was that it led to the idea of having such a show for a live audience, and the idea of expanding to a festival was put forward and acted on. The rest is history. Blues history.

Bernie And The First Blues Festival (1980)

As we moved towards a firm date, there were several twists and turns to be negotiated, but all obstacles were overcome. I was grateful to have three Blues artists that I could consult for advice and support: Marjorie Evans, George Smith, and Smokey Wilson. When I say WE pulled it off, I recognize that without a lot of people pulling together, nothing can happen. The First Annual KLON Blues & Gospel Festival, July 20, 1980 was just such an effort.

Step One – Getting Approval

The four people with "boots on the ground" jobs at KLON FM 88.1 largely took up the idea of a live outdoor Blues Festival after seeing (I think) the potential of the blues for raising support money for the station. The only real blues fan among them was Dan Jacobson, but I think that Robben Romano had a rebellious streak in her that liked originality. I couldn't really get a read on Henry Glenn, and Ken Borgers was a Jazz guy, and was behind ways to support the station. They discussed it among themselves and then took it to the community governing body headed by prominent socialite, political leader, mover and shaker Ms Harriett Williams.

Lightning struck, and the project was approved! Never mind that there was a miniscule budget to work with, I was appointed Festival Director (no pay guaranteed) and assigned to work with the City to set a location and date, and to then book the talent. I was pretty sure, after conversations with my "shadow cabinet" of Smokey, George, and Margie, that money would not be the highest priority, but getting a festival started would be the prime objective. Granted, that was more my feeling than a clear plan by the community. It was, as the Little Walter tune said, "Just a Feeling", but oh what a feeling.

I enthusiastically informed my buds of the project's go ahead. Ideas were thrown at me, you ought to do this and that, such as include Jazz – an idea quickly tossed after Margie commented you can get Jazz everywhere, this is our thing, the Blues. We don't get the exposure. I did go for the idea of including some Gospel. Working with KPFK's Gospel show host Prince Dixon, we came up with a few acts to open the festival. I then went about sounding people of their availability and willingness. I met very little reluctance.

Prince Dixon

Then, as could be anticipated, the bomb. Well, not quite that calamitous. I had met with Parks & Recs representative Henry Zimmerman, and he offered Blair Field as the site for the Sunday, July 20 fest. Problem was that Blair Field was a baseball diamond used for the Summer League, and the hardballers were hollering.

The city then offered immense Veteran's Stadium. I was not included in this conversation and was, frankly, pissed. This also meant going back to everyone and, in my mind, re-negotiating. That was not to prove a problem, but it my mind it was a portent of insults and pushing arounds to come. I was, in fact, furious that I was not included in the conversation and was prepared to quit. I talked to George Smith, and he calmly advised, "No, Bernie. Don't do that. This is too important." He was right, and I went back to booking.

Step Two – Booking 1

Who to book, what to pay (given the tiny booking budget), how many to book, what order, who can headline? Well, if you're going to produce any project in the arts, you gotta' learn to deal. And, you gotta' deal honestly because all you have to offer is your credibility. Hey, you're the man, and the target should anything go wrong.

I looked at what money I had to pay and decided that I could offer each lead artist (or most) $100, and each supporting artist $50. I honestly can't recall if this extended to the Gospel artists who opened the show, but I can't imagine not paying them equally either. Prince Dixon M.C.'d this segment, which followed his weekly Sunday broadcast. Then I put on a couple of unknown artists of my own choosing, who played short sets gratis. A little pressure from friends, which is no way to book talent, helped the selection. A lovely lady with a beautiful voice and a bit of stage fright sang a tune or two, Ms Noqula Jones.

I was also approached by an artist and teacher I knew named Guy Carawan. Guy had been a prominent member of the L.A. folk community before moving to Tennessee and teaching at the Highlander School. Does it ring a bell? This is the institute which taught a non-violent approach to Civil Rights action, among whose notable students were Dr. Martin L. King, Jr., and Ms Rosa Parks. Guy was further notable for adapting a gospel tune to Civil Rights aims and teaching it to the movement's youngsters. The tune became the anthem, "We Shall Overcome". I listened to Guy, who told me there was a wonderful vocalist from the Movement who was living in L.A. I put Cleo Kennedy and Guy Carawan on for a couple of Civil Rights songs.

Guy Carawan and Cleo Kennedy
Courtesy: Bernie Pearl

Then we let the Blues loose.

Step Three – Booking 2 – What's a KLON?

As a general philosophy of booking I looked to people I had worked with. I called Big Mama Thornton first, when the event was still planned at Blair Field. She said she was going out of town, but it sounded like she's be back in time, and she gave me a conditional yes at first. Subsequent calls never firmed the booking up and I had to drop the idea. Too darn bad. She was living in L.A. and still performing. I also put in a call to Lightnin' Hopkins in Houston. Unfortunately he was ill, and not travelling by then.

Next, I looked to local people able to play, George Smith prime among them, not only for his faith in me and the project, but because he was a giant musician, a marvelous performer, and a kind of local god. Margie Evans, who demanded the queenly sum of $150 for her performance, which I ceded. Smokey Wilson, without whom there would have been less reason to do it. He was at the center of the real blues still going on in South L.A., and a world-class performer. I called on old friend Pee Wee Crayton, an historic figure in the West Coast Blues.

Pee Wee Crayton

After agreeing, Pee Wee said, casually, "What about Big Joe?" It had never occurred to me that Big Joe Turner, one of the creators of R&R, would be interested in such a low-paying event. I had a lot to learn. It was about being there, doing what he did, being included and maybe adored. I did ask Big Joe, and he agreed without protest.

Big Joe Turner

While my focus was L.A.'s vibrant Black Blues scene, there were white artists who were largely named as the desired back up bands by several Black artists. Most significantly, the Hollywood Fats Band, featuring guitarist Michael Mann. Young, Jewish, from the Valley, and looking nothing like an all-star blues whiz, he was all that and more. The most highly-respected young blues burner and traditionalist on the L.A. scene. Went on to play with notables like Muddy Waters and Albert King. He led a band of all-star side men behind several artists- Larry Taylor, Fred Kaplan, Al Blake, Richard Innis.

Hollywood Fats
(Michael Mann)

In booking a back up band for George Smith, I assumed that he again wanted William Clarke, so I booked him and he selected the Night Owls as his band. When I informed George, he said that he wanted Doug MacLeod, whom I never had heard of.

Doug MacLeod

Having already committed to book Clarke, I planned to give him his own spot opening the Blues section, about two hours into the show, with a set of rousing Mississippi harp tunes, and then booked Doug for George's set. William showed up at my house, upset. I saw this as his opportunity to grab the audience by the ear, he saw it as a downgrade. Never quite got over it, but did a fine set regardless.

I had also made the acquaintance of the entertaining and sometimes outrageous one-man-band, Long Beach's own Blind Joe Hill. A unique act, Joe was perfect for an outdoor blues show. I wanted to bring in at least one of the musicians I saw laying down the real blues at Smokey Wilson's Pioneer Club, and I selected Curtis C.C. Griffin.

Curtis CC Griffin

A powerful vocalist and fierce guitarist he filled the bill. But, he surprised me. I announced him and instead of stepping to the mic, he came running from the back of the audience to the stage. It took a long time and the audience just wasn't that interested by the time he got to the mic.

Expect the unexpected. I also asked legendary singer, guitarist, and band leader Lowell Fulson to play. It was he who told the young pianist in his band, Ray Charles Robinson, to stop imitating Charles Brown and to do his own thing. Ray listened, and then some.

Lowell Fulson

Lowell had been very popular among Black audiences (B.B. King was a great fan) in the 1950's and '60's ("Tramp!" was a big hit), but had faded, and was almost unknown among white blues fans. He wouldn't play for less than $350. Not until the end of booking did I find enough to hire him. Universally respected and liked, and of undoubted historical importance, Lowell finally got his money.

The show of some 8 to 10 hours was almost booked with artists who would entertain and play a great variety of real blues. But, we didn't have a headline act. One we could afford and who might serve as a magnet to a wide audience. I thought of my old Ash Grove buddies, who were genuine stars in the 60's and 70's, and who still had a name that resonated. I was on the phone to Joseph Chambers. I was able to pay the Chambers Brothers an affordable fee, they did me a big favor, and I was satisfied that they would be the stars to attract audience and close this historic show. I wasn't wrong.

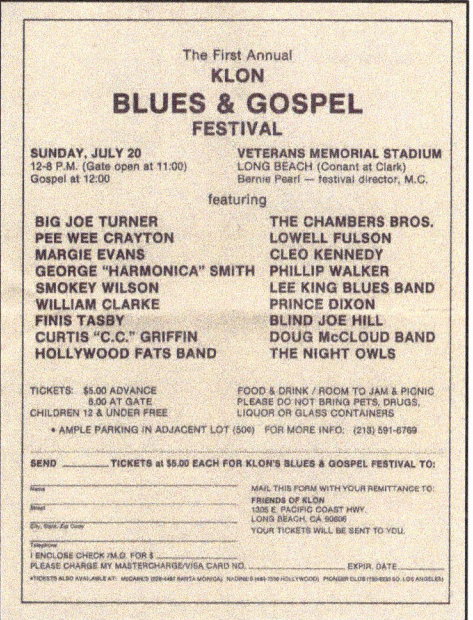

**Cover/Program, 1st Annual KLON Blues & Gospel Festival
Courtesy: Bernie Pearl**

All of the performers were local musicians at this 1st Festival.

The Day of the Festival

As people began arriving, the numbers were not impressive. Not overwhelming, but not a flop either. Dozens became hundreds, some 600 tickets sold, plus guests and others. Not the thousands I believed the show deserved – they were to come in the future – but still a hopeful number, and they were lively and enthusiastic.

1st Festival Entrance Ticket

As I gazed at the audience, I have to admit my heart swelled. It looked like America. I saw people of every color, hue, and identifiable ethnicity. This showed me that the music had a unifying magic and that we could be together and united behind something. No small thing in those times. I am something of an idealist and even a romantic, and thought that this turnout showed the unifying power and message of this music. A helluva big payoff by itself.

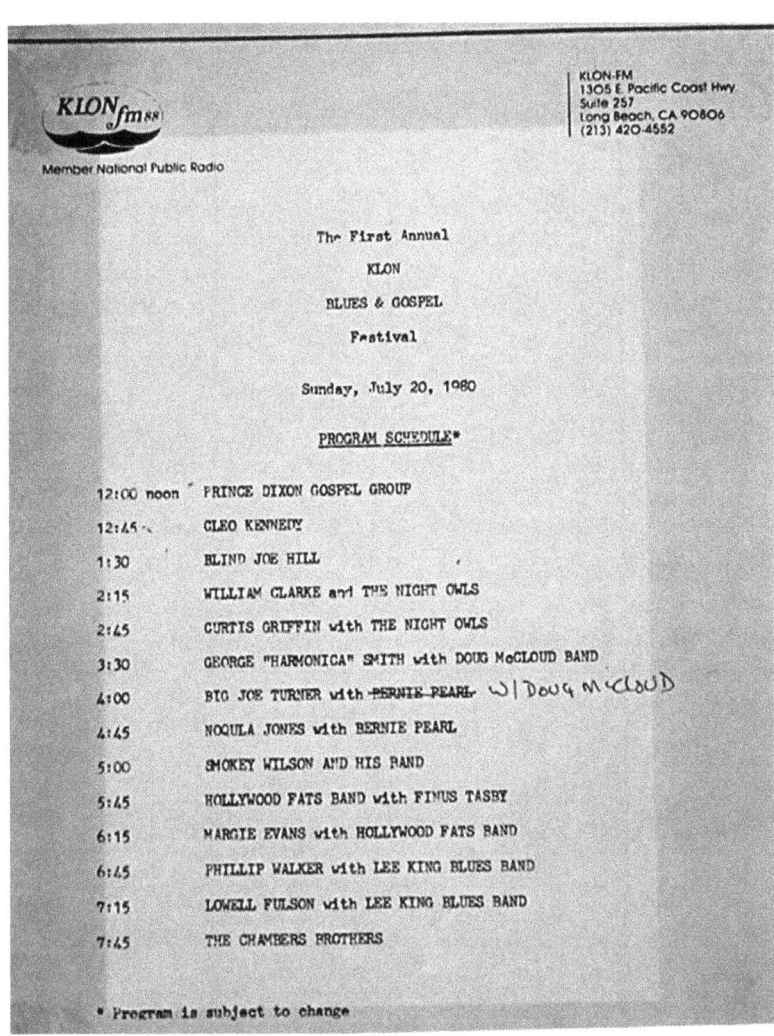

1st Festival Program Schedule

On the day of the 1st Festival, sunset in Long Beach was at 8:02 pm.[365] This was 15 minutes after The Chambers Brothers had started their 45 minute show, which ended about 8:30 pm.

It was dark when the Chambers Brothers took the stage and they dazzled with a great, satisfying and inspiring set of their blues/gospel/rock magic.

The moon shined bright as people made their way home from the enormous football stadium. That show opened up the Blues in Southern California, clubs, blues societies, competitor festivals. The Blues was back. KLON groused about not making any money. My thought was, were you asleep or just not paying attention. KLON FM 88.1 was truly born that day. The festival attendance doubled each of several succeeding years, and contributions bloomed. Their predominantly Jazz format drew new listeners, but the three hours on Saturday mornings of "Nothin' But the Blues" remained the most popular (and lucrative) show, and it grew too.

Did you not notice that the Earth stood still for just a moment on July 20, 1980 at the First Annual (I was optimistic) KLON Blues and Gospel Festival at Veteran's Stadium, Long Beach? People started to know what a KLON was.

1980, 1st Annual KLON Blues & Gospel Festival

All Photos In This Section Courtesy: Bernie Pearl

Smokey Wilson (right) and Sam King (left)

Smokey Wilson Plays The Guitar With His Teeth

George "Harmonica" Smith

Joe Turner, Pee Wee Crayton, Doug McLeod, Blind Joe Hill
(left to right)

Blind Joe Hill

Hollywood Fats (Michael Mann)

Pee Wee Crayton

Margie Evans

The Fruit Falls From the Tree

USC Extension I (1980)

Shortly after the 1980 1st KLON Blues Festival, I received a call from a colleague who taught traditional banjo styles at the Ash Grove School run by David Cohen and myself. We had started the school at the suggestion of John Cohen of the New Lost City Ramblers.

**New Lost City Ramblers
(left to right) Tom Paley, John Cohen, Mike Seeger
Courtesy: Smithsonian Folkways Records, Album FA 2494**

John told us of a school running in Chicago that taught the traditional styles of guitar, banjo, harmonica, etc. We jumped on it and named it "The School of Traditional Folk Music".

David Cohen and I were both guitarists exploring the traditional styles of many of the artists we were seeing on a regular basis at the club. There were those who knew and were able to teach other instruments. Stu Jamieson, an engineer by profession, was an excellent mountain-style banjoist who was our traditional (as opposed to Bluegrass style) banjo teacher. His wife, Gloria, worked at USC and proposed to the Adult Education Department that they ask me to teach a course on the Blues. I spoke with the chair, Chris Pasles, who also wrote music reviews for the L.A. Times. Based solely on Gloria's recommendation and our interview, Chris offered a once-a-week class in Blues history in the coming Fall session.

While I was not a historian per se, I did read a lot of material on the blues and felt I could present a series of non-academic lectures that would hold interest. My secret weapon was my intention to play a lot of recordings and bring in live guests. It actually worked out great. The only bump in the road was selecting a course name. I don't recall what my suggestions were, but Chris had already selected a name. He chose *Simply Blues*. Innocuous enough, but at the time there was a ritzy restaurant in Hollywood using the name, and it struck a chord with him. It struck me as being dilettante and off target. But, the one who writes the check…..

So *Simply Blue*s was posted and drew a decent number of enrollments. I enjoyed the preparation and the discussions in class, and I was able to bring in at least two notable live "informants". One was James "Shaky Jake" Harris, a recording artist from Chicago who knew all of the better-known names like Howlin' Wolf and Muddy Waters, and could speak authoritatively about them and the scene.

James "Shakey Jake" Harris

Jake was the uncle of one of the young and upcoming greats, Sam Maghett, who performed as Magic Sam, who had a tragically young death from natural causes. Jake also shared the origin of his name. He used to be called "Shake 'em Jake" because he loved gambling. In fact, and this is one really good reason to bring "informants" to class, you can get the real inside scoop (or a facsimile thereof). He said he really preferred gambling to being on stage. So often he'd do a number or two and then turn his show over to his nephew Sam and go backstage to gamble.

Magic Sam Maghett

That's how Magic Sam got his training and exposure. He made some very powerful recordings which really rank among the greatest of the so-called Westside Soul artists. Typically, born in Mississippi, raised in Chicago, putting emotionally charged songs over screamingly original and dazzling guitar riffs and solos, not cut from the same cloth as Muddy and company. Otis Rush is another of that school. Sam had a huge future, young, handsome, and a voice like a anguished angel. The course completed successfully, and I was asked to do a continuation the following session.

Another guest in that first session was Robert "Bumps" Blackwell, early producer of Little Richard's hits.

**Robert Bumps Blackwell
Guest At USC
Courtesy: Bernie Pearl**

I met Bumps at the Ash Grove when he was managing a Gospel act.

A Blues Society is Born (1980 – 1981)

At some point following that 1980 1st Festival, I got a call from KPFK blues host Mary Katherine Aldin (*Preachin' The Blues*). She said that Big Joe Williams was coming to town, needed a place to play, and we should get together a group to sponsor a concert with him. For the record, Big Joe Williams, from Mississippi, was a Blues revival on his own. He had never stopped playing and travelling, but as the first to record the classic *Baby, Please Don' Go*, he was among the first of the revival artists to start playing the clubs and college circuit in the early 1960's. He had an unique sound with his home-fashioned 9-string guitar, raucous playing style, and riveting delivery. An ideal blues paradigm, designed to entertain and hold audiences.

Big Joe Williams

Mary Katherine proposed that she, I, and Laurel Kenner, the blues host on KCRW FM, make an announcement that everyone interested in forming a Blues Society (there were the beginnings of a national move in this direction) get together at Barnsdall Park in East Hollywood. A lovely little park which famously was the site of a noted Frank Lloyd Wright building, an attraction in itself. We got together on a weekend afternoon, quite a few folks showed up. There was some music played, some brought picnics, and we talked among ourselves.

To follow up in a more organized way Mary Katherine had secured use of a meeting room at KPFK FM studios on Cahuenga Blvd, just west of Hollywood. Free-form discussion started to gel into concrete proposals for a blues organization. I, and my radio colleagues, made it clear that we did not want to be involved in running the group. A framework was worked out and a name was chosen. Not wanting to limit the outreach of the group, we all agreed to call it The Southern California Blues Society.

I didn't know most of the people there, but I did recognize one person who had taken my USC class. Betty Miller and her husband Jack had owned a club in Chicago and were ready to get involved here in LA.

Betty Miller

We were to become close friends over the years, and she and her husband ran The Music Machine, a club in west L.A, that was the site of many dozens of Blues shows.

The Music Machine at 1220 Pico Blvd
Courtesy: Marc Cantor

Betty and Jack knew the Chicago Blues scene from their days running a Blues club in Chicago. They were able to bring many of the Chicago Blues performers to play gigs in Los Angeles at their club as well as other places.

Betty took the Blues Society reigns for a long time. The Blues was on its' way in L.A. Big Joe got his showcase, and we had the key to Blues highway.

Jack and Betty Miller knew about hosting blues events from their experiences running a club in Chicago. These two also learned the names of many local Blues musicians through listening to *Nothin' but the Blues* on KLON FM. They also heard of other performers from attending local performances. Jack and Betty wanted to grow the Southern California Blues Society. Other members were also interested in extending the activities of the Society.

Beginning in 1980, Betty, Jack and other Society members began approaching club owners on the west side of Los Angeles. These clubs catered to local whites on the west side. A club owner would be approached to host a Blues concert performed by one or more local Blues musicians and sponsored by the Society. Gate proceeds would go to the Society. Bar revenues would go to the bar. By sharing in this manner, the Society would be able to raise funds for its activities.

Initially, white club owners on the west side of Los Angeles were resistant. Many excuses were offered. The Blues was an old, worn out format. Whites were not interested in hearing the Blues.

However, the Society had a secret weapon. *Nothin' But the Blues* was beginning to gain traction with white listeners up and down the coast of Southern California. Listeners were tuning into the radio show and were liking the Blues. As part of his program, Bernie would announce the Society sponsored shows on the west side of Los Angeles.

Finally, on Wed, April 13, 1981, the first Blues show was hosted by the Society on the west side of Los Angeles. This show was held at The Music Machine, 12220 Pico Blvd. Performers included Lowell Fulson and the Curtis Griffin Band.

Lowell Fulson   **Curtis Griffin**

Attendance at any Wednesday night show was likely to be poor. The performers, the Society and the hosting club made very little money. Fortunately, these performers were all living in Los Angeles and often had full-time jobs to earn a living. A second concert was held on Sat, Apr 16, 1981, at the Blue Lagoon Saloon, in Marina del Rey. Performers at this show were Lowell Fulson and Smokey Wilson, a Bluesman originally from MS, now living in Los Angeles.

The Play Is The Thing (1981)

Yerma

In early 1981 I got a phone call from Stephen Fisher, a theater director who was planning to stage a play by renowned Spanish playwright Federico Garcia Lorca, "Yerma", at the Odyssey Showcase in West L.A. The story of a woman, Yerma, her tyrannical husband, and a good man of the community. It concludes with the murder of the husband by his wife. It all takes place in a small peasant village in the Basque area of Spain.

He was calling me because he was planning to change the location from Spain to the American South, and he wanted to have live music that originated in the South, but did not want the usual fare that one might expect. He wanted authentic music that people had generally not heard before. Now, all that was well and good, but I was cautious about getting involved with a production that used dialect and drawls. He said he had been trained at the Royal Shakespeare Theater, and I decided to go see what was what at their first cast meeting at the theater.

I needn't have worried. The all-Black cast joked around with the clichés – I'm g'wan norf – and the like, but when it came down to reading, it was as Garcia Lorca had written it. Not a drawl to be heard. It was a lively group of serious actors. The director, Stephen Fischer, pointed out places for the music, which included some vocals and some dance movement.

While I am neither a songwriter nor choreographer, I thought I might just be able to bring something to the production. I had a pretty good record collection, and an idea of how to play "the songs that no one had heard", and I had been around members of just such a rural and traditional community who both sang and danced the music of their "forebears" as they called them.

Such a group had been organized to entertain wealthy White vacationers on their coastal island of St. Simons, Georgia. I don't know how much they earned for these performances, but it surely was far less than they deserved for bringing their precious heritage to light. Nonetheless, it brought in some amount more than they regularly earned.

They had been recorded by folklorist Alan Lomax on one of his trips South in 1959. The group, The Georgia Sea Island Singers, was led by a dynamic woman named Bessie (Elizabeth) Jones. There were five who came to the Ash Grove initially, Mrs. Jones, John Davis (called Moses by the group), Mrs. Emma Ramsey, Henry Morrison, and the youngest, Mable Hillary. Their return engagement saw John's brother Peter as a replacement for Henry. Someone mentioned 'drink' as a reason. Peter was delightful. He walked with

a severe limp and danced like a down-home Baryshnikov.

**George Sea Island Singers at The Poor People's March, 1968
(from left) Emma Ramsey, John "Moses" Davis,
Bessie Jones, Peter Davis
Smithsonian Institute, Diana Davies Photo Collection**

They introduced those of us who came to see them – the room was seldom full – to traditional song, both work song and religious, children's play songs and games (all rhythmic and enchanting), and religious dance movements (called "Shouts"). It was fascinating and something I had no idea of. I loved them and became friendly. My special friend was Mable, who loved to sing the Blues. The group did no Blues. While I didn't learn everything they were showing us, I did recall basics of two things that I thought I could bring to the production of "Yerma".

The Shouts involved four of the group, who circled the stage counter-clockwise in a shuffle step, never lifting their feet nor turning around, nor crossing their feet. They swayed side to side, bobbed up and down and sang, Mrs. Jones played the tambourine. It was fascinating and magical. I taught it to the cast of Yerma, who danced marvelously during a scene that took place by a river, evoked by a winding swath of white cloth – theatrical magic.

The second special thing I remembered was that the Shouts were led by Moses, who, seated, took a broomstick and used it to loudly tap counter-rhythms between his feet, which stomped a steady one-two. It was as compelling a scene as intended.

I also came up with several songs and tunes that were fresh to L.A. ears. My inspiration for these songs came from MS Fred McDowell and other Blues musicians.

One complication which I didn't anticipate was that the Director envisioned the lone musician as a character in the play and wanted him onstage. As a White guy, I didn't pass muster. I was deflated, but took it as something to be overcome. I did have a Black friend who could handle the music. My buddy Phil Wilkins played football for UCLA, and looked the athlete. He had studied with me and my friend Phil Boroff and was devoted to the Blues tradition.

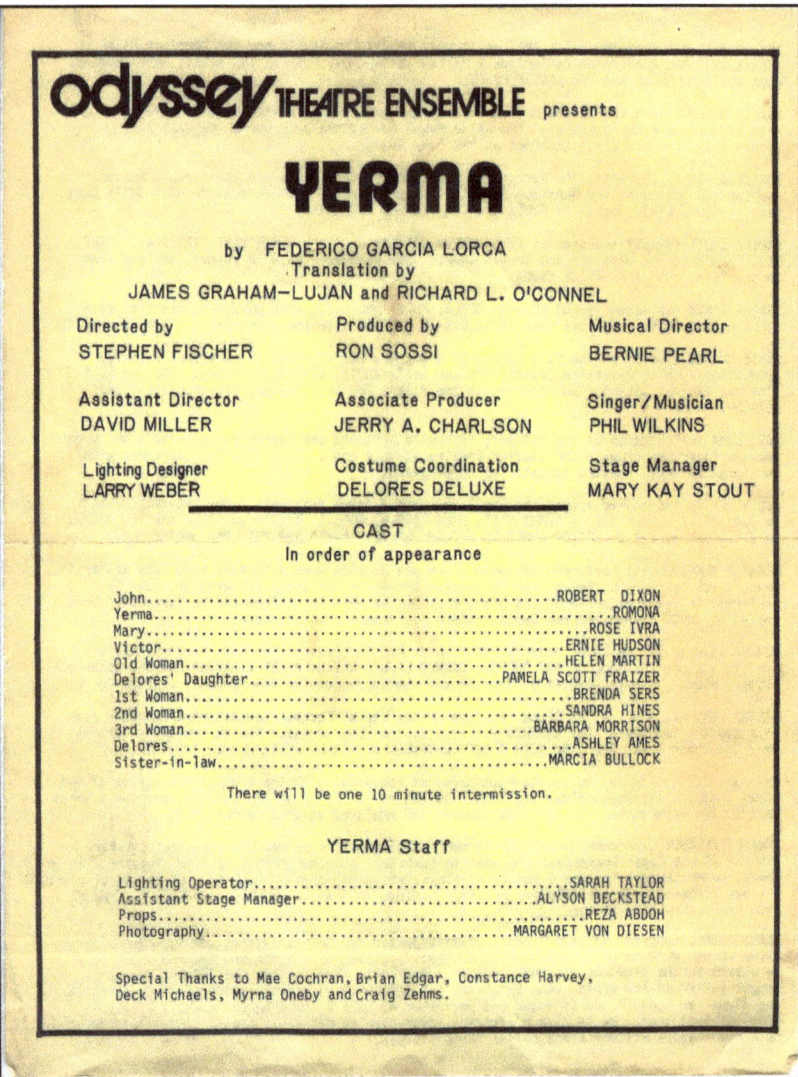

While neither of us was thrilled to be working for no pay, it was a worthwhile endeavor with its own rewards. He accepted, and did a fine job. Once the show opened I regularly attended. It all seemed to be going well, and Phil did great. However, one time I was approached by a cast member who asked if I could talk to Phil. From the start, the cast was asked to find appropriate rural work clothes. I went out and got me some used overalls. However, Phil was a good-looking guy and dressed to show off his good looks and athletic body. He had refused to get overalls. Instead, he wore designer jeans, and a couple of the cast objected. It was truly the director's job to handle issues like that, but it made me laugh.

I did get to be the musician one performance. Phil simply couldn't make it, and I was emceeing the second Long Beach Blues Festival. I got someone to bring on the final act in my stead, I changed into my overalls, and jammed to the theatre. Got there just in time for curtain. It was glorious!

Yerma 2 – I Meet Barbara

The cast of Yerma was a mix of actors at various stages of their careers and experience.

Romona, who went by a single name, played Yerma. Robert Dixon was so effective as the nasty husband that my wife Edie had to be restrained from going up to him and slapping him whenever she came to a show. She still talks about that.

Notable was Helen Martin, a veteran actress and, obviously, comedienne. Her role as the village elder drew laughs on just about every line.

Helen Martin

This was a pretty serious play, and laugh lines are needed to counter the grimness. Helen had it under control. She was later to show up in Charles Bronson's "Death Wish" film as the elderly lady who foiled the culprit with her hat pin. Still drawing laughs aplenty. Also notable was the "young stud" who steps in to counter the despicable, abusive husband, and provide some solace to Yerma, as played by Ernie Hudson.

Ernie Hudson

Ernie, surprisingly, knew who I was from visits to the Ash Grove, and provided strong support for my efforts. Handsome and muscular, he was, to whatever extent the play permitted, a hero. Ernie went on to a film career. Among his roles was as featured sidekick in the original "Ghostbusters". Others in the cast included Romona, who went by a single name, as Yerma. Robert Dixon was so effective as the nasty husband that my wife had to be restrained from going up to him and slapping him whenever she came to a show. She still talks about that.

All were receptive to what I was bringing to the production, but one stood out. A really good voice, and an understanding of the music and lyrics. Her name was Barbara Morrison. I went up to her to comment, and before I could say anything, she asked, *You married?* We connected right away.

**Long Gone Miles, Barbara Morrison, Bernie Pearl
Courtesy: Bernie Pearl**

As I came to find out over our forty years plus relationship, she had a natural way of putting people at ease. I've seen it at dozens of performances. Audiences which had no idea of what to expect would be excited to hear her before she sang a word. It was her manner. Another of Barbara's "what you gonna say 'bout that" lines came when I'd introduce her to a male musician or friend, even if she did it from her wheel chair in later years. *Oh, hello. Have I slept with you yet?* All tension flees the room laughing.

And she could sing, for sure. As we talked, it turned out she had been working with some folks I knew, artists in L.A. like Big Joe Turner, Eddie "Cleanhead" Vinson, and was vocalist with the Johnny Otis Show, following in the footsteps of Little Esther, Etta James, and Big Mama Thornton. She had her own way of filling those musical shoes, capably and with reverence.

Barbara and I became a team. As I would present new material, I'd teach it to her first and she would re-teach it (in perfect pitch and interpretation) to the cast. There was one occasion where I had brought something for the title character that just wasn't working. Barbara came up with an original song that was perfect for that moment. She always credited me for co-writing, but it was hers alone. It was called *I Ain't Got Nothin'*.

Director Fischer believed in the production to the extent that he attempted to bring it to New York's bustling off-Broadway scene. I was in a dilemma as Edie was pregnant and due that fall, just when the play was supposed to head East. The attempt didn't pan out, and I was present for the birth of my son in early December, 1982.

Who Was Barbara Morrison?

Barbara Morrison was a world famous singer. Morrison is featured on over 20 recordings. She dazzled fans of a wide array of genres from traditional Jazz and Blues to Gospel and Pop. Her voice was known worldwide. That melodic voice had a two-and-a-half-octave range. Her interpretations of familiar Jazz and Blues classics and original contemporary tunes were rich, unique, soulful and highly spirited. Equally as striking, Barbara Morrison had the ability to belt out down-home, soul-stirring Blues. Her impassioned renditions of old and favorite torch songs were breathtaking.

Barbara Morrison

Barbara Darlene Morrison was born at Beyers Memorial Hospital in Ypsilanti, Michigan, on September 10, 1949.[366]

Her father was Robert Earl Morrison. Constance Odessa Garner was her mother. At the time of her birth, Robert and Constance were not married.[367]

> *Our father was very smart and resourceful, not necessarily in an academic sense, but he had a real world, commonsense. ... My Dad always seemed to be a leader amongst his friends in whatever project they had going, constructing additions to our family home, or helping one of his friends with their individual goals. He drew people to him and most all of them remained loyal friends throughout his life.*[368]

> *Our mother was a beautiful woman with fair skin and long dark hair until it turned silver during the latter part of her life. Like many proud Black women, our mother's facile features and tone displayed the difficult life and times often experienced during that era ... Our mother had a solid education and was the rock that held everything together. Her sharp wit and stern, but seemingly angry discipline punctuated our upbringing, but our mother still managed that loving stare that indicated pride for what she had brought into this world.*[369]

Robert Morrison was drafted into the army to serve in the Korean War. When he left for Korea, Constance was pregnant with Barbara. Robert made Constance promise to wait for him.[370]

Constance moved to Detroit to obtain a job. Constance and Barbara lived with her aunt Isabel Garner and uncle Milton while in Detroit.[371]

With the underground railway, most of the people from Mississippi went to Chicago, and most of the people from Alabama went to Detroit, so we got all of their ways, mannerisms and stuff. Detroit is the place that people from Alabama came to, because we had Henry Ford, the Ford plant and General Motors. When they decided to pay Black people the same as white people, they flocked there.[372]

Constance Morrison fell on hard times. She gave Barbara away. When he returned from Korea, Robert looked for Constance and Barbara. He found both mother and daughter.

When he got out of the service he said he would buy us a house and I'd have a nice happy childhood. and did exactly what he said he was going to do. He bought a house and we all grew up in the same house—me and my brothers and sisters.[373]

When she fell on hard times, Constance Morrison was 22 years old. Having a child and lacking real employable skills made supporting a child difficult for Constance. Additionally, social pressures from having a child without a father in the home created even more difficulty for Constance. After Robert returned from Korea, Constance Morrison became a different and stronger person as a result of having to place Barbara in a different home. Constance and Robert insisted in keeping the family together, despite any economic or other family problems.[374]

Robert bought a house in Romulus, a very rural area near the Detroit airport.[375] Living in this area was like living in a rural area in the South.

My mother was from Alabama and I grew up in a rural area outside Detroit that was just as country as Alabama.

I knew about outhouses, coal stoves and wood stoves (that were used) to heat the whole house for us during the winter. I knew about chopping wood, and as a matter of fact (she rolls up her pant leg to reveal a scar) that is from chopping wood.'[376]

Robert was a Chevy factory worker. Constance worked as a nurse at Beyer Memorial Hospital in nearby Ypsilanti, about 14 miles from Romulus. Robert was also a great baseball player.

Work ethic was a constant requirement for all the members of the family. All members had to work and to contribute to the financial well-being of the family.

> *Both our parents worked most of their lives until illness gradually prevented them from carrying on. All the of children went to work at a young age, starting with Summer Job Programs, and following that up with whatever could be found. Barbara, who was the oldest of the siblings, had it the roughest when it came to working inside and outside the home, even though I think she enjoyed working at such a young age. I believe she worked harder during her childhood years than any grown woman could possibly have done during the same period. Barbara literally would do any type of work to support our family, including doing the grunt work required when working with elderly residents at nursing homes. I remember as a young child accompanying my father, or mother, depending on who was available and who's turn it was; with picking up Barbara late at night from one of the several, varied places she worked.*[377]

Church attendance was mandatory every Sunday. Initially Barbara's parents made her attend a local Methodist church until about twelve. After that, she was allowed to select any church she wanted. Barbara chose to attend a local Baptist church. *I learned a lot of Christian songs from the Baptist church because I was in the choir.*[378]

Robert was a great singer and also sang at church. He also had a doo-wop group [379]

> *His doo-wop group used to rehearse in the kitchen and my doll house was under the kitchen table. So I picked up all these songs—didn't know where they came from—and I would sing them just like they rehearsed them. And they used to laugh at me—they thought that was so funny.*[380]

But when he returned from the Korean War, Robert had a drinking problem. Sometimes, he did not return home from work.

> *My father would spend his whole paycheck down on the corner drinking wine with his friends. And my mother used to play Lee Morgan's "Sidewinder" every time he made it home with his paycheck. She put on Lee Morgan and we'd all get in a circle and dance [sings] "Bop, bop, Daddy came home with his paycheck, bop bop.*[381]

Barbara Morrison recorded her first appearance for radio in Detroit at the age of 9. She entered a contest on WERD of Atlanta. This station was the first Black radio broadcasting station in the United States. *I sang a Stevie Wonder song and got attention from the R&B community.*[382]

While living in Romulus, Robert and Constance had more children. Robert Earl Morrison, Jr, [called 'Man"], Pamela Delphine Morrison, Michael Edward Morrison, Richard Lee Morrison, and Ametta Morrison [called Angie]. All of these children were born at Beyer Memorial Hospital in Ypsilanti.[383] This hospital was the hospital in which Constance worked and in which Barbara was born.

**Barbara Morrison
High School Graduation**

When she graduated from high school, Barbara wanted to stay at home because her mother was pregnant. But Barbara had a scholarship to Eastern Michigan University. Robert, her father, wanted her to leave to go to college. *Baby, do me a favor. Let them see you go. Let them see you go to college. They're not gonna stand for that. They're gonna go too." And he was right. All my brothers and sisters graduated from college. ... and I moved to Ypsilanti and started going to Eastern.*[384]

After several years attending Eastern Michigan University, father Robert asked Barbara what she wanted to do. *My father always wanted me to be a singer. And I wanted to be a singer because he was a singer.*[385] *I said I want to be a singer.* Robert encouraged Barbara to follow her dreams. *"You won't be a singer. But I'll support you, I'll keep the family together, take care of your mom, sisters, and brothers, but I want you to know you can always come home.*[386]

Barbara financed a brand new 1972 Cougar and drove to CA in 1973. After a few days in CA, Barbara was singing in a rock band called L.A. Smog Control. This band was formed by a great musician who worked with the Jackson Five.[387]

And, then, Barbara would have a change of fortune. *I heard about an audition for a night club performer at the Rubaiyat, a prestigious jazz and R&B club in south central Los Angeles. This audition introduced me to Eddie "Cleanhead" Vinson.* Vinson was the same age as her father. Older Vinson took Barbara under his wing. *He dogged me into being a good girl. You better not be going to bed with none of them musicians.*[388]

Eddie "Cleanhead" Vinson

At first, Morrison wanted to sound like Barbara Streisand. Cleanhead Vinson counseled her to just be herself. About the same time, Morrison met Johnny Otis.

Johnny Otis

Otis gave her the same advice as given to her by Eddie Vinson.

Eddie used to tell me, 'Get your own sound, girl!' "Johnny said, 'Why are you singin' like Barbra Streisand? You need to learn your own people's music!'[389]

Being from the Detroit area, Barbara had wanted to be a Motown girl all her life. *Motown wouldn't give me the time of day. But I got attention in the jazz world. Of course, it's still a part of me.*[390]

From 1975 – 1977, Barbara Morrison was a member of The Mean Machine, a soul music band.[391]. Fellow member Tony Hithe played for some years with Johnny "Guitar" Watson. Hithe still plays around South Central Los Angeles, often backing Blues great Bobby Warren.

Mean Machine, circa 1977
Courtesy: Tony Hithe and Karen McCoy-Hithe

L->R: Tony Riley, drums; Carlos Pueblos, keyboards, Barbara Morrison, vocals, Denise Banks, vocals, Tony Hithe, guitar and vocals, Tracy Wright, bass

In 1975, Morrison was playing a gig at the Marlton Building in the Crenshaw District of south central Los Angeles. Her piano accompanist knew that band leader Johnny Otis was looking for a singer. He suggested that Barbara call Otis and gave her Otis' phone number. Barbara did not think she could get the job. So, Barbara Morrison simply threw away the phone number!

But, soon Johnny Otis called Barbara Morrison. Otis made an appointment for Morrison to record the next day. Still, Morrison did not think she would be hired. So, she simply did not show for the recording session. Otis then called Morrison and asked her, *do you have a screw loose?* Finally, Barbara came to a recording session at the studio.

Johhny Otis and Barbara Morrison, circa 1975

Barbara had never rehearsed or performed with the Johnny Otis Band. However, her father Robert had an extensive record collection. So, she was familiar with all the songs planned for the day. A complete LP was recorded that day by the Johnny Otis Band with vocalist Barbara Morrison. This record was released, but the details of the LP seem to be lost.[392]

Morrison subsequently joined the Johnny Otis Orchestra in 1975. She played with the Orchestra for the next 21 years until 1996.[393] Between the mid-1970s and early 1990s, Barbara Morrison recorded several albums with Johnny Otis.[394]

During her participation in the Johnny Otis Orchestra, Barbara Morrison had the opportunity to perform at Carnegie Hall in NYC. On Saturday, June 29, 1985, the Band performed at the world famous venue. Barbara Morrison received notice of her performance in the *NY Times*.

> *Mr. Otis himself sang the band's 1958 hit "Willie and the Hand Jive," while the singer Barbara Morrison demonstrated the proper wrist gestures. … Barbara Morrison delivered one song a la Esther Phillips and another with Ella Fitzgerald's blithe scat-singing.*[395]

In 1986, Morrison toured with the Philip Morris Superband, completing a 14-city one-month tour of Canada, Australia, Japan, and the Philippines. This band included jazz organist Jimmy Smith saxophonist James Moody, guitarist Kenny Burrell, trumpeter Jon Faddis and Grady Tate on drums. These musicians were the superstars of jazz at the time. Performing with these musicians indicated the super star status of Barbara Morrison herself. Barbara would remain lifelong friends with Kenny Burrell.

Since 1994, Morrison served as an adjunct associate professor of global jazz studies at UCLA.[396] She taught jazz vocal classes at UCLA's Herb Alpert School of Music.[397] Barbara was hired by Director Kenny Burrell. Burrell was one of the jazz superstars in the Philip Morris Superband that had toured with Barbara in 1986.

> *She was one of first hires made by then-director Kenny Burrell, her instinctual sense of song a valuable asset for the largely unexplored world of formal jazz education at the time. "Because of her vocal virtuosity and international name in the field, she has been one of our greatest examples to our students, who loved her teaching style and her personality," according to UCLA's current chair of Global Jazz Studies, Dr. Steve Loza.*[398]

In 1995, Morrison appeared in a televised tribute to Ella Fitzgerald with Mel Tormé, Diane Reeves, Stevie Wonder, Chaka Khan, Tony Bennett, Dionne Warwick and Lou Rawls.

Over the years, Morrison worked with Gerald Wilson, Dizzy Gillespie, Ray Charles, Ron Carter, Etta James, Little Esther Phillips, David T. Walker, Dr. John, Kenny Burrell, Terence Blanchard, Joe Sample, Cedar Walton, Nancy Wilson, Joe Williams, Tony Bennett, Keb' Mo, Count Basie Orchestra, Clayton-Hamilton Orchestra and Doc Severinsen. She performed at the Montreux Jazz Festival, Nice, Pori, North Sea, Darling Harbour, Sydney Opera House, Monterey, Long Beach, and in tributes to Dizzy Gillespie and Benny Golson.

After leaving Otis in 1996, Morrison joined Ray Charles's Orchestra and Doc Severinsen's orchestra, playing with both bands at the same time. This joint participation lasted for 7 years from 1996 until 2003. While playing with these Orchestras, Barbara also started performing on her own.[399]

So Barbara started experimenting by herself. She signed with the High Note record company. Morrison remained with this record company until her death.[400]

In addition to her multiple solo recordings, fans experienced the pleasure of Barbara Morrison's rich and vibrant tones on film soundtracks. Notable film and television appearances include the movie sound track for *The Hurricane* (starring Denzel Washington), Goin' Home: A Tribute to Duke Ellington and Johnny Otis's CD "Ooo Shoo Be Dooo". Additional credits include the hit NBC TV comedy *The Naked Truth*, *The Tonight Show with Jay Leno* and *The Dennis Miller Show*.

Beginning in 1998, Barbara Morrison performed for more than a decade at Pip's on La Brea Avenue, a jazz club in Mid-City.[401]

Pip's On La Brea at 1356 South La Brea Ave

After 7 years with the Ray Charles and Doc Severinson Orchestras, Barbara met the May Brothers. Barbara and the May Brothers worked at the Loews hotel in Los Angeles for about 6 years from 2003 until 2009. After this period, the May Brothers moved away from Los Angeles.[402]

In 2008, Morrison launched a 33 city tour of America. She was co-headliner in an all-star tribute to legendary composer Harold Arlen. Arlen was most recognizable for his genius behind the music for the classic film, *The Wizard of Oz*. That same year, she toured Australia.[403]

In addition to performing, Morrison dedicated her life to building the L.A. music community and fostering up-and-coming talent. In 2009, Morrison opened the Barbara Morrison Performing Arts Center in Leimert Park.

The Barbara Morrison Performing Arts Center

Two years later, in 2011, she founded the California Jazz & Blues Museum in the same area.⁴⁰⁴

> *I decided to come here to Leimert Park because it's one of the richest Black communities in the country. The community and Black businesses are getting more attention and even the kids are doing more. We have the Harmony Projects for kids 5 to 15 years old: these kids are doing it. The school across the street from my school? A graduate of that school [who] graduated from the University of Michigan; his kids played on the Miles Davis soundtrack. Our music schools are getting through to the top.*
>
> *Little kids, they don't know color. They come to me, even little white kids and little Mexican kids, they come in and ask if it's a place to be a musician. I take them into the museum and show that musicians can be all colors. To be a musician is not to be a person of color. It's to be a person of the arts. These are underprivileged kids with no color. Black lives do matter, all lives do matter. We have white people walking down the street: they don't care what color you are. They move to this community and now it's beginning to look like a mixture of people of all colors. It's all mixed up and it's beautiful.*⁴⁰⁵

Barbara Morrision was well known throughout the state of CA. In the Spring of 2011, newly sworn-in US Senator Kamala Harris presented a Certificate of Appreciation to Barbara Morrison.

**Awards Ceremony For Barbara Morrison, circa Spring, 2011
Courtesy: Rick Morrison
left->right: Kamala Harris, Barbara Morrison**

This Certificate from the US Senate was apparently presented at a fund raising dinner for Kamala Harris.

In 2011, Morrison began performing with Jack Hale, a guitarist, arranger and bandleader. However that activity did not last for long. In the Summer of 2011, Barbara Morrison experienced a major bout with diabetes. As a result of her diabetic condition, Morrison had one of her legs amputated.[406] Some time later, Barbara lost her second leg to diabetes. Most people would be deterred by being a double amputee in a wheelchair. But, Barbara Morrison was used to adversity.

> *The one thing about Barbara, even when she had both of her legs amputated, she approached it [her performances] with all of her might. All the way to the end. I saw her perform not too long before she went in the hospital. She was sounding just as good as she ever did. She was tried, trued and tested.*

She didn't discriminate," recalled Trible. *"She'd play at a hole in the wall or Disney Hall. She didn't have a thought that she was too good for a place. I think that's why she was somebody who was undeniable.*[407]

Even as a double amputee in an electric wheelchair, Barbara Morrison continued to perform with energy and passion.

In 2020, Barbara Morrison made her last recording: *Barbara Morrison: Standing on Their Shoulders*. This video was part of the *Southland Sessions* produced by KCET, the SoCal public media station. In the video, Barbara sings songs by Billy Holiday, Sarah Vaughan, Dinah Washington, and Ella Fitzgerald.[408]

A Mature Barbara Morrison

In early March 2022, Barbara Morrison was hospitalized for cardiovascular disease. Morrison died on March 16, 2022, at the age of 72.[409]

Subsequent to her death, Barbara Morrison received a special honor from the Los Angeles City Council. On Sept 10, 2022, the corner at 43rd St and Degnan Blvd was designated as Barbara Morrison Square. The Barbara Morrison Performing Arts Center is located at this corner.

Barbara Morrison Square Dedication Ceremony, Sept 10, 2022

**left of sign: Robert Sausedo, Community Build, Inc.
Yvonne Farrow, Dept of Cultural Affairs, City of LA
Heather Hutt, LA City Council Woman, 105h District
right of sign: Tim Morganfield, CEO**

LA City Councilmember Heather Hutt, of the LA City 10th District attended the ceremony and issued a proclamation commemorating the designation.

> *I am excited to have partnered with the City of Los Angeles Department of Cultural Affairs to celebrate the life and legacy of Barbara Morrison. Barbara Morrison was a musical trailblazer and international icon. Although she could have put her roots down anywhere in the world, Barbara chose to settle in Leimert Park; and she was a steady pillar in this community. I remember when this motion first passed to rename the intersection of 43rd Street & Degnan Boulevard as "Barbara Morrison Square," and to see this come to fruition is such an honor. We will forever love and remember Ms. Morrison; and we hope that this recognition will be a tribute to her legacy.*[410]

Barbara Morrison was one of the few singers who could sing the yellow pages or the obituaries with the ability to infuse personality and passion into her music.

The most important thing is for you to communicate and it doesn't matter how you say it, or how it comes out. It is not if you say it and the person that you are talking to understands what you meant. I am earthy and the way that I dress is earthy. (As for being) sensuous, I think that I can tap into stuff that a lot of people are afraid to say or to address. I think it is because I work a lot. Sometimes, like today (in the musical) in that scene with Johnny Otis when he discovered those people, I added, 'and then he discovered a little girl named Barbara Morrison,' because that works.[411]

Morrison specifically liked a single musical genre the best, *I like the blues. I think the blues are my forte, although I do like soft, sweet stuff. I like ballads which I think that I do very well. I like the idea of being able to do all of it. I just like to have fun. I always say that when I stop having fun, I am going to hang up my vocal chords."*[412]

Derrick Pipkin owned Pip's On La Brea during the period in which Barbara Morrison performed at the club.

Derrick Pipkin

On learning of the death of Barbara Morrison, Pipkin posted a photo of a smiling Morrison and offered his condolences.

Morrison captivated the hearts of us all. Her soulful voice was only surpassed by her beautiful spirit and radiance. She was the essence of a Sunday Kind of Love. She dedicated her life to being an inspiration not only through her music but through her words of motivation and encouragement. Her smile lit up a room and her presence brought a sense of warmth. A mentor, a friend, a legacy. She will be truly missed."[413]

When you watched Barbara Morrison perform and you sat in her company, she left no room for doubt that she was still having a lot of fun with her music.[414]

When asked, Barbara Morrison was very humble about her being a leader among the Black community.

> *I don't know if I have an answer. There are all kinds of role models around here. I'm a positive role model. I encourage people, I advise anyone to contribute something artistic to society. My father taught me to always follow through because you don't know what will happen. He told me you use everybody you can, but don't misuse anybody. And listen (to others), which is one of the hardest things for strong-headed people to do. Listen and choose and follow through, go all the way.*[415]

Johnny Otis had discovered several other notable female Blues singers prior to Barbara Morrison: Etta James and Little Esther.

Etta James

Barbara Morrison strongly felt that Etta James was a mentor. James gave meaningful and valued advice to Morrison.

> *Don't be jealous of nobody. Get out there and do your thing. She gained weight at one time, about 400 pounds, and she did not stop. Her attitude was, "Hey, I'm pretty good. Wait till you get like me and you'll be all right." She was cheesy like that.*[416]

Morrison was guided by these principles throughout the rest of her career and fame.

Barbara Morrison was quite an influence on her family. As her father Robert predicted, seeing Barbara depart for Eastern Michigan University motivated the others.

> *My parents stressed traditional education and all of us were expected to attend college for at least one year without question.*[417]

All of the other siblings attended college for at least 1 year.[418] Robert Earl Jr graduated from Northwestern University. Pamela was a graduate of Western Michigan University. Michael attended Eastern Michigan University but did not graduate. Rick Morrison graduated from Western Michigan University. Armetta/Angie also became a graduate of Western Michigan University.[419]

> *My sister Barbara had a tremendous work ethic. She could quickly find a job if dropped into a strange environment.*[420]

> *I strongly believe the example set by Barbara's incredible willpower and work ethic is where all of us siblings who came after her developed our own work ethic, loyalty, and belief of fairness towards others. Barbara set an example that was followed by the next youngest sibling and so on until all of us met the standard of being able to fend for ourselves and back each other up against whatever life had in mind to throw at us at any given moment.*[421]

Barabara Morrison was both role model and mentor for her other siblings. She did all that she could to help her siblings.

> *I believe we succeeded because of the high standards set by Barbara. I remember Barbara telling my oldest brother, who was having trouble with geometry, that she could teach him everything he needed to know about geometry from a pool table. I suppose it has something to do with the angles of the shots? But whatever it was, she indeed taught him geometry!*[422]

In 2009, Barbara Morrison was in the process of opening The Barbara Morrison Performing Arts Center in Leimert Park. Dave Pindeo built the stage for the Center. Through Dave, Barbara met Tim Morganfield. At the time, Tim owned and operated a production company. This company built stages and sets for high profile musical acts.[423]

Morrison needed some construction work completed at The Center. Dave introduced Barbara Morrison to Tim Morganfield. Tim had never heard of Barbara Morrison. When he told his ex-wife about Barbara, she became excited. She knew about Barbara Morrison.

So, Tim completed this first construction job for Barbara. He charged Barbara $2,500 for materials. Barbara only knew Tim by his first name. When she went to write the check, Morrison asked Tim his last name. Tim told Morrison that his last name was Morganfield. Barbara recognized that last name and asked Tim if he was related to McKinley Morganfield, commonly known as Muddy Waters. Tim admitted that Muddy was his cousin. Barbara Morrison took meeting a member of the Morganfield family as an omen. From that point onward, Barbara and Tim were family.

Tim Morganfield continued to work as a volunteer for Barbara. Tim completed production jobs at The Center for free. By way of appreciation, Barbara introduced Tim to a large number of people who needed production jobs completed. This jobs were charged for the work. After 6-7 months, someone told Barbara Morrison that Tim had experience running a business. Barbara came to involve Tim Morganfield more and more in the running of The Center.

Over the years, Barbara and Tim became friends. This pair would often meet for lunch or dinner and just talk about life. For Barbara, stepping out of the music world and talking about life was important. This type of discussion kept Barabara grounded in the real world. As a result of their friendship, Tim developed the kind of relationship with Barbara where he could talk to her straight out. Barbara herself recognized the need for such a relationship.

Tim Morganfield

Barbara Morrison

In 2011, when Barbara had both legs amputated, Tim Morganfield personally helped her to recover. Tim had a brother who had been a double amputee. His experience caring for his double amputee brother prepared and enabled Tim to support Barbara Morrison through her recovery. Tim was available to Barbara by phone 24 hours a day, 7 days a week. And, Barbara often did call Tim for emotional support at really odd hours.[424] Of course, this support further tightened the relationship between Barbara and Tim.

Barbara was a kind and giving person. She always wanted to give and did not seem to be able to discern when someone was taking advantage of her. She knew she needed protection against the weakness of her own generosity. As a big star, Barbara had people around that would often want to take advantage. As her friend, Tim provided a balance to all those people, helping Barbara to navigate all the pitfalls of being over generous and being a big star.

As a result of these years of friendship and frankness, Tim Morganfield was able to see the real Barbara Morrison.

> *Barbara was always giving to people. One time, she bought a van for a family. She would sit outside The Center, giving $100 bills to guys walking down the street. Another time, she gave a guy $20 to fetch coffee and told him to keep the change.*
>
> *At one point, Barbara encountered some young kids sitting out in Leimert Park getting stoned. These kids convinced Barbara to give them $10,000 to film a hip-hop video. I was able to intervene and prevent this give-away from happening. These stoned kids did not have the capability to produce a video. They were young, inexperienced, and mostly stoned.*

Upon the death of Barbara Morrison, Morganfield wanted to assume control of The Center. The Center was actually owned by Community Build, an organization started decades ago by Maxine Waters and colleagues. Tim Morganfield and Karen Clark had to bid on taking over The Center.

Tim Morrison

And

Karen Clark

This bid required that the pair describe their vision for The Center, their financial projections and prove the likelihood of solvency. Community Build granted approval to Morganfield and Clark. Also, Morrison's family agreed to allow continued usage of Barbara's name, likeness and image.[425]

Tim Morganfield became the CEO of The Barbara Morrison Performing Arts Center. Karen Clark became the Chief Financial Officer.

> *Barbara always wanted a stage for the community, a stage for people who never had the chance to perform onstage.*
>
> *She was a person who always tried to bring the community together. Creating The Barbara Morrison Performing Arts Center was to bring people together, as one. I am continuing to operate The Center, expanding its community outreach to obtain the goals of Barbara Morrison.* [426]

Several other individuals were part of the inner circle of Barbara Morrison. James Lamb was a trusted business and financial advisor. For several years, Morrison performed on Thursday nights at the LA Fitness Club bar in downtown Los Angeles. David Ross was the bass player in the band. Barbara and David became good friends. After the passing of Barbara Morrison, Ross played a significant role in creating the Barbara Morrison Scholarship at the UCLA School of Music. David solicited donors and raised sufficient capital to fund the scholarship.[427]

Barbara Morrison was a larger than life Blues and jazz singer. Her voice was distinct and filled with emotion when she sang. Morrison was a giving person, often at her own peril and risk. Despite growing up with adversity and experiencing adversity as an adult, Barbara Morrison never waivered in her ability to deliver a song with energy and feeling. Life was just a little bit brighter with Barbara Morrison singing her songs in all types of venues, large and small. While she is gone, Barbara Morrison will not be forgotten.

More Blues Festivals Follow

1981 2nd Annual Blues Festival Lineup

Clifton Chenier, Albert Collins, Pee Wee Crayton, Margie Evans, Blind Joe Hill, George Smith, Eddie "Cleanhead" Vinson, Smokey Wilson.

2nd

**Annual KLON Long Beach Blues Festival Program
Courtesy: Bernie Pearl**

1982 3rd Annual Blues Festival Lineup

Clarence "Gatemouth" Brown, Robert Cray, Johnny Littlejohn, Little Milton, Mighty Flyers with Rod Piazza, Johnny Otis Show, Esther Phillips, George Smith, Taj Mahal.

After listening to *Nothin' But The Blues* on KLON for about a year, and going to local clubs, Bruce Krell decided to attend a Festival. He chose the 3rd Festival in 1982. *I was impressed with the quality of the live music. As a result, I decided to get involved. I fully intended to participate in the 1983 Festival in any way that I could help.*

Johnny Otis   **Little Esther Phillips**
1982, 3rd Annual KLON Long Beach Blues Festival
Courtesy: Bruce Krell

Big Mama Drops In -- USC Extension II (1982)

I didn't cover the same material in the ensuing session as in the prvious year. There's plenty of material, recordings, and guest informants to keep people engaged, and many students re-enrolled. It felt like a success. This time, USC was also feeling good about the *Simply Blues* course (I never grew to like the title) and sent out press releases on it.

I had presented a "syllabus" (a grand name for my outline of topics to be covered) that included a session dedicated to "Women in the Blues". I had asked my radio colleague Mary Katherine Aldin (host of KPFK-FM's "Preachin' the Blues) to deliver the lecture. I believe I did share my pay for the evening with her, and her participation was most welcome, and appropriate. I'm not sure the small amount I paid her weighed all that heavily with her. I had also made a leap of faith, and asked Big Mama Thornton to be my guest and, unbelievably, she agreed! A press release must have been sent to the media and no one less than CBS-channel 2 responded that they wanted to feature this class on one of their Monday morning shows.

There were the expected back and forths, but at the end, both Big Mama and CBS were there that night. The producer of the segment was a young Black woman named Donna Brown, very professional and eager to make a special broadcast.

Donna Brown Guillaume

This event was in the early years of the career of Donna Brown. Since that time, Donna has become an Emmy-nominated television producer. Ms. Guillaume began her career in the Channel 2 Newsroom of KCBS. Donna then moved to the Los Angeles CBS Network Bureau of the *CBS Evening News*, becoming a top-notch researcher and interviewer unafraid of powerful or controversial material. She was then a producer on "Two on the Town," a news magazine, for five years at KCBS. Her documentary work as an executive producer includes "Unchained Memories: Reading from the Slave Narratives" on HBO. She served as consulting producer on "John Lewis: Get in the Way," which aired in 2023 on PBS.[428]

Big Mama had asked Pee Wee Crayton to join her, an unexpected bonus, plus her regular bassist Bill, who was also the regular bassist for Pee Wee. Palpable excitement. Big Mama was interviewed, and some of the music was recorded.

Simply Blues II At USC, 1982
(from left) Bernie Pearl, George "Harmonica" Smith,
bassist unknown, Big Mama Thornton, Pee Wee Crayton
Courtesy: Edie Pearl

But another aspect of the evening captures my attention.

I made my presentation to the class, and then called on my guest lecturer. Mary Katherine then went through some histories of women blues artists, complemented by musical samples. All very edifying. Then she came to an artist I had associated with Gospel music, Sister Bessie Jackson. It was revealed that Ms Jackson had also recorded bawdy party songs under the name, Lucille Bogan.

Lucille Bogan

Here's where the rubber meets the road. With Big Mama in full attention, the prim and academic Ms Aldin dropped the needle on an unexpurgated historic recording of Lucille Bogan's bawdy (an understatement) "Shave 'em Dry".

If you know of a bawdy tune, say by Tampa Red, put it out of your mind. Not in the same class as "Shave 'em Dry". By the time we got to the second verse, Big Mama was doubled over with hysterical laughter, I thought she was going to hit the floor. The class was roaring, no one louder than Willie Mae Thornton.

Shave em' Dry
By Jimmy James Yancy, c. 1924

I got nipples on my titties
Big as the end of my thumb
I got somethin' between my legs
That'll make a dead-man come

Baby won't you shave 'em dry
Want you to grind me baby
Grind me until I cry

Well I fucked all night
And all the night before, baby
And I feel like I wanna' fuck some more
Oh, great God, Daddy grind me honey
Shave me dry

And when you hear me holla baby
Want you to shave me dry

I got nipples on my titties
Big as the end of my thumb
Daddy say that?? and you can make 'em cum

Oh, daddy shave me dry
And I'll give you something baby
Swear it'll make you cry
I'm gonna turn back my mattress
And let you oil my springs
I want you to grind me daddy
Until the bells do ring
Oh daddy
Want you to shave 'em dry

oh great God daddy, if you can't shave 'em baby won't you try.
Now if fuckin' was a thing that would take me to heaven
I'd be fuckin' in the studio 'til the clock strikes eleven
Oh daddy, daddy shave 'em dry
I would fuck you baby, honey I would make you cry
Now your nuts hang down like a damn bell clapper
And your dick stands up like a steeple
your goddamn asshole stands open like a church door
and the crabs walks in like people
OWWW! Shit!
Baby won't you shave em dry

A big sow gets fat from eatin' corn
And a pig gets fat from suckin'
Reason you see this whore, fat like I am
Great God I got fat from fuckin'!
Ehhhh Shave 'em dry!

my back is made of whalebone and my cock is made of brass
And my fuckin' is made for workin' men's two dollars
Great God round to kiss my ass

Daddy shave em dry!

Without question, this was the finest sneak attack on propriety I've ever experienced. No one expected anything like this, and no one had ever heard such bawdy explicitness presented in such an austere atmosphere. It made Big Mama's night, and she sang beautifully when called on. The segment aired on Channel 2, without Lucille Bogan.

In the class, Big Mama Thornton showed up in a business suit. Big Mama was physically slight at the time (as the picture shows). When she had started as a Blues singer, Big Mama weighed 200 pounds![429]

Willie Mae Thornton

"Big Mama"

Yet, at the time of the USC course, Big Mama was thin and slightly, due to her cancer. However, she was still energetic and dynamic!

Blues Society Experiences Growing Pains[430] (1983)

Blues Society sponsorship of Blues concerts continued onward, mostly restricted to Mondays and Tuesdays by club owners on the west side of Southern CA. Attendance was low. Revenue to the Society, to the hosting club and to the performers was very low.

But, the west side listenership of *Nothin' but the Blues* was growing. As a result, attendance at the Long Beach Blues Festival was also growing. These two forces created a greater demand for Blues performances throughout the year at local clubs.

Finally, on Feb 24, 1983, the Society was able to host its first Thursday night performance at the Music Machine. Sippie Wallace, the Chambers Brothers, and Long Gone Miles performed at this event.

Sippie Wallace

The performers at this event actually paid into the attendance gate so that the hosting bar would see revenues.

Who Was Sippie Wallace?[431]

Beulah Thomas (Sippie) Wallace was born on Nov 1, 1898, in Houston, TX. Her parents were George W Thomas Sr and Fanny Thomas. Sippie was one of thirteen children. Thomas was a deacon at Shiloh Baptist Church. Beulah Thomas was nicknamed Sippie in grammar school because *My teeth were so far apart I had to sip everything.*

Sippie began singing and playing the organ at her father's church as a child. On summer nights, she would steal away from her home. During these nightly forays, Sippie listened to the ragtime sounds of the Blues singers in traveling tent-show bands through a flap in the canvas tent. On one of her many visits, some of the performers asked Sippie to fill an opening in the chorus line. With this invitation, her singing career began.

Sippie moved from Houston to Dallas with one of the tent shows. By the mid-1910s, she was participating in a wide variety of activities within the tent shows. She acted in plays, danced in the chorus line, performed comedy routines, and served as a snake charmer's assistant. Most importantly, Sippie begin singing solo ballads. She moved to New Orleans with Hersal Thomas, her younger brother and an exceptional pianist, to work with George W. Thomas, her older brother. George was a pianist, songwriter, and publisher. Jazz and ragtime were flourishing. Sippie found herself surrounded by young musicians, many of whom later became legends. Rehearsals in the Thomas house included King Oliver, Louis Armstrong, Sidney Bechet, Clarence Williams, and Johnny Dodds. While in New Orleans, Sippie married Frank Seals, but the couple soon divorced. She later married Matt Wallace.

In 1923, Sippie and younger brother Hersal moved to Chicago. With the help of older brother George, she met Ralph Peer, then general manager of OKeh Records. Okeh produced her first record within 3 months of the meeting. Sippie quickly moved to the top of the Black record industry, becoming a star with a national reputation. *Shorty George Blues* sold more than 100,000 copies. Sippie recorded more than forty songs for OKeh from 1924 to 1927. Her sidemen for these recordings included Louis Armstrong, Johnny Dodds, Clarence Williams, and others. Her song *Lazy Man Blues* was written by younger brother Hersal. Sippie herself composed *Special Delivery Blues*. *Mighty Tight Woman* and *Woman Be Wise* became classic Blues. *All of her songs spoke with earthy directness about love and relationships.*

During the Great Depression, musical tastes changed. As a result, the popularity of Sippie Wallace waned. Then, personal tragedies hit Sippie Wallace hard. Younger brother Hersal died of food poisoning in 1926. Several years later, older brother George was killed in a streetcar accident. During the mid-1930s, husband Matt Wallace died. This loss of family motivated Sippie to settle in Detroit. Here Sippie dedicated herself to singing gospel music.

Forty years later, the Blues revival of the 1960s began a resurgence of Wallace's career. Victoria Spivey, another Texas artist, persuaded Wallace to return to performing. Sippie and Victoria recorded a series of duets in 1966 In 1970, Spivey Records released the album *Sippie Wallace and Victoria Spivey*.

Feminists of the 1970s responded positively to the "tough-minded" lyrics of some of Wallace's songs. A young singer named Bonnie Raitt initiated renewed interest in Wallace. Raitt's debut album in 1971 included two Wallace songs. During the 1970s and 1980s, these two women recorded and toured together. In 1977 and 1980, Sippie Wallace performed at the Lincoln Center in New York. Atlantic Records released the album, *Sippie*, in 1982.

Sippie Wallace died on November 1, 1986, in Detroit. She was buried in Trinity Cemetery in Detroit.

The Blues Society Finally Takes Off (1983)

Finally, with the presentation of Clifton Chenier, the leading zydeco Blues musician from Louisiana, the attendance skyrocketed. This Blues concert was held at the Music Machine on Thursday, Aug 5, 1983.

Clifton Chenier

King of Zydeco

Everyone involved – the Society, the hosting club, and the performers, actually saw significant positive revenue.

By 1983, Blues Societies were sprouting up all over Southern California, from Santa Barbara to San Diego. Clubs in these areas could schedule big name Blues performers who were able to make the trip financially successful to the performers.

Attendance at the Long Beach Blues Festival was growing significantly. Listenership of *Nothin' but the Blues* was also increasing on the west side of Los Angeles. Bernie Pearl regularly announced all of the upcoming Blues performances at local clubs.

By 1984, attendance was large at Society-hosted and independent Blues performances in local clubs all over the west side of Southern CA. Local popular Blues performers found steady work playing in clubs. Big name Blues performers regularly came into the west side of Southern CA, playing regularly from Santa Barbara to San Diego. In Jan, 1984, Albert King played at the Music Machine. Performers such as BB King even performed at clubs such as the Music

Machine, the Seven Seas, Concerts By The Sea, McCabe's Guitar Shop, the China Club, and numerous other clubs.

While not directly involved in the shows at music clubs sponsored by the Southern CA Blues Society, Bernie Pearl did provide extensive support for those shows. *Nothin' but the Blues*, his radio show, was on KLON. This broadcast was received all over the west coast of SoCal. A demand for live Blues arose within those white audiences.

The KLON Blues Festivals with Bernie Pearl as MC and Artistic Director had an influence on the Blues Scene. These live and extended Blues performances further increased the demand for live Blues. Although a great venue to see live Blues, the Festivals were only once per year.

Annual performances left a huge unsatisfied demand in West Los Angeles, Hollywood, and East Los Angeles for live Blues through the remainder of the year. So, the club dates on the west side of Southern CA were scheduled more often and on high demand nights such as Friday and Saturday. Bigger named Blues performers could earn great money since these club performances on weekends were filled.

However, in order to attend the club performances, those interested in hearing the Blues had to be informed of the locations, dates and times. An internet did not exist back during the 1980s. Of course, *Nothin' but the Blues* hosted by Bernie on KLON was the source that most people consulted. Numerous printed sources were available for locating Blues performances. The Southern CA Blues Society published the *Blues Letter* bi-monthly. Local newspapers such as the *LA Weekly* and the *LA Reader* announced Blues performances.

1983 4th Annual Blues Festival Lineup

Bobby "Blue" Bland, Clifton Chenier, Johnny Copeland, Willie Dixon, Albert King, Jimmy McCracklin, Sonny Rhodes, Freddie Roulette, Koko Taylor.

In 1983, the KLON Long Beach Blues Festival had reached its largest attendance to date. Over 12,000 people attended.

**4th Annual KLON Long Beach Blues Festival
Courtesy: Wikipedia Commons**

As with all of the previous Festivals, Bernie Pearl served as both Artistic Director and Master of Ceremonies.

Bernie Pearl, Artistic Director

1983 Blues Festival

Courtesy: Bruce Krell

Bobby "Blue" Bland was the headliner of the 1983 Festival.

Bobby "Blue" Bland
1983 4th Annual KLON Long Beach Blues Festival

Albert King was another headliner of the 1983 Festival.

Albert King
1983 4th Annual KLON Long Beach Blues Festival
Both Photos, Courtesy: Bruce Krell

1983, 4th Annual Blues Festival Musicians

All Photos In This Section Courtesy: Bruce Krell

Willie Dixon (left) and Carrie Bell (right)

Koko Taylor

Johnny Copeland

Sonny Rhodes

Freddie Roulette

Jimmy McCracklin (left) and Lee King (right)

Clifton Chenier

Lee King (left) and Sonny Rhodes (right)

Albert Collins Visiting Back Stage

1983 4th Annual Blues Festival Details

Bernie Pearl Finds Albert King

I was driving down Pico Blvd. one day in the late 1960's, probably 1967. I was passing by the golf course (or park) where Century City was built later. I was listening to radio station KGFJ, an AM station geared toward the contemporary Black audience. The closest they got to the Blues was Otis Redding and other "Soul" artists, James Brown, and I'm not sure they even played an occasional B.B. King Blues.

I was shocked to hear a grinding, but modern, blues guitar. Loud, assertive, and knock-your-socks-off good. A style I had never heard before, backed by a really soulful band. I literally had to pull to the curb and listen. The song ended without the DJ announcing the artist. I raced home and called the station, something I had never done before, or since. I did my best to relate my impression of the music, but he knew exactly who and what I was talking about. He said, "Albert King", a name I had never heard before.

I asked about how I could contact him. He said it was on the Stax label. I don't recall if he gave me the studio number, but I recall immediately calling Stax. They answered and told me that Albert and his touring band were playing in San Francisco for Bill Graham and gave me the road manager's number. I called and found they were finishing their tour.). I was booking the Ash Grove at the time, and could discuss money. Albert King and his band would be available to come to the Ash Grove after the Fillmore (I assume that's where they were playing.) I'm sure they didn't ask for a big salary and we came to an agreement.

This was, I believe, Albert King's debut in Los Angeles, and he had just put out his commanding album, "Born Under a Bad Sign, (Stax 723, 1967). I later discovered that he didn't have the studio band, Booker T. and the MGs, with him. But his road band was well up to the task. Albert King was booked to open on a Tuesday night, I don't recall if they played more than one night, but oh what an opening.

The room was packed, SRO, and filled with an audience I had never seen there before. I guess "Hollywood Hippies" might describe them. White kids who were eager to rock to the real-deal electric Blues. And rock they did. They ate it up. How they know about Albert I really can only speculate, but they were there for him, and kind of knew what to expect. I guess word got around the Sunset Blvd. Rock scene that he was playing this club best known for its "Folk" offerings.

He was sensational and we re-booked him immediately for a multiple-night engagement on his next tour, which came fairly soon. Albert King was hot, hot, hot. We got along great, became friends, and I went to see him even after he began getting more substantial fees for his music.

Several years later I was visiting him in his dressing room at the Coach House in Orange County, and he told me he was thinking of moving from Memphis to California, and when he did, he wanted my band to back him. Flattering as this is, it posed a little bit of concern on my part.

You see, Albert could be hard on his band members, real hard, if they didn't play the way he wanted and expected on stage. He'd talk hard to them, maybe even cuss them out if he wasn't getting the music the way he wanted it played. The last thing I wanted was any sort of unhappiness or confrontation with him. However, it would have been an honor and good work credit, and I had some very good bandmates.

This never came about. I never heard more of it, and then the great Blues man passed away in Memphis Dec 21, 1993.

An Inside View Of The 1983 KLON Blues Festival

During the 3 months before the 1983 Festival, Bruce Krell worked diligently as a volunteer. *Every Friday, Saturday, and some Sundays, I would go accompany Bernie to various clubs all over Los Angeles. My job was to hand out flyers for the 4th Annual Blues Festival for those waiting in line to see a big named Blues musician. For example, I handed out flyers to those awaiting admission when Albert Collins played at China Club in Hollywood. When the music started, I was able to sit with Bernie and the musicians at their table in the club.*

After all of this effort, Bernie wanted to reward Bruce. *Bernie asked, What job would you like to do at the Festival? My answer was simple. I want to be the gofer for Albert King – run his errands through out the day. Bernie thought I was crazy. Why would a guy with a PhD want to spend the day running errands? My answer was simple – I would get to spend the day hanging out with Albert King!*

Bruce Krell and Albert King
1983 4th Annual KLON Long Beach Blues Festival
Courtesy: Bruce Krell

Who Was Albert King?

Albert King was one hell of a guitar player! King was often billed as King of the Blues Guitar. In 1983, Albert King (Albert Nelson) was one of the most popular Blues musicians in the country. Having Albert King as a headliner at the 4th Annual Festival brought nationwide attention to the Festival.

Albert Nelson King was born on April 25, 1923, to parents Albert King and Mary Blevins on a cotton plantation in Indianola, MS. He was one of 13 children. His father Albert King left the family when Albert was five. Mary Blevins then married Will Nelson. Albert was later adopted by his stepfather, Will Nelson.[432] The father Albert King was likely the father of Riley B "BB" King, who was born on Sept 16, 1925.

During childhood, Albert sang at a church with a family gospel group, in which his step father Will played the guitar. When he was 8 years old, his mother, Mary Blevins, and two sisters moved to an area near Forrest City, AK. Albert grew up picking cotton on plantations near Forrest City.[433] Young Albert picked cotton, drove a bulldozer, worked in construction, and held other jobs until he was able to support himself as a musician.[434]

While working at these jobs, Albert wanted to learn to play the guitar, just like his father had. He made his first guitar out of a cigar box, a piece of a brush, and a strand of broom wire.[435] He constructed this guitar using the string layout of a right-handed guitar.

However, Albert King was left-handed. So, Albert King turned his right-handed guitar upside down, teaching himself to play.[436] He would play a right-handed guitar upside down for the rest of his life! When bending the notes, Albert was forced to pull down on the strings rather than pushing the strings up. This technique gave a unique sound to the blues notes played by King.[437]

At first, King played with gospel groups -- most notably the Harmony Kings. After hearing Blind Lemon Jefferson, Lonnie Johnson, and several other blues musicians, he solely played the blues. In 1950, he met MC Reeder, who owned the T-99 nightclub in Osceola, AK. King moved to Osceola shortly afterward, joining The T-99's house band, the In the Groove Boys. The band played several local AK gigs besides The T-99, including several shows for a local radio station.[438] According to Albert himself, the In the Groove Boys were very limited. *We only knew three songs and we'd play them fast, medium and slow, that made nine songs. Somehow that got over all night long.*[439]

In 1953, Albert King moved north to Gary, Indiana. In Gary, King joined a band that also featured Jimmy Reed and John Brim.

Jimmy Reed

The Big Boss Man

Both Reed and Brim were guitarists, which forced King to play drums in the group. King played the drums on several of Reed's early recordings.[440]

Albert met Willie Dixon shortly after moving to Gary. Dixon, the bassist/songwriter, helped King schedule an audition at Parrot Records. King passed the audition and cut his first recording late in 1953. From these recordings, Parrot published his first single, "Bad Luck Blues"/"Be On Your Merry Way". This record sold a few copies, but made no significant impact. Parrot did not request any follow-up records or sign King to a long-term contract.[441] In 1954, King returned to Osceola and re-joined the In The Groove Boys at the T-99.[442]

In 1956, Albert King moved to Brooklyn, Illinois, just across the river from St. Louis, and formed a new band.[443] He became a popular attraction around the St. Louis nightclub scene alongside Ike Turner's Kings of Rhythm and Chuck Berry.[444] He signed to Little Milton's Bobbin label in 1959, releasing a few singles, but none of them charted.[445]

"Little" Milton Campbell, Jr

Blues Singer and Guitarist

However, Albert King caught the attention of King Records which released the single "Don't Throw Your Love on Me So Strong" in November 1961. This recording features musician Ike Turner on piano and became King's first hit, peaking at number 14 on the Billboard R&B chart.[446] Other recording attempts by King failed to obtain a position on the Billboard R&B chart.

With no apparent career prospects other than touring the club circuit in the South and Midwest, King moved to Memphis in 1966. King signed with the Stax record label.[447] His Stax single recordings were influential but did not initially generate any big hits. In 1967, Stax released the album *Born Under a Bad Sign*, a collection of the singles King recorded at Stax.[448] The title track of that album became King's best-known song and has been covered by several artists (including Cream, Paul Rodgers, and Jimi Hendrix). The production of the songs was sparse and clean and maintained a traditional blues sound while also sounding fresh and thoroughly contemporary.

In 1968, King was performing at Ike Turner's Manhattan Club in East St. Louis. Promoter Bill Graham was at the club looking for talent for his clubs in NYC (Fillmore East) and San Francisco (Fillmore West).

Bill Graham

Graham offered King $1,600 to play three nights at The Fillmore Auditorium in San Francisco.

I hadn't made $1,600 for three days in my life," Graham asked, 'How much deposit do you want?' I said, '$500.' I sent him a contract and he sent me a check for $1000. When I got there, I found out I was on the show with Jimi Hendrix and Janis Joplin. We started out at the old Fillmore but it was too small, so we had to move to Winterland. He kept us for three more weeks. People had been waiting to hear me play for a long time before I even showed my face out there."[449]

On June 25, 1968,[450] Albert King played at the Fillmore Auditorium in San Francisco. Following his success at the Fillmore, King became one of the few blues singers to attract large numbers of both black and white fans.[451]

King released the albums *Live Wire/Blues Power*, *Wednesday Night in San Francisco* and *Thursday Night in San Francisco* from the concerts.[452]

All of these albums were huge best sellers, promoting Albert King to the top of the list of Blues guitarists, second only to BB King.

Albert King was a unique individual. His signature bends were generated by pulling the strings downward on an upside-down, right-handed guitar using his left hand. In addition to this unique playing setup, Albert King did a lot of things differently. In an interview, Albert characterized many elements of his playing style:[153]

> *I do all of the vibrato with my hand. I don't use no gadgets or anything.*

> *I play single-note. I can play chords but I don't like 'em. I don't have time for them. I'm paying enough people around me to play chords.*

> *I have a tendency to bend two strings at one time ... Lots of times I don't intend to do that but I'm reaching for a bend and bring another one along. My fingers get mixed up, because I don't practice.*

> *I am the only guitarist who will start a song with a bent note, on "Angel of Mercy," for instance. I didn't plan that out. It's just what I felt and the way I recorded it. The bent note is my thing, man, and I'll put one anywhere it feels right. There are no rules.*

> *I like to mix volumes, treble and bass. There's a high, there's a mid-range and there's a bottom. If you don't ever mix that stuff up, you're not a complete player.*

> *First, you got to get in your mind what you want to play. If you hear a good lick – even if you're just rehearsing to yourself — and you feel it, then hit another one and another one and another one. The next thing you know you got 15 or 20 different licks you can hit and they all feel good. But if you rush right through, hitting them all, you're not even going to know what you did. You've got to take your time and learn your bag one lick at a time. And take your time in your delivery.*

> *Thanks to having played drums, I can tell immediately if a tempo is off.*

> *I have never used a pick. I couldn't hold one- my fingers were too big. I kept trying and the thing would fly across the house. I just always had a real hard time gripping it, so I learned to play without one.*

Albert Kng was once asked, *What is the single most common mistake young players make with the blues?* King's response was telling.

> *Overplaying. Definitely. Because they like to play loud and high all the time. And when you get ready to play chords, you got nothing to go to ... They play too loud, scream too high, and run too fast. See, when you overplay, you get too loud and people are gonna mistake what you're doing for a hole in the air.*

As Albert stated, his fingers were big. Those big fingers forced King not to use a pick and often caused him to bend two strings at once. His ability to repeatedly and clearly produce these same sounds is even more astounding given the size of his hands.

**Jeffrie Marks, Albert King and His Guitar Playing Hand
1983 4th Annual KLON Long Beach Blues Festival
Courtesy: Bruce Krell**

One of the benefits of working as Albert King's gofer was to be able to bring guests backstage to meet Albert.

Bruce Krell brought Jeffrie Marks, his girlfriend, to the Festival that year. Yes, Jeffrie is a girl.

> *My dad wanted to name my older brother (14 months older than I) Jeffrey, but got outvoted by my mother and other family members who wanted to name him Richard. When they were expecting me, my dad said he didn't*

care if they had a boy or girl but that the child was going to be named Jeffrey!! When I turned out to be a girl, he corrected the spelling to be, as he put it, a girl's name: Jeffrie. In spite of all that my family and friends always called me Jeff.

Bruce brough Jeffrie backstage to be photographed with Albert.

Jeffrie was tiny compared to Albert. Albert clearly stood at least a foot taller than Jeffrie. I asked Albert to put his guitar playing left hand next to Jeffrie's head. I was astounded. Albert's hand covered about ½ of her head. I closely examined Albert's hand. One of his fingers was as thick as two of my fingers placed side by side.

Normally, a person with big hands and thick fingers is expected to be clumsy and imprecise. Albert was anything but clumsy and imprecise. In fact, he was exactly the opposite. Consistently producing the same unique sounds of each song is just amazing given his playing an right-handed guitar upside down, his big hands, and his huge fingers.

Albert King could not read or write English. Bernie Pearl asked Albert to sign his copy of that first album, *Born Under A Bad Sign*.

Signature of Albert King
Courtesy: Bruce Krell

Albert would have been embarrassed to admit that he did not read or write English. So, Albert King just scribbled something unintelligible.

Inability to read and write led to some potential problems for Albert. Getting paid required that he know the terms and conditions of his contracts – which he could not read. Albert had a very simple solution to this problem.

Club owners were notorious at cheating the musicians, paying less than in the contract or not paying at all. He had been verbally told the amount he would receive at the time when the performance was scheduled. Albert ALWAYS got paid the agreed upon amount without any issues. Because, Albert had a solution. Albert King carried a large 45 pistol. When he went to collect payment for his performance from the club owner, Albert drew the pistol. He layed the pistol on top of the table, muzzle pointing towards the club owner. "Now, pay me." Albert King always got paid this way.[454]

Albert King also did not read or write music. A special approach was needed to enable Albert to record the music and the lyrics.

Albert knew the music and how to play the music. He had the Blues in his DNA. But, the lyrics were a problem. Allen Jones, the producer, was in the control room with headsets on. Albert would be down in the studio. Allen would tell Albert the pre-planned lyrics. Albert was given some time to get his phrasing together, putting. his Blues slant on the lyrics. Then, the recorders would start. Albert and the band would play. Albert would sing the lyrics with his phrasing. After completing that set of lyrics, the recorders were turned off. This process would begin again. Ultimately, Albert would have to remember both the music and the lyrics in order to repeatedly play the same version of the song in each live recording. His inability to read music and English lyrics forced him to have a crystal clear, sharp memory for both the music and the lyrics.[455]

Who Was Bill Graham?[456]

Bill Graham was a music promoter who played a key role in the discovery of Albert King and the Blues among young white music fans. Graham was also instrumental in the promotion of a number of important rock stars of the 1960s, including the Paul Butterfield Blues Band, Jefferson Airplane, Big Brother and the Holding Company, Country Joe and the Fish, and the Grateful Dead.

Bill Graham

Bill Graham was born Wulf Wolodi Grajonca on January 8, 1931, in Berlin, Germany. He was the youngest child and only son of lower middle-class Jewish parents, Frieda (née Sass) and Jacob "Yankel" Grajonca.[457,458] The parents had emigrated from Russia before the rise of Nazism.[459] Six children were in the Grajonca family. Jacob, his father, died in an accident two days after Graham was born.[460,461] Graham's family nicknamed him "Wolfgang" early in life.[462]

Due to the increasing peril to Jews in Germany and the death of Jacob, Frieda, Graham's mother, placed her son and her youngest daughter, Tanya "Tolla", in a Berlin orphanage. This orphanage sent Wulf and Tolla to France in a pre-Holocaust exchange of Jewish children for Christian orphans. Sonja and Ester, Graham's older sisters, stayed behind with their mother.[463]

After the fall of France, Graham was among a group of Jewish orphans spirited out of France. some of this group finally reached the United States. Tolla Grajonca came down with pneumonia and did not survive the difficult journey. Graham was one of the One Thousand Children (OTC), mainly Jewish children who managed to flee Hitler and Europe, came directly to North America. Parents of all the children in the OTC were forced to stay behind. Graham's mother was murdered in Auschwitz.[464]

At age 10, Graham settled into a foster home in the Bronx, New York. He was often taunted as an immigrant and called a Nazi because of his German-accented English. Graham worked on his accent, eventually able to speak in a perfect New York accent. He changed his name to sound more "American". "Graham" was the closest name in the phone book that matched to his birth surname, "Grajonca". Graham graduated from DeWitt Clinton High School and then obtained a business degree from the City College of New York.[465,466].

Graham was drafted into the United States Army in 1951, and served in the Korean War. He was awarded both the Bronze Star and Purple Heart as a result of being wounded. Upon his return to the States, Graham worked as a waiter/maître d' in Catskill Mountain resorts in upstate New York during their heyday. He regularly hosted poker games behind the scenes poker games. Graham felt that his experience as a maître d' and running the poker games was good training for his eventual career as a promoter.

In the early 1960s, Graham moved from New York to San Francisco to be closer to his sister Rita. He was invited to attend a free concert in Golden Gate Park, produced by Chet Helms and the Diggers. At this concert, Graham made contact with the San Francisco Mime Troupe, a radical theater group. After Mime Troupe leader R. G. Davis was arrested on obscenity charges during an outdoor performance, Graham organized his first concert, a benefit concert to cover the troupe's legal fees. The concert was a success.[467] Graham saw a future business opportunity as a music promoter.

Graham began promoting more concerts supporting peace movements, civil rights, farm workers and others causes. Most of his shows were performed at rented venues. Graham saw a need for more permanent location of his own.

Charles Sullivan was a mid-20th-century entrepreneur and businessman in San Francisco. Sullivan owned the master lease on the Fillmore Auditorium.

Charles Sullivan

Businessman, San Francisco

Ambassador Roller Skating Rink, 1949
Fillmore Auditorium, 1966

Graham approached Sullivan to host the Second Mime Troupe concert at the Fillmore Auditorium on December 10, 1965. Graham later secured a contract from Sullivan for the open dates at the Fillmore Auditorium in 1966. Graham credits Sullivan with giving him his break in the music concert hall business.

Graham continued to promote concerts starring the radical Mime Troup. After the success of the Mime Troupe shows at a number of locations, Graham parted ways with the Troupe. He went back to the Fillmore. Sullivan had died. The Fillmore was owned by Harry Shifs, a haberdasher. Eleven other promoters had already put in bids to lease the Fillmore. Graham had forty-one prominent citizens to write letters to Shifs. Shifs gave him a three-year lease at five hundred dollars a month.[468]

Graham hired an amazing staff. The staff was resourceful, successful, and popular. Perhaps most importantly, staff members maintained personal contacts with artists and fans alike. As a result, Graham became the top rock concert promoter in the San Francisco Bay Area. Rock concerts promoted by Graham were extremely successful.

From March 8, 1968, until June 27, 1971, Graham operated the Fillmore East in the lower east side of Manhattan. On July 4, 1968, Graham closed the Fillmore Auditorium. Graham opened the Fillmore West on the very next day, July 5, 1968, which he operated until July 4, 1971. These clubs were even more successful.

Bill Graham needed musicians to perform after he opened the clubs in 1968. Graham went looking. He found Albert King at Ike Turner's Manhattan Club in East St. Louis.

In 1971, Bill Graham decided to close both clubs. Graham continued to promote music concerts until his death on October 25, 1991.

Who Was Willie Dixon?[469]

Willie Dixon was the chief architect of the post WWII Chicago Blues. Thanks to Willie Dixon, Chess Records went from a struggling recording company to the leading publisher of the Chicago Blues sound. Willie was responsible for finding, recruiting and recording of the greats of Chicago Blues.

Willie loved the Blues. ... *the blues will always be because the blues are the roots of all American music. As long as American music survives, so will the blues ... Most of the blues artists today ...they tell you their expression and feeling. The story of the facts of life is a helluva thing.*[470]

Willie Dixon

Having both Albert King and Willie Dixon as performers at the 4th Festival further enhanced the national reputation of the Festival.

William James Dixon was an American blues musician, vocalist, songwriter, arranger and record producer.[471] He was proficient in playing both the upright bass and the guitar, and sang with a distinctive voice. Willie is perhaps best known as one of the most prolific songwriters of his time.

Dixon wrote or co-wrote more than 500 songs.[472] Several have become blues standards, including *Help Me*, *Hoochie Coochie Man*, *I Can't Quit You Baby*, *I Ain't Superstitious*, *I'm Ready*, *Little Red Rooster*, *My Babe*, and *Spoonful*.[473]

Dixon was born in Vicksburg, Mississippi, on July 1, 1915.[474] He was one of 14 children to Anderson Bell and Daisy Dixon.[475,476]

Anderson Bell   **Daisy Dixon, Baby Willie**
Both Courtesy: Willie Dixon

Daisy, his mother, often rhymed things she said. Willie soon began to imitate this habit. He wrote poems for himself. Willie Dixon sang his first song at Springfield Baptist Church at the age of four.[477]

Dixon was first introduced to blues when he served time on a prison farm in Mississippi as a young teenager. When he was about 12 years old, Willie, Shedrick Johnson and Leroy Wilson entered an old doctor's house. This gang took some old pipes that had been torn down. For this theft, Dixon and his friends were put in jail on a prison farm called Ball Ground Farm about 15 miles north of Vicksburg. *I heard these guys down there moaning and groaning these really down-to-earth blues. From these songs, I really began to find out what the blues meant to Black people. It gave them consolation to be able to think these things over ... and how they resented various things in life.*[478]

Later in his teens, Willie learned to sing harmony from Theo Phelps, a local carpenter. Phelps led the Union Jubilee Singers, a gospel quintet, in which Dixon sang bass. In addition to Willie, Melvin Short, Alonzo Phelps and Theo Phelps were in this group. This group regularly performed on the Vicksburg radio station WQBC.[479] Willie began adapting his poems into songs and even sold some to local music groups.

Dixon left Mississippi for Chicago in 1936.[480] He was 6 feet 2 inches tall and weighed over 250 pounds. In Chicago, Willie became a very successful boxer.

Boxer Willie Dixon

Courtesy: L V Dixon

He won the Illinois State Golden Gloves Heavyweight Championship (Novice Heavyweight Division) in 1937.[481],[482] Around 1939, Willie became a professional boxer, fighting under the name James Dixon. *I didn't have any training. I just knocked out every damn body and that was it. I won.* He worked briefly as Joe Louis's sparring partner. After four fights as a professional, he left boxing in a dispute with his manager over money.

Dixon met Leonard "Baby Doo" Caston at a boxing gym, where the pair would harmonize at times. Dixon performed in several vocal groups in Chicago. Caston persuaded Dixon to pursue music seriously.[483] Caston built Dixon's first bass, made of a tin-can and one string. Dixon's experience singing bass made the instrument familiar.[484] Willie also learned to play the guitar.

In 1939, Dixon was a founding member of the Five Breezes, with Leonard "Baby Doo"Caston, Freddie Walker, Joe Bell, Gene Gilmore and Willie Hawthorne.[485]

The Five Breezes
(left to right)
(front) Freddie "Cool Breeze" Walker, Willie Hawthorne
(rear) Dixon, Gene Gilmore, Leonard "Baby Doo" Caston
Courtesy: Willie Dixon

The group blended blues, jazz, and vocal harmonies, in the mode of the Ink Spots.[486] In Nov, 1940, the Five Breezes cut eight tracks that were released on the Bluebird label, a subsidiary of RCA that produced "race records".[487]

Dixon's progress on the upright bass came to an abrupt halt with the advent of World War II. He refused induction into military service as a conscientious objector and was imprisoned for ten months.[488] Willie refused to go to war to fight for a nation in which institutionalized racism and racist laws were prevalent.[489]

After the war, in 1945, Willie Dixon formed a group named the Four Jumps of Jive. This Quartet included Willie Dixon, Gene Gilmore, Bernardo Dennis, and Ellis Hunter.[490]

The Four Jumps Of Jive
(left to right)
Bernardo Dennis, Gene Gilmore, Dixon, Ellis Hunter
Courtesy: Willie Dixon

He then reunited with Leonard "Baby Doo" Caston, and Ollie Crawford, forming the Big Three Trio,[491,492] which recorded for Columbia Records.[493]

The Big Three
(top to bottom)
Willie Dixon
Leonard "Baby Doo" Caston
Ollie Crawford

The Big Three was regularly booked into show clubs seating 3000-5000 people. Featured artists played 2-3 week engagements rather than a string of one-nighters.[494]

In 1950, Dixon had made the most important move of his career, signing up with Chess Records in Chicago, as a recording artist.[495] Very quickly, Willie began performing less, becoming more involved with administrative tasks for the label. By 1951, he was a full-time employee at Chess, where he acted as producer, talent scout, session musician and staff songwriter. He was also a producer for Checker Records, the Chess subsidiary. His relationship with Chess was sometimes strained, but he stayed with the label until the early 1960s.[496]

During this time Dixon's output and influence were prodigious. *After awhile, Chess got to a place where they would always depend on me to have a song when somebody else ran short.*[497] From late 1956 to early 1959, Willie also worked in a similar capacity for Cobra Records. He produced early singles for Otis Rush, Magic Sam, and Buddy Guy.[498] From the late 1960s until the mid-1970s, Dixon ran his own record label, Yambo Records, and two subsidiary labels, Supreme and Spoonful. He released his 1971 album, Peace?, on Yambo and also singles by McKinley Mitchell, Lucky Peterson and others.[499]

Dixon is considered one of the key figures in the creation of Chicago blues. He worked with Chuck Berry, Muddy Waters, Howlin' Wolf, Otis Rush, Bo Diddley, Little Walter, Sonny Boy Williamson II, Koko Taylor, Little Milton, Eddie Boyd, Jimmy Witherspoon, Lowell Fulson, Willie Mabon, Memphis Slim, Washboard Sam, Jimmy Rogers, Sam Lay and others.

In his later years, Dixon became a tireless ambassador for the blues and a vocal advocate for its practitioners. He founded the Blues Heaven Foundation, which works to preserve the legacy of the blues and to secure copyrights and royalties for blues musicians who were exploited in the past.[500] Speaking with the simple eloquence that was a hallmark of his songs, Dixon claimed, *The blues are the roots and the other musics are the fruits. It's better keeping the roots alive, because it means better fruits from now on. The blues are the roots of all American music. As long as American music survives, so will the blues.*

In 1977, unhappy with the small royalties paid by Arc Music, Chess's publishing company, Dixon and Muddy Waters sued Arc. With the proceeds from the settlement, Dixon and Waters founded their own publishing company, Hoochie Coochie Music.[501]

Willie Dixon maintained a grueling touring pace until 1982. Tired of this constant, tiring touring, Willie moved to Los Angeles in that year. In Los Angeles, Dixon found greater opportunities that paid well without having to travel. He acted in commercials and became involved in movie soundtracks. Willie continued writing songs, working with artists, recording music, and performing in clubs in the Los Angeles area. His new songs often reflected an increased concern with social issues.[502]

Willie Dixon died of heart failure on January 29, 1992, in Burbank, California. Willie was buried in Burr Oak Cemetery, in Alsip, Illinois.

Who Was Bobby "Blue" Bland?[503]

Bobby Blue Bland was the ultimate Blues vocalist. He had to be that good, because he followed Albert King at the 1983 KLON Blues Festival. Bobby Bland had a long standing, established reputation as the leading vocalist of the Blues. Having Bland as the headliner at the 1983 Festival was another indicator that the KLON Festival was a national event for the Blues.

Bobby developed a sound that mixed gospel with the blues and R&B.[504] He was described as *among the great storytellers of blues and soul music... [who] created tempestuous arias of love, betrayal and resignation, set against roiling, dramatic orchestrations, and left the listener drained but awed.*[505]

**Bobby Bland
Lion of the Blues**

Bland was born Robert Calvin Brooks in the small town of Barretville, Tennessee.[506,507] to parents I. J. Brooks and Mary Lee Brooks. I. J. abandoned the family not long after his birth. When he was 6, his mother remarried to his stepfather, Leroy Bridgeforth.

Robert later acquired the name "Bland" from his stepfather who was also called Leroy Bland.[508] Robert dropped out of school in third grade to work in the cotton fields and never graduated from school.[509]

With his mother Mary Lee, Bland moved to Memphis in 1947, where he started singing with local gospel groups, including the Miniatures. Eager to expand his interests, Bland began frequenting the city's famous Beale Street, where he became associated with a circle of aspiring musicians. These musicians were collectively called the Beale Streeters. The Streeters included Earl Forrest, the founder, Richard Sanders, Rosco Gordon, and Johnny Ace. Sometimes, other members were included such as B.B. King, Junior Parker, and now Bobby Bland.[510]

The Beale Streeters
(left to right)
Earl Forest, Richard Sanders, Bobby Bland, Johnny Ace

In 1951, talent scout Ike Turner recorded Bland for Modern Records at Tuff Green's house in Memphis.[511,512] Because Bland was illiterate, this first recording was the one song that Bobby knew, *They Call It*

Stormy Monday.[513] Turner played the piano, backing Bland for his first two records. These records were released under the name Robert Bland.[514,515] Between 1951 and 1952, Bland recorded commercially unsuccessful singles for Modern and Sun Records, which licensed its recordings to Chess Records.[516]

Bland's recordings from the early 1950s show him striving for individuality. These unsuccessful records caught the attention of Duke Records.[517,518] Bobby signed a recording contract with Duke Records in 1950. However, Bobby's progress was halted for two years while Bland served in the U.S. Army. During his Army service, Bland performed in a band with the singer Eddie Fisher.[519]

Eddie Fisher

When Bland returned to Memphis in 1954, several of his former associates, including Johnny Ace, were enjoying considerable success. Bland joined Ace's revue.

In 1956, Bland began working with Junior Parker, also serving as his valet and driver. The modest Bland had also provided these services to Rosco Gordon and B.B. King. He wouldn't be a valet for long.[520]

Duke Records was now being run by Houston entrepreneur Don Robey.

Don Robey

Duke Records

Robey handed Bobby a new contract, which Bobby could not read So, Robey willingly helped Bobby sign his name to the contract. This contract gave Bland just half a cent per record sold, instead of the industry standard of 2 cents per record.[521]

This underhanded behavior was usual for Don Robey. Robey was half black, half Jewish, all gangster. He was the first African-American record mogul. A gambler and a hustler, Robey did not play fair. But he produce and distribute some of the greatest gospel, R&B and rock and roll records of the 1950s and '60s from a building at 2809 Erastus Street in the Fifth Ward of Houston. Duke/Peacock was raw, black Southern music for an audience more into jubilation than assimilation.[522]

In a back office, Robey he launched Peacock Records in 1949. Peacock first made its name in the gospel field, then hit big in R&B in 1953 *Hound Dog*, by Big Mama Thornton. Elvis Presley cover of this song would not become famous until 1956.

After he acquired the Duke label in the early '50s, Robey's stable of acts contained not only Clarence Gatemouth Brown, Bobby "Blue" Bland, Junior Parker, Johnny Ace, Roscoe Gordon, Memphis Slim, Johnny Otis, Big Walter and the Thunderbirds and O.V. Wright.

Robey's empire included the Buffalo Booking Agency, run by the irreplaceable Evelyn Johnson, which repped many Black entertainers, including B.B. King, out on the "chitlin circuit" and gospel highway. Robey insisted that his acts tour incessantly. If the performers had jobs they couldn't leave, like Austin's Bells of Joy in 1951, Robey sent out singers to pose as them. As a one-stop operation, Robey got a piece of everything and used strong-armed intimidation to make negotiations go his way.

He might've ripped me off but if it wasn't for Don Robey, nobody would've ever heard of me, said Clarence Gatemouth Brown.

Such sentiments fueled impresario greed across the board in the music business at the time. Getting paid to do something you love was a novel concept after the Depression and WWII. Robey allowed musicians to make records, and the style didn't matter as long as people were buying them.

Bland released his first single for Duke in 1955.[523] In 1956 Bland began touring on the Chitlin' Circuit with Junior Parker in a revue called Blues Consolidated. Initially, Bland doubled as Parker's valet and driver.[524] Bobby then began recording for Duke with the bandleader Bill Harvey and the arranger Joe Scott.

Bill Harvey

Orchestra Leader, Saxophonist

Bill Harvey was born in Winona, Mississippi. Harvey moved with his mother to Memphis, Tennessee, as a child.[525] He became the leader of the Bill Harvey Band, one of the most successful performing bands in Memphis immediately after World War II. This band established a residency at Mitchell's Hotel on Beale Street. In 1950, Harvey signed a deal with Don Robey at Peacock Records in Houston, Texas. His band was featured on many of the successful R&B records released by Peacock and Duke Records during the 1950s, including those by Marie Adams, Big Mama Thornton, Bobby "Blue" Bland, and Little Junior Parker.[526] He also led Clarence "Gatemouth" Brown's touring band.[527] In 1952, he signed with B.B. King to become the bandleader for BB King, a role he continued for the next four years.

In the Duke/Peacock recordings, Bland began asserting his characteristic vocal style and crafting the melodic big-band blues singles for which he became famous. He was often accompanied by the guitarist Wayne Bennett.[528] Unlike many Blues musicians, Bland did not play an instrument.[529].

Bland's first chart success came in 1957 with *Farther Up the Road*, which reached number 1 on the R&B chart and number 43 on the Billboard Hot 100. Bland's craft was most clearly heard on a series of early-1960s releases, including *Cry Cry Cry*, *I Pity the Fool* and *Turn On Your Love Light*. *I Pity the Fool* was number 1 on the R&B chart in

1961. *Turn On Your Love Light* became a much-covered standard by many bands. Despite credits to the contrary—often claimed by Robey—many of these classic works were written by Joe Scott.[530]

In 1963, *That's the Way Love Is* was Bland's last record to reach number 1 on the R&B chart. But Bobby continued to produce a consistent run of R&B chart entries through the mid-1960s. Bland's records mostly sold on the R&B market rather than achieving crossover success. Bland had 23 top ten hits on the Billboard R&B chart.[531]

Financial pressures forced the singer to cut his touring band. In 1968, the group disbanded.[532] Bland suffered from depression and became increasingly dependent on alcohol.[533] But, Bland stopped drinking in 1971. Duke Records, his record company, was sold to the larger ABC Records group.[534] This sale resulted in several successful and critically acclaimed contemporary blues and soul albums[535].

In 1973, Bland released the single *This Time I'm Gone for Good*. Hugely popular, this single took Bland back into the pop Top 50 for the first time since 1964 and made the R&B top 10 in late 1973.

In the late 70s and throughout the 80s most Blues artists were performing for white audiences. However, Bobby wanted to continue performing for Black audiences.[536] In 1985, Bland signed a contract with Malaco Records.[537] Malaco specialized in traditional Southern black music whose target audience was Black. Bland made a series of albums for Malaco, while continuing to tour and appear at concerts with B. B. King.

Despite occasional age-related ill health, Bland continued to record new albums for Malaco. He performed occasional tours alone and with B. B. King. He also performed at blues and soul festivals worldwide.[538]

Bland continued performing until shortly before his death. He died on June 23, 2013, at his home in Germantown, Tennessee, a suburb of Memphis. His family members described his cause of death as *an ongoing illness*. Bobby Bland was 83 when he died.[539,540,541,542] After his death, his son Rodd told news media that Bland had recently told him that the Blues musician James Cotton was Bland's half-brother.[543]

Call Him "Mr. Harmonica Smith" (1983)

On Oct 2, 1983, George "Harmonica" Smith died. Bernie Pearl relates the sudden shock to the Blues community and its response.

To say that George "Harmonica" Smith was respected and would be missed only diminishes his place in the Blues scene in Southern California and beyond. His stature among harp blowers and fans was nothing less than "Mr. Harmonica", the man who taught one and all how to play the modern Blues, Chicago-style. He revealed the elusive technique of blowing the Blues on the chromatic harp, and could play Little Walter tunes note for note. Born in West Helena, Arkansas, George Smith spent time in Chicago, making friends with many of the greats like Muddy and Wolf, and brought his huge history and prodigious musicianship to L.A.

His passing was sudden and shocking, even though we all knew he had a heart condition. He played with vitality and vigor until the end. We might have guessed that he knew his health outlook was not good when he took a bunch of us into McCoy's Studio in South L.A. to record an L.P., which would be titled *Pick Your Choice*. In his words, he wanted to bring attention to people who had earned it, but were not getting it. He even named me as his co-producer, though I really had no greater role than playing guitar on some tracks.

One-Man-Band Blind Joe Hill, down-home vocalist Long Gone Miles, guitarist Doug McLeod, guitarist Evans Walker, and harp man William Clarke with the Night Owls, all had songs on George's "Shoe Label" release. Smith himself was featured on three of the eight sides, "Misty", "Stockholm Swing", and "Bad Luck at My Door". It was to be his final recording. Participating studio musicians included Lloyd Glenn (original pianist on "Call It Stormy Monday Blues"), L.A. legend J.D. Nicholson and Mark Withers also on piano, Dennis Walker and Jerry Abrams, bass, and more.

The Blues community got together just two months after his funeral, and on December 4 of 1983 we put on a benefit show for his family at the Music Machine in West L.A. It featured a who's who of L.A.-based Blues artists: Big Joe Turner, Pee Wee Crayton, Cleanhead Vinson, Smokey Wilson, Lee Allen, Mickey Champion, Percy Mayfield, Margie Evans, Shaky Jake, Joe Houston, and Smith harp disciples Rod Piazza & the Mighty Flyers, and William Clarke. His daughter Darlene also sang. Also Doug McLeod, Bernie Pearl, J.D. Nicholson, and many more. I recall the place being full to the rafters. TG no Fire Department inspectors came by.

It was a huge success. I don't know how much money was raised, but the $6 admission, times at least 200-300, provided immediate help to the family.

1984 5th Annual Long Beach Blues Festival

This 5th occurrence of the KLON Blues Festival was significant for a number of reasons. At this Festival, BB King was the headliner. BB King was known as the *King of the Blues*. His presence gave a national prominence to this Festival. All of the other performers were the cream of the crop of Blues musicians from all over the US. This Festival was extended from 1 day to 2 days, the first KLON Blues Festival to be 2 days long. With 13,000 attendees, this Festival was the largest of all the Festivals. Attendance at successive Festivals would average around 8500.

Who Was BB King?[544]

BB King was considered the King of the Blues. By 1984, everyone who listened to the Blues knew BB King. Having BB at the 5th Festival announced that the KLON Long Beach Blues Festival was one of the premiere Blues festivals.

BB King, 1984 KLON Blues Festival
Photo Courtesy: Bernie Pearl

Riley B. King, known professionally as B. B. King, was an American blues guitarist, singer, songwriter, and record producer. He introduced a sophisticated style of soloing based on fluid string bending, shimmering vibrato, and staccato picking that influenced many later blues electric guitar players.[545,546]

Riley/B B King was born on September 16, 1925,[547] on a cotton plantation named Bear Creek in the unincorporated town of Berclair, MS.[548] This planation was owned by Jim O'Reilly.[549] Berclair is in Leflore County, near the city of Itta Bena, Mississippi.[550] Riley was the son of sharecroppers Albert and Nora Ella King.[551]

Around 1931, Nora Ella King left Albert King. Nora moved to Kilmichael in the hilly part of MS, east of the MS Delta, to be with her family. Nora took young Riley to live with her and the family. When Riley was 10 years old, Nora Ella died from diabetes. Nora was only 31 years old, blind and wasted from the diabetes.[552] From 1931, BB was raised by Elnora Farr, his maternal grandmother, in Kilmichael.[553]

Booker T Washington 'Bukka' White

Bluesman Bukka White was a first cousin of Nora Ella King, King's mother. Lula White, Bukka White's mother, and Elnora Farr, King's maternal grandmother, were sisters. Thus, BB King and Bukka White were second cousins. As a child, BB saw White perform many times.[554]

From 1936 to 1940, King was attracted to the Pentecostal Church of God in Christ because of its music. Rev Archie Fair, the local minister, performed with a Sears Roebuck Silvertone guitar during services and taught King his first three chords. Riley began teaching himself to play the guitar.[555] During this period, King attended and sang in the gospel choir at the Elkhorn School of the Elkhorn Primitive Baptist Church[556] in Kilmichael, MS.

Elkhorn Baptist Church (left), Elkhorn School (right)

King walked several miles a day to attend the one-room school heated only by a wooden stove.

Luther Henson, was a teacher at Elkhorn School.

Luther Henson, Elkhorn School

Henson taught Riley to be self-reliant, fair minded and devoted to self improvement.[557]

Disaster struck on Jan 10, 1940. Grandmother Elnora Farr died after a brief illness. At age 14, Riley King was alone in the world. He had to earn his own living. Riley tried to work the farm. At the end of his first crop year in Sept, 1940, Riley had earned $4.18 and still owed $7.54 to Edwayne Henderson, the farm owner. Later in that Fall, 1940, father Albert King moved his son to Lexington, MS. Riley lived with Albert, his wife and his half-siblings. Albert enrolled Riley in a segregated Black school.[558]

Riley/BB lived with Albert and his family until late 1941. For BB, Lexington was a big city with its population of 3,000. He didn't like the "big city" ways. Cruelty to Blacks was common. And, BB felt like a stranger in his father's home. He wanted to join his cousins back in Kilmichael. Riley rode his bicycle for 2 days to cross about 45 miles back to Kilmichael. Unfortunately, the cousins had moved away.[559]

In 1942, Riley took residence with the family of Flake Cartledge, a white farmer, in Kilmichael. He lived in a shack on the farm and worked. King walked to a local school. He also worked around the farm to earn money for food and clothing.[560] King's first guitar was bought for him by Flake Cartledge for 15 dollars. Cartledge withheld money from King's salary for the next two months until the debt was repaid.[561,562]

In the early 1940s, King honed his guitar skills and formed a gospel quartet, called the Elkhorn Singers. This group performed at local churches around Kilmichael.[563]

In November 1941, King Biscuit Time had first aired, broadcasting on KFFA in Helena, Arkansas. This radio show featured the Mississippi Delta blues. King listened to the show while on break at the Cartledge farm in 1942. By now a self-taught guitarist, King decided to become a radio musician.[564]

BB King moved by himself to Indianola in 1943, which he referred to as his hometown. Riley lived with his cousin Birkett Davis. He earned a living by driving a tractor on a plantation owned by Johnson Barrett.[565] In Indianola, King later worked at a cotton gin.[566]

Early in 1944, Riley King married Martha Denton. Riley and Martha lived with Cousin Birkett and his wife Delicia in a shared cabin on the Barrett Farm. Each couple raised cotton on adjacent tracts. King also continued to work as a tractor driver for Barrett.[567]

King was drafted into the U.S. Army in the Fall, 1944. He sang Blues for the troops stationed at Camp Shelby, in Hattiesburg, MS, and at Fort Benning, Georgia.[568] King was released after being ruled as "essential to the war economy" based on his experience as a tractor driver.[569,570,571] King returned to Indianola, earning a living doing odd jobs, including operating a tractor on the Barret Farm. He occasionally sang gospel in the local church and on streetcorners.[572]

In 1945, BB joined and played guitar with the famous St. John's Gospel Singers in Indianola.[573] This group regularly performed at area churches and on broadcasts by WJPM radio in Greenwood and by WJPR radio in Greenville.[574,575,576]

St. John's Gospel Singers

Back, from left:

Birkett Davis, O.L. Matthew, Riley King

Front, from left:

Ben Carvin, John Matthew

Source: BB King or Sawyer Book

Then, King had an unfortunate accident. In 1947, King damaged the tractor on the Barrett Farm. In panic over his possible liability to pay for the damages, BB decided to get out of town. BB hitchhiked to Memphis TN, to join cousin Bukka White. King deserted Martha and left the crops in the ground to rot. White hosted cousin Riley for the next ten months. King returned to Indianola in 1948. He worked hard, paying his debt for the tractor damage.[577]

Late in 1948, Riley King and Martha moved to West Memphis, Arkansas. Sonny Boy Williamson II (Alex Ford) still hosted and played the King Biscuit Time show.

Sonny Boy Williamson II (Alex Ford)

This show was that same daily Blues show on KWEM radio in West Memphis that initially motivated Riley. By way of an audition, Riley King played one song, live and on the air.[578] King then performed regularly on the radio program of Sonny Boy Williamson. As a result of these shows, BB began to develop an audience. King's popularity led to steady engagements at the Sixteenth Avenue Grill in West Memphis.[579]

Memphis, TN, was on the east bank of the MS River, across from West Memphis, AR. WDIA radio station in Memphis conducted a revolutionary music program specifically targeting Black audiences. Shortly thereafter in late 1948, King auditioned in the lobby of WDIA.[580] He was well received and was assigned a 15 minute spot on the station.[581] This radio spot identified Riley King as The Pepticon Boy. His show promoted Pepticon, an alcohol-laced health tonic.[582] This show became extremely popular and was expanded. Eventually, the WDIA show was renamed as the Sepia Swing Club.[583]

Beginning in 1949, Riley King began working at WDIA as a disc jockey, spinning vinyl in addition to performing live on air. After becoming popular as a disc jockey, Riley was renamed from The Pepticon Boy to the nickname "Beale Street Blues Boy". This nickname was later shortened to "Blues Boy", and finally further shortened to "B. B."[584,585]

 His local popularity on radio and around the area attracted the attention of Bullet Records, a small recording company. In 1949, King debuted his recordings on Bullet Records by issuing the single *Miss Martha King*. This song failed to chart well.

My very first recordings [in 1949] were[sic] for a company out of Nashville called Bullet, the Bullet Record Transcription company. I had horns that very first session. I had Phineas Newborn on piano; his father played drums, and his brother, Calvin, played guitar with me. I had Tuff Green on bass, Ben Branch on tenor sax, his brother, Thomas Branch, on trumpet, and a lady trombone player. The Newborn family were the house band at the famous Plantation Inn in West Memphis.

My infatuation with brass goes back even farther I'm kind of from the big-band era. I was crazy about Benny Goodman, I liked Count Basie, Duke Ellington, Jimmy Lunceford and all the big bands that had blues singers with them. Jay McShann had Walter Brown as a singer, Count Basie had Jimmy Rushing, Duke had Al Hibbler, Benny Goodman had Peggy Lee. All those were my favorites. I loved the sound of horns and all of that. I always wanted it, and I always had one or two horns, always.[586]

During one show in Twist, Arkansas in 1949,[587] a brawl broke out between two men, causing a fire. King evacuated with the rest of the crowd but returned to retrieve his guitar. BB later discovered that the two men were fighting over a woman named Lucille. He named the guitar Lucille, as a reminder not to fight over women or run into any more burning buildings.[588]

Ike Turner introduced King to the Bihari brothers while Ike was a talent scout at Modern Records. In 1950,[589] King began recording songs under contract with Memphis-based RPM Records, a subsidiary of Los Angeles-based Modern Records. Many of King's early recordings were produced by Sam Phillips for RPM Records.[590]

Sam Phillips, RPM, then Sun Records

Phillips would later record Elvis Presley, Johnny Cash, Jerry Lee Lewis, Roy Orbison and Carl Perkins under the Sun Records label.

While working at WDIA in 1950, BB King first met T-Bone Walker. *Once I'd heard him for the first time, I knew I'd have to have [an electric guitar] myself. 'Had' to have one, short of stealing.*[591]

Los Angeles Bluesman TBone Walker

Over the years, BB King took quite a bit more from T Bone Walker.

In the late 1940s and early 1950s, King was a part of the Blues scene on Beale Street. *Beale Street was where it all started for me.* On Beale Street, BB performed with Bobby Bland, Johnny Ace, and Earl Forest in a group known as the Beale Streeters.

3 O'Clock Blues had been a minor hit by Oakland CA Bluesman Lowell Fulson. BB King recorded, *3 O'Clock Blues* in August, 1951, for RPM Records, the subsidiary of Modern Records. This recording was at an improvised space in the Memphis YMCA. *That Ain't The Way To Do It* was also recorded at that same session. A 45 rpm record containing the pair of songs was released by RPM Records in Dec, 1951.[592]

On Feb 2, , 1952, *3 O'Clock Blues* charted as his first #1 song on the Billboard Rhythm and Blues hit parade chart. As a result of the success of *3 O'Clock Blues*, BB King obtained his first chance at a national audience. King signed with Universal Attractions, a booking agency. This agency arranged a tour for BB with stops at the Howard Theater in Washington, DC, the Royal Theater in Baltimore, the Regal Theater in Chicago, and the Apollo Theater in NYC.[593]

BB King wanted to play with an orchestra. In 1952, King teamed with the Bill Harvey Band, the most famous band in Memphis. This band became the road band for BB. He signed with the Buffalo Booking Agency of Houston, TX. Buffalo was owned by the infamous Don Robey and actually run by Evelyn Johnson.[594]

BB King and the Bill Harvey Band
(left to right) Johnny Ace (piano), Bill Harvey (sax), BB King (far right) Big Mama Thornton

Riley King and Martha King divorced in 1952, without any children. Also in 1952, *You Know I Love You* became the second #1 hit on the R&B hit parade chart released by BB King.[595]

In 1953, BB King resigned from playing and from the disc jockey roster at WDIA in Memphis. Robey and Johnson were so successful at obtaining gigs for BB King and the Bill Harvey Band that BB simply did not have the time to work at the station. BB King liked playing on the road and especially liked the greater income.[596]

From 1952 after the release of *You Know I Love You* until 1956, King released an impressive list of hits. His hits included *Story from My Heart and Soul* (R&B #9, 1952), *Woke Up This Morning* (R&B #3, 1953), *Please Love Me* **(R&B #1, 1953)**, Please Hurry Home (R&B #4, 1953), *When My Heart Beats Like a Hammer* (R&B #8, 1954), *Whole Lotta' Love* (R&B #8, 1954), *You Upset Me Baby* **(R&B #1, 1954)**, *Every Day I Have the Blues* (R&B #8, 1955), *Sneakin' Around* (R&B #14, 1955), *Ten Long Years* (R&B #9, 1955), *Bad Luck* (R&B #57, 1956), and *Sweet Little Angel* (R&B #8, 1956).[597]

Appearing on the R&B Roster indicated the popularity of the songs with Black audiences. At the time, most whites did not listen to this kind of music. These records were identified as *race records* by the producing companies and generally sold only in Black music stores.

These hits led to a significant increase in the weekly earnings of BB King, from about $85 to $2,500.[598,599] BB King and the Bill Harvey Band continued to play at major venues such as the Howard Theater in Washington and the Apollo in New York, as well as continued touring on the *Chitlin' Circuit*. This informal network of Black clubs and juke joints across the south and southeast US were the bread and butter for Blues musicians during the 1940's – 1960s. As Blues musicians moved from large venue to large venue, these smaller venues provided a source of income to pay travel expenses.

King assembled his own band, the B.B. King Review, under the leadership of Millard Lee in 1956.[600]

Millard Lee

Courtesy: Univ of Houston

Public Domain

This band initially consisted of Calvin Owens and Kenneth Sands (trumpet), Lawrence Burdin (alto saxophone), George Coleman (tenor saxophone),[601] Floyd Newman (baritone saxophone), Millard Lee (piano), George Joyner (bass) and Earl Forest and Ted Curry (drums), bassist Shinny Walker, his brother Cato Walker, the bus driver, and vocalist Evelyn "Mama Nuts" Young.[602] Onzie Horne was a trained musician enlisted as an arranger to assist King with his compositions. By his admission, King could not play chords well and always relied on improvisation.[603]

With 16 touring members, King needed transportation. BB purchased his first touring bus, "Big Red."[604]

Big Red and the BB King Touring Entourage

For BB King, 1956 became a record-breaking year, with 342 concerts booked and three recording sessions.[605] That same year he founded his own record label, Blues Boys Kingdom, with headquarters at

Beale Street in Memphis. With his own label, King became a producer for artists such as Millard Lee and Levi Seabury.[606]

BB King was married a 2nd time in 1958. King married Sue Hall. Sue was the daughter of Ruby Edwards,[607] the proprietress of Club Ebony back in Indianola, MS.

Club Ebony, Indianola, MS

Rev CL Franklin presided over the wedding, which was held in Detroit. Sue accompanied BB King in his life on the road.[608]

Bad luck and trouble followed Bluesman King in 1958. "Big Red", King's touring bus, collided with a butane truck on a bridge in TX. In the fiery wreck, the truck driver and his passenger died. Fortunately, the group on the bus were safe. Unfortunately, for BB, the company that insured the bus had been suspended several days before the accident. King was personally liable, even though he was not present. In a negotiated settlement, BB agreed to pay approximately $100,000 in damages ($ 1,092,263 in 2024).[609] BB King worked for many years to pay off the debt.[610]

In 1962, King signed with ABC-Paramount Records, which was later absorbed into MCA Records. (MCA was later absorbed into Geffen Records). King's recording contract was followed by tours across the United States, with performances in major theaters in cities such as Washington, D.C., Chicago, Los Angeles, Detroit, and St. Louis, as well as numerous gigs in small clubs and juke joints of the Chitlin' Circuit across the southern United States.[611]

In addition to changing record companies in 1962, BB King terminated his relationship with Buffalo Bookings. King signed with the New York City based Milt Shaw Booking Agency.

How Blue Can You Get by BB King was released by ABC-Paramount Records in 1963. Billboard had suspended the R&B Chart at this time. However, this recording reached number 97 on the Billboard Hot 100 chart in 1964.[612]

In November 1964, King recorded the album *Live at the Regal* at the Regal Theater in Chicago.[613] *Regal Live is considered by some the best recording I've ever had ... that particular day in Chicago everything came together."*[614]

Further bad luck and trouble hit the King of the Blues in 1966. Sue King filed for divorce. His replacement bus for Big Red was stolen. And the IRS slapped a $78,000 ($759,931 in 2024) lien on the future income of King for back taxes owed.[615]

However much he (and his wallet) desired a larger, more diverse audience, King still felt the need to connect to his own people, perhaps even feeling a measure of guilt for going uptown. Despite his emerging success with cross-over audiences, King continued to play clubs in the famed Chitlin' Circuit of Black clubs across the South throughout the 1960s.[616,617]

In 1966, BB King launched the ABC Bluesway series with the album *Blues Is King*.[618] This live album was recorded on Nov 5, 1966, at the International Club in Chicago. Future generations of Blues listeners would rank this album as one of his finest works.[619]

However, the fortunes of BB King were not doing so well in 1966. BB was playing to Black audiences that were actually shrinking in size. In 1966, Bernie Pearl went to see BB King 2 nights in a row at Gazzarri's on the Sunset Strip in West Hollywood, CA.

**Gazzarri's On Sunset
Original Home of the Doors**

On both nights, the house was pretty much empty. BB King and his band were not making any attempts to translate their music and style to the increasing Motown style. King chose to stay true to his form. On these 2 nights, band members wore suits and ties. His band included horns, unlike the Motown sound. Most importantly, BB King stayed true to his version of the Blues. King needed some way to reconnect with Black audiences and connect with a large and growing white audience.

Finally, a big break came for BB King. On Feb 26, 1967,[620] Bill Graham booked BB King into the Fillmore Auditorium in San Francisco. Bill Graham introduced BB King as *The King of the Blues*. This introduction was his first recognition with this title in front of a predominantly white audience. King was given his first standing ovation as he walked onto the stage at the Fillmore.[621]

In 1968, BB King had a dispute over money with Lou Zito his business manager. BB fired Zito and hired Sid Seidenberg, Zito's accountant, as his business manager. Seidenberg signed BB with Associated Booking. Associated Booking was operated by Joe Glaser. Glaser managed extremely popular Black musicians such as Louis Armstrong and Fats Domino.[622]

Realizing that his earnings would be forever limited by playing to an exclusively Black audience, King sought to break through to white listeners, achieving this feat by virtue of his own tenacity. In support of this goal, new manager Sid Seidenberg pushed King into a different type of venue. Blues-rock performers like Eric Clapton (once a member of the Yardbirds, as well as Cream) and Paul Butterfield were popularizing an appreciation of Blues music among white audiences.[623]

King gained further visibility among rock audiences as an opening act on the Rolling Stones' 1969 American Tour.[624] Bill Graham would later book King in both his Fillmore East and Fillmore West auditoriums.[625,626]

In 1969, his recording of *The Thrill Is Gone* was a crossover hit, appealing to both black and white audiences. This recording reached #3 on the R&B Charts and #15 on the Pop charts.[627]

My audience had started mixing before that, but that really pushed it over the top.... It was soon after that the Rolling Stones invited me to tour with them.... A lot of people heard me on that Rolling Stones tour that hadn't heard of me before." [628]

BB King won a 1970 Grammy Award for Best Rhythm and Blues Vocal Performance: Male for his version of "The Thrill Is Gone".[629] This song was also # 183 in Rolling Stone magazine's 500 Greatest Songs of All Time.[630]

From 1971 until his death in 2015, BB King maintained a highly visible and active career, appearing on numerous television shows and sometimes performing shows 300 nights a year.

In 1988, King reached a new generation of fans with the single "When Love Comes to Town". This song was a collaborative effort between King and the Irish band U2 on their *Rattle and Hum* album.

That same year, King joined U2 as the opening act on a 4 month world tour.[631]

BB King took the Blues from "*dirt floor, smoke in the air joints to grand concert halls. The Blues belonged everywhere beautiful music belonged.* He successfully worked both sides of the commercial divide, with sophisticated recordings and "raw, raucous" live performances.[632]

In 2006, King went on a "farewell" world tour, although he remained active afterward.[633]

On October 3, 2014, BB King completed a live performance at the House of Blues in Chicago. King did not feel well. A doctor diagnosed King with dehydration and exhaustion. King was actually suffering from high blood pressure and diabetes.[634,635,636] Eight remaining shows of his ongoing tour were canceled. King did not reschedule the shows.[637] That House of Blues show was his last show before his death in 2015.[638]

On May 14, 2015, at the age of 89,[639] BB King died in his sleep from vascular dementia. This condition was caused by a series of small strokes as a consequence of his type 2 diabetes.[640]

King's body was flown to Memphis on May 27, 2015. A funeral procession rolled down Beale Street with a hearse carrying his casket. A brass band marched in front of the hearse while playing *When the Saints Go Marching In.* Thousands lined the streets to pay their last respects.

King's body was then driven down Route 61 to his hometown of Indianola, MS.[641] King was laid in repose at the B.B. King Museum and Delta Interpretive Center, in Indianola. Mourners came to view his open casket.[642,643] On May 30, 2015, the funeral service was conducted at the Bell Grove Missionary Baptist Church in Indianola.[644] BB King was buried at the B.B. King Museum in Indianola.[645]

PBS has placed a complete video of the whole procession, service and burial online for future generations to pay respects to the King.[646]

Big Mama Maybe Sings Her Last Song (1984)

From 1980 - 1985, Bruce Krell spent a lot of time in clubs throughout south Central Los Angeles. In these clubs, Bruce could hear real Blues performed by some of the greatest Blues performers of the time. Many of these musicians had moved to Los Angeles.

One night in Feb, 1984, Bruce was sitting at home alone on a Saturday night with nothing to do. He decided to go out and hear some Blues. Bruce went to The Tiki Room down on Western Avenue in south central Los Angeles. That night, a thin haggard woman in a business suit sang one song as a guest performer.

I had gone to see Vernon Garrett, a well-known LA Bluesman, that had been announced as the performer of the evening. That night, the club was almost empty. Vernon was taking a break. Without any introduction, a thin, haggard woman walked on the stage. The band started playing behind her. She sang that song in a booming voice, full of the Blues.

After that song, I offered to buy the woman a drink. She sat down at my table. I said, That was a really great rendition of Hound Dog Man. You have a great voice. She responded, Thank you. I wrote that song. I then asked, What is your name? She told me, Willie Mae.

I had seen pictures of Big Mama Thornton, whose given name was Willie Mae. She was huge. This thin, haggard woman must be a different person. So, I asked, what is your last name? She said quietly and with amazing humility, Thornton. They used to call me Big Mama!

Given her current emaciated physical stature, I knew something had to be wrong. But, I didn't ask. Big Mama did not offer an explanation.

We sat. She slowly drank her beer. But, I was quietly amazed that she had delivered her song, singing her heart out with that booming voice, as usual. Big Mama was momentarily able to overcome whatever was causing her significantly dimiminished physical stature. But, just long enough to sing the one song that made her famous.

Willie Mae Thornton was literally wasting away from cancer. She likely had liver cancer, from all of her excessive drinking. She died of a heart attack on July 25th, 1984, at her home in Los Angeles. Her death was about 5 months after I had heard her sing at The Tiki Room. Given her poor health, that night just might have been the last live performance of Big Mama.

1985 6th Annual Blues Festival Lineup

Roomful of Blues, Otis Rush, Jimmy Smith, Lee Allen, Eddie "Cleanhead" Vinson, Linda Hopkins, Bo Diddley, The Blasters, Albert Collins, Papa John Creach, Joe Liggins & The Honeydrippers, Cash McCall Band, Charlie Musselwhite.

1985 KLON Blues Festival Signed Program Cover
Courtesy: Bernie Pearl

These hands on the cover are the hands of Henry Butler. Henry played piano in the band of Papa John Creach.

Blues Guitar Killers (1985)

Some of the hottest electric Blues guitarists in Southern California played at Madame Wong's, Chinatown, on Saturday, May 11, 1985. This group promoted themselves as The Blues Guitar Killers. The show ran from 9:00 p.m. until 1:00 a.m. Admission was $6.50 ($19.06 in 2024).

Madame Wong's was located on the 900 block of North Broadway in the Chinatown section of Los Angeles

. **Madame Wong's, Chinatown, Los Angeles, CA**
Courtesy: Chris Walter

In 1970, Madame Esther Wong and her husband George Wong opened Madam Wong's Restaurant on Sun Mun Way in Chinatown. Polynesian bands were originally featured. When that music attracted smaller and smaller crowds, Esther was persuaded in 1978 to book rock musicians for one month. Immediately her nightly crowd increased from as few as a dozen to about 350. Wong declared the restaurant a stage for rock, punk and new wave bands.

From 1980 until 1985, Madame Wong's Restaurant in Chinatown provided a venue for new and local groups and especially punk rock groups. Appearing on her stages were Oingo Boingo, the Police, X, the Motels, 20/20, the Knack, the Know, the Textones, the Go-Gos, the Plimsouls, the Kats, the Nu Kats, the Bus Boys, Plane English, the Naughty Sweeties and others. From 1978 – 1991, Esther Wong operated Madame Wong's Restaurant West in Santa Monica, CA. She closed the Chinatown location in 1985, a few months after the Blues Guitar Killers concert.

The Blues Guitar Killers consisted of 4 musicians from the Los Angeles area.

**Blues Guitar Killers
(from left)
Guitar Shorty, Bernie Pearl, Smokey Wilson, Tony Matthews
Courtesy: Edie Pearl**

"Guitar Shorty" refuses to tell his real name (David Kearney). But, audiences really don't mind because Shorty has a most amazing finale to his performances. He actually does acrobatics while playing his guitar! And he plays it for real!

Bernie Pearl is listened to each week by thousands of Blues fans on KI.ON/FM 88. But his guitar playing has been recognized by *Guitar Player Magazine* as .. *most .impressive* .. His specialty is electric slide and lap steel guitars.

Robert Lee "Smokey" Wilson hails from Mississippi Blues country. The dynamic singer/guitarist made his.reputation back home in the bands of Elmore James, Howlin' Wolf and Jirrmy Reed. His original interpretations of traditional Blues give ample reason for his noted guitar prowess.

Tony Matthews got his basic style from his uncle in rural Oklahoma. He honed those skills to razor-sharpness in the bands of Little Richard and Ray Charles, with whom he played for 10 years. A fine vocalist as well. At the time, Tony had a recently released album on the Alligator label, *Condition: Blue*. This album offered a chance for Tony to display his singing, playing and songwriting ability.

1986 Blues Festival Lineup

Big Twist and the Mellow Fellows, Guitar Showdown with Johnny Copeland, Buddy Guy & Matt "Guitar" Murphy, Super Harmonica Jam with James Cotton, Rod Piazza & Jr. Wells, Hank Crawford, Jimmy Johnson, Albert King, Robert Lockwood, Jr. & Pinetop Perkins, Little Milton, Rockin' Dopsie with Katie Webster, Koko Taylor.

Big Time Blues Productions (1986)

Bernie Pearl, Blues Festival 7 and The Beginning

After the first annual Blues festival was under our belts in 1980, KLON FM's facilities and personnel were moved to more suitable digs at Cal State U. Long Beach. Most important was the hiring of Dave Creagh, an experienced public radio General Manager. Dave began reshaping the station, bringing in experienced personnel and looking to boost the very low signal of the station.

Dave Creagh, General Manager

He also looked at what he had to work with on air. He immediately moved *Nothin but the Blues* to a three-hour spot on Saturday mornings, 9:00-noon. He brought in Steve Propes, an R'nB, R&R scholar and fanatic, to host an oldies counterpart for Sunday mornings. The instructional format was dropped in favor of largely Jazz content and news most of the week. He was connected to NPR, and looked to work with the network.

Dave also looked at the Blues Festival. He consulted with Dan Jacobson, who continued in an official paid position.

Dan Jacobson, Producer

Dave did not consult with me, a volunteer programmer. Dan and Dave worked out a plan whereby I would be paid a fee for booking, but the station would be in charge of everything else. He was a smart and energetic guy, wise to see that the Blues could continue to serve as a listener and donor magnet, including festival continuity, but underestimating my role. I asked him about this, and he replied, not unreasonably, that Dan was at the station and he could meet with him at will. He praised my work, but did not reward it. George Smith's words echoed in my brain, *Don't quit – it's too important.* The ball was rolling, I really didn't want to stop it.

The second festival took place, the name was altered to read, "The 2nd Annual Long Beach Blues Festival", the budget was raised, the location changed to a tree-lined triangle of grass on campus, and twice as many people bought tickets as the first event. I did the booking, and it was deemed a success by GM Creagh, and we headed towards a third, and then a fourth festival in the same sweet location. Attendance doubled each year. However, Dan wanted more input into the booking. We had a back and forth about some choices, as could be expected.

By the 1985 and 1986 Festivals, it was clear that this was not working, and attendance dropped. Sometime after the 1986 event (the 7th Annual) Creagh left to go to another radio post.

Creagh rose to become executive producer of National Public Radio's flagship evening news program *All Things Considered* after his start as a technical director on the show. He served on NPR's board of directors and was centrally involved with various aspects of system development, including the launch of new programs and concepts, including "Morning Edition," "Soundprint" and others. Creagh hired many nationally admired on-air talents, developed, ran and nurtured major market stations and other industry assets during his important 22-year public radio career. In the mid-1990s, as public broadcasting faced recurring assaults on government funding, along with increased resistance to perpetual pledge drives, Creagh helped launch and later served as senior vice president at the nonprofit Alliance for Public Broadcasting, which pioneered use of transaction-based fundraising for the industry.[647]

A new GM was appointed. Another experienced public radio hand, Rick Lewis, took the reins.

Rick Lewis, General Manager

Changes were afoot. Dan and Rick didn't see eye to eye, and Dan resigned. This left festival production open. The station had undertaken aspects of the production, with mixed results (to be polite) and he was looking engage an outside company to produce the 1987 Festival. These festivals were still the station's biggest listener boost, full house or not, and it served as the highest profile event on the LBSU campus. How much is that worth?

Still a year away, the festival was something of an orphan.

A New Production Company Gets Started

By the days of the 1986 Festival, there were auxiliary events leading up to the big 2-day weekend show. Galas, children's music events, film showings. The film event at Long Beach's venerable Art Theater ran into some problems with equipment. A quick-minded volunteer ingeniously came up with a solution – renting a hospital bed to prop up the screen, or something of the sort. The volunteer was a local attorney named Gene Kinsey. He was truly a problem-solving go-getter who could think out of the box. We became friends, and when the production of the next festival arose as a possibility, he proposed that we form a company and do it. It needed doing. Attendance had dipped and one more dip would probably do it in.

Gene and I talked, and he brought in local civic activist Tom Fields to do publicity and promotion, and when I mentioned this to my new KLON Jazz-host buddy from Denver, Bubba Jackson, he didn't have to think about it, he wanted in.

L Parker "Bubba" Jackson

Bubba was energetic, dependable, and was open to doing whatever was necessary to pull this off. We four got together in Gene's law office and did the legal paperwork to form a company. We called it, tongue in cheek, Big Time Blues Productions, and made an appointment to meet with GM Rick Lewis. Here goes nothing.

We met with Lewis, and he expressed skepticism as to our experience and ability. I guess my having conceived of the festival and actually pulled it off, with minimal help from the station, didn't make the scales balance in Rick's mind. After a period of hemming and hawing, Rick agreed and signed a win-win contract. We were in business. We were the producers of the 1987 8th Annual KLON Long Beach Blues Festival. No pay out front, but a decent bonus if we succeeded.

We all worked our tails off. My wife said Gene and I looked like we might have heart attacks, got tons of things donated to bring down expenses, including artists' trailers.

I booked Robert Cray to headline the Saturday show, with B.B. King headlining Sunday. Cray came very close to selling out the arboreal grassy campus venue.

Robert Cray

And, we had to post Sold-Out signs for B.B. on Sunday. Couldn't have been more successful. Rick Lewis and his lieutenants were sour-faced, and claimed that they lost money. They refused to pay us the agreed-upon bonus. Legal argumentation ensued. Things got a little nasty. I tried to stay out of the bickering. Things were not looking good for my future at KLON. I lasted until after festival 10, when they handed me my walking papers, playing only a minimal role in those remaining Festivals.

But, Big Time Blues was alive and looking.

1987 Blues Festival Lineup

Lonnie Brooks, Clarence "Gatemouth" Brown, Cephas & Wiggins, Jeannie & Jimmy Cheatham & The Sweet Baby Blues Band, Robert Cray, Snooks Eaglin, Etta James, B.B. King, Tony Matthews, Johnny Otis Show, Phillip Walker, Katie Webster

George Smith Harmonica Blowdown (1987)

In 1987 my wife and I decided to produce an all-harmonica show under the auspices of our DBA, Pearl Productions. I like doing shows, both live and radio, that have themes. We selected as the venue the Music Machine, by then run by Betty and Jack Miller. In my recollection, I had not heard of anybody doing this kind of a show previously. I could be wrong, and I supposed that I will hear from someone to contradict my assertion., but this was the first all-harp show on the West Coast in my recollection. It may well have preceded all others nationally. We'll keep an eye on the response.

There were good local harp blowers aplenty who would be eager to play, but we were mindful of our debt to George Smith. George had died in 1983.

George Harmonica Smith

It seemed proper to dedicate the event to him. In order to do so we needed his wife's permission. I asked Doug McLeod to arrange a meeting, he had remained in touch with her. I had met Christine Smith only a few times as she rarely attended George's shows. I knew that Doug was close and was trusted. We arranged to meet at the Smith house on Wadsworth St. Doug also mentioned that they were having a rough time financially, and I considered that as I drove to South L.A. from Long Beach.

We sat at the dining table I and ran my plan by the two of them. It was received well when I offered to split profits evenly after expenses. I walked away with permission to use George's name and a feeling that this was the right thing to do.

I began booking for the March 7, 1987 date. I selected some of the best local players and somehow obtained the services of renowned headliner Charlie Musselwhite. We included Blind Joe Hill, Harmonica Fats, Johnnie Dyer (a George disciple), Rod Piazza and the Mighty Flyers, Juke Logan, William Clarke Band, plus guitarists Smokey Wilson and Doug McLeod.

I cannot recall how much I paid the artists – it really couldn't have been much more than an honorarium, and the other expenses were minimal – but the show was a success, and I gave Christine Smith about 75% of the profits. In fact, I felt guilty about paying myself anything, but I had one small child at home and another on the way, with rent to pay.

I framed the show as a co-presentation with the Smith Family. The Annual George Smith Blues Harmonica Blowdown continued for several years, with the Smith family benefiting each year. Eventually I could not continue being the sole producer and provider of front-money, costs kept rising, and I turned it over to my Big Time Blues partners. I continued as booker and M.C. Ultimately, expenses grew to the place that no one was coming away with any money, and we simply shut it down. But, the Blowdown had spawned other harp-centric events. At least the fan base was not left standing in the rain.

There was one incident following the first Blowdown that caused me some unease. The morning after the show, I was still glowing when my phone rang and a woman's voice said, "Bernie Pearl?" "Yes". "Well, this is Mrs. B"….. I omit the full name, you'll see why in a moment…She continued, "You said this was a benefit for the family of George Smith", "Yes". "Well, I'm also family. George Smith was my husband too." I swallowed my shock and answered that the only family I have ever heard George talk about was the one he had with Christine.

The conversation continued for a while without anything new being said, Mrs. B. asserting her rights to family money, and me responding that I never heard of her, and that George had only spoken of Christine as his wife. The only variation came at the end of the call when Mrs. B. threatened to get a lawyer and sue me. I invited her to do so and hung up. I was disturbed. I called Doug, he might know something about George that I needed to know. He had never heard of this lady or her claims. I was at a loss. Then I thought of calling Johnnie T. Blackston, Fats' wife. Fats and George had been pals for decades, and she might know something. I made the right call.

Johnnie had connections in L.A. City government, and said, "I'll look into it."

She returned my call shortly, saying that this lady lived close by George and Christine and, while not married to him, she listed him as the father of her children. My jaw dropped. It dropped further when I took a call from Christine Smith who told me that she knew of this woman, and she had forgiven George. She was still upset about him having fathered children outside their marriage, but they remained together through it all.

I knew that George took every single gig that came his way. Every gig paid something, and I believe that the money went to support his family commitments to both families. My jaw no longer drops at the choices people make. It is a wild world out there. My hostility is reserved for those who opt to do harm to others. George was a man who did the best he could in all circumstances. I see him as a man of honor, let alone a genius musician.

Final Blues Festivals With Bernie Pearl

Bernie Pearl participated as artistic director and master of ceremonies in 3 more KLON Annual Long Beach Blues Festivals.

Attendance at these festivals was about 7500 Blues lovers.

1988 Blues Festival Lineup

Johnny Adams, Bobby "Blue" Bland, Ruth Brown, Albert Collins, James Cotton, Albert King, Kinsey Report with Big Daddy Kinsey, Lil' Ed & The Blues Imperials, Staple Singers, Johnnie Taylor, Walter "Wolfman" Washington.

1989 Blues Festival Lineup

Bobby "Blue" Bland, Charles Brown, Solomon Burke, Ronnie Earl & The Broadcasters, The Fabulous Thunderbirds, Grady Gaines & The Upsetters, Buddy Guy, John Hammond, John Lee Hooker, Johnny Shines, Terrance Simien & The Mallet Playboys, Koko Taylor.

1990 Blues Festival Lineup

Anson Funderburgh & The Rockets featuring Sam Myers, Ruth Brown, Albert Collins, Bo Diddley, Roy Gaines, Harmonica Fats (pseudonym for Harvey Blackston with the Bernie Pearl Blues Band, Etta James, Little Milton, Lonnie Mack, Yank Rachell, Otis Rush, Johnny Winter.

After the 1990 Blues Festival, Bernie Pearl and KLON FM went their separate ways.

Bernie and The Real Deal

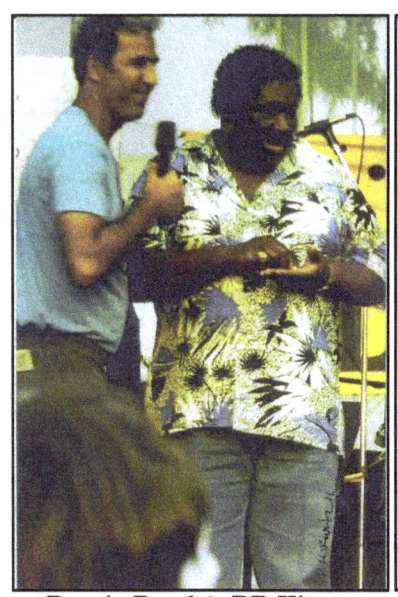

Bernie Pearl & BB King   Bubba Jackson & Bernie Pearl
Courtesy: David Horwitz

Willie Dixon & Bernie Pearl   Pee Wee Crayton, Bernie Pearl,
Courtesy: James Tamburro   Percy Mayfield At Ms Whis
Percy Mayfield's Last Performance

Barbara Morrison & Bernie Pearl
Courtesy: Bernie Pearl

Lowel Fulson & Bernie Pearl

Bernie Pearl & Freddie Roulette
Courtesy: Stan Weinstock

Bernie Pearl & Keb' Mo'

Bernie Pearl, R L Burnside, & Napolean Strickland

Bernie Pearl & Etta James

Bernie Pearl, Stevey Ray Vaughn & John Mayall

Johnny Copeland & Bernie Pearl

Bernie Pearl, Honeyboy Edwards, Mike Franks, Mike Barry

Harmonica Fats and Johnnie (1986 – 1999)

Weak Signal – Strong Message

Even after KLON FM 88.1 moved from LB City College to LB State College (now University), the signal was weak, and reached only the vicinity of Long Beach, South L.A. and Compton, largely Black residents and, surprisingly, up and down the coast, largely monied White residents. I did not program my show to reflect anybody's taste but my own. I had personal history or recollections of many artists, which I shared with my audience, and I conscientiously prepared my playlist each week, rife with blues, old and new. But, it had to be the Blues. I also threw in a little history, which people liked, as long as it was brief and to the point.

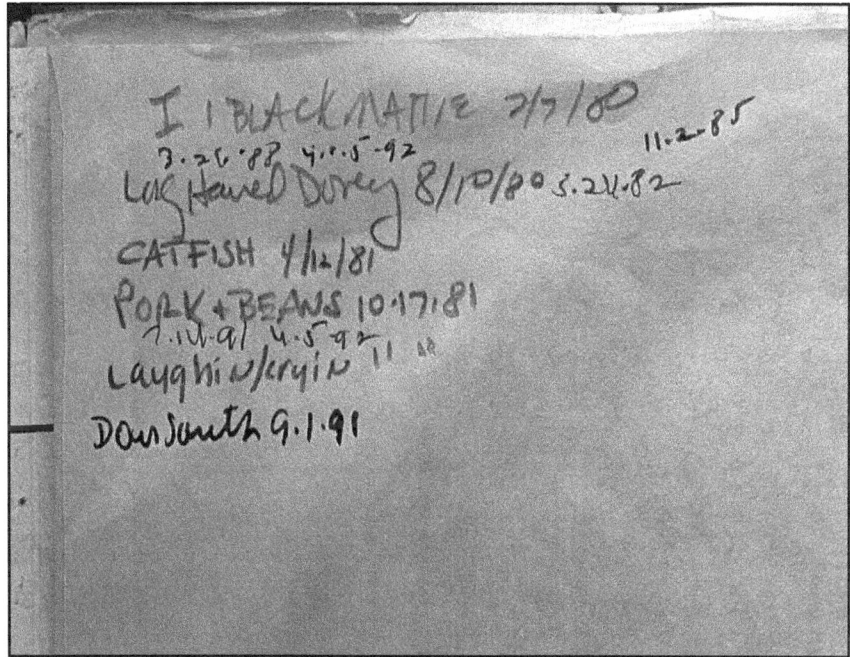

Playlist Notations On Record Sleeve Showing Dates On Air
Mississippi Delta Blues, Vol 2, Arhoolie Records
Courtesy: Bernie Pearl

Listeners would also call in and make requests, but I used my own personal library of LPs and simply could not anticipate their requests, even if I would have wanted to play them. The station did have a certain amount of Blues in its library, but there was no time to comb through it during the show.

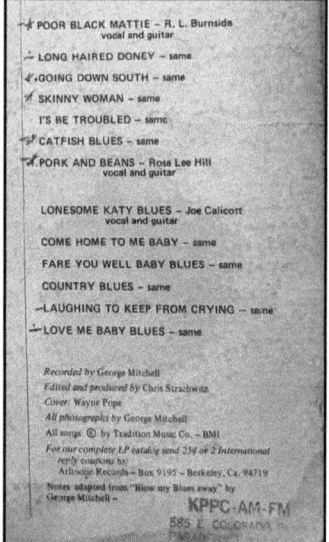

Periodic public radio fund-raising hours allowed more flexibility in airplay choices.

Front Cover, *MS Delta Blues*

Album Matching Playlist Above

Back, Song List, *MS Delta Blues* Showing KPPC Station Stamp

I began to get a sense of who was listening and where they were. I got messages from Terminal Island inmates (Federal), men and women who met and listened while they did their car stuff each Saturday morning, listeners from the Deep South who grew up with the music and told me stories of early B.B. King shows (25 cent admission, a sandwich and a beer included). That was new to me, and I loved hearing from them. My favorite came from a Watts resident who said that every Saturday morning, a man would lash a boombox to his bicycle, turn on the show full blast, and then pedal through the community. A town crier on steroids. The Blues was welcome news in many places, even on a Saturday morning.

Not everyone was pleased with my choices. Fans of local artists, both Black and White, would complain that I was not playing their music. I did consider what was being asked, but in most cases found that the music they wanted to hear was really not up to the standards I was comfortable with. There were times I relented, played their favorite, and regretted it.

There were some callers I enjoyed talking to, limited by the fact that I had to cue up the next record (it was in the days of needle and turntable). One woman, named Johnnie, was married to a Blues player named Harmonica Fats, and she was a pleasure to talk to. I later learned that she saved her housework for Saturday mornings, and woe be unto any of the grandkids if they interrupted her Blues.

Johnnie Tillmon
Wife Of Harmonica Fats

She was from rural Arkansas, and knew the Blues. Her persuasion was gentle, and I did air a couple of his 45's. Truthfully, they were not very good. The sound quality was sub-par, and the music was ordinary. She invited me to attend a show that he was part of in L.A., and I went. Again, I was not impressed, and I told her so, politely.

Time moved on, and I was playing a weekly Sunday afternoon gig with Barbara Morrison at a nice club in West Long Beach, Ms. Whis, where the band would play a set, Barbara would sing, and we'd have a guest artist each week. There was a week open and I called to see if Harmonica Fats was available, he was. I won't mention the pay because we all were working for very little, but it was not an issue. I felt I was taking a chance, but he was an experienced entertainer. And it was, after all, a Sunday afternoon in Long Beach.

Harmonica Fats
Courtesy: Edie Pearl

He came, did his thing very well, singing standards, Jimmy Reed, Fanny Mae, Little Red Rooster, etc. He was entertaining, but nothing to write home about. We talked, and he mentioned that he also had original songs, but reverted to standard tunes to please the audience. I told him he ought to do his own stuff, as everyone did the standards. Let me tell you, that opened a can of worms, but they were golden, shining worms.

Fats was a treasure-trove of great, Grammy personal, original songs, which really told his story in an unique way. Dozens of them. This led to a 15-year partnership including a co-owned, co-producing label, Bee Bump Records. Bee Bump produced his first CD, *I Had to Get Nasty*, with my full band. And two acoustic duo CDs, *Two Heads Are Better*, and *Blow, Fat Daddy, Blow*, both of which were nominated for W.C. Handy Awards for Best Acoustic Blues – both lost to an up and coming artist from L.A. named Keb' Mo', our friend. It led to our playing several national festivals, and two trips to Europe.

I kept artistic merit at the top of my playlist requirements throughout my years on the air. But, I learned that you have to leave space for originality and innovation.

320 Pounds of the Blues

Harvey "Harmonica Fats" Blackston was from rural McDade, Louisiana, near Shreveport. He said he didn't mind being called "Fats" because he always was fat. His wife always referred to him as Harvey. In his youth, according to his own account, he was wild, drank, chased women, and danced (he was amazingly light-footed on stage, even at 300+ pounds) while he blew his "harp" and sang. As he said, *I love to have fun. I love to entertain people.* While totally identifying with the harmonica, he was a limited player, but he meant every note he played. His expansive repertoire, jovial stage presence and humor made him a compelling stage presence and an in-demand entertainer after he moved to L.A. with his father, after WWII.

That didn't mean that music made enough to sustain him. He worked every day at a steady job, and went out to play at night. He married and divorced and, by the time I met him, he had remarried a woman with three children, Johnnie, and lived happily in his home "across the tracks" in the Watts area. Their house was literally across the street from the rails. He continued to work at the Clorox plant daily, often going out to play at night.

Johnnie tells a humorous story about how they met. She had a friend who knew that she loved the blues, and this friend invited her to a club one night to see this blues singer. They were seated and the show started, and Harmonica Fats was announced. He came out ready to play, and to clown. He could make his eyes bulge and could move around the stage in an entertaining way as he delivered classic and original tunes that spoke of his life. Johnnie wondered aloud to her friend, *What is this?*, but she was fascinated.

After Fats really got going, the crowd came along, and a lady next to Johnnie started yelling, "Blow, fat daddy, Blow!" Fats poured it on,

and before you knew it, he and Johnnie Tillmon added Blackston to her name. I liked the story so much that I insisted we call our second CD, *Blow, Fat Daddy, Blow*.

It was dedicated to her as she had passed away prior to the recording. *Blues for Mrs. B.* was his musical tribute on the CD. Mine was *Blues Kaddish*, the Hebrew term for a memorial prayer.

Harvey Blackston did not swear, drink, or chase women by the time I met him. But, that didn't mean he was not aware of women. Once, we were driving along and we saw a very attractive young woman sashaying down the street. You couldn't not notice, and we both took a good look. His comment was, *Holy Smokes!* Tells you something about the man. Fats was not very tall, but he was big-boned and just large all over. He did carry a lot of weight. He sometimes billed himself as *320 Pounds of the Blues*.

Fats had a calm and quiet demeanor, and I never saw him get angry or come anywhere near losing his cool. Regardless as to provocation he remained calm and under control. Johnnie once said, *I don't know how you guys put up with what you do. If it was me I'd be done killed somebody already and be sittin' in jail*. The lady was a truth-teller. Fats just chuckled. But, he did tell me of an incident at his work. A White co-worker at Clorox once came up behind him while he was operating a machine and said something very offensive – one can only imagine what that might have been. Fats said that without hesitation he turned and flattened the guy. The man then apologized, and never gave him reason to repeat. Fats turned back to his machine.

Going Acoustic

After we recorded *I Had to Get Nasty* on our own label, Bee Bump Records, and with our own money, Fats and I continued to play here and there with the band. I had gathered a wonderful group of musicians while working at Ms Whis in Long Beach, while working our Sunday gig with Barbara Morrison.

We backed just about everybody, from Charles Brown to Denise LaSalle to Percy Mayfield on his last gig ever, to Smokey Wilson. From raw and down-home to smooth and polished, we could cover the Blues. Big Terry De Rouen, from NOLA, on lead guitar, Hollis

Gilmore, from Arkansas, smooth but greasy and gritty sax, Albert Trepagnier, Jr, also from NOLA, on drums, Mike Barry, Oregon, who could play any style on bass, and myself on rhythm guitar, and band leader

Bernie Pearl Blues Band
(from left) Bernie Pearl (guitars), Hollis Gilmore (sax),
Harmonica Fats (harmonica, vocals),
Terry DeRouen (lead guitar), Mike Barry (bass),
Albert Trepagnier (drums)
Courtesy: Bob Aisley

If we needed a keyboard, we could call on Dwayne "The Gangster" Smith, blind and unlimited. For a more down-home piano style, Leon Blue stood ready. L.A. area was full of good musicians eager to play if called. Nothing like a steady gig to hold a band together.

Nasty was really a fine album, but it did not get the recognition I thought, and still think, it deserved. I looked at the festivals going on all over the US and the world, and took into account the number of bands competing for slots, and couldn't imagine how we could get the publicity needed to get the attention of bookers, good as I thought we were. I also took notice of how slim the solo/duo/acoustic ranks were. I thought that with his originality and audience-friendly shows, Fats and I could make a dent in the market. I ran it by him. He was absolutely opposed, saying it wasn't what he was used to. Yet, he was a Sonny Terry fan, and I cited Sonny's longevity on stage, with or without Brownie McGhee. He would not be moved.

I then resorted to dirty tricks. I talked to his wife. Johnny was a practical person, a trait which served her well when she engaged in social and political activism. She saw the logic and, apparently, agreed with the artistic premise that Fats could provide something unique that was not currently available. Fats, knowing he was outgunned, agreed to try it. It worked well enough to go in the studio and record some of his songs and some other more or less original material. Thus *Two Heads are Better* was released and gained some airplay and traction. We received a nomination for the W.C. Handy (Blues Foundation) Best Acoustic Album award, and earned general praise for keeping acoustic blues going.

We flew to Memphis for the ceremony. When we got there, we had no easy way to get to our hotel. On the same flight was an acquaintance from L.A. who was also nominated for the same award, Keb' Mo'. He saw our plight and offered his limo to get us to our room. We accepted, and he dropped us off.

**Keb' Mo', Harmonica Fat, Bernie Pearl, Handy Awards, 1995
Courtesy: Bernie Pearl**

After the ceremony, during which he was presented with the award, he offered us the opportunity of sitting in with him when he played the festival on the river front the next day. We had given up our room and had booked our tickets. It was a generous and kind offer from someone we didn't know that well. We declined his offer reluctantly and came home knowing we had met a brother.

We got local work as an acoustic duo as well. We had fairly steady work at Disneyland, a local fish house with a couple of locations, plus some club work. Not at the top of the business, but working at what we do, earning some steady money, and building our resume and reputation.

Johnnie Tillmon Blackston had diabetes. The disease progressed and as she declined I visited one day. She called me to her bedside. With Fats standing nearby she said, *Bernie, take care of my husband*. I responded, *I will, if he lets me*.

Mrs. Johnnie T. Blackston

Mrs. Blackston had come from Arkansas to L.A. She was married and had three children. She worked to support her family. I don't know if her husband worked as well, but I do know that one day he up and left, and in short order she lost her job. I never asked for details. It was a disaster. She was forced to apply for welfare. I don't know much about that, but for someone with kids who worked and had a reasonably secure life to have to go hat in hand to the County for help must have been humiliating.

Johnnie related just one of the humiliations a woman on welfare had to endure. One which she worked on and successfully helped to overturn in her later activist days. She called it the *No-Knock Law*. Welfare *enforcers* had the right to enter a recipients home at any hour, without knocking. They were looking for code violations, which included having a man in your house overnight. I suppose the premise was that if you had a man there, he could work and provide for you. This was shocking to me. It echoed slavery. Simply inhumane. She met adversity with calm and resolution.

She was a straight-forward person, who would tell you the truth. Once we were talking about the destruction of Watts during the 1965 "riots", also characterized as a rebellion. Evidence of the havoc remained in plain view even in the 1980's. Without blinking an eye she related that during the conflagration many of her neighbors took items they couldn't afford from the burning stores. *I saw my neighbors getting TV's, so I went and got me one too.*

She later formed a community group, largely women on welfare, that exerted pressure on City Hall. If it was known that the City Council was going to vote on or enact something that could go against the interests of the community, they could organize a large protest outside City Hall by simply calling each other on the phone, and taking the bus a few miles North and making some (political) noise within the Council's hearing. She also became an assistant to City Councilman Robert Farrell, my old UCLA pal. She had some clout. She even joined the Republican party because she felt the Democrats weren't doing anything for Black people. She would get calls from some of the high-placed GOPs who wanted to know what was happening on the street. She and Fats became staunch supporters and friends of Maxine Waters.

**Johnnie Blackston Speaking At A Political Event
Courtesy: Wisconsin Historical Society**

My wife Edie was volunteering at a Democratic Party convention in recent years, and spotted Ms Waters passing by. She knew that we had some connection with the Blackstons. My wife hailed her and reminded her of that. Edie adored Johnnie and brought up her name. The Congresswoman wistfully said that she wished she could call and get some advice from her now. Then she said, proudly, *You know I'm in one of Fats' songs!* Edie said she knew, she had been listening to it on the way to the arena. *In Love With Three Girls* has a refrain where Fats calls the three girls names. We all still get a kick out of howling, *Pearly Mae*, pronounced Pooly Mae, *Ruth*, pronounced Roof, *Maxine!*, as written.

The Obscene Phone Call

Quite possibly the funniest true story I've ever heard came from Johnnie when we were editing the cassette tape of our recent live sets with Fats and our guest Papa John Creach at Café Lido in Newport Beach. This is before we recorded CDs with either Fats or Papa. Fats, Johnnie, and I were sitting with engineer Doug Lohr in his home studio, when I told everyone that I had received an obscene call from a woman last night, my first and only one. I didn't go into details.

Some silence, and then Johnny said, "I had one of those once. I got a call, and a guy asked me to talk dirty so he could jack off. I said, what you want to do that for? He replied, cause I can't find no pussy. What you mean you can't find no pussy? Where do you live? He said, on Figueroa (a major street running through L.A.). You mean to tell me you can't go out on Figueroa and find no pussy? No, I can't find no pussy! Well, give me your address, I got 200 pound of pussy and I'll be right over! Click, dial tone. Incomparable.

Fats and I Part Company

After Johnnie died in 1995, I lost any leverage I had in doing things with Fats. He got an agent, a journalist well-known in South L.A., and made unreasonable demands for pay. He wanted to get what he was worth, he said. I responded, no one I know is getting what they're worth. He turned down a couple of decent gigs and I knew it was over. In addition, he hired a fellow to make sure I hadn't been cheating him out of royalties, and to check the records of our joint record company. I hadn't cheated him and the books and record showed not a trace of dishonesty.

What he [the auditor] did accomplish was to destroy any possibility of working together again. That was apparently OK with Fats. If he had thought about it, he would have known that my honesty was assured by the paralyzing fear of ever having to try explain to Johnnie Tillmon Blackston any discrepancy in the money. I am convinced that she could sense dishonesty by the way you walked into the room, the look on your face. No thank you – I'll pass on the cheating. He ended up firing his auditor. Fats died of the lung cancer which he knew he had and, I believe, decided not to treat at the start of 2000.

A final Johnnie Tillmon story. I was teaching at McCabe's and a new student showed up. Bill Phillips was a young attorney from the East who loved the blues. I mentioned Harmonica Fats and his wife Johnnie Tillmon. He knew her name. He had volunteered to advise the hotel workers' on strike in Las Vegas and had met her there. She stood up for them big time! He related that they were on a march when a group of "the boys" showed up in their suits and confronted the marchers, Johnnie at their head. The boys growled and put their hands in their jackets, as if….Soon after issuing their warnings to an unimpressed woman – she was great at showing no fear because she had none, the boys turned tail and slouched away. I imagine that she had faced threats before, and they knew they'd get nowhere. Maybe her placidity scared them.

Booksellers' Blues (The 1990s)

Show I – Las Vegas

My friend Scott Willevsky, who ran the Chelsea Book Store in Long Beach, told me of a booksellers' group which held large conventions nationally. Many of the larger retailers and publishers put on special events for promotion for the many potential buyers who attended. One seller he was associated with was contemplating doing a show at the upcoming Las Vegas meeting. He thought they might be interested in working with me.

Opportunity knocking. I got in touch with them, and they hired me to produce a show at the Shark Club. I already had my band, plus Harmonica Fats, eager to play Vegas – there were some avid slot-players amongst us. For a headliner I decided to call Roomful of Blues, which had lately reorganized and were playing all over. They accepted the gig. The package came in within the budget agreed on, including housing.

Roomful Of Blues
(from left) John Rossi, Duke Robillard, Ed Parnagoni, Rich Lataille, Greg Piccolo, Doug James; Al Copley at the piano

The literary crowd could party. The place was packed. We opened, and got them dancing. Fats was at his best and won the folks over. Then Roomful took over and, my playing and emceeing over, I went up to the balcony for a bird's eye view. The party was raging when someone pointed into the crowd and said, *Look there. That's Timothy Leary down there dancing.*

I'm sure there were other literary stars milling around, but Leary was a counter-culture hero. I recall that after we had retired, resting on our laurels, that there were reports of a big fight that broke out. We saw no sign of that as we packed up and bid farewell to Vegas. Exhausting, but worth the effort. Next year?

Show 2 – New York

The following year, I heard from the client. Destination was New York. We discussed finances and came to an agreement. I made sure there was enough to also pay the way of an assistant – there was no way to do this by myself. My friend Bob Aisley was willing, and the deal was set. I called Buddy Guy's management and arranged for him to headline. Opening act was Otis Clay, a soul-blues vocalist of quality, provided by Buddy's agent.

Buddy Guy　　　　　**Otis Clay**

We arrived early the morning of the show and checked into our hotel. We were shown to a room that hadn't been cleaned yet. It was a mess. Bob took the reins and made it clear that unless we were moved to a clean room, we were leaving. It had the desired effect. A clean room was ours. We made our way to the theater and had some trouble gaining entry – it was mid-afternoon, but they weren't yet open for business. We got in and had a look at the venue. It was a big place, we got shown around and then left to find somewhere to order the dressing room catering required by our artist contract, a large delicatessen variety. Found a place nearby and placed the order.

We returned to the theater for the show, deli in hand, and found out that Buddy had ordered pizza, which was on its way. I don't know what happened to the deli, maybe the band ate it. I went out to parking to check on Buddy's bus, his driver was grumbling that he had to pay $20 out of his pocket. That was no problem, as I had adhered to my policy of the Producer's Hundred: always have five $20 bills in your pocket at every show. A $20 bill can quickly solve a wide variety of issues that come up at shows. That was one instance among many, including the time that Bobby Bland wanted BBQ from a vendor at the Long Beach Blues Festival rather than what was provided in the dressing room – which was, no doubt, what his contract called for. Here's $20, now go get Mr. Bland his Q.

The show went great. Buddy was Buddy and the booksellers conventioneers loved it. Looking to next year.

Show 3 – Albert Collins

This third year looked to be a slam dunk. I had talked to Albert Collins, who lived in Las Vegas and had a tour bus. He was just a few hours away, and the money was good. The convention was in Orange County, our show at a local hotel.

Albert Collins

Master of the Telecaster

Courtesy: Collection of the Smithsonian National Museum of African American History and Culture, Gift of David D. Spitzer

The opener was popular roots band The Bonedaddys. Perfect for dancing and lighthearted partying. Albert would follow and knock 'em dead with the Blues.

The Bonedaddys, A World Beat Group

I stayed at the hotel the night before the show in order to be on top of things all day. I called Albert early to make sure that he got away with plenty of time to arrive, eat, maybe get some rest (I think he would do the driving) and do a sound check before the crowd arrived. One of the band members, pianist Leon Blue, lived in L.A. and arrived early. I called Albert a couple of times and he assured me that they were just about ready to leave. The day wore on, sound arrived and set up, and when some of the Bonedaddy contingent got there I became concerned. I called Albert. They were on the road and had a bus problem.

I frantically arranged for two of our crew to drive Hwy 15 to where they were stuck and bring the players and instruments to the gig, leaving someone on their end to take care of the bus problem. The emergency driver solution proved impractical and the Bonedaddys took the stage and wowed the crowd. No Albert. No response to calls. I paid the Bonedaddys to do another set. The crowd was happy, but the company I was working for was not, not to mention my own dissatisfaction, which kind of ate at my gut.

I stayed a second night at the hotel, not saying a word to my employers. I didn't ever find out what happened to Albert, whom I loved and respected, but whenever I saw him after that, he apologized for it. Even when I went to visit him in his home after he had been diagnosed with terminal cancer, he apologized again, but never an explanation. I'm guessing that he had become incapacitated, and simply couldn't make the trip and play. A sweet guy, a great player, a sad end.

I did no more bookseller shows. As they say, "That's Show Business".

We Go to Gemmrig – Where? (1993)

The Long Beach Blues Festival completely changed its focus after I left – alright, I was fired – after the festival in 1990. It had been moved to Labor Day Weekend, expanded to three days, offering luxury tickets, backstage passes for big donors, and other perks for the wealthier fans. You can't fault that as a motivation for a public-supported station, I suppose. It had wiggled so that one could sponsor air time in exchange for recognition, i.e. advertising. Again, you have to survive. I didn't listen, I didn't attend, and I paid as little attention as I could to the doings at KLON. They had arranged with Bubba Jackson, normally a Jazz DJ, to be interim host of *Nothin' But the Blues*. I had no beef with him.

Big Time Blues (BTB) wanted to do a smaller festival in Long Beach and we searched for a venue. The Long Beach Police Academy is located at the edge of massive El Dorado Park, near the 605 freeway. It had a building or two, and a shooting range for the cadets to hone their skills. I heard, but never experienced, that on occasion a stray bullet would find its way into the surrounding area. Whether that was true or not I can't say, but one could hear when target practice was going on.

It was a lovely small gated park which had trees on the grassy field, a covered area with picnic tables and a concrete floor, an outbuilding which opened to the park, and a kitchen. I believe they said it could hold 1,000 people. That looked like a squeeze to me, but there was ample space for hundreds to spread blankets if they chose to.

The park was named after an officer named Gemmrig. Most in Long Beach had never heard the name, nor knew how to get there. These challenges aside, it looked like a great place to set up a stage and put on a show. One crucial detail was that it was rented by the day, midnight to midnight. We would have to set up overnight, have the show, break down the equipment, clean the venue, including bathrooms, and be gone by 12:00. Rental fee was reasonable

But, the positives outweighed the difficulties. We decided to do it in July (date selected by availability) of 1993.

We did not have a budget to bring in the "name" artists, and have sold-out shows. But, Southern California was rife with blues artists, known and up and coming. Papa John Creach, Keb' Mo', Joe Houston, Smokey Wilson, Big Jay McNeely, James Harman, Canned Heat, and dozens more were on hand.

Papa John Creach   **Keb' Mo'**   **Joe Houston**   **Big Jay McNeely**

We also looked for touring artists needing a gig: Magic Slim, Louisiana Red, Freddie Roulette, and dozens of others. We regularly reserved space in the covered area to do special shows and art work for children. The kitchen area had local chefs offering delicacies. We brought in mobile potties to supplement the on-site bathrooms. We constructed a dance floor on the grass for line dancing. People could bring their own food, but we inspected for alcohol, which was prohibited by our ABC permit. It was, from one year to the other, relaxed, well-run, comfortable, and strictly blues.

I would often arrive at midnight, open the locked gate, supervise the set up of stage and sound, arrival of the portable potty trucks, the set up of tables in the vending area (T-shirts, artwork, etc.). Maybe catch a couple of hours sleep in my van, then M.C. the show, maybe play a set with someone, make sure that people left before the over-zealous cops started issuing tickets. Then stay on and help with general field and bathroom clean up and, finally, lock the gate. When I returned my key next day, I was sure to hear complaints about not leaving the park spic and span. I took it all in stride. I didn't quit, it was too important.

1993 Big Time Blues Festival: Artists

Courtesy: Daniel Perales

This Festival was the first Big Time Blues Festival.

Smokey Wilson

Freddie Roulette

1996 Big Time Blues Festival: Artists

Courtesy: Daniel Perales

James Harman

John Hammond

Long John Hunter

Magic Slim

2001 Big Time Blues Festival: Artists

Courtesy: Daniel Perales

This Festival was the last Big Time Blues Festival.

Sonny Rhodes

Arthur Adams

Hubert Sumlin and Bob Margolin

Kirk Fletcher

Big Time Blues Gets The Blues (2002)

One sour note. BTB went about its business, some little shows here and there, planning next year's fest. I woke up and smelled the coffee and realized that my buddy Bubba had been booking shows on his own. Again, nothing wrong with entrepreneurship, but our signed contract with each other stated that we must present all possible events to the group first, and one may not set up a competing business. I brought this to the partners' attention at our next meeting. Bubba was simply uninterested in discussing it. It was a situation of waiting for the other shoe to drop. The two lawyers had other business to tend to, but to me and Bubba Jackson, this was our business. He continued to stonewall and we came to a crisis point. I proposed formally that we remove him as an officer (vice-president) of BTB. My point was simple, you can do what you want, but you can't remain in the company if you're competing with it. He remained obdurate, and was voted off the board. It was, in effect, the end of BTB. He was angry, but had no defense. We were deflated, but went ahead with plans for the next fest, which was to be our last, summer of 2001. The world changed that September.

I remained at a distance from Bubba, a very sad thing for me as we had been very good friends for several years. I made a couple of attempts to put it behind us, but he wasn't having it. So it has remained. A sad thing. We must move on.

Some Interesting Gigs

The Berlin Blues (2005)

My daughter had made a friend whose parents were artists. Mom was an actress and playwright. Dad was a trained cellist who could play whatever was placed in front of him. He called me to let me know that a theater company he had worked with was looking for a blues guitarist for an upcoming production, and was I interested in talking to them? I was. I hadn't been involved in a play since Yerma, some 20 years earlier. I called the company and was given a time to come and audition. It was called Native Voices at the Autry. Based at the Autry Museum and adjacent theater in Griffith Park, it was dedicated to producing plays by indigenous playwrights in North America.

I arrived at the Wells Fargo theater with two acoustic guitars, and was told to go on stage. The space was a comfortable 99-seater. Two people took seats and after a little conversation, asked me to play. I obliged and played some of the Blues songs I knew. They were polite and said there was one other musician they were considering and they'd be in touch.

I didn't have to wait long – I got the gig. It was a union gig and although I was not a union actor, I would be paid as one. Great news. My previous theatrical work was unpaid, though gratifying in other ways. But, nothing spends like money, and we could use some at my home.

I worked under a Music Director whose job it was to guide me, and to compose the one major musical number in the play. But, it was up to me to improvise blues riffs to supplement the dialog and to fill in during scene changes. I was also asked to compose an "overture" to be played as people were seated and waiting for the play to start. The Music Director said he was looking for something lively and brief, and I came up with a little ragtime original that lasted about 2 minutes. He liked it, and the "Berlin Rag" was born.

The play was called "The Berlin Blues". The author, was Drew Hayden Taylor, an Ojibway (Chippewa) from Canada, had previously written two plays with "Blues" in the title, and they had used canned music. This time they wanted the Blues live.

The Berlin Blues

Drew Hayden Taylor

The play concerned the exploitation of Native culture by a Germany-based company, which by its nature attracted and corrupted native collaborators. This was a story of the conflict within the tribe, and with the exploiters. It was humorous and serious, and the music played an important role in moving the plot along. I even accompanied a couple of the actors' songs.

I loved all of it. I drew praise from the director during the "notes" portion of a run through, during which mistakes by the actors are cited. The director was amazed that I had no notes to be read. I was proud of myself. No missed cues.

I sat in the front row of the theater, left, and played my guitars without reinforcement. The theater had good acoustics, and the audience was there to listen. Every note could be heard.

We had several preview tune-up performances, and when opening night came we were excited and ready. The house was full, I played the overture, the director welcomed everyone and gave the native blessings to the gathering. Reviewers were there as well. The play went on, and everyone felt good about it.

Next day the reviews were read, and the cast was a little miffed with me (in a comradely way) because one of them singled out my playing as the best thing about the production. But, it was a fine cast and an interesting, entertaining, and meaningful production we all could be proud of.

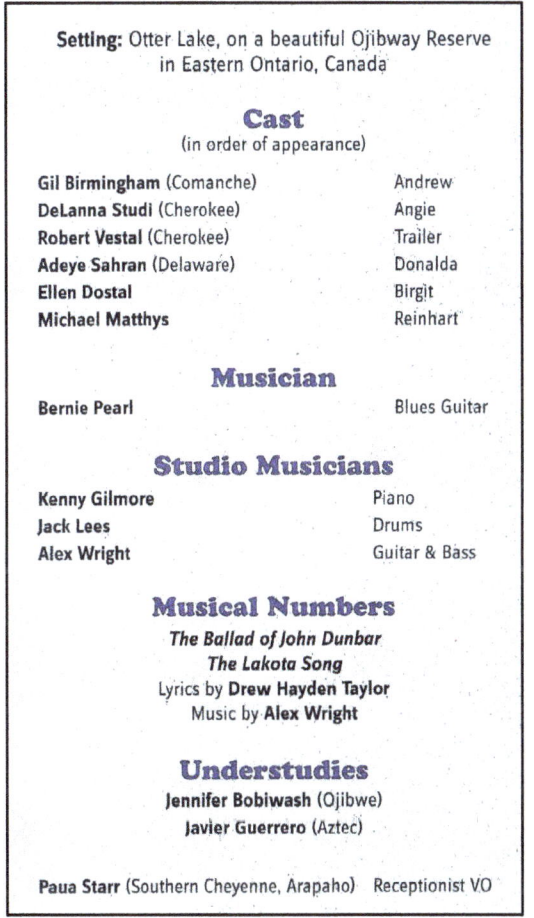

Cast and Crew. Berlin Blues

I was given one other musical task. After the first act there was a break. Across the modest plaza, opposite the theater was a small eatery, which also offered wine. During the intermission, many would go to the café, and some would order wine. In order to lure folks back in to see the second and final act, I was asked to play some Blues. That gave me a chance to play a full song on my National guitar, as loud as I could. I chose a Fred McDowell stomp-down, *Write Me a Few Lines*. It may or may not have served the purpose they intended, but I and those listening had a ball.

As a bonus, we flew to New York and did a couple of performances at the Native American Museum there, and then flew to D.C. for performances at the Smithsonian Museum..

A whole lot of fun. And I got paid too!

The Bible & the Blues

One day a few years ago I got a call from a Professor of the Old Testament at Loyola Marymount University. He said he had been given my name by the Los Angeles Blues Society (a different group than the Southern California Blues Society). He was looking for someone to collaborate on a lecture he was preparing that involved the Blues for an upcoming Catholic Conference in Anaheim, and was met with, *Oh, Bernie Pearl is your guy*. Very flattering.

Professor Daniel L. Smith-Christopher had opted to lecture on *The Book of Lamentations*, and to draw a parallel between it and the poetry and intention of the Blues.

Daniel Smith-Christopher

Loyola Marymount University

Professor, where have you been all my life? Really, I know very little of the details of the *Old Testament*, let alone its poetry, let alone *The Book of Lamentations*. But, I'm a sucker for intellectualizations and this guy sounded both serious and full of fun. We set up a meeting in his office. I brought my guitar.

We sat and he explained his lecture and how it would work with the music. It was a pretty simple plan. While citing theological scholars and other aspects of the *Bible*, he also elaborated on its similarity with aspects of Black history and civil rights evolution, and the Blues. Each segment ended with a theme or a moral, and that was my cue.

He wanted blues that would musically and lyrically echo his conclusions. Simple, really. All I had to do was come up with Blues songs that address themes like pain, and loneliness. The Professor also talked about the development of the blues, and of Gospel music. It was quite brilliant and not too abstract or arcane to understand, granting that it would be clearer if you knew your Bible.

I was drawn to seek mainly Blues by down-home artists recorded mostly in the 1950's, Mercy Dee Walton's *One Room Country Shack* fit the theme of loneliness like a glove, "*...a thousand miles from nowhere...*". Eddie Boyd's *Third Degree*, hopelessness, *Got me 'cused of murder, I never harmed a man*. And so on. I sang "*Tough Times, God Moves on the Water*, and more

Professor Smith-Christopher ended his talks with these words,

We admit we have the Blues - that we can Lament – because we know there is someone who cares, and who listens.

Then I lead the "congregation" in "Jesus on the Main Line" – just tell Him what you want!

This was a thoroughly enjoyable and unusual foray into previously unknown territory. When I made this contact I shared it with bassist Mike Barry, a practicing Catholic, and he wanted in. We both performed at the Catholic Convention to some 800 attendees, and over the years a couple of dozen times more to congregations large and small.

These unique opportunities don't pop up all the time, but when they do you have to embrace them.

And You Thought We Were Done! (2020-2021)

The Barbara Morrison Performing Arts Center

Barbara Morrison and I continued to stay in touch after the play *Yerma* closed, sometimes connecting me with band gigs, sometimes working together.

This continued for several years. She arranged for us to do Sundays at Ms. Whis in Long Beach, where we played with just about everyone.

She and I decided to try and co-produce a special Valentine's Day show featuring Mr. Cleanhead Vinson. Our lines got crossed, and our relationship suffered for several years, I'm sorry to say. We still loved and respected each other, but stopped working together, though I'd regularly get calls for gigs based on her recommendation. The strain of not communicating was too much, and we totally made up and healed on the occasion of our losing our dear friend Mrs. Tina Mayfield. Tina had been married to the great singer and writer Percy Mayfield. We had him as our guest artist at Ms. Whis on the Sunday before he passed away.

Percy Mayfield

Singer, Songwriter

Wrote "Hit The Road Jack"

Percy was related to another great song writing Mayfield, Curtis. Tina later took in and cared for blues great Lowell Fulson in his declining years. She was a force in the Blues community, creating and heading the L.A. Black Blues Society. There was nothing negative in her outlook, but simply looking to ensure Black participation in the rise of the Blues. A notable and unifying figure had passed and we mourned together.

Barbara had a vision and an ambition. She was thinking of establishing a Blues/Jazz Museum, with a performance space, back in her home turf near Detroit. Apparently, there was a space large enough to do this that was for sale. This didn't come to fruition. But, what she did was acquire use of a former small theatre with a stage and lots of potential, in the reviving cultural neighborhood of Leimert Park. She opened The Barbara Morrison Performing Arts Center.

The Barbara Morrison Performing Arts Center

When I got word about it I called. She immediately offered me Monday nights for a Blues night. We came up with a formula of my band opening the show, and then having an open jam session. We began, and it was a success.

This was in the Black community, and we attracted a mixed crowd that loved the Blues, and musicians aplenty, some of whom were unknown to me, but the standard of playing nothing but the Blues reigned supreme. I brought in my usual players: Big Terry DeRouen, Mike Barry, Albert Trepagnier, Hollis Gilmore. When Albert couldn't make it I used down-home, Alabama-born drummer Willie T. Brooks.

At one point Hollis became unable to play, and I was introduced to a tenor sax player I had heard of, Bobby "Hurricane" Spencer. Fit like a glove.

Bernie Pearl (guitar, vocals), Albert Trepagnier (drums), Mike Barry (bass), Bobby Spencer (saxophone)

Barbara Morrison Realizes Her Dream

Barbara also realized her dream of establishing a Jazz/Blues Museum. Just up the block was a space to house it and, somehow, she gathered the resources and the personnel to make it viable.

I am reminded that as a younger artist, though church-trained, she had admired Barbara Streisand's vocals most of all, and had attempted to sing like her. This changed. Eddie "Cleanhead" Vinson and his wife Bernice were one pair of her L.A. "parents", the other being Johnny and Phyllis Otis. When Cleanhead heard her great ability being used to emulate Ms. Streisand, he told her to get off it and sing the music of her own people, and to find her own direction.

Eddie "Cleanhead" Vinson   **Johnny Otis**

She took Vinson seriously and over the years developed her own style of Jazz and Blues interpretation. Her vocal ability and her inborn charisma made her one of the most in-demand performers in L.A. Her acceptance and popularity extended to Europe and Japan once she appeared on tour with Johnny Otis, Ray Charles, and others.

Barbara was kind, loving, and understanding to all, but she faced her own severe trials. Shortly after we had begun the Monday Night blues series, she told me that she was having a problem with her foot. One of her toes had turned black. She was diagnosed with diabetes. She began treatment and thus began a progressive series of amputations and surgical interventions over several years. Never a hint that she had these very serious issues, and continued to sing beautifully.

You could not tell from her singing or her optimistic joviality that this was happening. Never at any point. First, walking with a cane, a walker, then crutches, then a wheel chair, she remained herself. If she just came through a surgery, she might go directly to an engagement, or come to the Center to M.C. or sing. If she just stepped off a plane from Japan, she might head to a club engagement. Unreal, but factual. She had an iron will, and never gave into the negative.

We did not work together a lot, but when my CD that she sang on (*Take Your Time,* Bee Bump Music, BEBCD009) featuring a few of our duets, brought us a nomination for a *Blues Blast Magazine* Award, she wanted to go to the awards show back in Illinois. That meant each of us paying for the flight, car rental, hotel room, food while we were there. That didn't matter, she was going. Her being in a wheelchair and any other connected difficulties were discounted and never mentioned. In fact, I was never aware of any difficulties. What needed to be done, she did.

Her outgoing personality engaged people immediately, and by the time we got to the ticket counter to check in, she was already chatting and laughing with an airport helper pushing her chair. No artificiality at all. She believed in positivism as an article of her faith.

In fact, people have asked me over time, *How does she do it?* I've given some thought to the answer. It is a serious question. I've come up with this: First, she was a woman of faith. She was a believer. Second, she did not permit negativity in her life. You can talk about a problem with her, once. You dwell on your troubles, you need to find another shoulder. Example: A mutual friend got divorced and in time started keeping company with a man. As it turned out, this guy was less than the right guy for her. He was really, to be blunt, a low-down dog. She called to talk to Barbara, and Barbara listened, and then simply advised her to drop him – flat! When she called again to essentially complain about the same treatment, Barbara cut her off, permanently. She told me she couldn't be friends with anyone who didn't respect herself enough to walk away from abuse.

Barbara was not perfect. Once she got an idea, she ran with it, as far as it would go. She pulled off many successful events, but her belief in herself did have some drawbacks. It was hard for her to take advice. I'd pretty much stayed out of an advisory posture, but when she said she wanted to do a Mother's Day festival in the small park adjacent to her Center, I volunteered to meet with her and help plan it. I have some hands-on experience that I thought could help with the logistics. I was not going to get involved with booking or catering and the like, just wanted to help with the details. Neglected details can pop up and snag you. I recall not having steps for Big Joe Turner (and others) to access the stage at the First Blues Festival, you'll recall. We dodged disaster on that one.

We arranged to meet on her patio, and I was excited to help. My wife, who was eyewitness to everything I tried, and is quite calm, logical, and practical, wanted to participate. We both adored Barbara and wanted to help make this a success. When planning an event, especially a multi-faceted festival, regardless of size, you need a progressive plan to lay out and keep track of all of its aspects until the day of the event. Simple, no? No! We laid out the plan which had worked for my events. It called for periodic scheduled meetings and assigning tasks to individuals who would be responsible for carrying them out. We could tell that Barbara wasn't buying it, so we didn't push very hard. She planned everything herself, I believe.

The space could hold maybe 150 people and a stage, plus catering. I was opening the show, and we got there early. There was no one at the ticket table/artist sign-in. We asked. She forgot to assign it to anyone, so Edie and our friend Nancy took it over – all day. Everything else seemed to run OK. It was a modest turnout. I have no idea of what promotion or advertising was done, but I'm sure it lost money. I've stayed out of the helping-Barbara-plan business, but remained involved as a performer only, happily. I had a good time every time, and Edie got to enjoy the day too.

Another Grand Effort By Barbara

After the first Mother's Day outdoor festival, Barbara wanted to do another. She asked me if I would open the show solo, with some traditional acoustic blues, my specialty. I happily accepted. I didn't mention helping with planning this time.

Barbara had an ace in the hole – a gambling term that means (I think) you have a surprise for your fellow gamblers. Gambling is a fair metaphor for event production, in my opinion. Her surprise was that she had obtained the agreement of renown blues artist Keb 'Mo'. She had provided a great break for him early in his career by bringing him in as her guest artist at the famous Monterey Jazz Festival.

Keb' Mo'

I had booked him at my much smaller Big Time Blues Festival as he was gaining local notice, and had just signed a management contract. His manager didn't want him to do it, but he insisted. He didn't hurt his reputation that day. He was wonderful. And, Barbara had him coming. I was glad for her, and when she intimated that he was interested in having me join him for a tune or two I was doubly glad. That turned out to be not quite so, but it was a notable day regardless.

My concern, as always, was what was being done to promote this event? It had the potential of putting some money in her account, or pocket. Keb' was, for all intents and purposes, a star performer, bound to fill the place. When festival day came, there were people there, but not in the numbers I expected. Well, it's early, I told myself. It didn't get much better as the show progressed. Keb' showed up and we talked. He hadn't told her that he wanted me to play with him, and I accepted that in stride – it was always an outside chance in my mind. He was planning a set of his originals, which I didn't know anyhow.

Always friendly, he went about tuning up for his set, eyeing the sparse attendance. I couldn't figure that out. Given that he is not a traditional blues artist for a Black blues audience, I assumed that even modest notice in the general press would bring crowds to Leimert Park despite the aversion among many Whites to going into a Black neighborhood.

Keb' took the stage, played some of his songs and then, much to my surprise, called me up. I didn't know what tuning he was in, but he said, *Here, play this guitar*, and handed me one of his Nationals. He hit a Muddy Waters tune and we started to rock. Barbara heard us and made her way up to the stage and joined in. It was wonderful, with smiles all around.

But, I wondered why we were playing to 50 rather than 500? I know that Keb' wasn't happy with that as well. I got my answer a bit later when I asked Barbara about the publicity. She told me that she had put all of her money into advertising on KJLH, which plays only contemporary music for its mainly Black audience. I was speechless. He is known just about everywhere for his blues-based originals and traditional style playing. His music had been featured on Martha Stewart's show for years. The word didn't get out to the general public where it belonged. There was no third Mother's Day festival.

Pandemic Blues I – "Tuesday's Just As Bad"

By the end of March, 2020, Covid had hit California hard, and Governor Newsome had declared a shutdown of all public events. Restaurants, concert halls, arenas, clubs, many workplaces, and other gatherings were legally shuttered. People sheltered at home. Freeway traffic dipped to a trickle.

At first, in view of the ominous virus all around, it was almost a blessing to be at home. We had plenty of work to do at our house. I had amassed a huge pile of wood to be split for our fireplace. Our large garage was rendered all but unusable by mountains of tools, cloth, furniture, paint, music paraphernalia, and more piled over every square inch. Our side yard was a mountain of dirt, at the center of which was a huge tree stump and a network of deep-down roots that needed removal. We had also been collecting bricks over the years to make a large patio in that space once the dirt and stump had been removed. We had lots of work around here to keep a blues guitarist busy, let alone the need to keep your chops up with no playing dates. Time did not sit heavily on our hands, and we got to work.

Still, I missed having an outlet for playing the Blues, even after a day of assorted hard labor. Barbara Morrison had just the remedy. She proposed that we get together at her Center and do a series of sets that would be broadcast on the internet and made available on video for later showing. No audience, but there would be a working crew, and one or two specially invited guests. Her schedule was open on Tuesdays. She proposed that each show would open with a set of my acoustic country blues, followed by a set by her and me, with whatever accompaniment I had.

We had no budget, but my bassist Mike Barry was available and willing. Drummer Albert Trepagnier had a foot issue that prevented him from playing for a period of time, so we decided to try it as a duo. Barbara had always talked about doing a series based just on the Blues sung by women, and this seemed like a perfect opportunity. We decided to go ahead and try it, opening segment to be on the final Tuesday in July. We mulled over different titles and I came up with *Tuesday's Just as Bad*, the line following *They call it Stormy Monday...* from the T-Bone Walker classic. And a show was born.

I got to work on my acoustic blues material when I wasn't splitting wood, sorting through the garage mess, or digging out deep roots. I was busy. Best of all, I had a place to play live for a few ears and an unlimited internet audience.

I did my opening set on my two acoustic guitars, and then switched to electric for Barbara's set. As sometimes, and even more often than that, things don't work out as planned. Barbara knew dozens of songs, but I was looking to do a more traditional set with her. I had quickly prepared lists of songs from several women singers, from Bessie Smith, to Memphis Minnie, to Big Mama Thornton, to Koko Taylor, and more. But, Barbara's professional plate was already full. She taught Jazz vocals at UCLA, she ran her Center and the Jazz and Blues Museum, and did singing gigs of various types all the while managing her serious health issues.

Still, it was a challenge and a pleasure to have my set to prepare each week, and to work on whatever songs Barbara proposed for herself, and then have a professional, though unpaid, performance each Tuesday night. I even got to invite an acquaintance or two to sit in the almost empty house and enjoy a private show. Each segment was supposed to be aired live, and sometimes it was, sometimes not. I don't know if the re-airing was being done, but that really was out of my orbit.

We did 13 segments, stopping at the end of October. What am I gonna' do now? I wondered.

Mr. Whitmore Dances

One of the wonderful surprises that occurred during these Tuesday sessions was encountering a dancer I had not met before. I came to each session early enough to set up in a leisurely fashion, leaving enough time to deal with any issues, and still have time to kick back and "get my mind right" (Strother Martin, "Cool Hand Luke").

One evening there was a man sitting there. At first, I had the impression that he was a homeless man who just happened by. Barbara was extremely open and welcoming to all, so I wasn't surprised. This man was of fairly small stature, thin, bearded, grey-haired, and attired casually. He also had something in his hand. First impression was of a stick. A second look showed a wire on the stick. I asked him what it was, and he said *a diddly bow*. Wha….? I had seen the larger, front-porch version on film, and knew that Ellas "Bo Diddley" McDaniel had named himself after it. It was often the first musical instrument put together by many a future guitarist. It usually ended up earning a "whippin'" from Mama, because the wire was often what held Mama's broom together. With no baling wire available, the household broom would have to suffice. The whippin' hurt but the bow inspired.

This was smaller, hand-held, and wasn't going to result in any punishment. We talked further, and this man, Chester, turned out to be a dancer and choreographer who worked on TV and in movies.

Chester Whitmore

At some point I asked him if he'd care to dance. I do some very lively tunes that he could tap to. We went over some tunes, and he went to his car to get his tap shoes on, and we had a joyous time. I played Jesse Fuller's *San Francisco Bay Blues* because this was the first occasion I had to speak of Jesse to a fellow dancer in a Blues setting. It did my heart good. Chester Whitmore became a fairly frequent visitor to our set.

A Young Chester Whitmore

I mentioned that Jesse used to dance the *Buck and Wing*, and Chester said that was an old dance, and promptly demonstrated it. He could dance to anything we wanted to play.

Pandemic Blues 2

The ending of the Tuesday series at BMPAC in October left a gap in my life. I had completed most of the home projects by then, and what I had left did not fill that chasm. Even practice didn't do it. I slipped into a malaise, of the sort that many people had experienced during the pandemic. Even with the introduction of effective vaccines against the virus, I still had some internal demons to deal with. That ended with a call from Barbara Morrison proposing a Blue Monday series. This one, however, would follow a different pattern than the Tuesday shows. I was to do my acoustic set to open, and then switch to electric to back a different guest artist each week. She wanted guitar, bass, and drums. There would be a live audience.

I had to think about this. The trio was not much of a problem. Bassist Mike Barry was on board, and while drummer Albert couldn't do the first few shows, I found a fine substitute. He didn't know my acoustic material but was open to learning. A larger problem loomed: who would be my guests? I started a list of names. It was a pretty full list of names that expanded as we went on, but I had not worked with many of the artists, though most knew who I was.

Blue Monday Concert Series
Guest Artist Elizabeth Hangan

I decided to accept the challenge, very much as a drowning man is grateful for any assistance, no matter who tossed him a preserver. I needed to breathe, and Barbara's offer was breath itself.

The first three segments were to begin Monday, July 12, after the 4th of July weekend, and I had imagined a variety of artists I had worked with. The best laid plans…..the specific artists I had hoped for were not available. Plan B….I had no plan B. It was on me to figure this out. I called on three women vocalists. Long story short, it worked out great.

I wanted to make sure that we stayed with the blues, and asked that they choose their material with that in mind. Though all three were experienced performers, I asked one special thing from them all: I didn't want a "show" with bells and whistles. I wanted each to talk to the audience a little about why they were singing what they chose to sing. I wanted some intimacy. The theater was designed for it. Each understood what was being asked and brought the audience into the show. It was wonderful.

My acoustic sets were designed that way and, as long as you don't over do the talk, people find it interesting. A plus very often was that Barbara would join in with the featured performer at times, or would wheel up to the stage during my set and ask us to play a tune that she wanted to sing.

We did 25 consecutive Monday nights, each with a different guest artist, and each took the suggestion and drew their audiences in. We had Zydeco accordion, world-class harmonica players, startling guitarists, great vocalists, super piano players. Many had long drives to Leimert Park, but accepted nonetheless. They all wanted to play this series at Barbara's venue. It meant a great deal to them. Most all came to my house to rehearse their material in person. Professionalism was important.

Some were not normally featured performers, but people who could really bring it if asked. Each week was full of surprises, and each week a gift to the blues public.

I want to mention two which stand out in my mind.

Roy Lee Jones

I had seen a male vocalist there who sang well, but seemed a little off. It became clear that the band, fine musicians all, were not quite on the same page. I had his name on my list and decided to call Roy Lee Jones, Sr. The call went well, he accepted the October date.

When we talked about material, I expected some familiar tunes. But he had something else in mind. He asked if I knew any Howlin' Wolf songs. Of course I did, and named a few. He named a few, and we were off to the races.

Roy Lee Jones

Roy was also an actor, on TV and film, tall and handsome, and had a commanding stage presence. He was from Arkansas and had grown up with the Blues. We rehearsed, and did an all-Howlin' Wolf set. He knocked their socks off. Not imitating, but evoking Wolf in his own style.

Kee-Eso Pitchford

When Smokey Wilson passed away, at his funeral they announced a memorial get-together at Mr. Bell's Workshop following the service. I had heard of Bell's, but had never been there. Harmonica Fats played a lot with my band, but he also had his own band that played, as he said, "in the 'hood". The drummer was Franklin Bell.

Franklin Bobo Bell

Mr. Bell was a gas station owner and he did well and he loved the blues. When he retired, after Fats' passing, he and his wife decided to convert their spacious garage into a place to gather 'round the Blues. It was a legal juke joint in the 'hood. One pays a modest admission. A dinner buffet is provided (Grace is said before each meal), and one can get a bottle of water or a cold beer for free. No laws are being broken, and it is normally a friendly and trouble-free space. At Smokey's repast I met a guitarist from Mississippi whose blues name was Real Cool. I enjoyed talking with him and we became buds. He invited me to his birthday party at a hall on Manchester Bl. He had a young man running sound whom I had seen before, playing bass. This young man ran the sound with knowledge and gave me the best sound I ever had on my vintage Valco amp.

I asked for his name and was told Kee-Eso. I ran into Kee-Eso again at the Barnyard – a junkyard that becomes a (legal) juke joint on weekends – playing bass very well.

Kee-Eso Pitchford

When I began playing lap steel (not quite sacredly as yet) for Lester Lands' monthly Gospel Brunch, not two blocks from Mr. Bell's home, I heard several really impressive gospel singers.

One morning, Kee-Eso came in. We greeted each other warmly. Lester called him his nephew, and asked him to come up and sing. The young man took his guitar with him a wove a magic spell. Incredibly talented guitarist and dynamic gospel vocalist.

I knew he played the Blues too, and now I had heard him sing, I wondered if he'd agree to do both Blues and Gospel on a Monday night at Barbara's. I talked to him about that, and he said no problem. I told him our format, which included my trio backing him, and he said, oh, I'll bring my band. I said I just can't come up with the money to pay them, he said, no problem.

No problem indeed. In August, he played. The *Church Boys* (the ensemble's name) showed up and rocked the house, Kee-Eso Pitchford singing and playing like an angel possessed. No one was ready for this, including Barbara. After the set, I passed by her sitting at the back of the room. Understand that Barbara did not curse or use foul language, but she asked me, *Where did this mother fucker come from?* She was, totally taken with him, as was I and all in attendance.

I'm sure we can't imagine how many brilliant artists are out there, unrecognized.

Kee-Eso Pitchford worked a day job for the City of L.A. He does what he was born to do at other times.

Monday Blues Guest Artists at BMPAC 2021

We started the series with me, Mike Barry on bass, and Robert Gates on drums, as Albert had a foot issue that needed tending to. Albert rejoined the band perhaps after two months, say, in September. Date uncertain. We had rehearsals with almost all artists on the Friday prior, at my house. The rehearsals really made a difference, and we practiced on our own using You Tube on other days.

The trio opened each show with a set of acoustic blues. Once Albert rejoined us, our set included one or two songs from him. As circumstances led me to book all female vocalists in July, and I found it to give a coherence to the program and attempted to carry the idea forward, i.e. all keyboards, all guitarists, etc. It worked for a couple of months but ultimately I needed to return to a monthly program of more variety. Either way, the series was most satisfying and of a high quality.

During these shows, Barbara would often join the band for a song.

**Barbara Morrison, Bernie Pearl
Performing Live Together**

Each artist was reminded to give a little background to their material, trying to draw the audience in. It worked very well, and helped make this half-year of intimate concerts memorable and special.

Artists who performed during this series represented the finest in Los Angeles Blues right now.

1) 7/12/21 – Marguerite Love, vocalist

2) 7/19/21 – Dena Michals, vocalist

3) 7/26/21 – Elizabeth Hangan, vocalist

4) 8/2/21 – Jeff Paul Ross, Guitarist

5) 8/9/21 – Taywaun "Bud" Moore, Guitarist

6) 8/16/21 -- Job Striles, Guitarist, Vocalist
7) 8/23/21 – Kimberley Allison, Guitarist, Vocalist
8) 8/30/21 – Kee-Eso Pitchford, Guitarist, Vocalist
9) 9/6/21 – Dennis Gurwell, Zydeco Accordion, Vocals
10) 9/13/21 – Rob Rio, Boogie Woogie Piano, Vocals
11) 9/20/21 – Barbara Morrison, Vocalist

12) 9/27/21 – Mo Beeks, Piano, Vocals
13) 10/4/21 – Henry Carbajal, Guitar, Vocals
14) 10/11/21 – Michael Fell, Harmonica
15) 10/18/21 – Claudia Lennear, Vocalist

16) 10)25/21 – Roy Lee Jones, Sr., Vocalist
17) 11/1/21 – Ray Bailey, Guitar, Vocals
18) 11/8/21 – Delphia McKinley, Vocalist
19) 11/15/21 – Brophy Dale, Guitar, Vocals

20) 11/22/21 – Guitar Jack Wargo, Guitar, Vocals

21) 11/29/21 – R.J. Mischo, Harmonica, Vocals
22) 12/6/21 – Billy Watson, Harmonica, Vocals
23) 12/13/21 – Lester Lands, Guitar, Vocals
24) 12/20/21 – Dave Melton, Guitar, Vocals
25) 12/27/21 – Bernie Pearl Blues Band, Guitar, Bass, Drums, Vocals

Generally, these sessions followed a specific format. In Set 1, Bernie and the Band would perform. In this set, Bernie performed a wide range of music, from Lightnin' Hopkins to Albert King. Albert Trepagnier would perform at least 2 songs originally performed by Albert King. During Set 2, the guest musicians, outlined above, would perform, with backing from Bernie and the band.

**Claudia Lennear, Mike Barry, Bernie Pearl, Albert Trepagnier
Monday Blues, Oct 18, 2021**

Sadly, most of these unique and excellent Blues sessions were not recorded on audio or video. However, Bruce Krell did capture some of them. These recordings were a good opportunity to capture the state of Los Angeles Blues today.

Insights Into Barbara As A Person

Barbara and I had talked about a lot of things, but, our personal lives and relationships were not included. Funny little jokes, even little risqué' sayings came up, such as Cleanhead's referring to sex as *whatchamacallit* when performing. *Ain't had no whatchamacallit since my baby been gone.*

Once she talked about being on the road with Johnny Otis. When they were getting ready to leave to catch the plane home, she had a bunch of her clothes, including some underwear, left out of her luggage, and they needed to get to the airport-bound bus right away. So, they threw them into Johnny's luggage because hers had already been loaded. Bear in mind that Johnny was a Father figure for

Barbara, and his wife a Mother figure. When they got to Johnny's house, his wife, Phyllis, began unpacking his suitcase and discovered the underwear. She didn't wait for an explanation, drew the wrong conclusion and slapped Barbara. The mess was straightened out, and the familial tranquility was restored.

I don't recall whether we continued this discussion about the perils of the road or came back to it at another time. I surely didn't ask about it, but she made the statement that it was a hard and fast rule of hers not to get involved with anyone in the band she was working with, especially while on the road. She paused and said, *I just broke the rule one time*. Oh? She paused and said, *it was with B.B. King*. We both laughed. I may not have said it, but I thought, *Well if you're going to break the rule, might as well go for the top*. She said, it was just one time, but they stayed in touch.

I have the capricious thought that they must be having a laugh about it themselves up yonder.

Last Days of Barbara Morrison

Barbara left us in mid-March of 2022. She was coming to my daughter's wedding at our house on March 12. She was going to sing, *At Last*, for their first dance as a married couple, by my daughter's request. Deeply meaningful to all of us.

She had gone to the hospital in an emergency the day before the wedding, had undergone a stent surgery for a heart condition I didn't know she had, and was reportedly doing well. They had planned a second surgery, but she passed away before it could be done.

She certainly lived as fully and generously as she was able, and helped a lot of people. She provided opportunities for up and coming artists through her work. And, she had a spine of steel, and a golden voice. She always sang from her heart.

She was, as stated in the Book of Proverbs, a woman of valor, whose value is greater than rubies. She will be spoken of wherever people gather.

Barbara Morrison Performs Shortly Before Her Death

Our community has not recovered from her loss. It'll take a while, if ever.

Musicians I Have Known

This Bud's for You

While I have written of the musicians who played and recorded with the Bernie Pearl Blues Band for years, there were other notable players I'd like to mention who were also with me for a shorter while.

When I'd go to Smokey Wilson's Pioneer Club, there was a dynamic trombonist who used to appear with him. His name was Buddy Clemons. A large good-looking man with striking white hair and beard, he'd rock the joint with his playing. He also walked with a noticeable limp from a work-related accident in which his foot was severely damaged. The accident ended his days of toil and reputedly gave him a substantial settlement. Buddy had heard that I had put together a band and approached me about joining. I was surprised and didn't quite know what to say. I had a sax player already, which was new for me in itself. But, given that Ms Whis was a place where audiences are accustomed to, and even expected, horns with their blues, I asked him to come by and sit in.

I had room for another horn, if Buddy worked out. He came and blew his horn and the crowd ate it up. Buddy also made room for himself by singing. Much of the early afternoon crowd had been to church already and Buddy played it just right with extended versions of familiar songs straight out of a "church of the Blues" approach. He'd open his song on stage (really just a designated band space at crowd level) and then wander out into the seated crowd, extending the verses and preachin' the blues, and Alabama-born Buddy could preach! The audience, especially the women, hollered with joy and recognition. They'd stuff dollar bills into all parts of his attire – you know what I mean. That caused a little riff backstage once because the custom was for musicians to share all tips, and Buddy wasn't giving up nar' a dollar without a fight. We all just said go 'head on, and let it go.

Buddy Clemons really should have had his own band and show and, after a while, couldn't step back into a support role with the band. One big show we did, he simply refused to stop doing his own stage show while we were doing something else. It was embarrassing and frustrating and I decided that it couldn't go on, and I had to let him go. No animosity ever, he understood. I suspected that he was using something and just could not help himself. But, he was something else in front of an audience.

My original group did have a keyboardist, Dwayne Smith, and a saxophone, Freddie Clarke.

Freddie Clark had played the circuit around the South. He had played in Little Richard's band and when Grady Gaines came to the Music Machine and Richard showed up, Freddie was there too. He was a steady member of the Johnny Otis Show band, and he played Sundays with us at Ms Whis and elsewhere. He was an experienced veteran and a tremendous asset on the bandstand. Off the bandstand he had a drinking problem and I was getting reports that after some gigs he would hang out and drink and pester the wait staff. It was not part of what I had to offer an employer, and with sadness I replaced Freddie with Hollis Gilmore. Gil, as we called him, brought no liabilities with him, was a wonderful player and highly reliable. Freddie moved to Sebastopol when Johnny Otis moved his operation to the Bay Area and continued in his band.

I had also included a young, White former guitar student of mine, Robert Lucas, on harmonica and vocals.

Bernie Pearl and Robert Lucas

People loved Lucas. Freddie would rag on his overalls and pointy boots, but they were my "horn section", albeit an unusual one. At some point Robert left to join another band. He eventually made a career as a recording artist and front man for several working groups, including a later iteration of Canned Heat. It hurt me and Edie when we heard of his passing. He had struggled with drugs for a while. We were, in a fashion, his blues parents. He started with me as a teenager who took the bus to his lessons.

Maurice "Pops" Miller

I was fortunate to have been introduced to both pianist Dwayne Smith and drummer Maurice Miller by an extraordinary guitarist friend, Art Johnson. They all had been bandmates with Lena Horne, and all top artists with tons of high-level experience. Art was not only a friend, but a relentless supporter for many years of what I was attempting to do.

When I landed the gig at Ms Whis I asked both Dwayne and Maurice if they would consider doing it with me. The pay, as I have mentioned, was low, as the venue did not charge an admission at the door, but it was a very nice club and a musician always wants to keep active and to enjoy himself as well. It was a go for both. "Mo" or "Pops", as we called Maurice, was from East St. Louis, a music hot bed, and had played in famed pianist Memphis Slim's band. Both Ike & Tina, and B.B. King were on the East S.L. scene when he was with Slim. Mo never said he played with them, but seemed very familiar with them.

Mo came west, found it welcoming to his talents, and was seldom out of a job. Aside from his gig with Lena, he was in the cast of "Hair". He could drum, and he could sing. In fact, singing the Blues was one of the perks of the Ms Whis gig. It helped attract and keep "Pops" Miller on board for much of our early days at Ms Whis. He remained a friend and played many other gigs with me.

Mo also played alongside Matt "Guitar" Murphy (featured in the Blues Brothers movie),

Epilogue

When he plays live, Bernie Pearl is often introduced as the *Godfather of the Blues in Los Angeles*. This biography clearly justifies that title.

During that career, Bernie has acted as musician, show and record producer, master of ceremonies, artistic director, radio host and now author.

Bernie Pearl started his career in the Blues in 1958 at the Ash Grove in Los Angeles. At the Ash Grove, he was mentored by Lightnin' Hopkins, Mance Lipscomb, MS Fred McDowell, Rev Gary Davis, Sonny Terry and Brownie McGhee and dozens of others. These Bluesman gave Bernie a solid grounding in the oral tradition and playing mechanics of the rural Blues.

Bernie also performed and associated with many of the big names in modern urban Blues. Freddie King, Albert King, B B King, Otis Rush, Taj Majal, Keb' Mo', and dozens of others were a part of Bernie's musical sphere.

Nothin' But the Blues, created and hosted by Bernie, was the first all-Blues show on FM Radio in Los Angeles. This radio show led to his role as creator, artistic director and master of ceremonies of the Annual KLON Long Beach Blues Festival. As a result of the radio show and the Festivals, demand for Blues performances by affluent white residents of Los Angeles increased. Blues musicians found an extensive market for their shows throughout the area over a fifteen year period. Many of the musicians were finally able to make a living as a full-time Blues musician.

As a musician, Bernie Pearl has learned to play the Blues and to project the internal feelings of the Blues. Clearly, the Blues chose Bernie as its instrument.

If you go to hear the Blues somewhere in Los Angeles today, you are very likely to get a chance to hear Bernie play. Don't miss such an opportunity.

Bernie will be playing the Blues until he can no longer play.

Book References

Bradford, Perry, *Born With The Blues*, Oak Publications, 1965.

Bryant, Clora et al, *Central Avenue Sounds: Jazz in Los Angeles*, University of CA Press, 1998.

Collis, John, *The Story of Chess Records*, Bloomsbury, 1998.

Dance, Helen Oakley, *Stormy Monday: The T-Bone Walker Story*, Louisiana State University Press, 1987.

Davis, Mike and Jon Wiener, *Set the Night on Fire: L A in the Sixties*,Verso, 2020.

Dixon, Willie and Don Snowden, *I Am The Blues*, Da Capo Press, 1989.

Gordon, Robert, *Can't Be Satisfied: The Life and Times of Muddy Waters*, Little Brown & Co, 2002.

Handy, W C, *Father of the Blues*, Da Capo Press, 1941.

Iglauer, Bruce and Patrick Roberts, *Bitten By The Blues: The Alligator Records Story*, University of Chicago Press, 2018.

James, Etta and David Ritz, *Rage To Survive: The Etta James Story*, Da Capo Press, 1995.

Lipsitz, *George, Midnight at the Barrelhouse: The Johnny Otis Story*, University of Minnesota Press, 2010.

Lauterbach, Preston, *The Chitlin' Circuit and the Road To Rock 'N' Roll*, Preston Lauterbach, 2011.

O'Connell, Sean, Los Angeles's Central Avenue Jazz, Arcadia Publishing, 2014.

Oliver, Paul, *The Story of the Blues*, Chilton Book Company, 1969.

Otis, Johnny, *Upside Your Head! Rhythm and Blues on Central Avenue*, Wesleyan University Press, 1993.

Palmer, Earl, *Backbeat: Earl Palmer's Story*, Da Capo Press, 1999.

Pastras, Phil, *Dead Man Blues: Jelly Roll Morton, Way Out West*, University of CA Press, 2001.

Reed, Tom, *The Black Music History of Los Angeles – Its Roots*, LA Black Accent Press, 1994.

Sawyer, Charles, *B B King: From Indianola to Icon*, Schiffer Publishing 2022.

Sawyer, Charles, *The Arrival of BB King*, Da Capo Press, 1980.

Smith, R J, *The Great Black Way: L A in the 1940s and the Lost African American Renaissance*, Perseus Books Group, 2006.

Sporke, Michael, *Big Mama Thornton: The Life and Music*, McFarland & Co Inc, 2014.

Wilkerson, Isabel, *The Warmth of Other Sons: The Epic Story of America's Great Migration*, Vintage, 2011.

Zack, Ian, *Say No To The Devil: The Life and Musical Genius of Rev Gary Davis*, University of Chicago Press, 2015.

Dozens of other books referenced in the End Notes.

Appendix

Barbara Morrison's Family and Early Life

by Richard Morrison, Barbara's Brother

Barbara Morrison's Family and Early Life

by Richard Morrison, Barbara's Brother

Any description of our family would have to start with our mother and father, Constance Odessa and Robert Edward Morrison. Our mother was a beautiful woman with fair skin and long dark hair until it turned silver during the latter part of her life. Like many proud Black women, our mother's facile features and tone displayed the difficult life and times often experienced during that era. She of course packed on pounds occasionally, to support the bearing of her children. Our parents met each other near Ypsilanti, MI, around 1948, just after our mother graduated from High School, but before our father left for the Army. Our mother would eventually bear seven children; Barbara, Robert Jr. ("Man" was his nickname), Pamela, Michael, Richard, James (who I was told died at birth or shortly thereafter) and Armetta, known to all of us as "Angie."

Our mother had a solid education and was the rock that held everything together. Her sharp wit and stern, but seemingly angry discipline punctuated our upbringing, but our mother still managed that loving stare that indicated pride for what she had brought into this world. Our father was very smart and resourceful, not necessarily in an academic sense, but he had a real world, commonsense. He was certainly, smart enough to not let his children know they were as low on the socioeconomic class scale as we happened to be at the time. We always seemed stable and had what we needed.

I didn't realize how poor we were until, as a young man finding his way, I needed a couple of hundred dollars to pay a college bill and my mother told me we did not have it. That let me know I needed to start paying my own way. My Dad always seemed to be a leader amongst his friends in whatever project they had going, constructing additions to our family home, or helping one of his friends with their individual goals. He drew people to him and most all of them remained loyal friends throughout his life. He was a U.S. Army veteran who served in Korea and saw firsthand the horrors of war. He was very athletic and loved baseball and music, which he played and coached and sang until he couldn't. One of our family's most cherished memories, especially with Barbara who deeply loved our dad, was my father somehow getting us in to see a game of the 1968 World Series between the Detroit Tigers and the St. Louis Cardinals.

Dad was also a bit of a musician—a trait that inspired Barbara and helped lead to her later success. Our family had a secondhand organ, and later purchased a secondhand piano that my father would play, sing, and try with great patience to teach us rudimentary lessons. We all benefited, but looking back now it's so obvious how these special moments formed the basis for Barbara's incredible love for these authentic and beautiful sounds.

Both our parents worked most of their lives until illness gradually prevented them from carrying on. All the of children went to work at a young age, starting with Summer Job Programs, and following that up with whatever could be found. Barbara, who was the oldest of the siblings, had it the roughest when it came to working inside and outside the home, even though I think she enjoyed working at such a young age. I believe she worked harder during her childhood years than any grown woman could possibly have done during the same period. Barbara literally would do any type of work to support our family, including doing the grunt work required when working with elderly residents at nursing homes.

I remember as a young child accompanying my father, or mother, depending on who was available and who's turn it was; with picking up Barbara late at night from one of the several, varied places she worked. I strongly believe the example set by Barbara's incredible willpower and work ethic is where all of us siblings who came after her developed our own work ethic, loyalty, and belief of fairness towards others. Barbara set an example that was followed by the next youngest sibling and so on until all of us met the standard of being able to fend for ourselves and back each other up against whatever life had in mind to throw at us at any given moment.

My father thought experience was the best teacher and allowed us to make mistakes and find our own approach to life. He would talk with us about our trials, our worries, our dreams, offering his own unique perspective—while we were in the process of fully experiencing whatever he was trying to help us navigate through, whether those experiences turned either good or bad. My father was a practical man, but he never told us that our dreams were not achievable because of our station in life.

To be a beautiful, light skinned Black woman during that time in our history would ultimately create emotional baggage for her that was hard to overcome. She would rather crack a whip and let you know what was what through sometimes "harsh instruction." Our mother loved all of us very much but learned quickly when we did something wrong in our mothers 'opinion and adjusted accordingly. It was the way it was for those times.

My siblings and I were all born in Washtenaw County Michigan, at Beyers Memorial Hospital, which was in the City of Ypsilanti. We grew up in the City of Romulus in Wayne County, Michigan, about 20 miles West of Detroit off the Interstate 94 Expressway. It was a very small town. It's hard to imagine this now since we weren't "that" far from the big city back then, but my cousin who lived in the City of Detroit used to call our town "the country." Like we lived on a farm or something. The Detroit Metropolitan Airport is the City of Romulus's main claim to fame, as it's located inside the city limits. We all attended Romulus High School, in fact my mother, and most of us kids, were taught by some of the very same teachers.

My parents stressed traditional education and all of us were expected to attend college for at least one year without question. When it was all said and done every one of us attended college for at least three years. We achieved and earned college degrees ranging from an Associates of Arts Degree, to a Master's Degree. Most of us were academically inclined, with one of us always teaching or pushing the other, then handing it off to the next sibling down the line. Whoever needed that nudge or helping hand got it. I believe we succeeded because of the high standards set by Barbara. I remember Barbara telling my oldest brother, who was having trouble with geometry, that she could teach him everything he needed to know about geometry from a pool table. I suppose it has something to do with the angles of the shots? But whatever it was, she indeed taught him geometry!

So let's talk about Barbara!

Barbara

Barbara was such a beautiful young lady growing up. She developed early as a teenager. Looking older than she was probably helped in landing some of the jobs at Department Stores and the various Offices she worked at during her early years, certainly well into her teens. She set the standard for all of us—probably without even knowing it. I don't remember a single instance where my parents scolded Barbara about her grades, or anything having to do with school. Her good looks, high academic and extra-curricular activities also generated a lot of jealousy among her peers. Getting grades equal to the nerdy kids, being on the cheerleading squad, often working an afterschool job while also babysitting her younger siblings from time to time filled up her dance card during her Junior High and High School Years. As I remember it, I was the last person that Barbara hugged when she dashed out the front door of our house and jumped into her car to make the drive to Michigan State University. The same car, which a few years later would take her to Los Angeles to begin her career as a performing artist. Barbara began performing at a young age, from singing with my father and his friends, to winning beauty contests during her early days in Michigan, to striking out West and becoming a Jazz and Blues legend.

I am not bragging when I say she was a legend. This was proven to me when I came out to visit her in California after an unexpected illness had taken her legs. To me I was just being a helpful brother who was pushing his "Big Sis" around. But I quickly realized I couldn't push her wheelchair ten feet without someone wanting to touch her arm or shoulder to get her attention; or to ask for an autograph while telling her how much they loved her music. I had to step back and ask myself if this was the same person I grew up with as a kid? I finally realized that she had transcended far beyond just being my big sister. Through sheer willpower she had overcome losing her legs. I asked myself how many people could handle something like that with such grace and positivity? The person I knew from my youth was still there, but she was now also something else entirely. Someone who had the power to spread incredible joy through her music and personality. Laughing and sometimes making jokes about her situation. She also charmed almost anyone she performed for with ease, sending out wonderful sounds in her songs, which was at times downright gritty.

Now let's talk about the rest of the family!

Robert

My eldest brother Robert ("MAN") also set high standards. He was an excellent student, and an even better athlete. He participated in wrestling and football while in High School. He earned a full athletic scholarship to Northwestern University for wrestling. After graduation he moved to Texas and opened an independent Office for Allstate Insurance. Within a few short years, he had two children and had adopted another. His oldest daughter now has her own business and is married with two children of her own. His son took over his Insurance Office after his untimely death in 2021; and his youngest daughter recently earned her Doctorate from Howard University in December of 2023. Regarding the value of education, his family had continued the circle.

Pamela

My middle-sister Pamela displayed a lot of the traits you would expect to find in a middle child. She was protective of the Morrison name and was willing to do battle when needed. She was always very supportive. She was the kind of person who would almost give you the shirt off her back. I say "almost" because she could spot a fake person, or situation a mile off. If any of us were ever in trouble, like Barbara, she would be the one to call. She stood up and protected us our whole lives; when life changing situations inevitably happened, she would always come though without asking for reward, or attempting to take credit.

I don't think Pamela, like many middle children, was every appreciated for all she did for each of her family members. I know she helped each of us with our parenting, which sometimes included sacrificing her time, money, and strength to assist with whatever we were facing. When our mother died, and my little sister needed adult supervision, Pamela took over and kept the family home together. When my brother needed a short-term loan to expand his business, she made sure she was there at the most critical time with support.

When my own son needed a liver transplant, she was there to support me in every way imaginable for that stressful month I had to stay with him in the hospital. I realize now how much I had come to depend on her wise counsel and advice.

My sister had a long-time life partner/husband/friend/everything; someone that I have to mention, as he was like another brother blessed to our household. He and Pamela dated each other from the time she was in the 7th Grade, and he was in 8th Grade. They later married and never separated until her death in 2023, a year after Barbara. My sister had two children and was a grandmother of four. Her daughter works in Social Services as a Counselor and is a very smart and resourceful soccer mom. Like her mom, she doesn't miss a thing going on around her. Her son also has two children and he works for Amazon. He is one of the most genuine people you will ever meet and I think similar to me in that dedication, determination, and hard work are his strong suit. Again, our legacy. Pamela was so close to Barbara, they were always talking on the phone and making plans. I can picture the both now in Heaven, catching each other up on the gossip and planning for the day when we'll all be together again.

Michael

My brother Michael I believe was Barbara's favorite although she would never let on. I heard it in the way she called him "Digga!" which was a nickname she gave him, and it stuck until his passing at an early age. My brother was an Honor-Roll Student and extraordinary High School athlete. He was a High School all-American in baseball and basketball. He was also the quarterback and Captain of the football team. He earned a full scholarship to Eastern Michigan for basketball and ended up playing for Eastern for two years. He was also a middle-child and very protective of his family. I was always proud of how he went his own way, carved his own pathway, but still represented the family well until an unexpected illness took him from us far too soon. His incredible popularity was a tough act to follow. He had the prettiest girlfriends and knew everyone, and they knew him. Several of his longtime friends often remind me how they considered it an honor to be his friend in life, as I do.

I think what I remember the most about him is that he didn't seem to want to take credit, or get pats on the back, for being so protective of his family. I remember several incidents of him defending me and other family members during our younger days; and he just did it because, as he put it, "that was what he was supposed to do and there it is!" It was not a big deal to him because that's who he was in life. I can't say for sure that I would have stepped in the middle of some of the controversies and conflicts like he did—that takes a special person. But I loved and admired him at the same time because he was "'the man,' the guy everyone wanted to be."

Richard (Rick)

When I think about myself I had it made! I was carefree and happy growing up. I think I was blessed with a clear, and already set, pathway for me to travel. I just needed to grow up, get through High School and go to College. Only a few of my peers had this seemingly set obligation, or pathway, laid out by their family. A family that pushed them in a certain, pre-planned, direction. Although, at least in my mind, I didn't have to try very hard because of the solid reputation of my older siblings, I also knew I had to do more than just show up. I always felt that I was given the benefit of the doubt no matter what happened, because my last name was Morrison. Just showing up with the last name of "Morrison" carried with it certain benefits and privileges.

I was not a very good student. I lacked some of the academic focus that my siblings possessed, and it seemed I could get by because of my privilege, or just sheer luck. It seemed that others; teachers and even people in the community, gave me this grace because of the Morrison reputation. I remember doing very poorly on my SAT exams. I got bored during the test as it was stressful, so I just "Christmas-treed" the answers. But wouldn't you know it! I was accepted into Western Michigan University! This is where I learned to apply myself. Where my true academic study began. Even if others didn't grant me the grace I thought would always be there, I was blessed with a forward-looking sprit and the ability to overcome almost anything negative. Nothing could keep me down for very long. I could compartmentalize the good and bad news, never getting too excited or depressed. I took things in stride and was content. As long as I knew where I stood, knew what I had to face, then I also knew that I could overcome, and recover if need be. Coming back from adversity, both good and bad, was normal to me.

This would certainly not be true of 2020-2023, when all my older siblings passed away in succession during this period. This was, and remains the biggest emotional, and challenging time of my life! But even with this clear example of our own mortality; that the end appears to be closer now than the beginning, I would still describe myself as lucky! Whether it's luck that was made or given, it is luck that has left me blessed to be a Morrison, a great family that set an example for all of us; one that will continue through our ten nieces and nephews.

James

I did not have the pleasure of knowing my little brother as he only lived for a short time. I am told he still had a very emotional impact on my mother. He was greatly missed.

Armetta

My baby sister is one of my heroes whether she knows it or not. I have never told her this in so many words. I have always been so proud of her as she exhibited so many of the qualities of her older sisters. Like them she is a fighter. A fighter, not in the physical sense, but in her dedication and determination to overcome obstacles. Our parents passed away when she was still in High School. Yet she finished High School and College, later earning a master's degree. I always felt that Angie could do anything she set her mind to and focused on. We've all ran into people who sit around wishing someone else would get things done. Angie always focused on her goals and acted. She has overcome so much in life. She is her own worst critic, not really seeing how beautiful she is and too humble to realize all the things she brings to the table. She became pregnant mid-way through college and put together a Herculean effort to finish college as a single mother. When most people would have given up, she battled. She would tell you that she had a lot of help, but I would bet the house she would have made a way, with or without any help. I will always admire her for that. That is an example of the dedication and determination I speak of with our family. Apples don't fall far from trees as her two children are both excelling in life after their college years. Her daughter is an entrepreneur, and her son recently began his career as an engineer.

Conclusion

My hope is that anyone blessed with receiving a Barbara Morrison scholarship would take the time to understand the power of family and friends who come along at just the right time to supply that little extra nudge. That say those badly needed words of encouragement when all seems bleak. It takes more than talent and money to be a success. Barbara Morrison, my family's beloved "Big Sis," demonstrated that every day. Our hope is that a bit of Barbara's spirit travels with anyone who is fortunate enough to share in her legacy. So, to those recipients, thank you for applying, and thank you for allowing Barbara to share in your own life's journey.

Endnotes

[1] Biography of Jesse Fuller adapted from Wald, Elijah, "Jesse Fuller Profile", *Acoustic Guitar*, 1997, retrieved 8/6/2022, https://www.elijahwald.com/bluarch.html.

[2] Koenig, Lester, Liner notes to Jesse Fuller: San Francisco Bay Blues. Good Time Jazz S10051, 1963.

[3] Jesse Fuller, quoted at "Jesse Fuller: the Lone Cat – San Francisco Bay Blues", *The Immortal Jukebox*, retrieved 8/6.2022, https://theimmortaljukebox.com/2015/02/12/jesse-fuller-the-lone- cat/comment-page-10/.

[4] Harris, Dave, quotes By Jesse Cahn, childhood friend of Jesse Fuller, in "FotDellas", *One Man Band Book*, retrieved 8/6/2022, http://onemanbandbook.blogspot.com/2009/10/fotdellas.html.

[5] Koenig, Lester, Liner notes to Jesse Fuller: San Francisco Bay Blues. Good Time Jazz S10051, 1963.

[6] Interview, Barry Hansen, Sept 2, 2023, Long Beach, CA.

[7] *Southland Blues*, Jan, 1995.

[8] Al Lubiejewski, "BLUE BLAZES", *Jazz Erie*, Dec, 1996.

[9] Lauterbach, Preston, *The Chitlin' Circuit and the Road to Rock and Roll*, WW Norton and Co., 2011, p. p. 223.

[10] Zebrowski, Rafal, Dr., Anniversary of the Pale Settlement Decree, Jewish Historical Institute, retrieved 3/7/2024, https://www.jhi.pl/en/articles/anniversary-of-the-pale-settlement-decree, 243.

[11] Zebrowski, Rafal, Dr., Anniversary of the Pale Settlement Decree, Jewish Historical Institute, retrieved 3/7/2024, https://www.jhi.pl/en/articles/anniversary-of-the-pale-settlement- decree,243.

[12] "Modern Jewish History: The Pale of the Settlement", *Jewish Virtual Library*, American-Israeli Cooperative Enterprise (AICE), retrieved 3/7/2024, https://www.jewishvirtuallibrary.org/the-pale-of-settlement. [13] Wexler P. , "Yiddish—the fifteenth Slavic language. A study of partial language shift from Judeo-Sorbian to German", *Int. J. Soc. Lang.* 1991, pp. 9–150, 215–225. 10.1515/ijsl.1991.91.9.

[14] Aptroot M. "Yiddish language and Ashkenazic Jews: a perspective from culture, language and literature", *Genome Biol. Evol.* 2016, 8, pp.1948–1949. 10.1093/gbe/evw131.

[15] "Modern Jewish History: The Pale of the Settlement", *Jewish Virtual Library*, American-Israeli Cooperative Enterprise (AICE), retrieved 3/7/2024, https://www.jewishvirtuallibrary.org/the-pale-of-settlement. [16] "Modern Jewish History: The Pale of the Settlement", *Jewish Virtual Library*, American-Israeli Cooperative Enterprise (AICE), retrieved 3/7/2024, https://www.jewishvirtuallibrary.org/the-pale-of-settlement.

[17] Polonsky,Antony, "The Position Of The Jews In The Tsarist Empire, 1881-1905", *The Jews In Poland And Russia*, Vol 2, Ch. 1, p. 3, retrieved 3/7/2024, https://www.brandeis.edu/tauber/events/Polonsky_vol2%20_%20ch1.p df.

[18] *The Jewish Chronicle*, May 6, 1881, cited in Benjamin Blech, *Eyewitness to Jewish History*, Wiley; 1st edition, August 13, 2004.
[19] Sakalli, Seyhun, Ekatarina Zhuravskaya, and Irena Grosfeld, *Political and Economic Drivers of Pogroms*, retrieved 3/5/2024, https://cepr.org/voxeu/columns/political-and-economic-drivers- pogroms.
[20] Pogrom Archived February 6, 2010, at the Wayback Machine, based on Alina Cała, Hanna Węgrzynek, Gabriela Zalewska, *Historia i kultura Żydów polskich. Słownik*, WSiP.
[21] Polonsky,Antony, "The Position Of The Jews In The Tsarist Empire, 1881-1905", *The Jews In Poland And Russia*, Vol 2, Ch. 1, p. 5, retrieved 3/7/2024, https://www.brandeis.edu/tauber/events/Polonsky_vol2%20_%20ch1.p df.
[22] Weinberg, Robert, "The Pogrom of 1905 in Odessa: A Case Study" in *Pogroms: Anti-Jewish Violence in Modern Russian History*, John D. Klier and Shlomo Lambroza, eds., Cambridge,1992, pp. 248-89.
[23] Steiner, Edward A., "The Fellowship of the Steerage". *On the Trail of The Immigrant*. New York: Fleming H. Revell Company. 1906, pp. 35–38.
[24] "Los Angeles: The 1920s and the '30'", *Britanica*, retrieved 3/8/2024, https://www.britannica.com/place/Los-Angeles-California/The-1920s- and-30s.
[25] "From Elite Suburb to Immigrant Enclave", Jewish Histories in Multiethnic Boyle Heights, retrieved 3/9/2024, https://scalar.usc.edu/hc/jewish-histories-boyle-heights/from-elite- suburb-to-immigrant-enclave.
[26] Security National Pacific Collection, Los Angeles Public Library, retrieved 3/9/2024, https://scalar.usc.edu/hc/jewish-histories-boyle-heights/media/00011195.jpg
[27] Kagel, Jenna,"For Jewish Immigrants, Boyle Heights was a place for community building and a slice of the American dream", KCRW, 6/2/2021, retrieved 3/8/2024, https://www.kcrw.com/news/shows/greater-la/boyle-heights/jewish-american-enclave.
[28] "Jewish American Heritage", *East Side Los Angeles*, Los Angeles Conservancy, retrieved 3/9/2024, https://www.laconservancy.org/jewish-american-heritage/.
[29] The next 3 notes are extracted from Elliott, Wendy, "The Jews of Boyle Heights, 1900-1950: The Melting Pot of Los Angeles*", Southern California Quarterly*, Vol 78, No 1, The Historical Society of Southern California, Spring,1996, pp 1-10.
[30] Vorspan, Max and Lloyd P. Gartner, *History of the Jews of Los Angeles*, The Huntington Library, 1970, p.118.
[31] Sanchez, George, *Becoming Mexican American: Ethnicity, Culture, and Identity in Chicano Los Angeles, 1900-1945*, Oxford University Press, 1993 , p. 75.
[32] Sandberg, Neil, *Jewish Life in Los Angeles: A Window to Tomorrow*, University Press of America, 1986 , p. 28.
[33] "The Menorah Center", Jewish Histories in Multiethnic Boyle Heights, retrieved 3/9/2024, https://scalar.usc.edu/hc/jewish-histories-boyle- heights/the-menorah-center-3218-wabash-ave.
[34] "The Menorah Center", Jewish Histories in Multiethnic Boyle Heights, retrieved 3/9/2024.
[35] "The Menorah Center", Jewish Histories in Multiethnic Boyle Heights, retrieved

3/9/2024.
[36] Variety Boys and Girls Club, https://vbgc.org/history/.
[37] Tabenkin, Yad, *Habonim, Great Britain, 1929–1955*, 1999.
[38] Yaroslavsky, Zev, *Zev's Los Angeles*, Academic Studies Press, 2023, p. 20.
[39] *Nehije koelanoe chaloetsiem; Haboniem 60 jaa,* Ichoed Haboniem-Dror BeHolland, 2010 ; and, *"Over ons – Haboniem-Dror beHolland",* www.haboniem.nl (in Dutch), 21 August 2013, retrieved 6/4/2024..
[40] Yaroslavsky, Zev, *Zev's Los Angeles*, p. 20.
[41] Yaroslavsky, Zev, *Zev's Los Angeles*, p. 22.
[42] Yaroslavsky, Zev, *Zev's Los Angeles*, p. 25.
[43] Torok, Ryan, "A new home for historic labor zionist youth camp*", Jewish Journal,* 27 July 2011, *retrieved 6/4/2024; and.*Gruenbaum Fax, Julie, "Labor Zionist ideals live on at Gilboa", *Jewish Journal,* 14 December 2007, retrieved 2 May 2024.
[44] Yaroslavsky, Zev, *Zev's Los Angeles*, p. 24.
[45] Gruenbaum Fax, Julie, "Labor Zionist ideals live on at Gilboa", 14 December 2007.
[46] Pine, Dan, "Hike, swim, fix the world: Kids mix it up at Gilboa camp*", Jewish News of Northern California,* 15 January 2016 , 2 May 2024, https://www.jweekly.com/2016/01/15/hike-swim-fix-the-world-kids-mix-it-up-at-gilboa-camp/; and, Pink, Aiden, "What Jewish Camps Taught Your Kids About Israel This Summer", *The Forward,* August 5, 2019, retrieved 2 May 2024, https://forward.com/news/national/406175/what-jewish-camps-taught- your-kids-about-israel-this-summer/.
[47] US Works Progress Administration, 1939, https://tessa2.lapl.org/digital/collection/photos/id/1754.
[48] **Unless indicated otherwise**, this biography was adapted from Stone, Peter and Ellen Harold, "Sonny Terry (Saunders Terrell)", *CulteralEquity.org*, retrieved 7/3/2025, https://www.culturalequity.org/alan-lomax/friends/terry.
[49] Lomax, Alan, *The Land Where the Blues Began* , 1993.
[50] "Sanders (Sonny) Terry", *National Endowment for the Arts*, retrieved 7/4/2025, https://www.arts.gov/honors/heritage/sanders-sonny-terry. [51] "Sanders (Sonny) Terry", *National Endowment for the Arts*, retrieved 7/4/2025
[52] "Sanders (Sonny) Terry", *National Endowment for the Arts*, retrieved 7/4/2025.
[53] Alligator Records, "Sonny Terry", *Artists*, retrieved 7/9/2025, https://www.alligator.com/artists/Sonny-Terry/.
[54] Alligator Records, "Sonny Terry", retrieved 7/9/2025.
[55] Bastin, Bruce, *Red River Blues: The Blues Tradition in the Southeast* , 1989, p 266.
[56] Alligator Records, "Sonny Terry", retrieved 7/9/2025.
[57] **Unless indicated otherwise**, this biography was adapted from Stone, Peter and Ellen Harold, "Brownie McGhee", *CulteralEquity.org*, retrieved 7/4/2025, https://www.culturalequity.org/alan-lomax/friends/mcghee.
[58] "Brownie McGhee", *National Endowment for the Arts*, retrieved 7/4/2025, https://www.arts.gov/honors/heritage/brownie-mcghee.

59 "Brownie McGhee", *National Endowment for the Arts*, retrieved 7/4/2025.
60 "Brownie McGhee", *National Endowment for the Arts*, retrieved 7/4/2025.
61 "Brownie McGhee", *National Endowment for the Arts*, retrieved 7/4/2025.
62 "Brownie McGhee", *National Endowment for the Arts*, retrieved 7/4/2025.
63 "Brownie McGhee", *National Endowment for the Arts*, retrieved 7/4/2025.
64 Balfour, Alan, *Sonny Terry & Brownie McGhee' UK Souvenir Tour Programme*, April/May, 1977, retrieved 7/10/2025, https://earlyblues.org/british-blues-articles-and-essays-sonny-terry- brownie-mcghee/.
65 Balfour, Alan, *Sonny Terry & Brownie McGhee' UK Souvenir Tour Programme*, retrieved 7/10/2025.
66 **Unless indicated otherwise**, this biography was adapted from Stone, Peter and Ellen Harold, "Sonny Terry (Saunders Terrell)", *CulteralEquity.org*, retrieved 7/4/2025, **AND** Stone, Peter and Ellen Harold, "Brownie McGhee", *CulteralEquity.org*, retrieved 7/4/2025.
67 Identified by Bernie Pearl, who was at the Ash Grove at the time.
68 Balfour, Alan, *Sonny Terry & Brownie McGhee' UK Souvenir Tour Programme*, retrieved 7/10/2025.
69 "Brownie McGhee", *National Endowment for the Arts*, retrieved 7/4/2025.
70 "Brownie McGhee", *National Endowment for the Arts*, retrieved 7/4/2025.
71 "Brownie McGhee", *National Endowment for the Arts*, retrieved 7/4/2025.
72 Relayed by Sonny Terry to Bernie Pearl in a conversation, probably at the Ash Grove when the pair was performing at the club.
73 Alligator Records, "Sonny Terry", retrieved 7/9/2025.
74 "Brownie McGhee", *National Endowment for the Arts*, retrieved 7/4/2025.
75 Davies, Phil, "Brownie McGhee", *TIMS: this is my story*, retrieved 7/5/2025, https://tims.blackcat.nl/messages/brownie_mcghee.htm.
76 "Brownie McGhee", *National Endowment for the Arts*, retrieved 7/4/2025.
77 Album notes, *Sonny and Brownie*, A&M Records, 1973.
78 Personal communications between Brownie McGhee and Bernie Pearl.
79 Davies, Phil, "Brownie McGhee", retrieved 7/5/2025.
80 Personal observations of Bernie Pearl during performances.
81 Sanders (Sonny) Terry", *National Endowment for the Arts*, retrieved 7/4/2025.
82 "Brownie McGhee", *National Endowment for the Arts*, retrieved 7/4/2025.
83 As an example of scat singing, listen to the vocals starting at 1:40 in *Keep On Trucking'*.
84 Oakley, Giles, *The Devil's Music*, Da Capo Press,. 1997, pp 190/2.
85 Larkin, Colin, *The Virgin Encyclopedia of Popular Music*, Virgin Books, 1997, p 147.
86 Larkin, Colin, *The Virgin Encyclopedia of Popular Music*, p 147.
87 Cult, Steve, "Notes", *Blind Boy Fuller: Truckin' My Blues Away*, Yazoo Records, 1978.
88 Eagle, Bob and Eric LeBlanc, Eric, *Blues: A Regional Experience*, Praeger, 2013. p 278.
89 Larkin, Colin, *The Virgin Encyclopedia of Popular Music*, p 147.
90 Larkin, Colin, *The Virgin Encyclopedia of Popular Music*, p 147.
91 "Blind Boy Fuller: His Life, Recording Sessions, and Welfare Records",

Jas Obrecht Music Archive, Jasobrecht.com, retrieved 1/15/2025.
[92] Larkin, Colin, *The Virgin Encyclopedia of Popular Music*, p 147.
[93] Larkin, Colin, *The Virgin Encyclopedia of Popular Music*, p 147.
[94] Cult, Steve, "Notes", 1978.
[95] Russell, Tony, *The Blues: From Robert Johnson to Robert Cray*, Carlton Books, 1997, p 13.
[96] Oakley, Giles, *The Devil's Music*, pp 190/2.
[97] Oliver, Paul, *Blues Off the Record*, Da Capo Press, 1984, pp 95–98.
[98] Oakley, Giles, *The Devil's Music*, pp 190/2.
[99] Olstrom, Clifford, *Undaunted by Blindness* (revised ed), Perkins School for the Blind, 2012.
[100] Santelli, Robert, *The Best of the Blues*, Penguin Books, 1997, p 274.
[101] Blandy, J P, "Urethral stricture", *Postgraduate Medical Journal*, Vol 56, Issue 656, 1980, pp 383–418.
[102] Larkin, Colin, *The Virgin Encyclopedia of Popular Music*, p 147.
[103] Cult, Steve, "Notes", 1978.
[104] Galleran, Tadg, "Even White Boys Get The Blues", *Turnin' Up The Heat, King Brothers*, 1997.
[105] Hansen, Barry/Barrett, aka Dr. Demento, interview, Sept 2, 2023, Long Beach, CA.
[106] Some portions of this section adapted from: Bershaw, Alan, "Liner Notes", *King David and the Parables*, Wolfgang's, retrieved 8/28/2024, https://www.wolfgangs.com/music/king-david-and-the-parables/audio/20053892-3737854.html?tid=4873323.
[107] **Aug 25, 1964, Set 1**: https://www.wolfgangs.com/music/king-david-and-the-parables/audio/20053834-3737854.html?tid=4855712; **Aug 25, 1964, Set 2**: https://www.wolfgangs.com/music/king-david-and-the-parables/audio/20053891-3737854.html?tid=54295; **Aug 28, 1964**: https://www.wolfgangs.com/music/king-david-and-the-parables/audio/20053892-3737854.html?tid=4873323.
[108] Cohen, Carson, "Conversations with David Hershel Cohen", *David Hershel Cohen*, retrieved 6/7/2025, https://www.davidhershelcohen.com/conversationsdhc.
[109] https://www.davidhershelcohen.com/gallery1.
[110] Cohen, Carson, "Conversations with David Hershel Cohen, retrieved 6/7/2025..
[111] Cohen, David, "Liner Notes", *Circadian Symphony*, Circadia Records, 1996.
[112] Cohen, Carson, *David Hershel Cohen*, retrieved June 7, 2025, https://www.davidhershelcohen.com/.
[113] "The Wrecking Crew (music)", *Wikipedia*, retrieved 6/7/2025, https://en.wikipedia.org/wiki/The_Wrecking_Crew_(music).
[114] https://www.davidhershelcohen.com/gallery1.
[115] Cohen, Carson, "Music", *David Hershel Cohen*, retrieved 6/7/2025, https://www.davidhershelcohen.com/music1.
[116] "The Great Awakening 'Amazing Grace' (1969)", *Rare Bird's Rock and Roll Nest*, September 24, 2014, retrieved 6/7/2025, https://rarebird9.blogspot.com/2014/09/the-great-awakening-amazing- grace-

1969.html.
[117] Cohen David, "Liner Notes", 1996.
[118] Harris, George W, "Larry Carlton: Six Strings of Faith", *Jazz Weekly*, July 1, 2014, retrieved 9/2/2024, https://www.jazzweekly.com/2014/07/larry-carlton-six-strings-of-faith/. [119] *Discogs*, retrieved 9/2/2024, https://www.discogs.com/master/74352- Barbra-Streisand-Stoney-End.
[120] Price, "Just Because", *The Beatles Bible*, retrieved 9/2/2024, https://www.beatlesbible.com/people/john-lennon/songs/just- because/.
[121] Cohen, Carson, "Conversations with David Hershel Cohen", *David Hershel Cohen*, retrieved 6/7/2025, https://www.davidhershelcohen.com/conversationsdhc.
[122] Cohen David, "Liner Notes", 1996.
[123] Cohen David, "Liner Notes", 1996.
[124] Wright, Carol, "David Cohen Biography", *AllMusic*, retrieved 8/31/2024, https://www.allmusic.com/artist/david-cohen- mn0000641102#relatedArtists.
[125] "Kaleidoscope", *Wikipedia*, retrieved 8//20/2024, https://en.wikipedia.org/wiki/Kaleidoscope_(American_band).
[126] Strom, Yale, "The Mesmerizing Sounds of Klezmer", *Humanities: The Magazine of the National Endowment for the Humanities*, Winter 2024 retrieved 9/10/2024., https://www.neh.gov/article/mesmerizing-sounds- klezmer
[127] Mazor, Yaacov; Seroussi, Edwin, "Towards a Hasidic Lexicon of Music", *Orbis Musicae*, Vol 10, 1990, Tel Avi Univserity, pp. 118–43, retrieved 9/10/2024, https://arts.tau.ac.il/Researches/journals/asaf- music.
[128] Beregovski, M, "Yidishe klezmer, zeyer shafn un shteyger", *Literarisher Alamanakh "Sovetish"* (in Yiddish), Volume 12, Melukhe-farlag "Der Emes", 1941, pp. 412–450, retrieved 9/10/2024, https://archive.org/details/Beregovsky1941/.
[129] Beregovski, M, Yidishe klezmer, zeyer shafn un shteyger, 1941.
[130] "You Can Hear Strains Of Klezmer in Benny Goodman", *Princeton Info*, Nov 30, 2021, retrieved 9/17/2024, https://www.communitynews.org/princetoninfo/artsandentertainment/y ou-can-hear-strains-of-klezmer-in-benny-goodman/article_787a3bd7- e364-5b9f-ad4a-f54bcd0129ad.html.
[131] "Brotman, Stuart", *Klez California*, retrieved 9/30/2024, https://klezcalifornia.org/acadp_listings/stuart-brotman/.
[132] "Dr Craig Woodson", Museum of Making Music, retrieved 8/30/2024, https://www.museumofmakingmusic.org/more/appearances/dr-craig- woodson-2.
[133] "Dr Demento", *Wikipedia*, retrieved 8/30/2024, https://en.wikipedia.org/wiki/Dr._Demento.
[134] **Unless indicated otherwise**, this section adapted from "Lightnin' Hopkins", *Wikipedia*, retrieved Apr 17, 2024, https://en.wikipedia.org/wiki/Lightnin%27_Hopkins#cite_ref-Dahl_6-0. [135] Hayworth, Alan Lee, "Hopkins,Sam [Lightnin']", *Texas Facts*, Texas State Historical Association, Nov 9, 2020, retrieved Apr 17, 2024, https://www.tshaonline.org/handbook/entries/hopkins-sam-lightnin.
[136] "Lightnin' Hopkins", *New World Encyclopedia*, retrieved Apr 17, 2024, https://www.newworldencyclopedia.org/entry/Lightnin%27_Hopkins.

137 Hayworth, Alan Lee, "Hopkins,Sam [Lightnin']", *Texas Facts*.
138 "Lightnin's Texas Blues and Boogie", *Cultural Crossroads*, Houston Institute for Culture, retrieved Apr 17, 2024, https://www.houstonculture.org/cr/lightnin.html.
139 "Lightnin' Hopkins Songs, Albums, Reviews, Bio & More", *AllMusic*.
140 Dahl, Bill, "Frankie Lee Sims: Biography", *AllMusic*, retrieved Apr 17, 2024, https://www.allmusic.com/artist/frankie-lee-sims- p125539/biography.
141 Hayworth, Alan Lee, "Hopkins,Sam [Lightnin']", *Texas Facts*.
142 "Lightnin' Hopkins Songs, Albums, Reviews, Bio & More", *AllMusic*.
143 "Lightnin' Hopkins Songs, Albums, Reviews, Bio & More", *AllMusic*.
144 Colin Larkin, ed., *The Guinness Who's Who of Blues* (Second ed.), 1995, Guinness Publishing, pp. 181/3.
145 "Lightnin's Texas Blues and Boogie", *Cultural Crossroads*.
146 Colin Larkin, ed., *The Guinness Who's Who of Blues* (Second ed.), pp. 181/3.
147 "Lightnin' Hopkins Songs, Albums, Reviews, Bio & More", *AllMusic*.
148 Hayworth, Alan Lee, "Hopkins,Sam [Lightnin']", *Texas Facts*.
149 Russell, Tony,*The Blues: From Robert Johnson to Robert Cray*, Carlton Books,1997, p. 64.
150 Adapted from: Encyclopedia of Arkansas, retrieved 9/10/2024, https://encyclopediaofarkansas.net/entries/howlin-wolf-631/.
151 Adapted from: "Hubert Sumlin", Wikipedia, retrieved 9/10/2024, https://en.wikipedia.org/wiki/Hubert_Sumlin.
152 Kitts, Jeff and Brad Tolinski, *Guitar World Presents the 100 Greatest Guitarists of All Time*, Hal Leonard, 2002, p. 37.
153 **Unless indicated otherwise**, adapted from Minton, John, *Lipscomb, Mance (1895-1976)*, Texas State Historical Association, retrieved 5/21/2024, https://www.tshaonline.org/handbook/entries/lipscomb- mance.
154 "Mance Lipscomb", *Same Passage*, retrieved 5/21/2024, https://samepassage.org/mance-lipscomb/.
155 Stoker, David, "Mance Has A Song For Every Day Of The Year", *Ft Worth Star Telegram*, Jun 28, 1969, p. 24.
156 Lipscomb, Marice, *Mance Lipscomb*, Da Capo Press, 2009, and Norman Charles, "Mance Lipscomb – Farmer and Songster".
157 Lipscomb, Mance, *I Say Me For A Parable*, 157 Lipscomb, Marice, *Mance Lipscomb*, Da Capo Press, 2009, and Norman Charles, "Mance Lipscomb – Farmer and Songster".
158 Lipscomb, Mance, *I Say Me For A Parable*, 158 Lipscomb, Marice, *Mance Lipscomb*, Da Capo Press, 2009, and Norman Charles, "Mance Lipscomb – Farmer and Songster".
159 Lipscomb, Mance, *I Say Me For A Parable*, ed Glen Alyn, WW Norton, 1993, summarized in Charles Norman, "Mance Lipscomb – Farmer and Songster", *Reverb Racoon*, retrieved 5/22/2024, https://reverbraccoon.com/2020/11/11/mance-lipscomb-farmer-and- songster/, and **verifed in the actual book by this author.**
160 Lipscomb, Mance, *I Say Me For A Parable*, 160 Lipscomb, Marice, *Mance Lipscomb*, Da Capo Press, 2009, and Norman Charles, "Mance Lipscomb – Farmer and

Songster".

[161] McDowell, Fred, opening vocal accompaniment, Side 1, I do not play no rock'n'roll, Capital Records, 1969, ST-409/403.

[162] York, Joe and Scott Barretta, *Shake 'Em On Down: The Blues According To Fred McDowell*, The Southern Documentary Project, Center for the Study of Southern Culture, Univ of MS, 2024, 1:56, https://southdocs.org/project/shakem/.

[163] York, Joe and Scott Barretta, *Shake 'Em On Down: The Blues According To Fred McDowell*, 11:05.

[164] "MS Fred McDowell Biography", *Index of Musician Biographies*, retrieved 3/27/2024, https://musicianguide.com/biographies/1608001112/Mississippi-Fred-McDowell.html.

[165] Birth of the Blues: MS Fred McDowell", from *Frets Magazine*, retrieved 3/28/2024, https://js.guitartricks.com/forum/t/30890/p/249278.

[166] Welding, Pete, "Fred McDowell, *Blues Unlimited,* 1965, quoted in Albert McCarthy, *MS Delta Blues* Liner Notes, Vinyl Me Please, Jan 12, 2018, retrieved 5/21/2024, https://www.vinylmeplease.com/blogs/magazine/fred-mcdowells-mississippi-delta-blues.

[167] McDowell, Fred, *Frets Magazine*, April, 1988.

[168] Larkin, Collin, ed. , *The Guinness Who's Who of Blues* (Second ed.). Guinness Publishing, 1992, p. 262.

[169] "Birth of the Blues: MS Fred McDowell, *Frets Magazine*."

[170] Welding, Pete, "Fred McDowell, *Blues Unlimited,* 1965.

[171] McDowell, Fred, *MS Delta Blues*, back cover, Arhoolie F1021.

[172] Welding, Pete, "Fred McDowell, *Blues Unlimited,* 1965, quoted in Albert McCarthy, *MS Delta Blues* Liner Notes, Vinyl Me Please, Jan 12, 2018, retrieved 5/21/2024, https://www.vinylmeplease.com/blogs/magazine/fred-mcdowells-mississippi-delta-blues.

[173] "Mississippi Fred McDowell Biography", *Musician Biographies*, retrieved 3/7/2024, https://musicianguide.com/biographies/1608001112/Mississippi-Fred-McDowell.html.

[174] Birth of the Blues: MS Fred McDowell", from *Frets Magazine*, js.guitartricks.com.

[175] McDowell, Fred, *MS Delta Blues*, back cover, Arhoolie F1021.

[176] "Birth of the Blues: MS Fred McDowell".

[177] "Mississippi Fred McDowell Biography", *Musician Biographies*.

[178] "Mississippi Fred McDowell Biography", *Musician Biographies*.

[179] "Mississippi Fred McDowell Biography", *Musician Biographies*.

[180] Larkin, Collin, ed. , *The Guinness Who's Who of Blues* (Second ed.). Guinness Publishing, 1992, p. 262.

[181] York, Joe and Scott Barretta, *Shake 'Em On Down: The Blues According To Fred McDowell*, 13:35.

[182] York, Joe and Scott Barretta, *Shake 'Em On Down: The Blues According To Fred McDowell*, 30:45 – 31:45.

[183] "Mississippi Fred McDowell Biography", *Musician Biographies*.

[184] Atlantic LPs 1346, 1348, 1352 and 1351, "Atlantic Records Discography: 1959",

JazzDisco.org, retrieved 5/21/2024, https://www.jazzdisco.org/atlantic-records/discography-1959/.
[185] "Mississippi Fred McDowell Biography", *Musician Biographies*.
[186] "Mississippi Fred McDowell Biography", *Musician Biographies*.
[187] York, Joe and Scott Barretta, *Shake 'Em On Down: The Blues According To Fred McDowell*, 16:17 – 17:20.
[188] Bastin, Bruce, *Red River Blues: The Blues Tradition in the Southeast*, University of Illinois Press, 1986, p 330.
[189] Harold, Ellen and Peter Stone, *Reverend Gary Davis*, ACE. The Association for Cultural Equity, April 30, 2005, retrieved 7/16/2025, https://www.culturalequity.org/alan-lomax/friends/davis.
[190] Grossman, Stefan, *An Interview With Reverend Gary Davis*, Stefan Grossman's Guitar Workshop, retrieved 7/16/2025, https://www.guitarvideos.com/interviews/rev-gary-davis.
[191] The Gale Group, "Gary Davis", Black History: Biographies, retrieved 7/16/2025, https://secure.cbn.com/special/blackhistory/bio_garydavis.aspx.
[192] Evans, Allen, "Liner Notes", *The Sun of Our Lives: Gary Davis Recorded 1955–57*, World Arbiter, 2005.
[193] Harold, Ellen and Peter Stone, *Reverend Gary Davis*, retrieved 7/16/2025.
[194] Eagle, Bob and, Eric LeBlanc, *Blues: A Regional Experience*, Praeger, 2013, pp 285-286.
[195] Zack, Ian, *Say No to the Devil: The Life and Musical Genius of Rev. Gary Davis*, University of Chicago Press., 2015, p 8.
[196] Harold, Ellen and Peter Stone, *Reverend Gary Davis*, retrieved 7/16/2025.
[197] Grossman, Stefan, *An Interview With Reverend Gary Davis*, retrieved 7/16/2025.
[198] Harold, Ellen and Peter Stone, *Reverend Gary Davis*, retrieved 7/16/2025.
[199] Grossman, Stefan, *An Interview With Reverend Gary Davis*, retrieved 7/16/2025.
[200] Zack, Ian, *Say No to the Devil: The Life and Musical Genius of Rev. Gary Davis*, p 9.
[201] Grossman, Stefan, *An Interview With Reverend Gary Davis*, retrieved 7/16/2025.
[202] Zack, Ian, *Say No to the Devil: The Life and Musical Genius of Rev. Gary Davis*, p 15.
[203] Harold, Ellen and Peter Stone, *Reverend Gary Davis*, retrieved 7/16/2025.
[204] Grossman, Stefan, *An Interview With Reverend Gary Davis*, retrieved 7/16/2025.
[205] Harold, Ellen and Peter Stone, *Reverend Gary Davis*, retrieved 7/16/2025.
[206] The Gale Group, "Gary Davisretrieved 7/16/2025.

[207] McNeil, WK, *Encyclopedia of American Gospel Music*, Routledge, 2013, p 97.
[208] *Rev Gary Davis*, Arbiterrecords.org, January 31, 201, retrieved 7/16/2025, http://arbiterrecords.org/music-resource- center/rev-gary-davis/.
[209] Harold, Ellen and Peter Stone, *Reverend Gary Davis*, retrieved 7/16/2025.
[210] The Gale Group, "Gary Davis", retrieved 7/16/2025.
[211] Harold, Ellen and Peter Stone, *Reverend Gary Davis*, retrieved 7/16/2025.
[212] The Gale Group, "Gary Davis", retrieved 7/16/2025.
[213] The Gale Group, "Gary Davis", retrieved 7/16/2025.
[214] Grossman, Stefan, *An Interview With Reverend Gary Davis*, retrieved 7/16/2025.
[215] Zack, Ian, *Say No to the Devil: The Life and Musical Genius of Rev. Gary Davis*, 2015, p 35.
[216] The Gale Group, "Gary Davis", retrieved 7/16/2025.
[217] Zack, Ian, *Say No to the Devil: The Life and Musical Genius of Rev. Gary Davis*, 2015, p 30.
[218] The Gale Group, "Gary Davis", retrieved 7/16/2025.
[219] The Gale Group, "Gary Davis", retrieved 7/16/2025.
[220] Zack, Ian, *Say No to the Devil: The Life and Musical Genius of Rev. Gary Davis*, 2015, p 37-38.
[221] The Gale Group, "Gary Davis", retrieved 7/16/2025.
[222] Russell, Tony, *The Blues: From Robert Johnson to Robert Cray*, Carlton Books,. 1997, p 105.
[223] Grossman, Stefan, *An Interview With Reverend Gary Davis*, retrieved 7/16/2025.
[224] The Gale Group, "Gary Davis", retrieved 7/16/2025.
[225] Bastin, Bruce, *Red River Blues: The Blues Tradition in the Southeast*, p 242.
[226] Zack, Ian, *Say No to the Devil: The Life and Musical Genius of Rev. Gary Davis*, 2015, p 41.
[227] Bastin, Bruce, *Red River Blues: The Blues Tradition in the Southeast*, p 242.
[228] Zack, Ian, *Say No to the Devil: The Life and Musical Genius of Rev. Gary Davis*, 2015, p 61.
[229] Zack, Ian, *Say No to the Devil: The Life and Musical Genius of Rev. Gary Davis*, 2015, p 62.
[230] Zack, Ian, *Say No to the Devil: The Life and Musical Genius of Rev. Gary Davis*, 2015, p 64.
[231] Zack, Ian, *Say No to the Devil: The Life and Musical Genius of Rev. Gary Davis*, 2015, p 65.
[232] Zack, Ian, *Say No to the Devil: The Life and Musical Genius of Rev. Gary Davis*, 2015, p 87.

[233] Zack, Ian, *Say No to the Devil: The Life and Musical Genius of Rev. Gary Davis*, 2015, p 66.
[234] Zack, Ian, *Say No to the Devil: The Life and Musical Genius of Rev. Gary Davis*, 2015, p 76.
[235] Grossman, Stefan, *An Interview With Reverend Gary Davis*, retrieved 7/16/2025.
[236] Zack, Ian, *Say No to the Devil: The Life and Musical Genius of Rev. Gary Davis*, 2015, pp 76-77.
[237] Zack, Ian, *Say No to the Devil: The Life and Musical Genius of Rev. Gary Davis*, 2015, p 77.
[238] Zack, Ian, *Say No to the Devil: The Life and Musical Genius of Rev. Gary Davis*, 2015, pp 81.
[239] Zack, Ian, *Say No to the Devil: The Life and Musical Genius of Rev. Gary Davis*, 2015, pp 78-79.
[240] Zack, Ian, *Say No to the Devil: The Life and Musical Genius of Rev. Gary Davis*, 2015, p. 83.
[241] Larkin, Colin, ed., *The Guinness Who's Who of Blues (2nd ed.)*, Guinness Publishing, 1995, p 102.
[242] Harold, Ellen and Peter Stone, *Reverend Gary Davis*, retrieved 7/16/2025.
[243] Zack, Ian, *Say No to the Devil: The Life and Musical Genius of Rev. Gary Davis*, p 163.
[244] Bromberg, David, "I Belong To The Band," and "Tryin To Get Home" plus an interview about Gary Davis, youtube.com, July 17, 2020, retrieved 7/16/2025.
[245] Bromberg, David, "I Belong To The Band," and "Tryin To Get Home" plus an interview about Gary Davis, youtube.com, July 17, 2020, retrieved 7/16/2025.
[246] Harold, Ellen and Peter Stone, *Reverend Gary Davis*, retrieved 7/16/2025.
[247] Zack, Ian, *Say No to the Devil: The Life and Musical Genius of Rev. Gary Davis*, p 235.
[248] Zack, Ian, *Say No to the Devil: The Life and Musical Genius of Rev. Gary Davis*, p 259.
[249] Zack, Ian, *Say No to the Devil: The Life and Musical Genius of Rev. Gary Davis*, p 235.
[250] **Unless indicated otherwise,** this biography adapted from "Bukka White", *Blues Trail Marker, Houston, MS*, MS Blues Trail, retrieved 7/18/2025, https://msbluestrail.org/blues-trail-markers/bukka-white.
[251] Photograph by Kelly Hart; © Northwestern University. Courtesy of Berkeley Folk Music Festival Archive, Charles Deering McCormick Library of Special Collections, Northwestern University Libraries.

[252] The Yellow Shark, "Cabale Creamery, 2504 San Pablo Avenue, Berkeley", *Berkeley in the Sixties*, Aug 1, 2009, retrieved 10/15/2024, https://berkeleyfolk.blogspot.com/2009/08/cabale-creamery-2504-san- pablo-avenue.html.
[253] Govenar, Alan,, *Lightnin' Hopkins – His Life and Blues*, Chicago Review Press, Inc. 2010.
[254] General organization based on "Willie Mae 'Big Mama' Thornton", *Encyclopedia of Alabama*, Auburn University, undated, retrieved 4/23/2025, https://encyclopediaofalabama.org/article/willie-mae-big-mama- thornton.
[255] "Willie Mae 'Big Mama' Thornton", *Encyclopedia of Alabama*, undated.
[256] Personal experience of Bernie Pearl when he performed with Big Mama Thornton.
[257] Dasgupta, Pubali, "Six definitive songs: The ultimate beginner's guide to Big Mama Thornton", *Faroutmagazine.co.uk*, December 11, 2020, retrieved 4/24/2025, https://faroutmagazine.co.uk/big-mama-thornton- 6-best-songs/.
[258] Dasgupta, Pubali, "Six definitive songs: The ultimate beginner's guide to Big Mama Thornton", December 11, 2020.
[259] Terkel, Studs, "Willie Dixon, Sunnyland Slim and Big Mama Thornton discuss their careers in the blues and describe some of their songs", *StudsTerkel.wfmt.com*, 1970, retrieved 4/25/2025, https://studsterkel.wfmt.com/programs/willie-dixon-sunnyland-slim- and-big-mama-thornton-discuss-their-careers-blues-and-describe.
[260] Zabo, Marta, "The Untold Truth of Big Mama Thornton", *Grunge.com*, October 3, 2022, retrieved 4/24/2025, https://www.grunge.com/1036721/the-untold-truth-of-big-mama- thornton/.
[261] Spörke, Michael , *Big Mama Thornton: The Life and Music*, McFarland, 2014, p 7.
[262] Terkel, Studs, "Willie Dixon, Sunnyland Slim and Big Mama Thornton discuss their careers in the blues and describe some of their songs", 1970. [263] Strachwitz, Chris, "Big Mama Thornton Interview", undated, retrieved 4/23/2025, https://arhoolie.org/big-mama-thornton-interview/.
[264] Strachwitz, Chris, "Big Mama Thornton Interview", undated.
[265] "Big Mama Thornton - Part 1: 1920s to the 1950s", *The Struggles and Triumphs of Bessie Jones, Big Mama Thornton, and Ethel Waters*, library.yale.edu, retrieved 4/24/2025, https://onlineexhibits.library.yale.edu/s/ohamstruggles/page/bmt1.
[266] Oakley, Giles, *The Devil's Music*, Da Capo Press, 1997, p 214.

267 Strachwitz, Chris, "Big Mama Thornton Interview", undated.
268 Strachwitz, Chris, "Big Mama Thornton Interview", undated.
269 Spörke, Michael , *Big Mama Thornton: The Life and Music*, p 70.
270 Strachwitz, Chris, "Big Mama Thornton Interview", undated.
271 Strachwitz, Chris, "Big Mama Thornton Interview", undated.
272 Strachwitz, Chris, "Big Mama Thornton Interview", undated.
273 Bronson, Fred, *The Billboard Book of Number 1 Hits*, Billboard Books, 1985.
274 Santelli, Robert, *The Big Book of Blues*, Chrysalis Books, 1994, p 464.
275 Hill, Charles, "Who Owns "Hound Dog"?", *Charlesd A. Hill Mediation*, April 12, 2016, retrieved 4/24/2025, https://nashville- mediator.com/who-owns-hound-dog/.
276 Herzhaft, Gerard, *Encyclopedia of the Blues, 2nd Edition*, University of Arkansas Press, July 1, 1997.
277 "City Auditorium - Houston, TX", ScottyMoore.net, July 26, 2012, retrieved 4/24/2025, http://www.scottymoore.net/houstonAud.html.
278 Strachwitz, Chris, "Big Mama Thornton Interview", undated.
279 "Liner Notes", *Big Mama Thornton: Ball 'N' Chain*, Arhoolie Records, CD 305, 1965-1969.
280 Spörke, Michael , *Big Mama Thornton: The Life and Music*, p 154.
281 Big Mama Thornton - Part 1: 1920s to the 1950s",
The Struggles and Triumphs of Bessie Jones, Big Mama Thornton, and Ethel Waters, library.yale.edu.
282 Shearer, Cynthia, "The Thinning of Big Mama", *Oxford American*, February 15, 2017, retrieved 4/25/2025, https://oxfordamerican.org/magazine/issue-95-winter-2016/the- thinning-of-big-mama.
283 Gaar, Gillian G, "The Summer of Love ... and music at Monterey!", *goldminemag.com*, August 17, 2017, retrieved 4/24/2025, https://www.goldminemag.com/articles/the-summer-of-love.
284 Mahon, Maureen, "Listening for Willie Mae 'Big Mama' Thornton's Voice: The Sound of Race and Gender Transgressions in Rock and
Roll", *Women and Music: A Journal of Gender and Culture*. Vol 15, 2011, pp 1– 17, http://muse.jhu.edu/journals/women_and_music/v015/15.mahon.htm. 285 Denise, Lynnée, *Why Willie Mae Thornton Matter*, University of Texas Press, 2023,. p 370.
286 Spörke, Michael , *Big Mama Thornton: The Life and Music*, p 70.
287 E-mail correspondence, Bernie Pearl, received 4/28/2025.
288 *Wolfgang's*, retrieved 4/28/2025, https://www.wolfgangs.com/music/?t=Big%20Mama%20Thornton.
289 Spörke, Michael , *Big Mama Thornton: The Life and Music*, p 156.
290 Spörke, Michael , *Big Mama Thornton: The Life and Music*, p 123.

[291] Johnson, Maria, "You Just Can't Keep a Good Woman Down: Alice Walker Sings the Blues", *African American Review*. Vol 30, Issue 2, 2010, pp. 221–236.
[292] Spörke, Michael , *Big Mama Thornton: The Life and Music*, p 70.
[293] Personal experience, Bruce Krell, 1983-1984,
[294] "Big Mama Thornton: Biography | Billboard", *www.billboard.com*, archived from the original on June 3, 2016., retreived 4/24/2025, https://web.archive.org/web/20160603025816/http:/www.billboard.com/artist/281663/big-mama-thornton/biography.
[295] Gaar, Gillian, *She's a Rebel: The History of Women in Rock & Roll*, Seal Press, 1992, p 4.
[296] Spörke, Michael , *Big Mama Thornton: The Life and Music*, p 147.
[297] Talevski, Nick, *Rock Obituaries: Knocking on Heaven's Doo*, Omnibus Press, 2010, p 403.
[298] Spörke, Michael , *Big Mama Thornton: The Life and Music*, p 147.
[299] Shearer, Cynthia, "The Thinning of Big Mama", February 15, 2017.
[300] Neff, Robert; and Anthony Connor, *Blues*. D. R. Godine, 1975.
[301] U.S. Farm Security Administration/Office of War Information Collection, Prints and Photographs Division, Library of Congress, retrieved 9/24/2024 https://loc.gov/pictures/resource/cph.3b22541/.
[302] US Supreme Court, *Morgan v. Virginia*, 328 U.S. 373 (1946).
[303] US Supreme Court, *Boynton v. Virginia*, 364 U.S. 454 (1960).
[304] Barbieri, Serena, "Lynching of John Campbell", Lynching in Texas, retrieved 9/24/2024, https://www.lynchingintexas.org/items/show/3. [305] Allen, Brandon, "Third Ward, Houston, Texas", *Black Past*, Sept 14, 2019, retrieved 9/25/2024, https://www.blackpast.org/african-american- history/third-ward-houston-texas-1837/.
[306] Kooper, Ivan Koop, "Lightnin' Hopkins: Texas Blues Man", *The Rag Blog*, Nov 11, 2020, retrieved 9/25/2024, https://www.theragblog.com/ivan-koop-kuper-music-lightnin-hopkins- texas-blues-man/.
[307] Kooper, Ivan Koop, "Lightnin' Hopkins: Texas Blues Man", *The Rag Blog*, Nov 11, 2020.
[308] Photograph by Barry Olivier; © Northwestern University. Courtesy of Berkeley Folk Music Festival Archive, Charles Deering McCormick Library of Special Collections, Northwestern University Libraries.
[309] Bonner, Brett, "Smokey Wilson", Living Blues #130, Nov/Dec, 1996, pp. 14-15.
[310] Talamantez, "Andy T", and Smokey Wilson, "Liner Notes", *Round Like An Apple: The Big Town Recordings 1977-1978*, Ace Records, 2006, p. 3.
[311] Talamantez, "Andy T", and Smokey Wilson, "Liner Notes", *p. 4.*
[312] Talamantez, "Andy T", and Smokey Wilson, "Liner Notes", *p. 5.*
[313] Talamantez, "Andy T", and Smokey Wilson, "Liner Notes", *p. 7.*
[314] *Celebration of Life*, Robert Lee "Smokey" Wilson, Oct 1, 2014, 12 pm.
[315] "In Memoriam: Smokey Wilson", *Blind Dog Radio*, retrieved 9/27/2024, https://blinddogradio.blogspot.com/2015/09/in-memoriam- smokey-wilson-july-

11-1936.html.
[316] Talamantez, "Andy T", and Smokey Wilson, "Liner Notes", *pp. 6-7.*
[317] Talamantez, "Andy T", and Smokey Wilson, "Liner Notes", *p. 6.*
[318] "Smokey Wilson", *Artists*, Blind Pig Records, retrieved 10/22/2024, https://www.blindpigrecords.com/artists.
[319] Talamantez, "Andy T", and Smokey Wilson, "Liner Notes", *p. 6.*
[320] "Smokey Wilson", *Artists*, Blind Pig Records, retrieved 10/22/2024, https://www.blindpigrecords.com/artists.
[321] "In Memoriam: Smokey Wilson", *Blind Dog Radio*, retrieved 9/27/2024.
[322] Talamantez, "Andy T", and Smokey Wilson, "Liner Notes", *p. 6.*
[323] Bonner, Bret, "Editorial", *Living Blues*, #240, Dec 2, 2015, retrieved 10/22/2024, http://digital.livingblues.com/publication/?i=282718&article_id=2338542&view=articleBrowser.
[324] Talamantez, "Andy T", and Smokey Wilson, "Liner Notes", *p. 7.*
[325] Talamantez, "Andy T", and Smokey Wilson, "Liner Notes", *p. 7.*
[326] "In Memoriam: Smokey Wilson", *Blind Dog Radio*, retreived 9/27/2024.
[327] Talamantez, "Andy T", and Smokey Wilson, "Liner Notes", *p. 8.*
[328] Talamantez, "Andy T", and Smokey Wilson, "Liner Notes", *p. 11.*
[329] Talamantez, "Andy T", and Smokey Wilson, "Liner Notes", *p. 11.*
[330] Krell, Bruce, *Sam King, Interview*, Aug 11, 2023, at the home of Sam King.
[331] "Episodes", *Boboquivari*, Internet Movie Database (IMDb), retrieved 5/23/2025, https://www.imdb.com/title/tt1446518/?ref_=ttep_ov_bk. [332] "Discovering the Impact of Freddie King", BluesChronicles.com, retrieved 5/19/2025, https://blueschronicles.com/discovering-the-life- and-impact-of-freddie-king-one-of-the-three-kings-of-blues/.
[333] O'Neal, Jim and Van Singel, Amy, *The Voice of the Blues: Classic Interviews from Living Blues Magazine*, Routledge, p. 359.
[334] "Freddy King – Country Boy", *Discogs*, retrieved 5/20/2025, https://www.discogs.com/master/992255-Freddy-King-Country-Boy- Thats-What-You-Think.
[335] Dixon, Willie and Don Snowden, *I Am the Blues: The Willie Dixon Story*, Da Capo, 1989, p 111.
[336] International Repertory of Music Literature, "Freddie Kng, the Texas Blues Guitar Icon", bibliolore, Apr 9, 2025, retrieved 5/20/2025, https://bibliolore.org/2025/04/09/freddie-king-the-texas-blues-guitar- icon/.
[337] Pruter, Robert, *Chicago Soul*, University of Illinois Press, p. 236.
[338] "Freddy King Sings", *Discogs*, retrieved 5/2025, https://www.discogs.com/master/563675-Freddy-King-Freddy-King- Sings.
[339] Schwie, Hank, "Freddie King", *last.fm*, retrieved 5/20/2025, https://www.last.tm/music/Freddie+King/+wiki.
[340] Schwie, Hank, "Freddie King", *last.fm*, retrieved 5/20/2025.
[341] Van Beveren, Amy and Laurie Jasinski, "Freddie King: The Legendary Blues Guitarist", retrieved 5/20/2025.
[342] Hardy, Laing, Barnard and Perretta,. *Texas Music*, Schirmer Books, p. 251.
[343] Hayner, Richard, "The Texas Pop Festival", texaspopfestival.com, retrieved

5/20/2025.
[344] Head, James, "Texas International Pop Festival", *Handbook of Texas Online*, Oct 26, 2015, Texas State Historical Association, retreived 5/20/2025, https://www.tshaonline.org/handbook/entries/texas- international-pop-festival-1969.
[345] "Freddie King – Getting' Ready", *Discogs*, retrieved 5/25/2025, https://www.discogs.com/master/319097-Freddie-King-Getting-Ready. [346] "Freddie King", *Discogs*, retrieved 5/25/2025, https://www.discogs.com/artist/323162-Freddie-King?superFilter=Releases&subFilter=Albums.
[347] "Freddie King Concert History", *Concert Archives*, retrieved 5/20/2025, https://www.concertarchives.org/bands/freddie-king.
[348] Nakamoto, Satoshi, "King of Blues: the Life and Legacy of Freddie King", *Blues Guitar Lab*, June 21, 2023, retrieved 5/20/2025, https://medium.com/@satoshinakamotosglab/king-of-blues-the-life- and-legacy-of-freddie-king-4c651d9f82a0.
[349] "Freddie King – Burglar", *Discogs*, retrieved 5/20/2025, https://www.discogs.com/master/292697-Freddie-King-Burglar. [350] "Freddie King – Larger Than Life", *Discogs*, retrieved 5/20/2025, https://www.discogs.com/master/237851-Freddie-King-Larger-Than- Life.
[351] Ward, Ed, "Freddie King and the Harsh 'Business' of the Blues", *Music Reviews*, National Public Radio, July 14, 2010, retrieved 5/2025, https://www.npr.org/2012/04/12/150496715/freddie-king-rock-hall- inductee-patriarch-of-blues-rock.
[352] Westervelt, Eric, "Freddie King: Patriarch of Blues Rock", *Music News*, National Public Radio, April 12, 2012, retreived 5/20/2025, https://www.npr.org/2012/04/12/150496715/freddie-king-rock-hall- inductee-patriarch-of-blues-rock
[353] Ward, Ed, "Freddie King and the Harsh 'Business' of the Blues", retrieved 5/2025.
[354] Ayo, Vicki Welch and William DeLaVergne, *Boys from Houston II: Deep in the Heart*, CreateSpace Independent Publishing Platform, 2015.
[355] Ayo, Vicki Welch and William DeLaVergne, *Boys from Houston II: Deep in the Heart*, 2015.
[356] "Liberty Hall", *Liberty Hall Web Site*, retrieved 5/20/2025, http://houstonrocksme.com/liberty%20hall.html.
[357] Ayo, Vicki Welch and William DeLaVergne, *Boys from Houston II: Deep in the Heart*, 2015.
[358] Smith, William Michael, "Live at Liberty Hall", *Houston Post*, Apr 29, 2009, retrieved 5/20/2025, http://www.houstonpress.com/music/live- at-liberty-hall-6586510.
[359] Wood, Roger, *Down in Houston: Bayou City Blues*, University of Texas Press, 2012, p 48.
[360] August, Mike, "The Cosmic Cowboys Come to Texas", *The Wimberly View*, May 14, 2025, retrieved 5/21/2025, https://www.wimberleyview.com/article/3444,the-cosmic-cowboys- come-to-texas.

361 *6th Annual Long Beach Blues Festival Program*, p. 15.
362 *Blues Letter*, The Southern California Blues Society, Jan-Feb, 1991.
363 *Southland Blues*, Feb, 1991.
364 *Southland Blues*, Jan, 1995.
365 *Sun Today*, retrieved 10/17/2024, https://www.suntoday.org/sunrise-sunset/1980/july/20.html.
366 Silsbee, Kirk, "This time, it's Barbara Morrison's turn for a favor", *Los Angeles Times*, September 10, 2011, retrieved 5/27/2025, https://www.latimes.com/entertainment/music/la- et-barbara-morrison-20110910-story.html.
367 Morrison, Richard, *Barbara Morrison's Family and Early Life*, received 6/3/2025, p. 1.
368 Morrison, Richard, *Barbara Morrison's Family and Early Life*, received 6/3/2025, p. 1.
369 Morrison, Richard, *Barbara Morrison's Family and Early Life*, received 6/3/2025, p. 1.
370 Interview with Barbara Morrison, Wrightson, Erica Zora, "Conversation with Barbara Morrison", *Unframed*, Los Angeles County Museum of Modern Art, June 23, 2016, retrieved 5/28/2025, https://unframed.lacma.org/2016/06/23/conversation-barbara- morrison.
371 Interview with Barbara Morrison, Fancher, Lou, "Jazz Legend Barbara Morrison Is Just Getting Started", *San Francisco Classical Voice*, Dec 14, 2020, retrieved 5/27/2024, https://www.sfcv.org/articles/artist- spotlight/jazz-legend-barbara-morrison-just-getting-started.
372 Montaque, Joe, "Barbara Morrison is Howlin' The Blues", *Riveting Riffs Magazine*, March, 2008, retrieved 5/27/2025, http://www.rivetingriffs.com/Barbara%20Morrison%20Interview%20with%20Riveting%20Riffs%20Magazine.html.
373 Wrightson, Erica Zora, "Conversation with Barbara Morrison", June 23, 2016.
374 Morrison, Richard, phone conversation, 6/9/2025 and email communicataion, 6/11/2025.
375 Interview with Barbara Morrison, Fancher, Lou, "Jazz Legend Barbara Morrison Is Just Getting Started", Dec 14, 2020.
376 Montaque, Joe, "Barbara Morrison is Howlin' The Blues", March, 2008, retrieved 5/27/2025.
377 Morrison, Richard, *Barbara Morrison's Family and Early Life*, received 6/3/2025, p. 1.
378 Wrightson, Erica Zora, "Conversation with Barbara Morrison", June 23, 2016.
379 Wrightson, Erica Zora, "Conversation with Barbara Morrison", June 23, 2016.
380 Wrightson, Erica Zora, "Conversation with Barbara Morrison", June 23, 2016.
381 Wrightson, Erica Zora, "Conversation with Barbara Morrison", June 23, 2016.
382 Interview with Barbara Morrison, Fancher, Lou, "Jazz Legend Barbara Morrison Is Just Getting Started", Dec 14, 2020.
383 Morrison, Richard, *Barbara Morrison's Family and Early Life*, received 6/3/2025, p. 1.
384 Wrightson, Erica Zora, "Conversation with Barbara Morrison", June 23, 2016.

385 Wrightson, Erica Zora, "Conversation with Barbara Morrison", June 23, 2016.
386 Interview with Barbara Morrison, Fancher, Lou, "Jazz Legend Barbara Morrison Is Just Getting Started", Dec 14, 2020.
387 Interview with Barbara Morrison, Fancher, Lou, "Jazz Legend Barbara Morrison Is Just Getting Started", Dec 14, 2020.
388 Interview with Barbara Morrison, Fancher, Lou, "Jazz Legend Barbara Morrison Is Just Getting Started", Dec 14, 2020.
389 Meija, Brittany, "Barbara Morrison, "jazz and blues legend who left a lasting imprint on L.A., dies", *Los Angeles Times*, March 16, 2022, retrieved 5/27/2025, https://www.latimes.com/california/story/2022- 03-16/barbara-morrison-la-jazz-blues-legend-dies.
390 Interview with Barbara Morrison, Fancher, Lou, "Jazz Legend Barbara Morrison Is Just Getting Started", Dec 14, 2020.
391 Personal conversation, Tony Hithe, member of The Mean Machine.
392 Lipsitz, George, *Midnight at the Barrelhouse*, Univ of MI Press, 2010, p. 108.
393 Wrightson, Erica Zora, "Conversation with Barbara Morrison", June 23, 2016.
394 Eagle, Bob and Eric LeBlanc, *Blues: A Regional Experience*, Praeger, 2013, p 84.
395 Pareles, John, "For Johnny Otis's Band, A 30-Year Repertory", *The New York Times*, July 4, 1985, p. 25.
396 Meija, Brittany, "Barbara Morrison, "jazz and blues legend who left a lasting imprint on L.A., dies", March 16, 2022.
397 Hutt, Heather, "CD 10 Mourns the Loss of Leimert Park Legend Barbara Morrison", *Los Angeles City Council*, Mar 17, 2022, retrieved 5/27/2025, https://cd10.lacity.gov/articles/cd10-mourns-loss-leimert- park-legend-barbara-morrison.
398 Ross, David, "Barbara Morrison: A Remembrance", *Jazz Salon*, 2025, retrieved 6/4/2025, https://jazzsalon.org/barbara-morrison-a- remembrance/.
399 Wrightson, Erica Zora, "Conversation with Barbara Morrison", June 23, 2016.
400 Wrightson, Erica Zora, "Conversation with Barbara Morrison", June 23, 2016.
401 Meija, Brittany, "Barbara Morrison, "jazz and blues legend who left a lasting imprint on L.A., dies", March 16, 2022.
402 Wrightson, Erica Zora, "Conversation with Barbara Morrison", June 23, 2016.
403 Montaque, Joe, "Barbara Morrison is Howlin' The Blues", retrieved 5/27/2025.
404 Billboard.com, "Barbara Morrison, Celebrated Jazz Singer, Dies At 72", *The Neighborhood News Online*, Mar 24, 2022, retrieved 5/27/2025, https://theneighborhoodnewsonline.net/history/memory/1470- billboard-com.
405 Interview with Barbara Morrison, Fancher, Lou, "Jazz Legend Barbara Morrison Is Just Getting Started", Dec 14, 2020.
406 O'Connell, Sean, "Jazz Chanteuse Barbara Morrison Had A Leg Amputated, Needs Your Help", *LA Weekly*, July 29, 2011, retrieved 6/4/2025, https://www.laweekly.com/jazz-chanteuse-barbara-morrison- had-a-leg-amputated-needs-your-help/.
407 Ross, David, "Barbara Morrison: A Remembrance", retrieved 6/4/2025.
408 Interview with Barbara Morrison, Fancher, Lou, "Jazz Legend Barbara Morrison Is Just Getting Started", Dec 14, 2020.
409 Meija, Brittany, "Barbara Morrison, "jazz and blues legend who left a lasting

410 "Office of Councilwoman Heather Hutt Celebrates The Life and Legacy of Icon, Barbara Morrison", *Heather Hutt*, City of Los Angeles, Oct 20, 2022, retrieved 6/4/2025, https://cd10.lacity.gov/articles/office- councilwoman-heather-hutt-celebrates-life-and-legacy-icon-barbara- morrison.
411 Montaque, Joe, "Barbara Morrison is Howlin' The Blues", retrieved 5/27/2025.
412 Montaque, Joe, "Barbara Morrison is Howlin' The Blues", retrieved 5/27/2025.
413 Meija, Brittany, "Barbara Morrison, "jazz and blues legend who left a lasting imprint on L.A., dies", March 16, 2022.
414 Montaque, Joe, "Barbara Morrison is Howlin' The Blues", retrieved 5/27/2025.
415 Interview with Barbara Morrison, Fancher, Lou, "Jazz Legend Barbara Morrison Is Just Getting Started", Dec 14, 2020.
416 Interview with Barbara Morrison, Fancher, Lou, "Jazz Legend Barbara Morrison Is Just Getting Started", Dec 14, 2020.
417 Morrison, Richard, *Barbara Morrison's Family and Early Life*, received 6/3/2025, p. 2.
418 Morrison, Richard, *Barbara Morrison's Family and Early Life*, received 6/3/2025, p. 2.
419 Morrison, Richard, Phone Conversation with Bruce Krell, 5/28/2025.
420 Morrison, Richard, Phone Conversation with Bruce Krell, 5/28/2025.
421 Morrison, Richard, *Barbara Morrison's Family and Early Life*, received 6/3/2025, p. 1.
422 Morrison, Richard, *Barbara Morrison's Family and Early Life*, received 6/3/2025, p. 1.
423 Unless indicated otherwise, the story of Tim Morganfield and Barbara Morrison provided in an interview with Morganfield on 5/27/2025.
424 Morrison, Richard, phone conversation, 6/9/2025.
425 Shelby, Kimberly, "Barbara Morrison: Still a Performer at the Center of Hearts", *Los Angeles Centinel*, Mar 2, 2023, retrieved 6/4/2025, https://lasentinel.net/barbara-morrison-the-performer-at-the-center-of- hearts.html.
426 Shelby, Kimberly, "Barbara Morrison: Still a Performer at the Center of Hearts", *Los Angeles Centinel*, Mar 2, 2023, retrieved 6/4/2025, https://lasentinel.net/barbara-morrison-the-performer-at-the-center-of- hearts.html.
427 Morrison, Richard, phone conversation, 6/9/2025.
428 "Donna Brown Guillaume: Producer", *Conscience of the Congress: A Documentary*, Progressional Black Caucus Foundation, retrieved 12/3/2024, https://www.cbc50years.org/index.php/donna-brown- guillaume-producer
429 Spörke, Michael, *Big Mama Thornton : The Life and Music*. McFarland, 2014. 188 pages.
430 Details in this section provided in Krell, Bruce, "Interview with James Tamburro", March 16, 2023. Jim Tamburro was one of the primary participants in the formation and growth of the Southern CA Blues Society.
431 Adapted from: Parker, Donna, "Sippie Wallace: The Texas Nightingale of the Blues", Texas State Historical Association, July 25, 2017, retrieved 5/13/2025, https://www.tshaonline.org/handbook/entries/wallace- beulah-thomas-sippie.
432 Kelton, Jim (Univ Of Ark, Fayetteville), "Albert King (1923-1992)", *Encyclopedia*

of Arkansas, Central Arkansas Library System, Jul 11, 2023, retrieved 10/25/2024, https://encyclopediaofarkansas.net/entries/albert- king-617/.
[433] "Albert King, Indianola", *Mississippi Blues Trail.org*, retrieved 10/23/2024; and, "Albert King", *Memphis Music Hall of Fame, memphismusichalloffame.com*. February 20, 2015., retrieved October 19, 2019. [434] "Albert King, Indianola", *Mississippi Blues Trail.org*, retrieved 10/23/2024.
[435] "Albert King", *Memphis Music Hall of Fame, memphismusichalloffame.com*. February 20, 2015., retrieved October 19, 2019.
[436] "Albert King, Indianola", *Mississippi Blues Trail.org*, retrieved 10/23/2024.
[437] "Albert King", *Brooklyn Legends*, retrieved 10/23/2024, http://www.histarch.illinois.edu/Brooklyn/HSOBI/AlbertKing.htm. [438] Erlewhine, Stephen, "Albert King", *Biography*, All Music, retrieved 10/23/2024, https://www.allmusic.com/artist/albert-king- mn0000617844#biography.
[439] West, Kirk, "An Interview with Albert King", *Guitar World, July* 1991, retrieved 11/5/2024, https://alanpaul.net/2014/05/an-interview-with- albert-king/.
[440] Erlewhine, Stephen, "Albert King", *Biography*, All Music..
[441] Russell, Tony, "Albert King*", The Blues from Robert Johnson to Robert Cray*, Carlton Books, 1997, pp 72-73.
[442] Erlewhine, Stephen, "Albert King", *Biography*, All Music..
[443] "Albert King", *Brooklyn Legends*.
[444] Watrous, Peter, "Albert King, a Master of the Blues, Is Dead at 69". *The New York Times.*, December 23, 1992, retrieved 10/23/2024.
[445] The Best St. Louis Blues Musicians of All Time", *www.stlmag.com*. June 1, 2012, retrieved 10/23/2024.
[446] Obrecht, Jas, *Rollin' and Tumblin': The Postwar Blues Guitarists*, Hal Leonard, 2000, pp 349.
[447] Russell, Tony, "Albert King*", The Blues from Robert Johnson to Robert Cray*, Carlton Books.
[448] Russell, Tony, "Albert King*", The Blues from Robert Johnson to Robert Cray*, Carlton Books.
[449] "Albert King", *Stax Records*, April 2019, retrieved 10/23/2024, https://staxrecords.com/artist/albert-king/.
[450] "Albert King Postcard", Wolfgang's, retrieved 11/26/2024, https://www.wolfgangs.com/posters/albert-king/postcard/BG126.html [451] "Albert King", *Stax Records*, April 2019, retrieved 10/23/2024, https://staxrecords.com/artist/albert-king/.
[452] Erlewhine, Stephen, "Albert King", *Biography*, All Music.
[453] Quotes extracted from: West, Kirk, "An Interview with Albert King", *Guitar World, July* 1991, retrieved 11/5/2024, https://alanpaul.net/2014/05/an-interview-with-albert-king/.
[454] Krell, Bruce, *Sam King, Interview*, Aug 11, 2023, at the home of Sam King.
[455] Krell, Bruce, *Sam King, Interview*, Aug 11, 2023, at the home of Sam King.
[456] Adapted from "Phil Graham", Wikipedia, retrieved 11/12/2024, https://en.wikipedia.org/wiki/Bill_Graham_(promoter).
[457] "Bill Graham profile", Jewishvirtuallibrary, Jewishvirtuallibrary.org; accessed

11/12/2024. https://www.jewishvirtuallibrary.org/jsource/judaica/ejud_0002_0008_0_07786.html.

[458] Skolnik, Fred, "GOS – HEP", *Encyclopaedia Judaica*, Volume 8, Thomson Gale. , 2007, p. 30, https://books.google.com/books?id=fEEOAQAAMAAJ

[459] Harrington, Richard, "On the Beat; Bill Graham, Lead Act at Last", *Washington Post*, Oct 7, 1992, retrieved 11/12/2024.

[460] Lambert, Bruce, "Bill Graham, Rock Impresario, Dies at 60 in Crash", *The New York Times*, October 27, 1991, p. 34.

[461] Harrington, Richard, "On the Beat; Bill Graham, Lead Act at Last", *Washington Post*, Oct 7, 1992.

[462] Graham, Bill; Greenfield, Robert. *Bill Graham Presents: My Life Inside Rock and Out*, Delta, 1992, pp. 37, 128–129, 153–154, 156, 544.

[463] Harrington, Richard, "On the Beat; Bill Graham, Lead Act at Last", *Washington Post*, Oct 7, 1992.

[464] "A more personal Bill Graham on display at CJM", *J. Jewish Community Federations*. March 11, 2016, https://www.jweekly.com/2016/03/11/a-more-personal-bill-graham-on-display-at-cjm/.

[465] Lambert, Bruce, "Bill Graham, Rock Impresario, Dies at 60 in Crash", *The New York Times*, October 27, 1991, p. 34.

[466] Kipen, David, "Flawed look at career of blacklisted director", *San Francisco Chronicle*, August 29, 2001.

[467] "Chronology of San Francisco Rock 1965-1969", San Francisco Museum, Sfmuseum.org, http://www.sfmuseum.org/hist1/rock.htmlg/hist1/rock.html.

[468] Hertzberg, Hendricks, "Unpublished file for *Newsweek*, October 28, 1966" at the end of "The San Francisco Sound, New music, new subculture", *Politics: Observations and Arguments, 1966-2004*, Penguin Press, 2004.

[469] Adapted from "Willie Dixon", Wikipedia, retrieved 10/23/2024, https://en.wikipedia.org/wiki/Willie_Dixon#.

[470] Dixon, Willie and Don Snowden, *I Am the Blues*. Da Capo Press, 1990, p 5.

[471] Eder, Bruce, *Willie Dixon: Biography, Credits, Discography*, AllMusic.com, retrieved 10/223/2024, http://www.allmusic.com/artist/willie-dixon-mn0000959770.

[472] Dixon, Willie and Don Snowden, *I Am the Blues*. 1990, p 247.

[473] Herzhaft, Gerar, "Willie Dixon", *Encyclopedia of the Blues*, University of Arkansas Press, 1992, pp. 436–478.

[474] Eder, Bruce, *Willie Dixon: Biography, Credits, Discography*, AllMusic.com.

[475] Palmer, Robert, *Deep Blues*, Penguin Books, 1982, p. 166.

[476] Dixon, Willie and Don Snowden, *I Am the Blues*. 1990, p 150.

[477] Long, Worth, *"The Wisdom of the Blues—Defining Blues as the True Facts of Life: An Interview with Willie Dixon*, *African American Review.*, Vol 29, Issue 2, 1995, pp. 207–212.

[478] Dixon, Willie and Don Snowden, *I Am the Blues*. 1990, p 25.

[479] Dixon, Willie and Don Snowden, *I Am the Blues*. 1990, p 34.
[480] Palmer, Robert, *Deep Blues*, 1982, p. 166.
[481] Snowden, Don, *Willie Dixon: Chess Box (Box set booklet)*, Chess Records/MCA Records, 1997.
[482] Dixon, Willie and Don Snowden, *I Am the Blues*. 1990, p 46.
[483] Eder, Bruce, "Leonard Caston", *Biography of Leonard Caston*, Rovi Corporation, 2010, retrieved 10/23/2024, https://www.allmusic.com/artist/p63195..
[484] Long, Worth, *"The Wisdom of the Blues—Defining Blues as the True Facts of Life: An Interview with Willie Dixon,* 1995, pp. 207–212.
[485] Dixon, Willie and Don Snowden, *I Am the Blues*. 1990, p. 49.
[486] Colin Larkin, ed., *Guinness Encyclopedia of Popular Music (First ed.)*, Guinness Publishing, 1992, p 706.
[487] Dixon, Willie and Don Snowden, *I Am the Blues*. 1990, p. 43.
[488] Eder, Bruce, *Willie Dixon: Biography, Credits, Discography*, AllMusic.com.
[489] Baird, Jim, "Book Review: *Willie Dixon: Preacher of the Blues.*" *Journal of American Folklore*, Vol 127, 2014, pp 100–101.
[490] Colin Larkin, ed., *Guinness Encyclopedia of Popular Music (First ed.)*, Guinness Publishing, 1992, p 706.
[491] Palmer, Robert, *Deep Blues*, 1982, p. 166.
[492] Dixon, Willie and Don Snowden, *I Am the Blues*. 1990, p. 47.
[493] Colin Larkin, ed., *Guinness Encyclopedia of Popular Music (First ed.)*, Guinness Publishing, 1992, p 706.
[494] Dixon, Willie and Don Snowden, *I Am the Blues*. 1990, p. 59.
[495] Mitchell, Ed and Mark Blake, "Willie Dixon: the life and legacy of the blues' greatest songwriter", *Classic Rock*, June 30, 2021, retrieved 10/23/2024, https://www.loudersound.com/features/willie-dixon-i-am- the-blues.
[496] Colin Larkin, ed., *Guinness Encyclopedia of Popular Music (First ed.)*, Guinness Publishing, 1992, p 706.
[497] Dixon, Willie and Don Snowden, *I Am the Blues*. 1990, p. 87.
[498] Dixon, Willie and Don Snowden, *I Am the Blues*. 1990, pp 103-112.
[499] Dixon, Willie and Don Snowden, *I Am the Blues*. 1990, p. 244.
[500] Colin Larkin, ed., *Guinness Encyclopedia of Popular Music (First ed.)*, Guinness Publishing, 1992, p 706.
[501] Mitsutoshi Inaba, *Willie Dixon: Preacher of the Blues*. Scarecrow Press, 2011, p, 67.
[502] Dixon, Willie and Don Snowden, *I Am the Blues*. 1990, p. 218.
[503] Adapted from "Bobby Bland", Wikipedia, retrieved 11/12/2024, https://en.wikipedia.org/wiki/Bobby_Bland#.
[504] "Bobby 'Blue' Bland", *Livinblues.com*, archived from the original on August 24, 2007, https://web.archive.org/web/20070824184215/http://www.livinblues.com/bluesrooms/bobbybland.asp.

505 Russell, Tony, "Bobby 'Blue' Bland Obituary". *The Guardian*, June 24, 2013, retrieved 11/12/2024, https://www.theguardian.com/music/2013/jun/24/bobby-blue-bland. 506 *Bobby Blue Bland Historic Marker*, Tennessee Historical Commission, dedicated 1/24/2015, Barretville, TN.
507 Friskics-Warren, Bill, "Bobby (Blue) Bland, Soul and Blues Balladeer, Dies at 83", *The New York Times.*, June 24, 2013, retrieved 11/12/2024, https://www.nytimes.com/2013/06/25/arts/music/bobby-blue-bland-soul-and-blues-balladeer-dies-at-83.html
508 Friskics-Warren, Bill, "Bobby (Blue) Bland, Soul and Blues Balladeer, Dies at 83", *The New York Times.*, June 24, 2013.
509 "Bobby 'Blue' Bland dies: Rhythm-and-blues singer was 83", *Bangor Daily News.*, retrieved 11/12/2024, http://bangordailynews.com/2013/06/24/living/bobby-blue-bland-dies- rhythm-and-blues-singer-was-83/.
510 Russell, Tony, "Bobby 'Blue' Bland Obituary". *The Guardian*, June 24, 2013.
511 Turner, Ike; Cawthorne, Nigel, *Takin' back my name : the confessions of Ike Turner*, The Archive of Contemporary Music, Virgin, 1999,. p. 51, retrieved 11/12/2024, http://archive.org/details/takinbackmynamec00turn.
512 Cotten, Lee, *The Golden Age of American Rock 'n Roll: 1952-1956*, Popular Culture Inc, 1995.
513 Turner, Ike; Cawthorne, Nigel, *Takin' back my name : the confessions of Ike Turner*, p. 51.
514 Farley, Charles, *Soul of the Man: Bobby "Blue" Bland*. University Press of Mississippi, 2011, pp. 38, 111-115, https://books.google.com/books?id=TTtp27sjB7YC&q=bobby+bland+ike+turner+modern&pg=PA38.
515 McArdle, Terence, "Bobby 'Blue' Bland dies: Rhythm-and-blues singer was 83", *The Washington Post*, June 25, 2013.
516 "Bobby "Blue" Bland", Memphis Music Hall of Fame", retrieved 11/12/2024, *memphismusichalloffame.com, https://memphismusichalloffame.com/inductee/bobbybluebland/*.
517 Cotten, Lee, *The Golden Age of American Rock 'n Roll: 1952-1956*, Popular Culture Inc, 1995.
518 "Bobby Bland", *The Daily Telegraph*, June 24, 2013.
519 "Bobby Blue Bland: November 1973 Interview", SoulMusic.com, https://web.archive.org/web/20130702061615/http:/www.soulmusic.com/index.asp?S=1&T=38&ART=2919.
520 "Bobby -Blue- Bland", Memphis Music Hall of Fame, retreived 12/27/2024, https://memphismusichalloffame.com/inductee/bobbybluebland.
521 "Bobby Bland", *The Daily Telegraph*, June 24, 2013.

522 Adapted from Corcoran, Michael, *Ghost Notes: Pioneering Spirits of Texas Music*, TCU Press, 2020.
523 "Biography at BobbyBlueBland.com", archived from the original on October 21, 2016. retrieved 11/12/2024, https://web.archive.org/web/20161021143352/http:/www.bobbyblueblа nd.com/.
524 "Bobby Blue Bland", *Pbase.com Soulful Impressions*, retrieved 11/12/2024, http://www.pbase.com/soulfulimpressions/bobby_bland.
525 Eagle, Bob; LeBlanc, Eric S, *Blues – A Regional Experience*, Praeger Publishers, 2013, pp. 224–225.
526 "45 Discography for Duke Records", *Global Dog Productions*, 12/27/2024, http://www.globaldogproductions.info/d/duke.html.
527 Lauterbach, Preston, *The Chitlin' Circuit and the Road to Rock'n'Roll.*, W. W. Norton, 2011, p. 202.
528 "Bobby Bland", *The Daily Telegraph*, June 24, 2013.
529 "Bobby Bland", BBC News, June 24, 2013, https://www.bbc.co.uk/news/entertainment-arts-23035845.
530 "Bobby 'Blue' Bland", *Livinblues.com*, archived from the original on August 24, 2007, https://web.archive.org/web/20070824184215/http:/www.livinblues.co m/bluesrooms/bobbybland.asp.
531 Colin Larkin, ed, *The Guinness Who's Who of Soul Music* (First ed.), Guinness Publishing, 1993, pp. 21/22.
532 Colin Larkin, ed, *The Guinness Who's Who of Soul Music* (First ed, pp. 21/22.
533 "Bobby 'Blue' Bland", *Livinblues.com*, archived from the original on August 24, 2007.
534 Colin Larkin, ed, *The Guinness Who's Who of Soul Music* (First ed, pp. 21/22.
535 Farley, Charles, *Soul of the Man: Bobby "Blue" Bland.* University Press of Mississippi, 2011, pp. 183-200.
536 Russell, Tony, "Bobby 'Blue' Bland Obituary". *The Guardian*, June 24, 2013.
537 Colin Larkin, ed, *The Guinness Who's Who of Soul Music* (First ed, pp. 21/22.
538 "Bobby Bland", BBC News, June 24, 2013.
539 Friskics-Warren, Bill, "Bobby (Blue) Bland, Soul and Blues Balladeer, Dies at 83", *The New York Times.*, June 24, 2013.
540 Marshall, Matt , "BREAKING: Bobby "Blue" Bland Passes Away", *American Blues Scene Magazine*, June 23, 2013, archived from the original on Dec 9, 2013. retrieved 10/12/2024, https://web.archive.org/web/20131209221853/http://www.americanblue ssscene.com/2013/06/bobby-blue-bland/.

541 Adrian Sainz, "Bobby 'Blue' Bland, known for 'Further On Up the Road' and 'Turn on Your Love Light,' dies, *The Associated Press*, January 15, 1992, Windsorstar.com, archived from the original on June 24, 2013, retrieved 11/12/2024, https://archive.today/20130624234524/http://www.windsorstar.com/entertainment/Singer+Bobby+Blue+Bland+dies+known+Further+Road+Turn+Your+Love/8568124/story.html.

542 "Blues legend Bobby "Blue" Bland dies", WREG-TV, June 24, 2013,. retrieved 11/12/2024, http://wreg.com/013/06/23/blues-legend-bobby-blue-bland-dies/.

543 Friskics-Warren, Bill, "Bobby (Blue) Bland, Soul and Blues Balladeer, Dies at 83", *The New York Times.*, June 24, 2013.

544 Adapted from "BB King", Wikipedia, retrieved 11/12/2024, https://en.wikipedia.org/wiki/B._B._King.

545 Komara, Edward M, *Encyclopedia of the Blues*, Routledge, 2006, p. 385.

546 Dahl, Bill, "B.B. King", *AllMusic*, retrieved 11/12/2024, http://www.allmusic.com/artist/bb-king-mn0000059156/biography. 547 Herzhaft, Gérard, "B.B. King". *Encyclopedia of the Blues.* Translated by Brigitte Debord (2nd ed.). University of Arkansas Press, 1997, pp. 108– 110.

548 B.B. King Birthplace", HMdb.org, retrieved 11/22/ 2024, https://www.hmdb.org/m.asp?m=173997.

549 Sawyer, Charles, *B.B's Life | The Life of Riley*, President and Fellows of Harvard College.

550 Dahl, Bill, "B.B. King", *AllMusic*, retrieved 11/22/2024, http://www.allmusic.com/artist/bb-king-mn0000059156/biography. 551 Troupe, Quincy, "BB King: American Blues Musician, b. 1925", *Jazzandbluesmasters.com*, June 4, 1958, retrieved 11/22/2024, http://www.jazzandbluesmasters.com/bbking.htm.

552 Sawyer, Charles, *B.B's Life | The Life of Riley*, President and Fellows of Harvard College.

553 Troupe, Quincy, "BB King: American Blues Musician, b. 1925", *Jazzandbluesmasters.com*, June 4, 1958, retrieved 11/22/2024, http://www.jazzandbluesmasters.com/bbking.htm.

554 Kostelanetz, Richard; Reiswig, Jesse, eds *The B. B. King Reader: 6 Decades of Commentary* (2nd ed)., Hal Leonard, 2005,. p. 4, 7, *https://archive.org/details/bbkingreader6dec00kost/page/4.*

555 Silliman, Daniel, "How the church gave B.B. King the blues", *The Washington Post*, May 15, 2015, retrieved 11/22/2024, https://www.washingtonpost.com/news/acts-of-faith/wp/2015/05/15/how-the-church-gave-b-b-king-the-blues/.

556 Sawyer, Charles, *B.B's Life | The Life of Riley*, President and Fellows of Harvard College.

557 Sawyer, Charles, *B.B's Life | The Life of Riley*, President and Fellows of Harvard College.

558 Sawyer, Charles, *B.B's Life | The Life of Riley*, President and Fellows of Harvard College.

559 Sawyer, Charles, *B.B's Life | The Life of Riley*, President and Fellows of Harvard

College.
[560] Sawyer, Charles, *B.B's Life | The Life of Riley*, President and Fellows of Harvard College.
[561] "B.B. King Biography and Interview", *achievement.org*. American Academy of Achievement, retrieved 11/22/2024, https://www.achievement.org/achiever/b-b-king/#interview.
[562] Troupe, Quincy, "BB King: American Blues Musician, b. 1925", *Jazzandbluesmasters.com*, June 4, 1958, retrieved 11/22/2024, http://www.jazzandbluesmasters.com/bbking.htm.
[563] "Riley 'BB' King", National Endowment For The Arts, retrieved 11/22/2024, https://www.arts.gov/honors/heritage/riley-bb-king.
[564] Weiner, Tim, "B.B. King, Defining Bluesman for Generations, Dies at 89". *The New York Times*, May 15, 2015.
[565] Sawyer, Charles, *B.B's Life | The Life of Riley*, President and Fellows of Harvard College.
[566] Danchin, Sebastian, *Blues Boy: The Life and Music of B.B. King*, University Press of Mississippi, 1998, p. 1.
[567] Sawyer, Charles, *B.B's Life | The Life of Riley*, President and Fellows of Harvard College.
[568] "Riley 'BB' King", National Endowment For The Arts.
[569] "B.B. King - Lower Mississippi Delta Region (U.S. National Park Service)". National Park Service, retrieved 11/22/2024, https://www.nps.gov/locations/lowermsdeltaregion/b-b-king.htm. [570] Carroll, Ward, "BB King was booted out of the Army for being a tractor driver", *We Are The Mighty*, February 5, 2020,
retrieved 11/22/2024, https://www.wearethemighty.com/mighty-trending/bb-king-was-booted-out-of-the-army-for-being-a-tractor-driver/.
[571] "B.B. King Fast Facts", CNN. retrieved 11/22/2024, https://www.cnn.com/2013/06/24/us/b-b-king-fast-facts/index.html.
[572] "Riley 'BB' King", National Endowment For The Arts.
[573] Sawyer, Charles, *B.B's Life | The Life of Riley*, President and Fellows of Harvard College.
[574] "Riley 'BB' King", National Endowment For The Arts.
[575] "Historical marker placed on Mississippi Blues Trail", *Pittsburgh Post-Gazette, Associated Press.*, January 25, 2007.
[576] B.B. King: National Visionary", National Visionary Leadership Project. retrieved 11/22/2024, http://www.visionaryproject.org/kingbb/.
[577] Sawyer, Charles, *B.B's Life | The Life of Riley*, President and Fellows of Harvard College.
[578] Sawyer, Charles, *B.B's Life | The Life of Riley*, President and Fellows of Harvard College.
[579] Troupe, Quincy, "BB King: American Blues Musician, b. 1925", *Jazzandbluesmasters.com*, June 4, 1958, retrieved 11/22/2024, http://www.jazzandbluesmasters.com/bbking.htm.
[580] Sawyer, Charles, *B.B's Life | The Life of Riley*, President and Fellows of Harvard College.

581 "B.B. King – KWEM 1948", KWEM Radio, retrieved 11/22/2024, http://www.kwemradio.com/BBking.html.
582 Sawyer, Charles, *B.B's Life | The Life of Riley*, President and Fellows of Harvard College.
583 *Encyclopedia of African American Popular Culture*, Edited by Jessie Carney Smith, ABC-CLIO, 2011, pp. 805–806.
584 Larson, Thomas, *History of Rock & Roll.*, Kendall/Hunt, 2004, p. 25.
585 Sawyer, Charles, *B.B's Life | The Life of Riley*, President and Fellows of Harvard College.
586 Robbins, Wayne, "Talk to the Boss: His Majesty, Mr King", *Blues Access*, no 37, Spring 1999, retrieved 11/22/2024, http://www.bluesaccess.com/No_37/bb_talk.html.
587 Sawyer, Charles, *The Arrival of BB King*, Da Capo Press, 1980, p. 74.
588 Kerekes, Jim; O'Neill, Dennis, "B.B. King: Lucille Speaks", January 3, 1997, retrieved 11/22/2024, https://web.archive.org/web/20111116041531/http://www.worldblues.com/bbking/prairie/lucille.html.
589 Sawyer, Charles, B.B's Life | The Life of Riley, President and Fellows of Harvard College.
590 Kostelanetz, Richard; Reiswig, Jesse, eds, *The B. B. King Reader: 6 Decades of Commentary* (2nd ed)., Hal Leonard, 2005,. *pp. 4, 7.*
591 Dance, Helen Oakley; and B.B. King. *Stormy Monday*, Louisiana State University Press, 1987, p. 164.
592 Sawyer, Charles, B.B's Life | The Life of Riley, President and Fellows of Harvard College.
593 Sawyer, Charles, *B.B's Life | The Life of Riley*, President and Fellows of Harvard College.
594 Sawyer, Charles, *B.B's Life | The Life of Riley*, President and Fellows of Harvard College.
595 Sawyer, Charles, B.B's Life | The Life of Riley, President and Fellows of Harvard College.
596 Sawyer, Charles, B.B's Life | The Life of Riley, President and Fellows of Harvard College.
597 Sawyer, Charles, B.B's Life | The Life of Riley, President and Fellows of Harvard College.
598 Kostelanetz, 2005, p. 146.
599 Lime, Harry, *B.B. King : King of the Blues!*, Lulu.com, p. 5, https://books.google.com/books?id=zzWfDwAAQBAJ.
600 Sawyer, Charles, *B.B's Life | The Life of Riley*, President and Fellows of Harvard College.
601 "George Coleman: This Gentleman can PLAY", *All About Jazz*m retrieved 11/22/2024, http://www.allaboutjazz.com/php/article.php?id=1078.
602 Sawyer, Charles, B.B's Life | The Life of Riley, President and Fellows of Harvard College.
603 "Liner Notes", *U2 Rattle and Hum* DVD, 1988.
604 Sawyer, Charles, B.B's Life | The Life of Riley, President and Fellows of

Harvard College.
[605] Sawyer, Charles, B.B's Life | The Life of Riley, President and Fellows of Harvard College.
[606] Danchin, Sebastian, *Blues Boy: The Life and Music of B.B. King*, 1998, p. 1.
[607] Jennie Gunn, Carroll Gunn, and John Gunn, "Club Ebony", *Mississippi Encyclopedia*, retrieved 11/24/2024, https://mississippiencyclopedia.org/entries/club-ebony/.
[608] Sawyer, Charles, B.B's Life | The Life of Riley, President and Fellows of Harvard College.
[609] Sawyer, Charles, *The Arrival of BB King*, p. 79.
[610] Sawyer, Charles, B.B's Life | The Life of Riley, President and Fellows of Harvard College.
[611] Kot, Greg."King of the Blues", *Chicago Tribune*, May 16, 2015, pp. 1, 5.
[612] Sawyer, Charles, B.B's Life | The Life of Riley, President and Fellows of Harvard College.
[613] Sawyer, Charles, B.B's Life | The Life of Riley, President and Fellows of Harvard College.
[614] Kot, Greg."King of the Blues", *Chicago Tribune*, May 16, 2015, pp. 1, 5.
[615] Sawyer, Charles, B.B's Life | The Life of Riley, President and Fellows of Harvard College.
[616] Richards, Tom, "It's Not Easy Being B. The Trailblazing Reign of B.B. King", *Houston Press*.
[617] de Vise, Danial, *King of the Blues — The Rise and Reign of B.B. King,* 2021.
[618] "Riley 'BB' King", National Endowment For The Arts.
[619] Sawyer, Charles, B.B's Life | The Life of Riley, President and Fellows of Harvard College.
[620] "BB King Postcard", Wolfgang's, retrieved 11/25/2024, https://www.wolfgangs.com/posters/b-b-king/postcard/BG052.html. [621] Sawyer, Charles, B.B's Life | The Life of Riley, President and Fellows of Harvard College.
[622] Sawyer, Charles, B.B's Life | The Life of Riley, President and Fellows of Harvard College.
[623] McArdle, Terence, "B.B. King, Mississippi-born master of the blues, dies at 89", *The Washington Post*, May 15, 2015, retrieved 11/24/2024, https://www.washingtonpost.com/entertainment/music/bb-king-mississippi-master-of-the-blues-dies-at-89/2015/05/15/36e7529a-c5da-11df-94e1-c5afa35a9e59_story.html.
[624] McShane, Larry, "B.B. King Dead at 89: Blues guitarist whose sound defined music for generations passes away in sleep". *Daily News*, May 15, 2015, retrieved

11/24/2024, http://www.nydailynews.com/entertainment/music/b-b- king-dead-89-article-1.2223075.

625 Richards, Tom, "It's Not Easy Being B. The Trailblazing Reign of B.B. King", *Houston Press*, Oct 14, 2021, retrieved 11/22/2024,
https://www.houstonpress.com/music/review-king-of-the-blues-the-rise- and-reign-of-bb-king-12074903.

626 de Vise, Danial, *King of the Blues — The Rise and Reign of B.B. King*, Atlantic Monthly Press, 2021.

627 Sawyer, Charles, B.B's Life | The Life of Riley, President and Fellows of Harvard College.

628 "Riley 'BB' King", National Endowment For The Arts.

629 Sawyer, Charles, B.B's Life | The Life of Riley, President and Fellows of Harvard College.

630 Rolling Stone Magazine Lists 500 Greatest Songs of All Time", Sun Records, July 15, 2010, retrieved 11/24/2024, http://www.sunrecords.com/news/rolling-stone-magazine-lists-500- greatest-songs-of-all-time.

631 Sawyer, Charles, B.B's Life | The Life of Riley, President and Fellows of Harvard College.

632 Kot, Greg."King of the Blues", *Chicago Tribune*, May 16, 2015, pp. 1, 5

633 Brown, Mick, "BB King Interview: The Last of the Great Bluesmen", *The Daily Telegraph*, May 18,
2009, https://web.archive.org/web/20090519193112/http:/www.telegraph.co.uk/culture/music/rockandpopfeatures/5343853/BB-King- interview-the-last-of-the-great-bluesmen.html.

634 Tour Update", *bbking.com*, May 30, 2015, retrieved 11/24/2024,
https://web.archive.org/web/20150430052505/http://www.bbking.com/. 2014/10/08/tour-update/.

635 Kreps, Daniel, "B.B. King Coroner's Report: No Evidence of Poisoning", *Rolling Stone*., July 14,
2015, https://www.rollingstone.com/music/news/b-b-king-coroners- report-no-evidence-of-poisoning-20150714.

636 Ellis, Ralph, "B.B. King "in home hospice care"", CNN, May 2, 2015, retrieved 11/24/2024, http://www.cnn.com/2015/05/01/us/bb-king-in- home-hospice-care/.

637 B.B. King Cancels Remaining 8 shows", *bbking.com*, October 4, 2014, retrieved 11/24/2024,
https://web.archive.org/web/20150507064711/http://www.bbking.com/ 2014/10/04/b-b-king-cancels-remaining-8-shows/.

638 "Tour Update", *bbking.com*. October 8, 2014,
https://web.archive.org/web/20150430052505/http://www.bbking.com/ 2014/10/08/tour-update/.

639 Weiner, Tim, *The New York Times*, May 15, 2015.

640 Ellis, Ralph, CNN, May 2, 2015.

[641] Alter, Charlotte, "B.B. King Buried in Indianola, Mississippi", *Time*, retrieved 11/24/2024, https://time.com/3902436/bb-king-funeral/. [642] "Music And Tears At BB King Memphis Procession", *Sky News*, retrieved 11/24/2024, http://news.sky.com/story/1492063/music-and- tears-at-bb-king-memphis-procession.
[643] "Beale Street says goodbye to B.B. King", *WMC Action News 5* May 15, 2015, retrieved 11/24/2024, http://www.wmcactionnews5.com/story/29171363/beale-street-says- goodbye-to-bb-king.
[644] "BB King's funeral draws hundreds as Obama says country 'has lost a legend' | US news", *The Guardian. Associated Press* in Indianola, Mississippi. January 1, 1970, retrieved 11/24/2024, https://www.theguardian.com/us-news/2015/may/30/bb-king-funeral- mississippi.
[645] "Beale Street says goodbye to B.B. King", *WMC Action News,* May 15, 2015.
[646] "BB King's Funeral Procession", *American Masters*, PBS, https://www.pbs.org/wnet/americanmasters/b-b-kings-funeral- procession/6536/.
[647] "National Public Radio Pioneer Dave Creagh Dies", *Watauga Democrat*, Dec 30, 2011, retrieved 12/11/2024, https://www.wataugademocrat.com/blowingrocket/news/national- public-radio-pioneer-dave-creagh-dies/article_87fd2214-57fe-5660-bf74- 8bf9ce1d27ef.html.

www.ingramcontent.com/pod-product-compliance
Lightning Source LLC
Chambersburg PA
CBHW040244010526
44119CB00057B/814